Experimenting with Housing Allowances

Experimenting with Housing Allowances

The Final Report of the Housing Assistance Supply Experiment

Ira S. Lowry, editor
The Rand Corporation

OG &H Oelgeschlager, Gunn & Hain, Publishers, Inc.
Cambridge, Massachusetts

International Standard Book Number: 0–89946–200–6

Library of Congress Catalog Card Number: 83–2346

Printed in the U.S.A.

Library of Congress Cataloging in Publication Data

Lowry, Ira S.
Experimenting with housing allowances.

Includes index.
1. Housing subsidies—United States. 2. Housing subsidies—Wisconsin—Brown County. 3. Housing subsidies—Indiana—Saint Joseph County. 4. Housing policy—United States. I. Title. II. Title: Housing allowances.
HD7293.L659 1983 363.5′8 83–2346
ISBN 0–89946–200–6

CONTENTS

FIGURES

TABLES

FOREWORD

For decades, the concept of housing allowances as a way of delivering housing assistance to low-income families has been on the table of national housing policy deliberations—but always eliminated from serious consideration because of great uncertainties as to possible design, effects, and costs.

This book replaces speculation with reliable evidence. It summarizes the findings of a ten-year study of housing allowances, their effects on recipients, their effects on housing markets, and their costs and administrative problems. Carefully managed field trials show that although allowances are not a panacea, they tend to meet the housing needs of most recipients more equitably and at lower cost than do present federal programs. Further, many of the dangers perceived for such a program proved to be groundless. For example, the dangers of market disruption that for so long inhibited serious consideration of an allowance program turn out to be negligible.

The evidence provided by the study enabled the President's Commission on Housing to recommend (in April 1982) a major shift in federal housing policy, from providing construction and operating subsidies to public authorities and private developers to providing allowance-like payments to needy families who would then choose their housing in the open market.

Whatever the immediate legislative fate of the Commission's recommendations, sound legislation in the 1980s to help lower-income families must reflect the findings of HUD's Experimental Housing Allowance Program, of which the Housing Assistance Supply Experiment was a major element. Going beyond the specifics of housing allowances, the experiment reveals that much of existing federal housing policy is based on an obsolete view of low-income housing problems and their causes. Both the objectives and the means of federal policy are ripe for reconsideration. Perhaps the single most important finding is that given cash allowances, most needy families tend to allocate only a small fraction to improved housing as opposed to other budget needs.

As Secretary of the Department of Housing and Urban Development during the formative period of this study, I am pleased to have played a part in an undertaking so rare in the annals of government—a carefully planned and scientifically executed attempt to gather reliable evidence about the consequences of a major shift in federal policy before it was adopted—and so fruitful in its results. The next task is the widest possible dissemination and consideration of these findings. We now have them. Let's use them.

James T. Lynn
Washington, D.C.
October 1982

PREFACE

This book is the comprehensive final report on the Housing Assistance Supply Experiment (HASE), a ten-year study of housing allowances conducted by The Rand Corporation under the sponsorship of the Office of Policy Development and Research, U.S. Department of Housing and Urban Development (HUD). The study was one of several elements of HUD's Experimental Housing Allowance Program (EHAP), undertaken in 1972 pursuant to a congressional mandate.

The Supply Experiment conducted full-scale allowance programs in two metropolitan housing markets (Green Bay, Wisconsin, and South Bend, Indiana), using administrative records and field surveys to address five issues:

- Factors determining eligibility for and participation in the allowance program.
- Effects of the program on those who participated in it and on their housing.
- Effects of the program on the housing markets and communities in which it operated.
- Costs of the program, including both allowance payments and administration.
- The effectiveness and efficiency of the administrative methods used in the program.

Our findings on these issues have been presented in over 60 interim reports and notes and in seven final topical reports.[1] This volume summarizes and integrates those findings to help the reader assess the strengths and weaknesses of housing allowances as a tool of federal housing policy.

---

[1]Appendix A lists 32 reports, 116 notes, and 20 professional papers prepared by Rand's staff that document research methods and findings. Appendix B lists 75 codebooks, 34 audit reports, and a three-volume user's guide that documents the data collected by HASE.

ACKNOWLEDGMENTS

Conducting the Supply Experiment has required close cooperation among a number of institutions and dedicated efforts by their staffs over a period of ten years. We are grateful for their support, advice, and technical contributions. The institutions are HUD's Office of Policy Development and Research, the sponsoring agency; local governments and housing authorities in Brown and St. Joseph counties, where the experiment was conducted; the housing allowance offices, nonprofit corporations established in those places to administer the experimental programs; and HUD's Region V office (Chicago), which administered the annual contributions contracts under which the two allowance programs operated. We regret that the individuals of these institutions who have earned our respect and gratitude are too numerous to name here.

We are also heavily indebted to the many citizens of Brown and St. Joseph counties who granted us lengthy interviews—some as often as four times—in the interests of policy research whose benefits to them were remote; and to the participants in the experimental programs who cooperated with research inquiries beyond their obligations as allowance recipients. Besides bearing the inconveniences entailed in our inquiries, both groups have entrusted us with personal information whose confidentiality we have and will continue to guard meticulously.

We should also record our appreciation for the careful work of other organizations that contributed directly or indirectly to our research. These include the survey research organizations that conducted fieldwork for Rand: Urban Opinion Surveys, a division of Mathematica, Inc., which conducted the first cycle of surveys in Brown County; the National Opinion Research Center of the University of Chicago, which conducted the remaining three cycles there; Westat, Inc., which conducted all four cycles in St. Joseph County; and Chilton Research Services, Inc., which conducted a special survey in both counties in 1979 under contract to the housing allowance offices. Others who have been helpful in various stages of the experiment are Abt Associates, Inc., contractors to HUD for the Housing Allowance Demand and the Administrative Agency experiments; and The Urban Institute, contractors to HUD for an integrated analysis of data from all the experiments.

This report draws directly or indirectly on data gathered, organized, and analyzed by Rand's staff for the Supply Experiment over a period of ten years, a group now numbering several hundred (see Appendix E). Ira S. Lowry, principal investigator of the Supply Experiment, planned and edited this report. Others, named below, helped organize the material and drafted portions of the text as indicated:

Chapter	Principal Author	Contributors
I	Ira S. Lowry	Donna Betancourt
II	Ira S. Lowry	Charles W. Noland
III	Ira S. Lowry	James L. McDowell
IV	Michael P. Murray	Grace M. Carter, Sinclair B. Coleman, James C. Wendt
V	John E. Mulford	Lawrence Helbers, James L. McDowell
VI	C. Lance Barnett	Carol Hillestad, C. Peter Rydell
VII	Ira S. Lowry	Donna Betancourt, Carl Hensler
VIII	G. Thomas Kingsley	Sheila N. Kirby, W. Eugene Rizor, Priscilla Schlegel
IX	Ira S. Lowry	Kevin Neels
Appendix		
A	Donna Betancourt	Jane Abelson
B	Patricia Boren	Christine D'Arc, Ann W. Wang
C	James L. McDowell	
D	Ira S. Lowry	
E	Donna Betancourt	Jane Abelson

The draft of this book was reviewed by Bernard J. Frieden (Massachusetts Institute of Technology), John Gardner (Office of Policy Development and Research, HUD), Thomas K. Glennan (Rand), Howard Hammerman (Office of Policy Development and Research, HUD), Stephen O. Kennedy (Abt Associates, Inc.), Edgar O. Olsen (University of Virginia), Raymond J. Struyk (The Urban Institute), Harold W. Watts (Columbia University), and Barbara R. Williams (Rand). Many others at Rand and HUD reviewed parts of the draft. Although we are unlikely to have satisfied all reviewers on all points they raised, their comments led to many improvements in both substance and exposition.

Gwen Shepherdson prepared most of the draft text and tables and also the final production copy. Karen J. Stewart and Dolores Davis prepared or corrected some parts of the draft. Jane Abelson edited copy and supervised production of this volume.

As noted, the Supply Experiment was sponsored by the U.S. Department of Housing and Urban Development, whose officers secured funding for the experiment and guided its operations over a period of 10 years. We can best acknowledge our appreciation for HUD's continued support through six changes of departmental administration by listing the officers of HUD whose positions entailed direct responsibility for oversight of the Supply Experiment.

Secretaries

George Romney (1969-73)
James T. Lynn (1973-75)
Carla A. Hills (1975-77)
Patricia Roberts Harris (1977-79)
Moon Landrieu (1979-81)
Samuel R. Pierce, Jr. (1981-present)

*Assistant Secretaries, Policy Development and Research**

Harold B. Finger
Michael H. Moskow
Charles J. Orlebecke
Donna E. Shalala
E. S. Savas

Deputy Assistant Secretaries, Research

Rudolph G. Penner
John C. Weicher
Claude Barfield
Raymond J. Struyk
Michael A. Stegman
Benjamin F. Bobo

Directors, Division of Research

John H. Betz
Jerry J. Fitts
Terrence L. Connell

Government Program Managers (HASE)

Charles Field
Gilmer L. Blankespoor
Martin D. Levine
Howard M. Hammerman

*Formerly, Research and Technology.

I. INTRODUCTION

The Housing Assistance Supply Experiment, conducted by The Rand Corporation under sponsorship of the U.S. Department of Housing and Urban Development (HUD), was a full-scale test in two metropolitan housing markets of a housing allowance program to help low-income families with their housing expenses. It is the largest, longest, and possibly the most complex "social experiment" ever conducted.

Between 1974 and 1980, over 25,000 households in Green Bay, Wisconsin, and South Bend, Indiana, enrolled in an experimental program that provided them with monthly cash payments on condition that they occupy decent, safe, and sanitary dwellings. The experiment was designed to reveal how such a program would affect both participants and nonparticipants who were competing for housing in the same market.

Using data from program administration and from annual marketwide surveys of landlords, renters, and homeowners, Rand researchers analyzed patterns of voluntary participation, changes in housing consumption among participants, market responses to participants' attempts to obtain better housing, community attitudes toward the program, and program costs. This book summarizes the experimental findings and explores their implications for national housing policy.

The Supply Experiment was one of several experiments undertaken by HUD to learn whether housing allowances were a desirable supplement or alternative to traditional federal housing programs that subsidize local authorities and private investors who build and operate low-rent housing. The results of these tests were reviewed in 1981 by the President's Commission on Housing, which recommended that housing allowances (also known as "housing vouchers" and "housing payments") be adopted as the principal form of federal housing assistance.[1] Legislation pursuant to that recommendation has been drafted by HUD for submission to Congress in 1982. Consequently, the experimental findings presented here are directly relevant to current decisions about national housing policy.

---

[1]The Commission's final report (1982) recommends a "Housing Payments Program" that is essentially an adaptation of the Sec. 8 Existing Housing program to include the payment formula used in the Supply Experiment.

HOW HOUSING ALLOWANCES WORK

Housing allowances are cash payments to low-income households that help them with their housing expenses and encourage consumption of better housing. Allowances are "demand subsidies," in contrast to "supply subsidies" that encourage private developers or public authorities to build or operate low-rent housing, or that encourage lenders to accommodate low-income homebuyers.

Many variations are possible, but the following features jointly distinguish housing allowances from alternative forms of housing assistance:

- Allowance entitlement pertains to a specific household, not to a specific dwelling. When an assisted household moves, its allowance moves with it.
- Allowance recipients find their housing in the private market. They negotiate the terms and conditions of occupancy with housing suppliers, and are entirely responsible for fulfilling such agreements. The administering agency makes no commitment to housing suppliers, and has no contingent liability for recipients' performances.
- The allowance is at least indirectly earmarked for housing consumption, which distinguishes it from a general income transfer. The earmarking device may be either a minimum consumption standard or graduated compensation for increased consumption.

In short, housing allowances provide low-income families with the means to pay for decent housing on condition that they obtain it from the private market by their own efforts. The concept applies as readily to homeowners as to renters. An allowance program does not sponsor housing construction or rehabilitation, although private developers, landlords, or the participants themselves might undertake such actions in response to the program.

THE EXPERIMENTAL HOUSING ALLOWANCE PROGRAM (EHAP)

HUD began its Experimental Housing Allowance Program in 1971, pursuant to direct Congressional mandate. The circumstances leading to that mandate are worth noting inasmuch as they strongly influenced the purposes and design of the experimental program.

Historical Background

The Housing Act of 1968 (Public Law 90-448, 82 Stat. 476) culminated two decades of increasing federal involvement in housing markets that had been aimed at stabilizing the construction industry, renewing decayed urban neighborhoods, and improving housing conditions generally, but especially for low-income families. These goals had been pursued through a bewildering assortment of capital grants, interest subsidies, direct loans, rent-supplement payments, and mortgage insurance plans directed to local public authorities, nonprofit housing sponsors, private developers, financial institutions, and housing consumers.

Taking stock at the end of 1968, The President's Committee on Urban Housing (Kaiser Committee) noted the proliferation of programs designed to subsidize specific housing projects as distinguished from housing consumers, who benefited only as tenants of subsidized projects. The Committee suggested that providing housing assistance directly to needy families would be a better long-run solution to the problems then addressed by project subsidies:

> A housing allowance . . . system would permit the consumer to make his own choices in the market place, a freedom which tends to enhance personal dignity. By relying on market forces, it should bring about a better matching of consumer demands and housing supply. Low-income consumers would make their own decisions on location and housing style rather than having others make these decisions for them. The project subsidy programs are now largely insulated from the healthy influences of market forces. In addition, by allowing recipients of housing assistance to make their own decisions on location, public controversy over the location of subsidized projects would be avoided. Distribution of the benefits of housing allowances could be made more equitably than is possible under project subsidy programs. Lastly, it is possible, though not certain, that a housing allowance approach would eliminate administrative processing of projects and would involve lower administrative expenses for government than do the present project subsidy programs.
>
> Several factors militate against a full-scale housing allowance program and have led to [our] conclusion that such a subsidy system initially be attempted on an experimental basis only. There is a strong need to stimulate new construction as quickly as possible and the project subsidy approach best lends itself to this purpose. In addition, the immediate adoption of a massive housing allowance system would be likely to inflate the cost of existing housing considerably, at least in the short run. The large infusion of new purchasing power would result in a bidding up of housing prices for the existing standard inventory. Consequently, any large-scale housing allowance system would have to be introduced gradually. Such a system might also require strong programs of consumer education and vigorous

> attacks on racial discrimination in order to work effectively. Despite these possible shortcomings, the potential merits of the housing allowance approach are such that it should be tried promptly on the experimental basis suggested (The President's Committee on Urban Housing, pp. 71-2).

During the next two years, several housing allowance proposals were introduced in Congress, and in the Housing and Development Act of 1970, Congress mandated an experiment "to demonstrate the feasibility of providing families of low income with housing allowances to assist them in obtaining rental housing of their choice in existing standard housing units."[2]

The Congressional mandate for experimentation acquired additional momentum because of a general dissatisfaction with the results of existing federal housing assistance programs, including several created by the Housing Act of 1968. Between 1970 and 1973, insistent questions were raised by the Congress, the Comptroller General, and the press about policy objectives, the feasibility of program missions, equity in the allocation of assistance, the effectiveness and honesty of program administration, and the long-run costs of current project commitments (see, for example, Lilly, 1971; and "The Bankruptcy of Subsidized Housing," 1972).

The Administration's concerns about these issues reached such a pitch that in January 1973, HUD Secretary George W. Romney imposed a moratorium on new subsidy commitments under existing programs, explaining that:

> It had become crystal clear by 1970 that the patchwork, year-by-year, piecemeal addition of programs over a period of more than three decades, had created a statutory and administrative monstrosity that could not possibly yield effective results even with the wisest and most professional management systems (Romney, p. 7).

The moratorium was Secretary Romney's valedictory. His successor, James T. Lynn, ordered a massive review of the entire structure of HUD's housing assistance programs and of the fundamental premises of federal housing policy.[3] He also expressed a lively interest in housing allowances as an alternative. On 19 September 1973, President Nixon sent a special housing message to Congress, in which he asserted:

---

[2]Public Law 91-609, 84 Stat. 1770, Sec. 504. This provision was sponsored by Sen. Edward W. Brooke of Massachusetts. The experimental authority was later broadened at HUD's request to include homeowners (Housing and Community Development Act of 1974, Public Law 93-383, 88 Stat. 633, Sec. 804).

[3]Much of the material gathered for the National Housing Policy Review was subsequently published (U.S. Department of Housing and Urban Development, 1976).

> Leaders of all political persuasions and from all levels of government have given a great deal of thought in recent years to the problem of low income housing. Many of them agree that the Federally-subsidized housing approach has failed. And many of them also agree on the reasons for the failure.
>
> The main flaw they point to in the old approach is its underlying assumption that the basic problem of the poor is a lack of housing rather than a lack of income. Instead of treating the root cause of the problem—the inability to pay for housing—the Government has been attacking the symptom. We have been helping the builders directly and the poor only indirectly, rather than providing assistance directly to low income families.
>
> In place of this old approach, many people have suggested a new approach—direct cash assistance [to low-income families for housing expenses]. . . . Not surprisingly, our recent housing study [The National Housing Policy Review] indicates what others have been saying: of the policy alternatives available, the most promising way to achieve decent housing for all of our families at an acceptable cost appears to be direct cash assistance (Nixon, pp. 807-8).

Thus, the Experimental Housing Allowance Program was planned in a period of great ferment in federal housing policy. Those plans were further shaped by a new sense of the possibilities of applying experimental science to the problems of government. Until the mid-sixties, experimentation in government essentially meant launching new national programs whose designs reflected at best purely theoretical analyses of probable effects but which might have provided for systematic evaluation after the programs were operating. The new idea was that the essential features of a contemplated national program could be tested by a carefully designed experiment conducted on a relatively small scale, the results of which would allow much more precise estimation of the effects of the full-scale counterpart and provide valuable guidance on program rules, administrative requirements, and costs if a national program were adopted.

The intellectual model for these social experiments, as they came to be called, was the clinical trial in medical research. In clinical trials, a therapy of unknown effectiveness is administered under controlled conditions to a carefully chosen sample of ailing persons; others get alternative or no treatment. Even if detailed causal links between the treatment and the subject's response cannot be identified, clinical trials enable experimenters to assess the statistical effectiveness of the treatment as against alternative or no treatment of the same ailment.

The application of this concept of experimentation to issues of social policy began with the New Jersey Income Maintenance Experiment, initiated in 1967 by the Office of Economic Opportunity. This enterprise was intended to show *scientifically* whether the guarantee of a minimum income would adversely affect the recipient's efforts at gainful employment. It was also expected to yield guidance in setting the optimal terms of such a guarantee and reliable estimates of the national cost of such a program (Kershaw, 1972; and Lampman, 1976).

By 1972, several such social experiments were either under way or planned. The list soon included experiments with educational vouchers, health insurance, manpower training, contracting for public services, congestion tolls for the use of public facilities, control of drug abuse, and the administration of criminal justice. Each of these enterprises raised new issues of experimental design with respect to sampling, analogue treatments, clinical or statistical controls, ethical and legal constraints, and generalization from experimental findings (Bennett and Lumsdaine, 1975; Reichen and Boruch, 1974; Rivlin, 1974; and Rivlin and Timpane, 1975).

In 1971, HUD's Office of Research and Technology[4] began to plan the housing allowance experiment mandated by Congress in the light of growing dissatisfaction with existing housing programs, a broad base of Executive and Congressional interest in housing allowances, and escalating methodological standards for experimentation. The result of these heady influences was the largest formal social experiment ever conducted, whether measured by budget, numbers of participants, number of experimental sites, duration, or (arguably) complexity.

The Elements of EHAP

As it developed during 1971-73, HUD's experimental program had four major components:

- The Housing Allowance Demand Experiment (HADE), conducted by Abt Associates, Inc. This experiment offered three-year allowances to a scientific sample of low-income renter households in Pittsburgh, Pennsylvania, and Phoenix, Arizona. Its purpose was to test the effects of alternative benefit formulas and earmarking devices on both acceptance rates and the housing consumption of participants. The terms of the allowance were therefore systematically varied between treatment groups, and the responses of these groups were

[4]Headed by Assistant Secretary Harold B. Finger. In 1973, the Office of Research and Technology became the Office of Policy Development and Research, headed by Finger's successor, Michael K. Moskow.

compared both with each other and with control groups that were not offered allowances.

- The Housing Assistance Supply Experiment (HASE), conducted by The Rand Corporation. This experiment offered allowances for up to ten years to all low-income renters and homeowners in Brown County, Wisconsin (metropolitan Green Bay), and St. Joseph County, Indiana (metropolitan South Bend). Its purpose was to test the market and community effects of a full-scale program. Identical program rules applied in both sites, but the sites were chosen for contrast in market characteristics. Both the allowance program and the local housing market were monitored for several years after the program began. During that time, enrollment was continuously open to all eligibles.
- The Administrative Agency Experiment (AAE), conducted by Abt Associates, Inc. This experiment offered two-year allowances to a limited number of low-income renter households in eight geographically scattered sites, including both urban and rural communities.[5] The purpose of the experiment was to test alternative styles of program administration and gather data on administrative costs in operational settings. In each site, the program was administered by an existing local agency (such as a housing authority or welfare department), pursuant to broad guidelines set by HUD.
- The Integrated Analysis, conducted by The Urban Institute. The staff of the Institute participated in the design of all three experiments, and arrangements were made to furnish them with data from each for an integrated analysis of the advantages and disadvantages of housing allowances as a method of delivering housing assistance, including the costs of a national program.

THE CHARTER AND MOTIVATION OF THE SUPPLY EXPERIMENT

The Supply Experiment is thus only one element of a broader program of experimentation involving twelve geographically scattered sites, three research contractors, and eight local public agencies. It was not intended to deal with all the research questions pertinent to

[5]The sites of the AAE were Salem, Oregon; Tulsa, Oklahoma; Jacksonville, Florida; San Bernardino County, California; Springfield, Massachusetts; Peoria, Illinois; Burleigh, Stutsman, Morton, and Stark counties, North Dakota; and Durham County, North Carolina.

housing allowances, only to learn about their market and community effects. Specifically, its research charter as specified in 1973 (Lowry, 1980, pp. 10-11) contained four elements:

- *Supply responsiveness.* How will the suppliers of housing services—landlords, developers, and homeowners—react when allowance recipients attempt to increase their housing consumption? Specifically, what mix of price increases and housing improvements will result? How long will these responses take to work themselves out to a steady state? How will the responses differ by market sector?
- *Behavior of market intermediaries and indirect suppliers.* How will mortgage lenders, insurance companies, and real-estate brokers respond to an allowance program? Will their policies help or hinder the attempts of allowance recipients to obtain better housing and those of landlords to improve their properties? What happens to the availability, price, and quality of building services and of repair and remodeling services? What seem to be the reasons for changes in institutional or industrial policies?
- *Residential mobility and neighborhood change.* In their attempts to find better housing (or better neighborhoods), will many allowance recipients relocate within the metropolitan area? What factors influence their decisions to move or to stay? What types of neighborhoods will the movers seek and succeed in entering? Do moves by allowance recipients set in motion a chain of moves by nonrecipients—either into neighborhoods vacated by recipients or out of neighborhoods into which recipients have moved?
- *Effects on nonparticipants.* How will households not receiving housing allowances—particularly those whose incomes are within or just above the range of eligibility—be affected by the program? Specifically, will the increased housing demands of allowance recipients cause an increase in housing prices for nonrecipients? Whether or not such price increases occur, will nonrecipients perceive personal hardships or benefits from the program? How will they perceive and react to allowance-stimulated neighborhood changes?

This charter reflects the policy issues that motivated the Supply Experiment.

The most important of those issues was the widespread belief that subsidizing the housing demand of low-income families would be highly inflationary unless actions were also taken to increase the supply of adequate housing. Some housing analysts thought that the landlords of allowance recipients would raise rents to capture all or most of the allowance, with little change in the quality of housing services offered. Some thought that enrollees would compete with ineligibles for the limited supply of adequate housing, driving up rents in that sector of the market for both participants and nonparticipants. Others thought that because the allowances were "portable," renter enrollees could bargain effectively with their landlords about rents and repairs; and that the market would respond rapidly to any evidence of an increased demand for well-maintained housing by repairing and improving existing dwellings and perhaps even building new ones.

The policies and practices of market intermediaries—mortgage lenders, real-estate brokers, rental agents, home-repair and maintenance contractors, and insurance companies—were expected to influence the outcome of a housing allowance program. These intermediaries could encourage or discourage home purchases, steer participants to or away from particular neighborhoods, open or close certain classes of rental housing to participants, facilitate or impede home improvement, and so on. It was especially unclear whether or not receipt of housing allowances would improve low-income families' credit ratings and thus make such families more desirable either as rental tenants or home purchasers.

Neighborhood effects were also a matter of interest and concern. Because the allowances were portable, some thought that enrollees from low-income neighborhoods would move in search of both better dwellings and better neighborhoods. Because low-income enrollees would in most places include many members of racial minorities, the effect of such moves would be to promote both economic and racial integration in the destination neighborhoods. The other side of the coin, however, could be a collapse of the housing market in the neighborhoods of origin, or racial tensions in the neighborhoods of destination. Others doubted that an allowance program would result in much interneighborhood mobility, particularly by members of racial minorities; they were convinced that racial barriers were more attitudinal than economic. Still others were intrigued by the possibility that housing improvements made by recipients or their landlords might affect adjoining properties, whose owners would be encouraged to improve or maintain dwellings that might otherwise have been allowed to deteriorate.

Finally, the possibility of adverse side effects, such as rent inflation or disruption of neighborhood social patterns led some to speculate about community hostility toward such a program and its beneficiaries. Others thought that the community would view this mode of housing assistance favorably because it did not concentrate the poor in "projects," or because it would lead to general neighborhood improvement. Some thought that landlords would find rent collection and property maintenance easier when they had assisted tenants, whereas others speculated that landlords would be hostile to allowance recipients, as many are to welfare recipients.

MAJOR DESIGN ISSUES AND THEIR RESOLUTION

Designing an experiment to assess the market and community effects of a full-scale program entailed tradeoffs between precise measurement of effects, generality of findings, credibility of evidence, expense, and risks to the host communities. During 1972-73, Rand and HUD staffs jointly weighed many alternatives before settling on the chosen design. The key issues and their resolutions are discussed below.

Program Scale and Duration

The obvious way to test the effects of a full-scale program is to conduct one. The obvious drawback to that approach is its expense and the risk it imposes on the host community. We examined various alternatives, including computer simulation of a full-scale program, using nonexperimental data; analysis of naturally occurring analogues to the market stimulus expected from an allowance program; micro-experiments to test the responses of individual landlords and homeowners to a hypothetical program; and experiments at the neighborhood scale within larger housing markets. None of these approaches seemed likely to provide reliable and generally credible evidence of the effects of an actual program when so little was known about how eligibles would respond to the allowance offer, how they would communicate their housing demands in the open market, and how the suppliers of housing would respond.

We did conclude that housing markets are essentially local, so that nearly all the relevant conditions of a national program could be created in a single metropolitan market. We therefore decided to conduct experimental programs in selected local markets, offering allowances to all those likely to be eligible under a permanent national program. Using the income eligibility standards of the public housing program, but including homeowners as well as renters, we estimated that about a fifth of all households in a typical metropolitan housing market would be eligible; however, we were unsure how many would participate.

Analyzing the economics of both household planning and investment in housing improvement, we concluded that the appropriate climate of expectations could be created only by a long-term program, even though most market effects should be apparent in the first few years of its operation. HUD agreed to fund a ten-year allowance program in each experimental site, but we planned to monitor only the first five years. It was stipulated that in the event of adverse community consequences, program growth could be stopped without violating commitments to those already enrolled; and that unexpected outcomes might either shorten or lengthen the monitoring period.

Site Selection

It was generally agreed that an allowance program might work differently in different housing markets. Three market characteristics that seemed likely to have strong effects were scale, structure, and current condition.

By offering more alternatives to consumers, a large market should enhance the value of allowance portability to participants in an allowance program. In addition, supporting services such as home repair contracting and mortgage lending should be better organized and more specialized. On the other hand, relations between landlords and tenants are more likely to be impersonal, or even hostile, so that tenant-initiated requests for dwelling repairs might fall on less responsive ears.

Market structure describes the degree to which a local housing market is subdivided into essentially noncompeting classes of suppliers, demanders, and dwelling types. One significant subdivision is between rental housing and owner-occupied homes; another is between racially segregated neighborhoods. The significance of strongly bounded submarkets is that the program's stimulus to each submarket must be absorbed within it, rather than diffused marketwide, so the potential for program-generated supply-demand imbalances is greater in a divided market.

Current market condition refers to the balance between the supply of housing services offered in a market and the demand from the resident population for those services. Market condition is roughly gauged by vacancy rates, which are high when supply is excessive relative to demand, low when supply is short. Imbalances are to some degree self-corrected by price movements; but the efficiency and speed of adjustment in housing markets are matters of controversy. Introducing housing allowances into a "tight" market might have quite different price effects than introducing them into a "loose" market.

Although the relevance of these market characteristics to our experimental purposes was widely accepted, they posed a dilemma for experimental design. With a limited experimental budget, not all combinations of market scale, structure, and condition could be tested. In fact, the expense of a marketwide, ten-year allowance program limited us to very few sites.

After thorough analysis of the possibilities and both their analytical and budgetary implications, HUD and Rand agreed to conduct the experiment in only two sites, both with under 250,000 inhabitants (about 75,000 households). One site should have a relatively "tight" market overall, but one that was not divided along racial lines; the other should be a racially segregated but relatively "loose" market. Sites of the first type are mostly found among the nation's smaller, rapidly growing metropolitan areas. Sites of the second type are mostly larger, older metropolitan areas whose central cities have been losing white and gaining minority populations. However, no two metropolitan areas are precisely alike, and no sample of two, however carefully chosen, can provide direct evidence about program effects in places not sampled.[6] Generalization from the Supply Experiment therefore requires nonstatistical inference, mediated by an analytical interpretation of the observed outcomes in the experimental sites.

Program Design

Although there was consensus on the basic features of a housing allowance program, many variants were plausible and some were to be tested by the Demand and Administrative Agency experiments. What versions should be tested in the Supply Experiment?

Our commitment to a full-scale, open-enrollment program ruled out intrasite variation in program design, but we did have the option of varying program rules between sites. We concluded that such variation would cloud answers to a more central question, whether response to an allowance program varied with site characteristics. HUD and Rand therefore agreed to run identical allowance programs in the two sites.

The design we chose reflected a priori judgments as to the eligibility rules, allowance formula, and earmarking methods that would be

[6]Although the limits to generalization from a two-site sample are particularly conspicuous in our experimental design, the principle is broadly applicable. For example, social experiments that focus on the behavior of individuals do not usually sample the entire universe of individuals to which inferences will be made, but choose their samples in one or a few places. In these cases, generalization implicitly postulates that individual behavior is unaffected by its local context.

most effective in promoting the desired responses by participants and suppliers of housing services, constrained to some degree by legislation governing the funds available for program operations.[7] Essentially the same design was the "center" from which the Demand Experiment tested variations.

All low-income households residing in our sites were eligible to participate except those whose assets exceeded $20,000 ($32,500 for households headed by elderly persons) and those consisting of single persons under 62 years of age (unless disabled, handicapped or residentially displaced by public action). Income limits for eligibility were integral to the allowance formula; a household became ineligible when its allowance entitlement was zero.[8]

The allowance formula was designed to enable all participants to afford the full cost of decent, safe, and sanitary housing in their communities without undue constraint on other expenditures. From market surveys, we estimated the "standard cost of adequate housing" (designated R^*) for each size of household.[9] A household's allowance entitlement (A) equaled that standard cost less one-fourth of the household's adjusted gross income (Y):

$$A = R^* - .25Y.$$

The income limit (Y^*) implicit in this formula is

$$Y^* = 4R^*,$$

at which value $A = 0$.

---

[7]Although allowance payments in the Demand Experiment were funded out of EHAP appropriations, the EHAP budget could not cover the costs of two ten-year, full-scale allowance programs. Program operations in the Supply Experiment therefore were funded from Sec. 23 (Leased Public Housing) appropriations, whereas data collection and analysis were funded from the EHAP budget.

[8]The asset limits were set high to enable homeowners with low current incomes to qualify; the limits were subsequently indexed to offset inflation. Under legislation passed in 1976, singles under 62 were admitted to the program after August 1977. For administrative reasons, a household was not enrolled unless its allowance entitlement exceeded $10 monthly; but once enrolled, it remained eligible so long as entitlement exceeded zero.

[9]For each dwelling size, we estimated the minimum gross rent (including all utilities) at which half or more of the dwellings available would meet program standards for domestic equipment, safety, and sanitation. Usually, the estimate was close to the median rent for all dwellings of that size. A similar measure of the standard cost of adequate housing, designated C^*, was used in the Demand Experiment.

In HUD's Sec. 8 rental assistance program, which operated concurrently with the Supply Experiment, participants paid 15 to 25 percent of their adjusted gross incomes toward the rents of the dwellings they occupied, and HUD paid the remainder. However, dwellings whose rents exceeded the "fair market rent" (*FMR*) set by HUD for each local housing market were not eligible for occupancy by participants. In 1975, the HASE schedule of R^* exceeded the HUD schedule of *FMR* by about 4 percent in Brown County. In St. Joseph County, *FMR* exceeded R^* by about 16 percent.

As we soon learned, developing equitable rules for income accounting in such a program is no easy task. Essentially, we annualized the current monthly income of all household members unless there was clear reason to believe that current income was inappropriate as a predictor for the ensuing six months. An important innovation was imputation of income to homeowners' equities in their properties; for an enrollee owning a debt-free $20,000 home, that imputation added about $1,000 to annual income, reducing allowance entitlement by $250 annually. Various income adjustments and exclusions were inherited from Sec. 23 legislation, the net effect of which was to reduce gross income by a minimum of 5 percent and, for large families, by as much as $1,500.

Allowance payments did not automatically follow enrollment. Under the rules adopted by the Supply Experiment, payments were made to enrolled households only while they occupied dwellings that met minimum standards for space, domestic facilities, safety, and sanitation; that requirement was enforced by periodic housing inspections. Enrollees whose dwellings were inadequate could either arrange to repair them or move to adequate dwellings. There was no time limit for action, but payments did not commence until adequate housing was obtained, and were suspended if a once-adequate dwelling fell below standard.

A key feature of the program was that the amount of the allowance did not depend on actual housing expenditures.[10] Those who obtained adequate housing cheaply would have more cash left for other purposes; those who spent more on housing, whether by choice or because they were unable to locate a less expensive but adequate dwelling, would have less money for other things. The program thus provided its participants with a strong incentive to "economize" on housing, paying no more than necessary to obtain a dwelling that (a) met program standards and (b) otherwise suited the household's preferences.

In short, allowances were only weakly earmarked for housing consumption. Once minimum standards were met, participants were neither penalized nor rewarded for additional housing consumption. That design reflected our understanding of low-income "housing problems": Some low-income families spent little on housing and lived in substandard dwellings. Others lived in adequate dwellings but spent

---

[10]Allowance payments could not exceed the recipient's total housing expenses, but this circumstance rarely arose. Typically, the allowance amounted to about half of total housing expense.

inordinate fractions of their incomes for housing. The allowance plan was designed to ameliorate both circumstances.

Program Administration

The allowance program described above would last for ten years, during which thousands of applicants and enrollees would be tested for initial and continuing eligibility, thousands of dwellings would be periodically inspected, and millions of dollars would be disbursed in monthly allowance payments. Effective administration would clearly require a quasi-permanent staff and careful procedural planning. If the program was to serve its experimental purposes, its operating rules had to be both explicit and stable and its record system had to serve analytical as well as administrative needs.

After considering alternatives, HUD and Rand agreed that our administrative objectives would be served best by establishing a nonprofit corporation in each site—the housing allowance office (HAO)—to administer the program under Rand's guidance. To meet the requirements for Sec. 23 funding, HUD entered an annual contributions contract with a local housing authority in each site, which in turn delegated program administration to the HAO. Each HAO was governed by a Board of Trustees composed of members of The Rand Corporation and community leaders.[11]

Before program operations began, a detailed manual of procedures was developed jointly by the Rand and HAO staffs.[12] With minor exceptions reflecting local circumstances, the program rules, administrative procedures, and record systems of the two HAOs were identical. Changes in either site required Rand's approval in all cases and HUD's approval in some cases.

As a result of these measures, we knew, throughout the experimental period, exactly what the program rules were and when they changed, and we were able to forestall HAO policies that might have subverted experimental purposes in order to solve administrative or local political problems.

---

[11]At the end of the five-year experimental period, the Rand members withdrew from the board; they were replaced by local residents who would guide the program through its remaining five years.

[12]A permanent reference edition of the manual was published by Rand (Katagiri and Kingsley, 1980). It deletes material pertinent only to "start-up," and incorporates all rule and procedural changes that were approved during the five-year experimental period.

Data Collection

We planned to collect the information needed to assess the market and community effects of the allowance program from two main sources: HAO administrative records and annual field surveys of the communities in which the programs operated.

The HAO administrative records included a file of all applications for enrollment; the data on household characteristics, income, and assets of those who enrolled (updated semiannually); records of all evaluations of enrollees' current or prospective dwellings; and a record of each administrative action affecting a household's program status or allowance entitlement. These records were maintained by the HAOs in machine-readable form, and were periodically copied and forwarded to Rand for analysis.

The community surveys were directed to a marketwide probability sample of about 2,000 residential properties in each site, chosen from a larger number surveyed at "baseline," before the program began. The surveys included annual interviews with the owners and occupants of each property, and initial and terminal field observations of the property and the neighborhood in which it was located. In addition, data on all neighborhoods were gathered from public records and by field observation.

The owners of rental properties were asked to supply information about the property itself, its finances, operating policies, revenues, expenses, and repairs or improvements during the preceding year. Their tenants were asked about household composition and income, the characteristics of their dwellings, their views on their housing, landlords, and neighborhoods, their rents and other housing expenses, and for a five-year history of household composition, residence, and employment. Homeowners were asked to supply both property and household information. After the allowance program began in each site, all respondents were asked about their knowledge of the program, its effects on them and the community, and their attitudes toward it. Interviews typically lasted about 90 minutes and gathered about 500 items of information.

The field observations of properties and neighborhoods recorded their physical characteristics and condition. Public records yielded additional detail about public and commercial facilities, the availability of services, and environmental quality.

Although formal surveys were essential to collect systematic data on events of known importance to our research, we were concerned that such surveys might miss unexpected events or subtle aspects of community response. We therefore assigned resident observers to each site who learned the local social and political structure and developed a network of informal sources that they tapped for information on community events and attitudes that might affect either the allowance program or our research.

Because the empaneled properties formed an annually updated probability sample of the entire housing stock, they also formed annual samples of owners and occupants. Because we returned to empaneled properties each year, we could compile time-series at both the dwelling and property level, showing changes in property, occupancy, ownership, or financial characteristics.

As noted earlier, we were initially unsure how long we would need to monitor the local market in order to reliably estimate long-run program effects. We planned for six annual survey cycles, with the reservation that either more or fewer might be needed. After assessing the first two years of program experience, we recommended to HUD that the surveys be terminated after the fourth annual cycle; thus the market data gathered by survey cover approximately the year preceding the allowance program and the first three years of its operation. We judged, and HUD agreed, that the information gained from additional surveys would not justify their cost.

Analysis Plans

Before either the survey fieldwork or the allowance program began, we prepared explicit analysis plans for each topic in our research charter, specifying what data were needed and how they would be used. Those plans guided the design of survey samples and interview instruments, and influenced the design of the HAO record system.

Not surprisingly, our analysis plans changed considerably over the course of the experiment. Interim findings altered our judgment as to the relative importance of the various research questions, and new issues were added to our charter by agreement with HUD (see below, "Midcourse Corrections"). Experience with the data informed us about their suitability for various kinds of analysis. Some analytical schemes proved disappointing when applied, and we thought of better methods. However, the initial planning exercise apparently provided sound guidance for data collection; at least, we have few retrospective regrets concerning the amount or kinds of data that were collected.

Given the extensive changes, there would be little point in detailing our initial analysis plans.[13] However, two often misunderstood features of those plans warrant explication.

[13]Interested readers can consult Lowry, 1980.

- *Measuring market responsiveness to increased housing demand.* We expected the housing allowance program to increase the demand for housing services; we planned to measure the market's response to that stimulus, whether in the form of price increases, output increases, or both.[14] From a research perspective, a relatively large demand "shock," compressed in time, would be experimentally efficient because it would result in a relatively large market response, which would be easier to measure reliably than a small response. However, if supply were inelastic, that response would be in the form of price increases rather than output increases. Experimental efficiency had to be balanced against the risk of damage to the host community.

Programmatically, the relevant market stimulus was that which would result from a full-scale housing allowance program. Allowing for considerable uncertainty as to eligibility and participation rates, our scenarios never yielded program-induced demand changes that were large enough to "shock" an entire metropolitan housing market, although submarket shocks were plausible if program-induced demand were focused in a few strongly bounded submarkets. We thought that the hazards to the community were minimal, and urged rapid enrollment in the allowance program so as to compress the demand change in time and thus provide stronger market signals.

More cautious advice prevailed, and program procedures were planned to build up enrollment slowly over a two-year period so as to reduce the risk of large initial price increases. As it worked out, the demand increases generated by the allowance program were so small that not even submarkets were visibly affected. Some critics view that outcome as evidence of poor planning, arguing that we should have created a stronger demand stimulus in order to generate a larger and more readily measurable market response. Our conclusion is that the observed small market stimulus is intrinsic to the type of housing assistance that motivated the experiment.

- *Distinguishing program effects from background events.* Social experiments that are designed to estimate the effect of

[14]Technically, we sought to estimate the price elasticity of the supply of housing services, which is the ratio of output change to price change, both expressed as percentages, during a specified period of time. When demand for a commodity increases in a competitive market, the commodity becomes scarce and its price is bid up. At the higher price, producers usually find it profitable to increase output, whereupon the price tends to fall again. The price movements equilibrate the quantity demanded with the quantity supplied. At different stages in this process, the measured supply elasticity has different values.

> programmatic treatments on the behavior of those treated have revealed the dangers of simple before-and-after comparisons. Behavioral change occurs even in the absence of treatment, as individuals or households move through life and are subjected to a variety of uncontrolled background influences. Further, it is very difficult to devise a sampling procedure that does not select for treatment those who are most favorably predisposed toward the purposes of the treatment; the others refuse to participate or drop out of the experimental program.

One of the best guarantees against erroneous inference is to match treatment groups with control groups that are subject to the same background influences and whose attrition is unmotivated by the characteristics of the treatment. Such control groups were used in the Housing Allowance Demand Experiment. However, for the Supply Experiment, that approach to experimental control was manifestly inappropriate. The subject of treatment was not an individual but a housing market; and for the reasons explained earlier (see "Site Selection"), only two markets were chosen for treatment. Even had resources permitted, it would not have been technically feasible to select and monitor a control group of housing markets subject to the same nonprogram influences as our chosen experimental sites. The absence of formal control groups has led some observers to label the Supply Experiment a "demonstration" rather than an "experiment."

Because empirical controls were infeasible, we planned instead to use statistical and analytical controls. We anticipated using enrollment and disbursement records to measure the market stimulus provided by the allowance program, and annual housing market surveys to measure changes in market prices and the flow of housing services; our problem was to distinguish marketwide changes directly or indirectly attributable to the program from those that would have occurred in its absence. Background influences might include changes in the local population's size or composition, changes in incomes either because of local events (closing a factory) or national ones (a general business recession), inflation in housing prices, revisions in other transfer programs, and so on. Insofar as such events were identified as relevant, they could also be measured.

To link marketwide "effects" back to program "causes," we needed a well-articulated model of the intervening market processes, and direct observations of both exogenous and intervening variables where possible. The principal test of that model's validity would be intersite comparisons. A robust model would explain different outcomes in the two sites entirely by differences in initial conditions and specifiable exogenous events.

The function of scientific investigation is never to establish exact truth, but to narrow the range of uncertainty. Whether the Supply Experiment is termed a "demonstration" or an "experiment," the appropriate test of its design is whether it narrowed the range of uncertainty about the market effects of housing allowances more than could have been done by a different expenditure of the same resources. We are confident that the experiment passes that test.[15]

MIDCOURSE CORRECTIONS

The design for the Supply Experiment was formally approved by HUD in October 1973, by which time field operations had begun in Brown County, the first site to be selected. Baseline surveys there were conducted during the winter and spring of 1973-74, and the allowance program began enrollment in June 1974. The second site, St. Joseph County, was approved in April 1974;[16] baseline surveys were conducted during the fall and winter of 1974-75, and enrollment began late in December 1974.

Between the beginning of enrollment and the end of the five-year experimental period (June 1979 in Brown County, December 1979 in St. Joseph County), there were many minor changes in administrative procedures, but few changes in program rules. The two most important are noted below.

Because the allowance program was funded under Sec. 23, which was designed for rental assistance, homeowners were at first enrolled under a cumbersome lease-leaseback contract with the HAO that qualified them as renters under the law. Some eligible homeowners balked at the arrangement. Subsequent legislation enabled us to dispense with lease-leaseback formalities; beginning in October 1975, the HAOs were authorized to enroll and make payments to homeowners as such.

Section 23 also prohibited assistance to single persons under 62 unless they were handicapped, disabled, or residentially displaced by public action. Subsequent legislation eased this restriction. Beginning

[15]That the experiment substantially narrowed uncertainties about market effects is attested by comparing experimental outcomes with preexperimental predictions by various housing economists, and to program simulations conducted by both the National Bureau of Economic Research and The Urban Institute while the experiment was under way. For a review of these predictions and simulations, see Barnett and Lowry, 1979.

[16]At that time, only the city of South Bend had agreed to participate in the program. By mid-1976, all of St. Joseph County had entered the program.

in August 1977, the HAOs were authorized to enroll all single persons under 62, but only up to 10 percent of total enrollment; the 10-percent limit was never reached during the five-year monitoring period.

These midcourse rule changes complicate our analysis of participation dynamics, but both occurred soon enough to enable a genuine test of a general entitlement program open to all low-income renters and homeowners on equal terms. Although annual contribution contracts contained participation ceilings, they were set high enough so that all eligible applicants during the first five program years could be enrolled.

The research agenda also evolved during the course of the experiment. It was soon apparent that the scale, duration, and open enrollment features of the Supply Experiment's allowance program offered opportunities for administrative analysis that were not available in the other experimental allowance programs. Early in 1976, HUD added administrative research to our charter; the work was to focus on the determinants of administrative cost, the reliability of the means test, and related issues of administrative effectiveness and efficiency.

By the end of 1977, we had collected and analyzed enough data to reach tentative answers to many of the research questions that had motivated the experiment.[17] We also by then had enough experience with the data to reassess their potential uses.

The key conclusion from early analysis was that contrary to general expectations, the allowance program had not noticeably perturbed the housing market in either site and was unlikely to do so in the future. Because the measurement of market effects was the core of the HASE research charter, it was appropriate to reconsider the research agenda for the remainder of the experiment. During the summer of 1978, HUD and Rand considered how best to use the time and resources remaining. Our joint conclusions were embodied in a contract, signed in September 1978, covering the remainder of the experiment.

One important decision was to terminate field surveys at the end of the fourth annual cycle, so that the final wave of interviews and field reports coincided with the allowance program's third year of operation. However, Rand's supervision of the allowance program and our analysis of program records continued through five full years of program operations.

The data collection plan meshed with a revised research agenda. Although we would still seek closure on the questions about market and community effects that dominated the original experimental

[17]The *Fourth Annual Report of the Housing Assistance Supply Experiment,* 1978, summarizes interim findings on all research questions.

charter, most of the remaining resources would be devoted to analysis of two new topics: the dynamics of eligibility and participation, and the program's effects on participants.

Although these topics had been incidentally treated insofar as they bore on the measurement of market stimulus, it was now clear that only the Supply Experiment surveyed the general population of its sites, so could reliably describe the set of households that were eligible to enroll; enrollment was continuously open to all eligibles only in the Supply Experiment, and the program's duration would permit estimation of long-term trends in enrollment, participation, and termination, leading to a steady-state program size and composition.

The Supply Experiment also offered special opportunities for analyzing the program's effects on its participants. Its allowance program was the only one that enrolled homeowners, the only one that tracked participants for more than two years, and the only one that gathered detailed data on the housing-market context of participants' decisions. In this case, however, there were also comparative disadvantages: Unlike the Demand Experiment, the Supply Experiment lacked the analytical benchmark of a formal control group of eligibles who were not permitted to enroll; and no program variations were tested in the Supply Experiment. We did, however, have detailed survey data on unenrolled eligibles, and much larger samples of enrollees than were available to the Demand Experiment.[18]

COMPLETING THE EXPERIMENT

The fourth and final wave of marketwide field surveys was conducted in Brown County during 1977, but we continued to monitor the allowance program there through its fifth year, ending in June 1979. In St. Joseph County, the fourth and final wave of surveys was conducted during 1978, and we monitored program operations through December 1979.

Appendix B of this book describes the research files we constructed from survey and program records. Here, we only note that editing the raw data, transcribing it to machine-readable records, organizing the records into efficiently processable research files, auditing those files, and deriving analytical variables from groups of data elements was a massive, time-consuming task. Although it began for each survey dur-

[18]At the end of the first five years of program operations, the two HASE allowance programs jointly had enrolled over 25,000 households, ten times the number selected for participation in the Demand Experiment.

ing or shortly after the field period, file development was not completed until the end of 1980 and documentation continued into 1981.

Meanwhile, analysis proceeded on the data that were available, testing and refining both methods and hypotheses. The earliest publications were mostly methodological; but between 1974 and 1980, HASE published over 60 research notes and reports of interim findings. As the data files accumulated, our investigations became both wider (integrating data from different but concurrent surveys or files of program records, analyzing time-series, making cross-site comparisons) and deeper (using more elaborate statistical methods to capture elusive relationships). That research culminated in seven final reports, one for each major topic on our agenda.[19]

This comprehensive final report is based mainly on the seven final topical reports mentioned above. It abstracts and interprets the main findings from each, avoiding methodological detail. Chapter II introduces the reader to our experimental sites and Ch. III summarizes the history of the allowance program conducted in each. This background will help the reader understand and evaluate the research findings reported in Chs. IV through VIII. Chapter IX integrates those findings and explores their policy implications.

Most of the statistics and tables in this book first appeared in other HASE publications. To avoid excessive cross-referencing, we do not identify such publications, indicating instead the primary data source. At the end of each chapter is a list of references that may be consulted for more detail, particularly for methodological detail. Where appropriate, these are cited also in the main text and in table notes.

KEY FINDINGS FROM THE EXPERIMENT

Not all readers will be equally interested in all aspects of the Supply Experiment. To guide the selective reader, we offer below a chapter-by-chapter precis of the findings.

The Experimental Sites (Ch. II)

For some years before the experiment began, Brown County's flourishing economy and growing population had combined to keep vacancy rates low and property values high. As St. Joseph County's

[19]In all, HASE published over 280 reports, technical notes, and professional papers. Appendix A indexes 169 that deal with experimental design and research findings. Appendix B lists 109 codebooks and audit reports and a three-volume *User's Guide* that documents the data collected by HASE.

manufacturing industries declined, it lost population, especially in the urban core; vacancy rates were high and property values were low. However, rents were about the same for comparable dwellings in the two counties. In both places, low-income households allocated large shares of their budgets to housing expenses; those with moderate incomes spent very little more for housing.

Our analysis of these housing markets at baseline cast doubt on two widely accepted scenarios of allowance program effects: that an allowance program would powerfully stimulate housing demand, and that such a demand change would promptly be reflected in rents.

The Housing Allowance Program (Ch. III)

Through the first five program years, over 25,000 households enrolled in the two allowance programs and over 20,000 received one or more allowance payments. At the end of year 5, about 11,500 households were enrolled and nearly 9,500 were receiving monthly payments.

During those five years, the program provided financial assistance to 11,350 renters and 8,650 homeowners. At the end of year 5, the average monthly payment was $97, augmenting the average recipient's gross income by 25 percent.

Nearly half of all enrollees joined the program while living in dwellings that met program standards; thus, their allowances mainly helped them meet existing housing expenses (which usually greatly exceeded the legislative norm of one-fourth of adjusted gross income). But nearly 11,000 dwellings were repaired or improved to meet program standards, and about 5,000 households improved their housing circumstances by moving. Over 300 renters bought homes after enrolling in the program.

The programs grew rapidly during their first three years; thereafter, growth was much slower because terminations nearly offset new enrollments. However, growth resumed during the sixth and seventh program years, perhaps because the 1980-81 recession increased the number of income-eligible households.

Eligibility and Participation (Ch. IV)

About 28 percent of all renters and 17 percent of all homeowners in the two counties were usually eligible for assistance under program rules, but about a third of the eligibles became ineligible each year and were replaced by newly formed or newly eligible households. At the end of year 3, about 41 percent of the currently eligible renters and 27 percent of the currently eligible homeowners were enrolled and receiving payments. Current recipients thus constituted about 6.5 percent of all households and a third of all eligible households.

The main reasons for nonparticipation were the small entitlements of those who were only marginally or briefly eligible, and the unwillingness of some whose dwellings were unacceptable to either repair them or move to better housing. The neediest were most likely to participate, but more of them would have participated in the absence of minimum housing standards.

Among those who had to repair or move in order to qualify for payments, about two-thirds did so and one-third dropped out. Overall, over 80 percent of the enrollees eventually qualified for payments. Most of those who dropped out could have recovered repair costs from their first few allowance payments.

Effects on Participants (Ch. V)

Participation in the program increased the likelihood of occupying standard housing from about 50 to about 80 percent, and reduced preenrollment housing expense burdens from about 50 percent of gross income to about 30 percent. In addition to making required repairs, two-fifths of the renters moved to larger or better dwellings and three-fourths of the owners voluntarily improved their dwellings each year. However, the average participant increased his housing expenditures by only 8 percent over his estimated expenditures absent the program.

Enrollees were able to meet program standards without much increase in expenditure because their housing defects were mostly minor health and safety hazards, rather than major structural defects or lack of basic domestic equipment. Repairs were generally made by the participants themselves, their friends, or their landlords, rather than by professional contractors. The average cost of repairing a failed dwelling was about $100, including an imputed wage for unpaid labor. Although allowances augmented the typical renter's income ($4,100) by about a fourth and the typical owner's income ($4,600) by a sixth, recipients chose to spend only a fifth of the extra money on housing. Thus, four-fifths of all allowance payments were allocated to nonhousing consumption.

Although the fiscal mechanism is different, the public housing program has about the same effect as housing allowances on participants' housing and nonhousing consumption. However, the public cost per dollar of participant benefit is over twice as high for public housing as for housing allowances. An unrestricted cash grant would be more efficient than the allowance program in delivering benefits to participants, but would have negligible effects on housing quality.

Market Effects (Ch. VI)

A full-scale open-enrollment allowance program had no perceptible effect on rents or property values in either a tight housing market (Brown County) or a loose market (St. Joseph County). One reason was that the program increased aggregate housing demand by less than 2 percent. Another was that it proved relatively easy and inexpensive to transform substandard to standard dwellings. When a renter joined the program without moving, his rent typically increased by less than 2 percent, even though his landlord may have made minor repairs to bring the dwelling up to program standards. Nonparticipants' rents were unaffected.

The program had little effect on the physical appearance or social composition of residential neighborhoods. Even in neighborhoods where participants made up a fifth or more of all residents, the housing improvements were inconspicuous because program standards were not concerned with cosmetics. Though many renters moved, the origins and destinations of the moves were too diffuse to alter neighborhood populations. The degree of racial segregation did not change perceptibly because of the program.

Because required repairs were inexpensive and could usually be completed with amateur labor, neither home improvement lenders nor home repair contractors were salient actors in the program. Real-estate brokers and mortgage lenders were involved in home purchases by participants, but few renter enrollees sought to buy homes. Those who did so usually obtained financing either from a mortgage bank or the seller of the property; commercial banks and thrift institutions were conspicuously uninterested in lending on low-valued properties.

Community Attitudes (Ch. VII)

Brown and St. Joseph counties offered very different political and social environments for the proposed experimental program. The former was a conservative community, remarkably free of competing interest groups and inexperienced with federal assistance programs. The latter was less a "community" than a network of overlapping interest groups—jurisdictional, political, economic, and ethnic—and had participated in similar federal programs. Although negotiations to operate the program in the two sites followed very different patterns, the outcomes in terms of public knowledge and attitudes were quite similar.

After three years of experience with the program, a majority of all household heads and 90 percent of all participants thought it was a "good idea." Landlords were less enthusiastic, but a majority of those whose tenants included recipients approved of the program. In general, the public approved of who got help, what the help was for, and how the program was run. However, only participants were very conscious of program-induced housing or neighborhood effects. Virtually no one perceived negative consequences, such as rent increases, property deterioration, or undesirable new neighbors.

Program Administration (Ch. VIII)

The allowance programs were administered by nonprofit corporations under the supervision of Rand and HUD. Hiring staff locally at prevailing wages, these housing allowance offices (HAOs) performed their functions promptly, equitably, and humanely at the surprisingly low cost of $163 per recipient-year (1976 dollars).

We attribute this administrative success to several factors. One is the intentionally limited nature of HAO administrative functions, which made workloads controllable and susceptible to routine procedures. Another was the administrative style, which stressed formal procedures, careful training, thorough and conspicuous checks on both clients' submissions and staff work, and a management information system that closely tracked individual performances as well as workloads and costs.

Lessons from the Supply Experiment (Ch. IX)

Much discourse on federal housing policy is based on two widely held beliefs: (a) that most poor people live in seriously substandard dwellings, and (b) that they do so because they cannot afford adequate housing. Evidence from the Supply Experiment strongly qualifies both propositions. Both in our sites and elsewhere, seriously overcrowded, under-equipped, or dilapidated dwellings are now rare. The much more common health and safety hazards could be corrected inexpensively by the dwellings' occupants if they were aware of them and concerned about them.

However, housing expenses are quite burdensome for low-income families, typically absorbing about half of their incomes. We judge that low-income households in our sites and probably elsewhere would much prefer help with their present housing expenses to any substantial increase in their housing consumption.

A housing allowance program serves that function, and at the same time requires the beneficiaries to bring their dwellings up to standards that are embodied in most local housing codes but are rarely enforced by local authorities. Although housing allowances are effective and efficient remedies for both the housing expense and quality problems of low-income families, they do not contribute much to other objectives of federal housing policy, such as neighborhood improvement, racial and economic integration, homeownership, stabilization of the construction industry, and liquidity of housing investments.

The experimental program was open to nearly all low-income households, regardless of family composition or housing circumstances. Nationally, about a fifth of all households would be eligible under Supply Experiment rules, and we estimate that about a tenth would actually participate. However, the size of a national program could be varied substantially by adopting broader or more restrictive eligibility rules, offering higher or lower benefits, or applying different housing standards.

We strongly recommend additional research and field testing for housing standards that are applied in both federal housing assistance programs and local housing codes. Those in common use represent a consensus of expert opinion; but their premises are largely untested and their consequences in the field are, except for the housing allowance experiments, poorly documented.

In the experimental program, assistance was conditional on both need and performance. Among those who were eligible, the needier were much more likely to participate than the less needy. It is also clear, however, that more of the neediest would have participated in the absence of performance requirements (housing standards). We leave it to the reader to decide whether the housing improvements achieved by the program warrant excluding those who were unable or unwilling to meet the program's housing standards.

REFERENCES

Barnett, C. Lance, and Ira S. Lowry, *How Housing Allowances Affect Housing Prices,* The Rand Corporation, R-2452-HUD, September 1979.

Bennett, Carl A., and Arthur A. Lumsdaine, eds., *Evaluation and Experiment: Some Critical Issues in Assessing Social Programs,* Academic Press, New York, San Francisco, and London, 1975.

Fourth Annual Report of the Housing Assistance Supply Experiment, The Rand Corporation, R-2302-HUD, May 1978.

Katagiri, Iao, and G. Thomas Kingsley, eds., *The Housing Allowance Office Handbook,* The Rand Corporation, N-1491-HUD, July 1980.

Kershaw, David N., "A Negative-Income-Tax Experiment," *Scientific American,* Vol. 227, No. 4, October 1972, pp. 19-25.

Lampman, Robert J., "The Decision To Undertake the New Jersey Experiment," in Institute for Research on Poverty, *The New Jersey Income Maintenance Experiment,* Vol. I, Academic Press, New York, San Francisco, and London, 1976, pp. xi-xx.

Lilly, William, III, "Policy Makers Condemn Housing Programs; Seek Alternative to Builder-Subsidy Approach," *National Journal,* 24 July 1971, pp. 1525-43.

Lowry, Ira S., ed., *The Design of the Housing Assistance Supply Experiment,* The Rand Corporation, R-2630-HUD, June 1980.

Nixon, Richard M., "Special Message to the Congress Proposing Legislation and Outlining Administration Actions To Deal with Federal Housing Policy," *Public Papers of the Presidents of the United States,* U.S. Government Printing Office, Washington, D.C., 1975, pp. 800-13.

President's Commission on Housing, *The Report of the President's Commission on Housing,* U.S. Government Printing Office, Washington, D.C., 1982.

President's Committee on Urban Housing, *A Decent Home,* U.S. Government Printing Office, Washington, D.C., 1982.

Reichen, Henry W., and Robert F. Boruch, eds., *Social Experimentation: A Method for Planning and Evaluating Social Intervention,* Academic Press, New York, San Francisco, and London, 1974.

Rivlin, Alice M., "How Can Experiments Be More Useful?" *American Economic Review,* Vol. 64, No. 2, May 1974, pp. 346 54.

Rivlin, Alice M., and P. Michael Timpane, eds., *Ethical and Legal Issues of Social Experimentation,* The Brookings Institution, Washington, D.C., 1975.

Romney, George, "Remarks Prepared for Delivery . . . at the 29th Annual Convention Exposition of the National Association of Homebuilders," *HUD News,* Washington, D.C., 8 January 1973.

"The Bankruptcy of Subsidized Housing," *Business Week,* 27 May 1972, pp. 42-8.

U.S. Department of Housing and Urban Development, National Housing Policy Review, *Housing in the Seventies,* 2 vols., U.S. Government Printing Office, Washington, D.C., 1976.

II. THE EXPERIMENTAL SITES

The sites for the Supply Experiment—Brown County, Wisconsin, and St. Joseph County, Indiana—were chosen principally for contrast in market characteristics that we thought were especially likely to influence the results of a housing allowance program and that also vary considerably among the metropolitan areas where a national program might operate.[1] In the following pages, we describe each site and contrast their characteristics, including some that did not enter into site selection but were potentially or actually important for the experiment.

The two sites were chosen after a thorough canvass of all metropolitan areas in the nation whose 1970 populations were under 250,000, and after site visits to and negotiations with a smaller list of suitable candidates (HASE Staff, 1980a and 1980b; Dubinsky, 1980). Most of the statistical evidence used in screening came from advance reports of the 1970 censuses of housing and population. Our baseline surveys of residential properties and their owners and occupants, conducted in 1974 for Brown County and in 1975 for St. Joseph County, confirmed that the two sites met our selection criteria not only in 1970 but also in mid-decade when the allowance program began. Those surveys also provided many details about household populations and housing markets that were not available from the decennial census.

Below, we describe the two counties at baseline, just before the allowance program began in each place. After an orienting sketch of each county, we contrast first their household characteristics, then their housing characteristics. Next, we examine housing market conditions at baseline, including utilization of the stock, property values, and rents. We then show how those conditions had affected consumers' choices as to tenure and housing consumption, highlighting differences that might affect program development. The chapter concludes by reviewing the implications of all these site characteristics for the experiment.[2]

---

[1]See Ch. I, "Major Design Issues and Their Resolution."

[2]Housing market characteristics were especially important for our analysis of the market effects of the allowance program, discussed in Ch. VI. At the end of that chapter, we consider whether the findings for Brown and St. Joseph counties can be extrapolated to U.S. housing markets generally. In that connection, we compare the experimental sites with a national sample of metropolitan areas, specifically with respect to eligibility rates, allowance entitlements, age of the housing stock, vacancy rates, and the presence of racial minorities. See Table 6.19 and Figs. 6.6 and 6.7.

TWO METROPOLITAN HOUSING MARKETS

Brown County was selected as an example of a metropolitan area with a growing urban center whose housing market was undivided by racial segregation. St. Joseph County was chosen as an example of an area with a declining urban center and a segregated minority population. Table 2.1 shows the population statistics that supported these choices.

Table 2.1

POPULATION CONTRASTS AT BASELINE: BROWN COUNTY (1974) AND ST. JOSEPH COUNTY (1975)

Area	Number of Persons	Average Annual Growth (%)		Households	
		1960-70	After 1970	Number	Percent Black or Latin
Brown County					
Green Bay	88,500	3.3	.2	28,100	1.9
Rest of county	81,900	1.2	3.0	19,800	.6
Total	170,400	2.4	1.5	47,900	1.4
St. Joseph County					
South Bend	112,500	- .5	-2.2	39,300	18.6
Rest of county	123,000	1.2	.6	36,300	1.3
Total	235,500	.3	- .8	75,600	10.4

SOURCE: U.S. Bureau of the Census, *Census of Housing: 1970* and *Census of Population: 1970*; and estimates by HASE staff from weighted records of the baseline surveys of households in each site.

Although the two places differ substantially in population size, neither is large relative to the national norm for Standard Metropolitan Statistical Areas, which in 1970 averaged about 600,000 inhabitants. Because the cost of an open-enrollment allowance program increases linearly with population size, we restricted our search to places with under 250,000 inhabitants.[3] Within that constraint, our two sites were remarkably different not only as indicated by the selection criteria, but in other ways as well.

---

[3]The Housing Allowance Demand Experiment, which enrolled a predetermined number of households by invitation, could be and was conducted in larger places: Pittsburgh, Pennsylvania, and Phoenix, Arizona. See Ch. I, "The Elements of EHAP."

Brown County, Wisconsin

Rapid growth in employment and population has given Brown County a persistently tight housing market. Because of the population's racial homogeneity, the market is unsegregated. These two features characterize about a fourth of the metropolitan areas in the nation, many of which also resemble Brown County in other, less salient respects.

Figure 2.1 maps Brown County's political subdivisions. Mostly flat farmlands and woodlands, the county is bisected diagonally by the Fox River and its estuary, Green Bay (an arm of Lake Michigan). The city of Green Bay is an important lake port and transshipment point for bulk goods moving through southern and eastern Wisconsin. Urban employment in Brown County is concentrated in the manufacture of paper, paper-mill machinery, lumber and wood products, office equipment, automobile parts, cheese and other dairy products, and in wholesale trade. Rural employment is mostly in diversified farming and dairies. The lakeshore is a popular vacation retreat, with numberous small resorts and summer cottages.

Shaded areas on the map mark the jurisdictions that were populated at urban densities in 1970. These include the city of Green Bay, with a population of 87,780, and four adjoining suburbs: De Pere city (13,400), Howard village (4,900), Allouez town (13,800), and part of Ashwaubenon (9,300 in the urban part). The remainder of the county contained 29,100 inhabitants in 1970, of which 18,900 were classified as rural nonfarm residents living in open country or small villages (Pulaski, Denmark, Wrightstown). The remaining 10,100 persons lived on farms. The countywide total in 1970 was 158,000 persons.

The county's population grew by 26 percent between 1960 and 1970, and three-fourths of the growth was in the urban center—Green Bay and adjoining suburbs. Green Bay grew mostly by annexation, the population within its 1960 boundaries increasing by only 8 percent. Since 1970, the city's boundaries and population have changed very little, but the surrounding suburbs continue to grow. For 1975, the Wisconsin Department of Administration estimated a countywide population of 170,400, up by 8 percent since 1970.

A remarkable feature of Brown County (and one of the reasons we chose it as an experimental site) was its ethnic homogeneity. Over 98 percent of its population were white and nearly two-thirds were of northern European or Scandinavian ancestry, Germany being the nation of origin most frequently identified. The remaining 2 percent includes some 1,700 American Indians, many of whom lived on a reservation in Hobart town; and about 370 blacks and 640 Latin

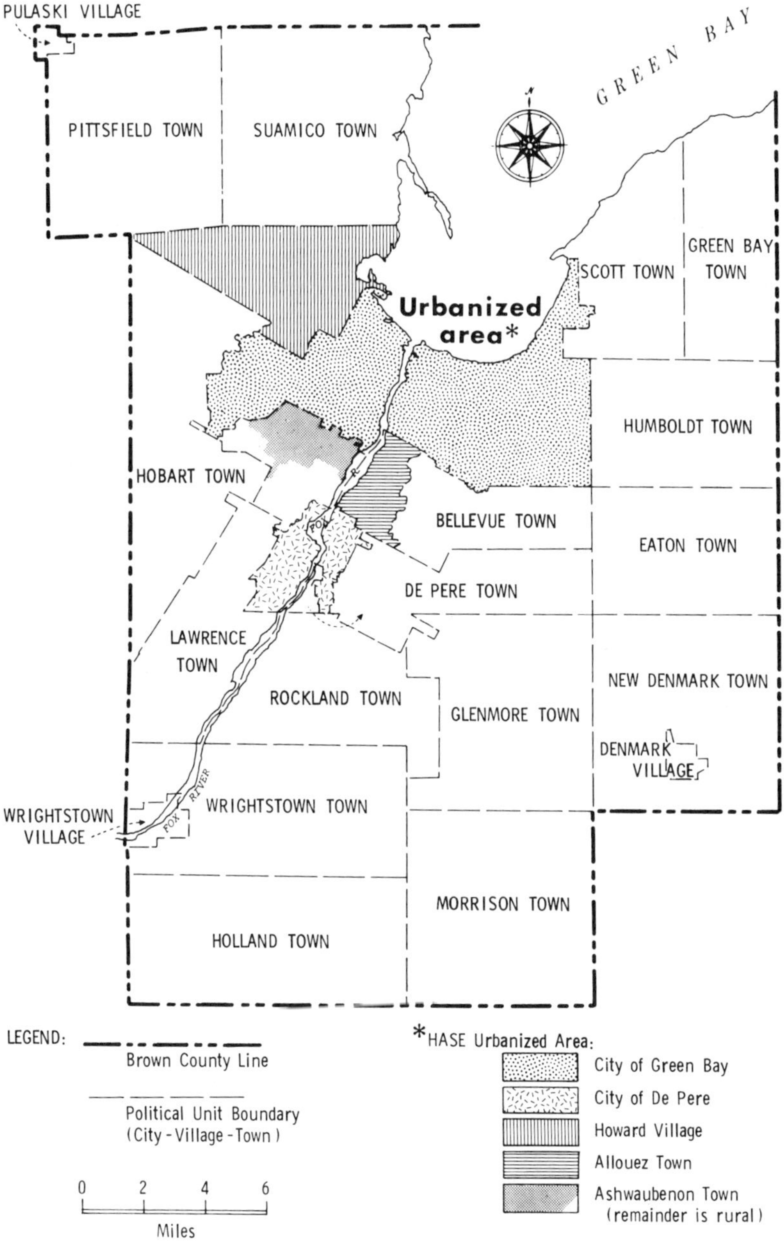

Fig. 2.1—Political subdivisions of Brown County, Wisconsin, and HASE urbanized area, 1974

Americans who lived in either Green Bay or its suburbs but nowhere formed a large ethnic enclave.[4]

The residents of Brown County accurately perceive their community as being homogeneous, generally prosperous, and socially conservative.[5] Their lives are marked by an orderliness reminiscent of Sinclair Lewis's novel, *Main Street,* and for much the same reason: Residents share a common set of values. This consensus is partly due to the absence of a demographic or economic basis for factionalism. The county lacks racial minorities or an unskilled underclass whose interests might clash with those of the majority; it lacks the aggressive jurisdictional rivalry that, in St. Joseph County, has pitted Mishawaka against South Bend; and it lacks competing economic interests with conflicting scenarios of progress.

Brown County has few formal political groups and organizations. To be sure, politics is played, influence is wielded, and decisions are made. But, more often than not, such business is transacted in athletic rooms, service club meetings, and during social gatherings. The county is unfamiliar with confrontation politics, usually arriving at major public decisions by informally working toward consensus.

St. Joseph County, Indiana

St. Joseph County was chosen as an example of a metropolitan area whose central-city growth rate was slow or negative, resulting in a surplus of deteriorating housing there; and one with a residentially segregated racial minority—in this case, blacks living in South Bend. About half of all the nation's metropolitan areas share these characteristics.

The county lies on the northern border of Indiana, about 30 miles southeast of Lake Michigan. Like Brown County, St. Joseph is generally flat and consists mostly of farms and woodlands. Its northeast corner is cut by the meandering St. Joseph River (see Fig. 2.2), which empties into Lake Michigan at Benton Harbor.

In earlier days, the river was an important means of transportation, and the county's only dense urban settlement developed at South Bend. Today, the location is significant primarily because it lies in a

[4]Population figures cited here for Brown County are based on the 1970 censuses of housing and population. A special census of Green Bay only, conducted early in 1976, indicates that the city's population had grown by less than 1 percent since 1970, and that the city contained 118 blacks and 823 persons of other nonwhite races, including native Americans but excluding Latin Americans.

[5]This account of the social and political structure of Brown County (and the similar account for St. Joseph County) are based primarily on discussions with and written reports from Rand's resident observers, whose functions were described in Ch. I. For more detailed treatment, see Ellickson and Kanouse, 1979.

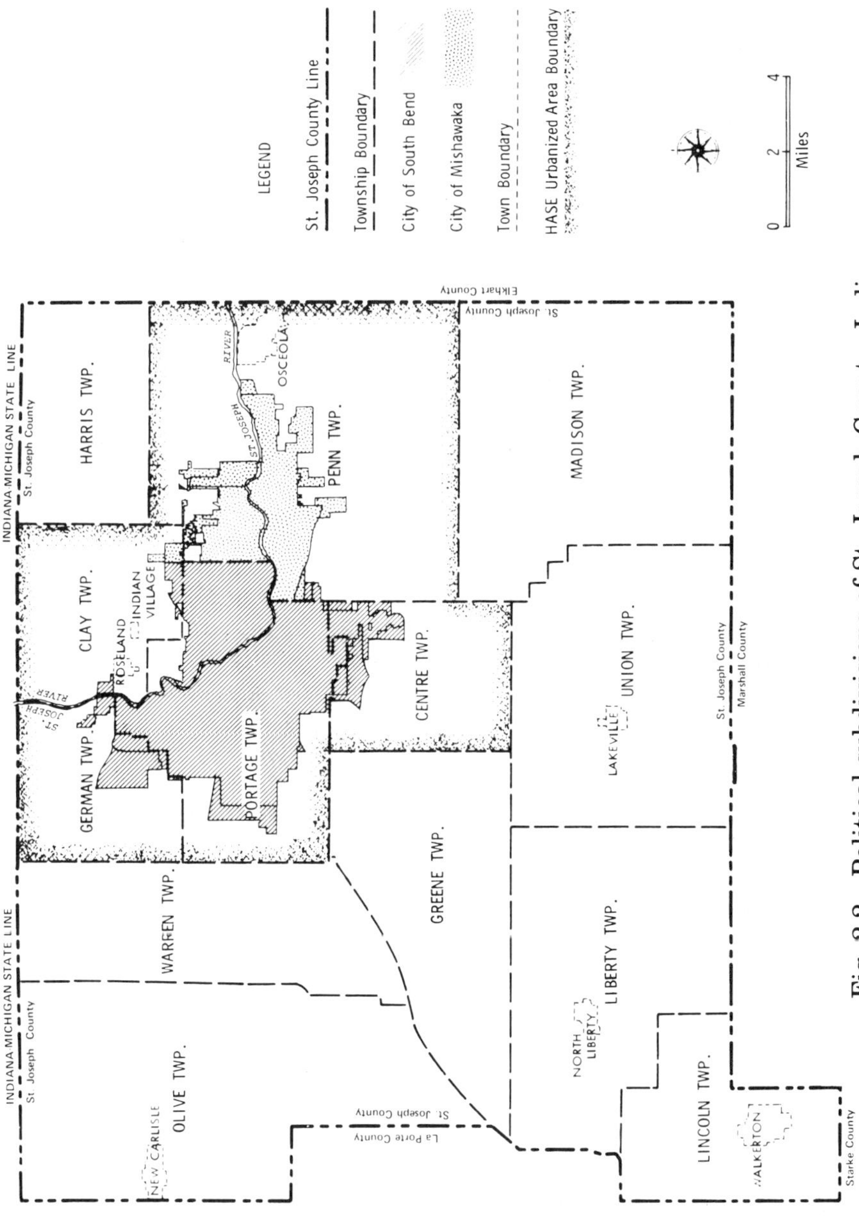

Fig. 2.2—Political subdivisions of St. Joseph County, Indiana, and HASE urbanized area, 1975

major rail and highway corridor connecting Chicago and Gary, at the toe of Lake Michigan, to Toledo and Detroit, on Lake Erie.

As recently as 1950, the local economy was dominated by manufacturing establishments employing 55,400 persons, about half the county's total employment of 110,000. By 1970, manufacturing employment had decreased to 32,500 out of a county total of 102,900, mostly because of a loss of jobs in the transportation equipment industry. The remaining manufacturing employment was predominantly in cyclically unstable industries: transportation equipment, electrical and nonelectrical machinery, and primary and fabricated metals.

Much of the slack in the local economy was taken up by growth in trucking, warehousing, and wholesale trade and by the development of business and financial services with a regional or national market. The local economy was also considerably affected by the presence of the University of Notre Dame (8,600 students), a campus of Indiana University (5,000 students), and several smaller colleges. These may partly account for the surprising growth in service and miscellaneous employment, which in 1975 accounted for 20 percent of all jobs in the county. Fewer than 1,000 people were employed in agriculture, although eight times that number still lived on farms.

In 1970, the county had 245,000 inhabitants, of which half (125,000) lived in South Bend. The adjoining city of Mishawaka contained another 35,500 inhabitants. The rest of the urban area, consisting of portions of five townships (shown in Fig. 2.2), contained 59,000 inhabitants. Altogether, this urbanized area accounted for about 90 percent of the county's population. The rest of the county contained about 25,000 inhabitants, a third of whom lived on farms.

Between 1960 and 1970, the county's population grew by about 3 percent, a net outmigration of 17,000 persons offsetting most of the natural increase. South Bend lost about 5 percent of its 1960 population during the decade, while the remainder of the county grew by 12 percent. After 1970, South Bend's losses were no longer offset by suburban growth; by 1975, estimates of the county's population ranged from 241,000 to 236,000 persons, down several percentage points from 1970.[6] However, because of declining household size, the number of households actually increased slightly.

Another important demographic feature of St. Joseph County was its racial and ethnic composition. HASE surveys conducted in 1975

---

[6]The U.S. Bureau of the Census, working from indirect indicators of population change, estimates that by mid-1975 the county's population had decreased to 241,000 (U.S. Bureau of the Census, 1976). The HASE surveys conducted early in 1975 did not cover those in institutions or group quarters. Data from our sample of households imply a household population of about 227,000 persons, to which we would add an estimated 8,500 persons not in households, to reach a total of 235,500 inhabitants early in 1975.

did not cover those living in group quarters; but of the estimated 227,000 persons living in households, about 21,000 were black and 2,000 were of Latin-American descent. The remaining white inhabitants were mostly of northern- or eastern-European origin and have, to a greater degree than in Brown County, retained their ethnic identities. Thus, parish churches and neighborhood political clubs often have an explicit ethnic association.

Whereas the county as a whole had about the same number of inhabitants in 1960 and 1975, its black population increased from 14,000 to at least 21,000, and the number of households headed by blacks increased from 3,200 to 7,100. In 1975, over 90 percent of the county's black households lived in South Bend, where they constituted nearly 18 percent of all households; two-thirds lived in seven census tracts that were more than one-fourth black (see Fig. 2.3). Most of the county's remaining blacks lived in census tract 111, an unincorporated area adjoining South Bend's western boundary. Generally, the neighborhoods with the largest black populations were also those where housing conditions were poorest and property values lowest.

St. Joseph County's economy and demography combine to give it many characteristics of much larger metropolitan areas. It is racially and ethnically diverse. Its industrial history led to strong labor unions and also left a legacy of skilled workers prematurely retired by factory closings. It has an intense political life, with Democratic and Republican parties vying for local as well as state and national offices. Its government is organizationally complex beyond any obvious need, and its civil service is frankly political in staffing and performance. Its intellectual and social life is leavened by the presence of five universities and colleges with a combined enrollment of more than 16,000 students.

It is understandably difficult for the county's residents to share the broad sense of community that we observe in Brown County. Instead, allegiances form among smaller groups of people with common backgrounds, interests, grievances, or values. Such groups often coalesce around an issue of concern to their members, then retreat from the political arena once that issue is resolved. Many groups clash regularly and publicly; but the heat thus generated seldom radiates beyond the immediate participants. Indeed, those unaffected by the issue at hand, and even the participants themselves, often view public controversy more as a dramatic performance than as a way of reaching public decisions.

The adversary style of local politics is evident in the rivalry between South Bend and Mishawaka. Mishawakans publicly congratulate themselves on their insulation from the poverty, crime, drug abuse, and social tensions that they believe afflict South Bend, and

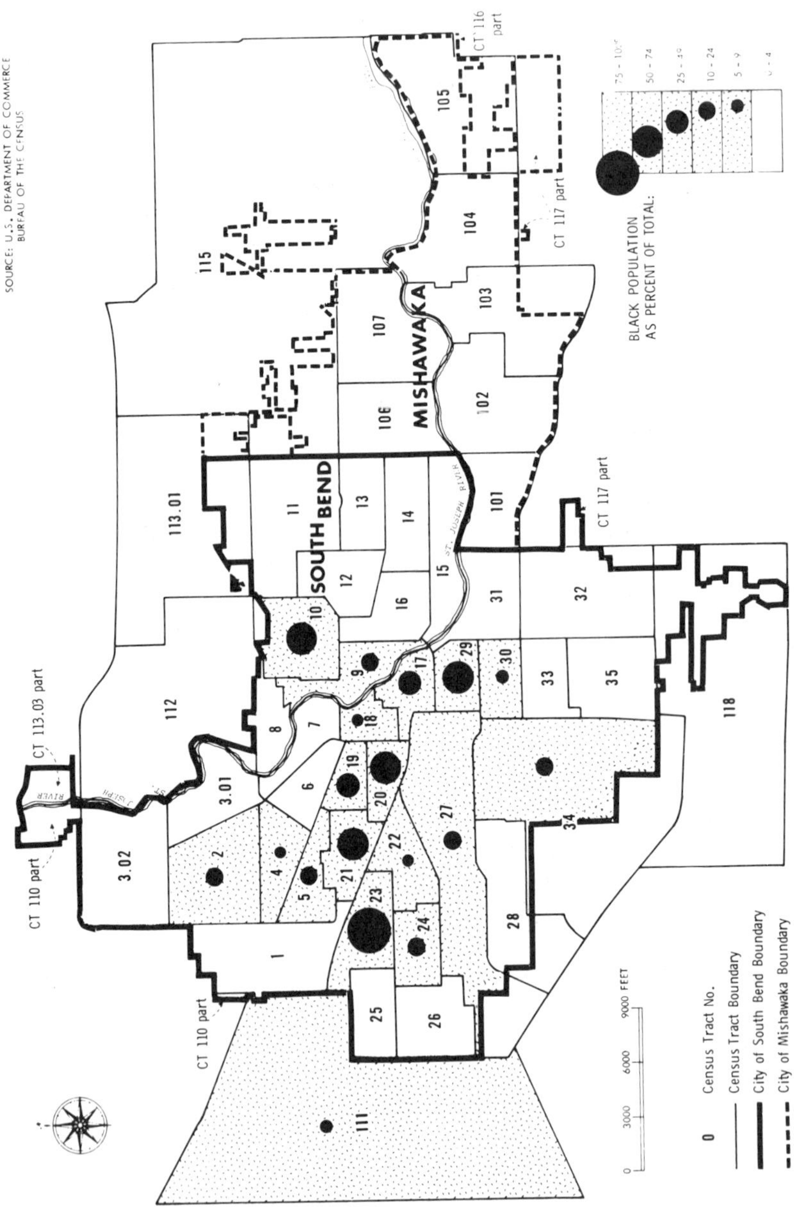

Fig. 2.3—Census tracts in South Bend, Mishawaka, and adjacent areas, and distribution of black population in 1970

are especially wary of threats to their sovereignty. The adversary style is also conspicuous in the remarkably aggressive contests for public office throughout the county. Even in office, officials have engaged in protracted feuds, trading accusations and calling for each others' resignations.

CONTRASTS IN HOUSEHOLD CHARACTERISTICS

For our purposes, perhaps the most important difference between the populations of Brown and St. Joseph counties was the presence in the latter of a residentially segregated black population. But the different demographic and economic histories of the two places also reflect in other characteristics, such as the types and size of households, the employment statuses of household heads, and household incomes. Those differences in turn affected local housing markets and influenced the allowance program's role in each community.

Briefly, Brown County's households were more traditionally organized than those in St. Joseph County, with earlier marriages, larger families, and fewer working wives. Their jobs paid less but provided steadier incomes, enabling earlier retirement. These intercounty differences were partly traceable to different racial mixes in the two counties. As compared with whites in St. Joseph County, the black minority had many more single-parent households, less labor-force participation, and lower incomes.

Life-Cycle Stage

Table 2.2 divides the households in each site according to stages in the household life cycle. That cycle typically begins when a young single person moves from the parental home to form a new household. Marriage may be the occasion for this move, but if not it usually follows within a few years, and the couple bear and raise children who also leave home in due course. The cycle ends with a widow or widower living alone. Most of those who depart from the normal sequence do so because of a divorce or separation during the child-rearing years; these are assigned to Stage 8.[7]

In both counties, it is striking that about half of all households did not contain children under 18. St. Joseph County had the larger pro-

[7]See McCarthy, 1979a and 1979b, for definitions of life-cycle stages, explanations of their social significance, and further analysis of household characteristics in each site, including residential mobility.

Table 2.2

Distribution of Households and Selected Demographic Characteristics by Life-Cycle Stage: Brown County (1974) and St. Joseph County (1975)

Stage in Life Cycle[a]	Percent of All Households		Average Age (years) of Male or Only Head		Average Number of Members	
	Brown County	St. Joseph County	Brown County	St. Joseph County	Brown County	St. Joseph County
1. Young single head, no children	8.6	10.4	25.4	29.8	1.65	1.31
2. Young couple, no children	7.3	7.8	26.4	28.2	2.01	2.13
3. Young couple, young children	26.0	19.2	31.5	30.0	4.53	4.42
4. Young couple, older children	10.2	10.8	38.9	38.2	5.16	4.77
5. Older couple, older children	11.8	7.7	51.8	51.9	5.46	4.66
6. Older couple, no children	18.0	18.0	62.8	62.7	2.27	2.28
7. Older single head, no children	13.0	18.0	67.1	65.0	1.23	1.35
8. Single head with children	5.1	8.1	37.2	35.1	3.60	3.43
All stages[b]	100.0	100.0	44.3	45.1	3.39	2.96

SOURCE: Tabulation by HASE staff of weighted records from the baseline surveys of households in each site.

NOTE: Entries for Brown County are based on a 1974 sample of 3,722 households, excluding most landlords and all occupants of federally subsidized housing units, mobile homes, and rooming houses. Entries for St. Joseph County are based on a 1975 sample of 2,774 households, excluding most landlords and all occupants of rooming houses but including mobile-home residents.

[a] Age divisions are as follows: Young heads are under 46; young children are under 6; older children are between 6 and 18; older heads are 46 or over.

[b] Totals include an estimated 66 households in Brown County and an estimated 242 households in St. Joseph County that were not classifiable by life-cycle stage.

portion of childless households (54 percent, vs. 47 percent in Brown County), primarily because of an abundance of elderly single persons living alone or with other adults. Brown County, on the other hand, had a relatively large number of young couples who had just begun their families (Stage 3).

Life-cycle stages tend to group households whose heads are of about the same age, so the counties did not differ much in the average age of those in each stage. But it does appear that St. Joseph County's young people stay single longer (Stage 1) and once married, postpone child-bearing (Stage 2). Couples in St. Joseph County who did have children had fewer than their counterparts in Brown County, as reflected in average household sizes for Stages 3, 4, and 5.

Labor Force Participation

Table 2.3 describes household employment status by life-cycle stage for the two counties. At every stage except Stage 7, household heads in Brown County were more likely to have jobs than their counterparts in St. Joseph County. The households in Stage 7 were mostly elderly single persons living alone; that more of them in St. Joseph County had jobs probably reflects the lack of an income large enough to support retirement. For instance, many who were employed in manufacturing for most of their working years lost their pension rights when the factories closed or their jobs disappeared.

In both counties, wives and older children often worked. This practice was more common in St. Joseph County, partly offsetting the more frequent unemployment of household heads there. Overall, Brown County came out ahead, with 1.3 employed persons per household, versus 1.2 for St. Joseph County. Only 16 percent of all Brown County households had no employed member, versus 22 percent in St. Joseph County. Both figures, of course, include households of retired persons.

Incomes

Figure 2.4 compares income distributions for each life-cycle stage in the two counties. Because more of its households were in their peak earning years, Brown County's median household income exceeded that of St. Joseph County by just over $500. But stage by stage, the advantage was with residents of St. Joseph County, despite its having fewer earners per household. For example, in Stage 3 household median income was higher in St. Joseph County by $800, and in Stage 4 by

Table 2.3

Employment Characteristics of Households by Life-Cycle Stage: Brown County (1974) and St. Joseph County (1975)

Stage in Life Cycle[a]	Percentage of Households with:						Average Number of Workers	
	Male or Only Head Employed		Wife Employed		No Members Employed			
	Brown County	St. Joseph County	Brown County	St. Joseph County	Brown County	St. Joseph County	Brown County	St. Joseph County
1. Young single head, no children	83.7	80.6	(*b*)	(*b*)	7.1	13.2	1.40	1.04
2. Young couple, no children	90.9	86.7	67.2	74.5	1.8	4.9	1.59	1.67
3. Young couple, young children	95.6	85.8	30.6	25.2	2.4	8.7	1.30	1.19
4. Young couple, older children	97.9	94.6	48.6	48.8	1.1	2.1	1.74	1.74
5. Older couple, older children	92.3	89.0	34.2	56.0	1.2	4.9	2.15	1.80
6. Older couple, no children	61.2	56.8	27.1	36.3	29.6	31.5	1.07	1.10
7. Older single head, no children	35.3	41.7	(*b*)	(*b*)	57.5	50.5	.51	.70
8. Single head with children	56.4	55.8	(*b*)	(*b*)	35.6	37.4	.75	.91
All stages	77.9	71.0	36.5[c]	42.3[c]	16.3	22.2	1.30	1.19

SOURCE: Tabulation by HASE staff of weighted records from the baseline surveys of households in each site.

NOTE: Entries for Brown County are based on a 1974 sample of 3,722 households, excluding most landlords and all occupants of federally subsidized housing units, mobile homes, and rooming houses. Entries for St. Joseph County are based on a 1975 sample of 2,774 households, excluding most landlords and all occupants of rooming houses but including mobile-home residents.

[a] See Table 2.2, note *a*, for age divisions.

[b] Not applicable.

[c] Base for percentage includes only households headed by a married couple.

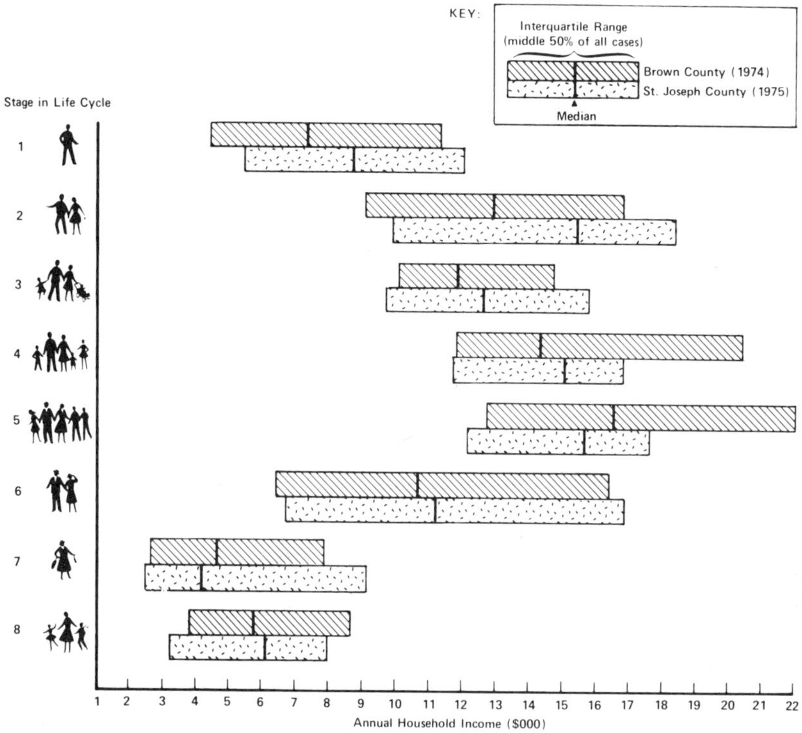

SOURCE: Baseline surveys of households in each site.

Fig. 2.4—Income distributions for households by life-cycle stage: Brown County (1974) and St. Joseph County (1975)

$700. Even in Stage 5, where Brown County households led by $900, income per employed household member was higher in St. Joseph County by $1,000.

Racial Differences

The intercounty comparisons above include nearly all households in each place. In St. Joseph County, it is important to distinguish the black minority, whose social and economic characteristics differ sharply from those of the white majority. Some perspective on the significance of this minority population for housing issues can be gained from Table 2.4, which characterizes black and white households in the county as of 1975.

The black household heads were younger and a large proportion had children under 18. It is especially notable that over a fourth consisted of a single parent with minor children; the corresponding figure for whites was 6 percent. The races also differed sharply in employment status and income. Only 58 percent of black household heads were employed, compared with 72 percent of white household heads; and white households averaged a fourth more employed members than black households. These disparities were reflected in household income; half of all black households had incomes under $7,328, but the median for white households was $11,422.

CONTRASTS IN HOUSING CHARACTERISTICS

The baseline housing stocks of Brown and St. Joseph counties are compared in Table 2.5 and Fig. 2.5. They differ in ways that reflect population growth and residential construction over the past century. Events of the past 25 years are particularly pertinent to understanding the current mixtures of structural type, tenure, and condition.

Briefly, Brown County's rapidly growing and prospering population has created a dependable market for new homes; and the county's older housing, still in demand, has generally been kept in good repair. In St. Joseph County, there have been important population shifts but (since 1960) little net growth. Suburbanization has been served by new construction, but the central city has accumulated a surplus of deteriorating older homes, once owner-occupied but now rented or vacant.

Brown County

In 1974, there were about 49,000 housing units in Brown County, 70 percent of which were single-family houses. Most of the remaining units (20 percent) were in small multiple dwellings; only 10 percent of the total were on properties with more than five units, the largest being mobile-home parks. There were only 45 properties with more than 19 conventional housing units on them; of these, only two federally subsidized rental projects exceeded 100 units.

The county's development history is reflected in the left-hand panel of Fig. 2.5, which shows that 58 percent of all housing units standing in 1974 were built after World War II, and nearly a fourth after 1964. Older homes predominated on farms and in urban neighborhoods

Table 2.4

SELECTED HOUSEHOLD CHARACTERISTICS BY RACE OF HOUSEHOLD HEAD: ST. JOSEPH COUNTY, 1975

Household Characteristic	Race of Male or Only Head	
	Black	White
Demographic Characteristics		
Average age (years) of male or only head	40.6	45.7
Average number of household members	3.13	2.94
Percentage of all households:		
Without children	43.3	55.4
Single head	26.4	28.6
Married couple	16.9	26.8
With children	56.7	44.6
Single head	25.5	6.4
Married couple	31.2	38.2
Economic Characteristics		
Percentage of male or only heads employed	57.9	72.2
Percentage of wives employed	51.6	42.2
Percentage of households with no employed members	29.6	21.5
Average number of workers	.97	1.21
Median income ($) in 1974	7,328	11,422

SOURCE: Tabulation by HASE staff of records from the baseline survey of tenants and homeowners in Site II.

NOTE: All entries except median income are based on samples of 432 black and 2,272 white households. Median income estimates are based on samples of 390 black and 2,039 white households who reported total household income in 1974. Latin Americans, native Americans, and Orientals, altogether accounting for less than 2 percent of all households, are excluded from this tabulation.

Table 2.5

Residential Properties and Housing Units by Type of Property and Occupancy Status of Unit: Brown County (1974) and St. Joseph County (1975)

Type of Property	Number of Properties	Number of Housing Units, by Occupancy Status				Percentage Distribution	
		Owner-Occupied[a]	Renter-Occupied	Vacant	Total	Properties	Housing Units
Brown County, 1974							
1 unit	34,389	31,950	2,085	354	34,389	87.9	69.8
2-4 units	4,380	1,969	7,425	360	9,754	11.2	19.8
5-19 units	231	37	1,822	123	1,982	0.6	4.0
20-99 units	43	2	1,520	89	1,611	0.1	3.3
100+ units	2	--	255	15	270	(*b*)	0.6
Mobile-home park[c]	13	807	--	90	897	(*b*)	1.8
Rooming house[d]	40	10	326	29	365	0.1	0.7
Total	39,098	34,775	13,433	1,060	49,268	100.0	100.0
St. Joseph County, 1975							
1 unit	62,373	54,548	5,720	2,105	62,373	94.8	78.3
2-4 units	3,169	1,295	5,176	914	7,385	4.8	9.3
5-19 units	179	39	1,037	188	1,264	0.3	1.6
20-99 units	28	39	987	161	1,187	(*b*)	1.5
100+ units	27	1,098	3,998	506	5,602	(*b*)	7.0
Mobile-home park	18	1,681	--	172	1,853	(*b*)	2.3
Rooming house	5	1	25	8	34	(*b*)	(*b*)
Total	65,799	58,701	16,943	4,054	79,698	100.0	100.0

SOURCE: Reconciliation by HASE staff of sampling and survey records for the baseline surveys of landlords, tenants, and homeowners in both sites.

NOTE: Estimates are based on sample data, but the samples cover all known residential properties in each site at the time of the surveys. Rented rooms in private homes are not counted as separate units. Mobile homes outside of mobile-home parks are counted in the property-size categories in which they occur. In Brown County, vacancies in 1,230 federally subsidized units were estimated without survey data.

[a] Includes owner-occupied units in cooperatives and condominiums and units occupied by resident landlords on rental properties. Also includes mobile homes owned by the occupant even though the vehicle may be in a rented space.

[b] Less than 0.1 percent.

[c] Mobile-home parks have five or more mobile-home spaces. Vacancies refer to vacant spaces rather than vacant vehicles.

[d] Rooming houses have five or more units that lack either complete kitchen facilities, a private bath, or a separate entrance.

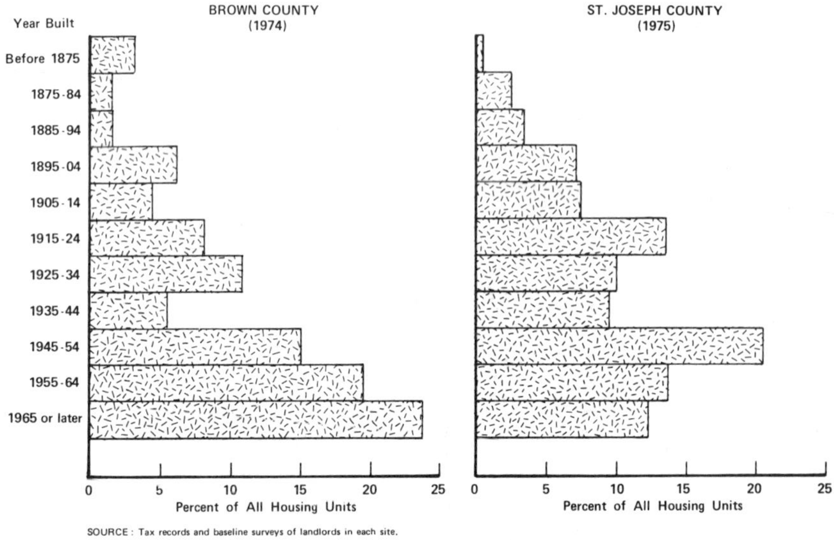

Fig. 2.5—Distribution of housing units by year built: Brown County (1974) and St. Joseph County (1975)

along the Fox River; newer ones predominated on the urban fringe. Even in the oldest neighborhoods there was usually a pleasing mixture of old and new, large and small homes, and single-family houses and small multiple dwellings; and the neat monotony of suburban tracts was likely to be broken by farmhouses surviving from earlier times.

Seventy percent of the county's housing units were owned by their occupants. Nearly all were single-family houses. The exceptions were 2,600 small multiunit properties with resident landlords, a few duplexes, one ten-unit cooperative, and about 860 mobile homes occupying rental spaces. The rental market, making up about 30 percent of all housing units, was dominated by 4,380 properties, each with two to four units. About 40 percent began as single-family houses, the rental units being added later. There were also about 2,100 single-family houses for rent; most of them were built for owner occupancy between 1915 and 1954, then were rented out when the original owners died or moved away.

After 1965, many investors in Brown County built directly for the rental market. About 74 percent of all units on properties with five or more units, and 27 percent of those on properties with two to four units, were less than 10 years old in 1974.

Very few of these new rental developments were subsidized. At the end of 1973, the county had 287 units of low-rent public housing and 203 units of private or nonprofit rental housing assisted under either Sec. 221(d)(3) or Sec. 236 of the National Housing Act. There were also 700 owner-occupied single-family homes assisted under Sec. 235 of the same act.[8]

Because so much of Brown County's housing was built recently, most dwellings—both owner-occupied and rental—were modern in design and unlikely to need major repairs. Although the urban part of the county contained pockets of obsolete or dilapidated housing, there were no large, seriously decayed neighborhoods. Four older neighborhoods in Green Bay had deteriorated enough to arouse local concern, reflected in the formation of neighborhood committees to seek ways to improve them. In 1975, the city government supported these efforts by allocating $250,000 of a federal grant to low-interest home improvement loans and to a fund for purchasing deteriorated houses and rehabilitating them for resale. There have been no major residential clearance programs in Green Bay (or elsewhere in the county), although several hundred older homes were removed between 1970 and 1972 to make way for a new bridge across the Fox River.

St. Joseph County

Although St. Joseph County's population was about 1.4 times Brown County's, its larger size was not reflected in higher residential densities or a greater incidence of renters. Seventy-eight percent of its dwellings were single-family houses, more than in Brown County (see Table 2.5). Properties with two to four units, common in Brown County, were relatively rare in St. Joseph County. There were many more large multiunit properties, although few were high-rise. Including large mobile-home parks, there were 35 properties in the county with 100 or more housing units on them. The largest is a private development of nearly 800 townhouses and apartments.

As shown in Fig. 2.5, much of St. Joseph County's housing was built during an earlier era of industrial expansion (roughly, 1880 to 1930). South Bend, in particular, had a large inventory of frame houses built early in this century for newly arrived factory workers. It also had

[8]After 1973, an additional 68 units of public housing and 387 units of housing assisted under Sec. 221(d)(3) or Sec. 236 were completed. The Farmers Home Administration has financed a few rural units that are not included in these counts.

streets of once-stately homes built for the owners and managers of then-prosperous businesses.

The great depression of the 1930s ended South Bend's industrial expansion, although the city prospered again during World War II. The precipitous postwar decline in manufacturing jobs dampened the building boom of the postwar decade. Suburban development proceeded slowly after 1955, hampered by a growing surplus of competing housing in older neighborhoods. Still, 46 percent of the housing units standing in 1975 were built after World War II.

As South Bend lost population, many older single-family homes passed from owner occupancy into the rental market, and others were vacated altogether. About 1965, the city began to systematically demolish the worst of the vacated structures and to clear sites for public housing or industrial parks. At the same time, developers (often aided by federal subsidies) began to build new rental housing on the urban fringe. These were mostly low-rise townhouses and garden apartments on large landscaped sites. By 1975, there were over 7,000 dwellings on properties with 20 or more units; two-thirds of these were built after 1964.

About 74 percent of all homes in St. Joseph County were owner occupied. These include over 1,100 dwellings on cooperative or condominium properties, over 1,600 mobile homes occupying rented spaces, and about 1,300 landlords' dwellings on rental properties. Excluding mobile homes, the rental inventory was composed in roughly equal parts of single-family homes, duplexes and small multiple dwellings, and apartments or townhouses on larger properties.

The rental properties included about 1,150 units of low-rent public housing and about 1,300 units of private rental housing assisted under Sec. 221(d)(3) or Sec. 236 of the National Housing Act.[9]

Until 1975, there were also about 200 privately owned single-family homes and small multiple dwellings leased by public authorities for occupancy by low-income families, but this program was phasing out during our survey. Fewer than 300 homeowners were assisted with their mortgage payments under Sec. 235.

Nearly a fourth of all landlords in St. Joseph County were renting out properties they used to occupy themselves, mostly single-family houses. A large proportion of these were in older blue-collar neighborhoods of South Bend, especially the area west of the river that now houses most of the city's blacks. East of the river and in Mishawaka there were still many pleasant neighborhoods of older homes in good repair; and on the urban fringe there were typical postwar tracts of owner-occupied homes, as well as the large rental developments described above.

---

[9]About 600 cooperative units are also federally subsidized under Sec. 221(d)(3).

St. Joseph County had relatively more deteriorated housing than Brown County, and the shabbiest housing was much more concentrated. Despite South Bend's demolition and clearance programs, there were neighborhoods of up to 25 blocks in which most homes were badly deteriorated and those still in good condition were blighted by their surroundings. The pattern of decay partly reflects the age of the houses and their originally modest amenities, features making them unappealing to present-day consumers. But more important were the years of neglect because of high vacancy rates, low market values, and the low incomes of those who occupied them.

CONTRASTS IN MARKET CONDITION

The main reason for the Supply Experiment was to learn about the market effects of a full-scale allowance program. Many people believed that those effects would differ sharply in tight and loose housing markets. We therefore chose Brown County as an example of a tight market and St. Joseph County as an example of a loose one, relying on the evidence of 1970 vacancy rates reported by the Census of Housing. The baseline surveys we conducted in 1974 and 1975 not only reassured us that vacancy rates still differed between the counties, they enabled us to probe more deeply into current market conditions, including the relationships between vacancies, rents, and property values. Below, we summarize our findings.

Housing Vacancies and Tenant Turnover

Housing vacancies, if appropriately measured, are useful indicators of the balance between housing supply and demand in a local market. They signal landlords, builders, and homeowners, respectively, whether rents should go up or down, whether new construction would be profitable, and whether the sale of an existing home will be easy or difficult.

The traditional measure of market condition is the current vacancy rate: dwellings vacant on a particular day expressed as a fraction of all dwellings. Evidence from both HASE and the (national) Annual Housing Survey suggests that average vacancy duration is a better measure of market condition than is the vacancy rate (Rydell, 1979c). The average annual vacancy duration equals the average annual vacancy rate divided by the average annual turnover rate. The annual turnover rate is the number of move-ins (alternatively, the number of move-outs) per 100 dwellings during a year.

The vacancy rate is easier to estimate and is equivalent to vacancy duration for comparing markets with identical turnover rates. However, turnover varies considerably between housing markets, and dramatically between sectors of a single market. For example, the 1975 turnover rate for rental dwellings in the northeastern region of the United States was 36.5 move-ins per 100 dwellings; in the western region, the corresponding figure was 61.6. In both regions, the turnover rate for homeowner dwellings was about a fifth of the rate for rental dwellings—6.0 in the northeast, 13.1 in the west (Rydell, 1979c, Table 2.1). Although the frequency of moving may partly reflect market tightness, we think it mainly reflects population characteristics that vary both regionally and between different sectors of local markets. Standardizing vacancy rates for turnover differences yields vacancy duration, a better measure of market condition.

Table 2.6 shows baseline vacancy rates, turnover, and vacancy duration for rental and homeowner dwellings in Brown and St. Joseph counties. The latter is divided into central South Bend and the rest of the county, two areas whose market conditions differ sharply.[10] Corresponding data for the United States are included for comparison.

At baseline, the rental vacancy rate for St. Joseph County was twice that for Brown County, and the homeowner vacancy rate was three times as large. In each case, figures for the two sites bracket national data for 1975. Within St. Joseph County, both rental and homeowner vacancy rates were substantially higher in central South Bend than elsewhere.

Average vacancy durations show the same general patterns, but reveal the similarity of market conditions for rental and homeowner dwellings within each area except central South Bend. There, the typical homeowner dwelling, once vacated, remains empty for nearly 26 weeks, as against 11 weeks for a rental dwelling.

Although a more detailed analysis shows that vacancy rates and turnover varied considerably within Brown County's rental stock, depending on type of structure, age of building, and rent level, vacancy durations varied little there (*Third Annual Report,* Table 4.6). At least since 1960, housing demand had grown moderately and smoothly (see Table 2.1, above). The county's housing market appears to have achieved a moving equilibrium in which the supply of dwellings tracks growing demand without large surpluses or shortages. Its submarkets are therefore uniformly tight.

---

[10]The area we designated as central South Bend is nearly congruent with the shaded portion of the city shown in Fig. 2.3: It excludes shaded census tracts 2 and 111, and includes unshaded tracts 6, 7, 15, 28, 31.

Table 2.6

HOUSING VACANCIES AND TURNOVER AT BASELINE: BROWN COUNTY (1973), ST. JOSEPH COUNTY (1974), AND THE UNITED STATES (1975)

Area	Number of Habitable Units	Average Vacancy Rate (%)	Annual Turnover per 100 Units	Average Vacancy Duration (weeks)
Rental Housing[a]				
Brown County	14,700	5.1	65.6	4.0
St. Joseph County	16,400	10.6	57.4	9.6
Central South Bend	8,000	12.3	59.5	10.7
Rest of county	8,400	8.9	55.3	8.4
United States	27,145[c]	6.0	51.5	6.1
Homeowner Housing[b]				
Brown County	31,700	.8	7.4	5.6
St. Joseph County	57,000	2.4	9.9	12.6
Central South Bend	13,600	4.2	8.5	25.7
Rest of county	43,400	1.9	10.2	9.7
United States	47,444[c]	1.2	9.9	6.3

SOURCE: Entries for Brown and St. Joseph counties were estimated by HASE staff from records of the baseline surveys of landlords and homeowners in each site. Entries for the United States were estimated from published data of the Annual Housing Survey; see Rydell, 1979c, for details.

[a] For HASE sites, excludes mobile-home parks, rooming houses, farmhouses, and federally subsidized dwellings; for the United States, excludes seasonal dwellings and others held off the market.

[b] For HASE sites, excludes mobile homes; for the United States, excludes seasonal dwellings and others held off the market.

[c] Entries are in thousands of dwellings.

Over the same period, South Bend was losing population while the rest of St. Joseph County was growing slightly. It has an excess supply of housing, concentrated in central South Bend, especially in the homeowner market there. Until its population stabilizes or resumes growth, the excess supply can only be reduced by demolition or conversion to nonresidential use. Although the city has been demolishing vacant, dilapidated dwellings since 1965, those removals have been offset by further population losses.

Balancing Supply and Demand

Housing rents and residential property values balance the demand for housing against the available supply. Achieving such a balance is a complicated process. On the demand side, every household needs a place to live; but size, quality, and location are negotiable, depending on household income, tastes, and housing prices. On the supply side, the owners of vacant dwellings are anxious to rent or sell them for whatever the market will bear, but generally have a "reservation price" below which they will not go.

We have seen that the demand for housing units, measured approximately by the number of households, has been growing steadily in Brown County. The added demand has been met by new construction, which at the same time extends the range of choice as to size, quality, and location for those whose incomes enable them to afford new housing.

In St. Joseph County, there has been little recent growth in population, hence little increase in demand for housing units. But some residents want and can afford new homes in desirable locations, so residential construction on the urban fringe has continued despite the accumulating surplus of older homes in central South Bend and parts of Mishawaka.

New homes will not be built in a community unless builders believe they can sell or rent them for enough to fully cover construction costs or, in the case of rental units, to cover operating costs plus the annual cost of the invested capital. Once a dwelling is built, however, its value or rent may rise or fall with changes in the overall demand for housing units or for units of a particular kind.

The looser housing market in St. Joseph County should depress housing prices, since consumers have a bargaining advantage when many alternatives are available. Our data show that this advantage is more salient for homebuyers than for renters, which may explain the high frequency of ownership in St. Joseph County for types of households that usually rent in Brown County. Renters occupying single-family houses were also more common in St. Joseph County.

Below, we compare baseline property values and rents for similar housing units in the two sites and show something of the historical process that led to current conditions.

Property Values

Our surveys of homeowners and landlords asked them when they acquired their properties and what they were then worth, as well as their current market values. We have used their responses to estimate trends in the values of owner and rental properties over the 13 years preceding baseline in each site.[11] Figure 2.6 summarizes our findings.

In both sites, current-dollar property values increased because of general price inflation. When the effects of that inflation are removed, our data indicate that the real values of both rental properties and owner-occupied homes were nearly stable in Brown County between 1960 and 1973. This stability indicates a long-run equilibrium in the county's housing market, maintained by increasing the supply as the demand for housing grew. In 1973 dollars, the equilibrium prices were about $11,000 per rental dwelling and $24,000 per homeowner dwelling.

St. Joseph County's record differs. There, the real value of rental property dropped by about 15 percent from 1961 to 1974. Homeowner properties first rose then fell sharply in average value; the peak-to-trough difference is about 18 percent. One reason for the erratic behavior of the annual series plotted in Fig. 2.6 is that the average encompasses two submarkets that behaved differently. We estimate that the real value of rental property fell by 24 percent in central South Bend, but by only 4 percent elsewhere in the county. For homeowner properties, real values fell by 40 percent in central South Bend, but increased by 2 percent elsewhere.

In 1974, just before the allowance program began, the typical rental dwelling in St. Joseph County would have sold for about $7,700 and the typical owner-occupied home for about $19,500. In central South Bend, single-family houses, far from new but habitable without major renovation, could be bought for as little as $10,000.

---

[11]Value changes for successive cohorts of rental properties between their dates of acquisition and the date of the baseline survey in each site were adjusted for capital improvements since acquisition. The adjusted value changes were then overlaid like shingles on a time-line to estimate average rates of change for each year. For more details on rental property values, see the *Third Annual Report,* 1977, pp. 67-70. For more details on homeowner properties, see Helbers, 1980, pp. 21-8.

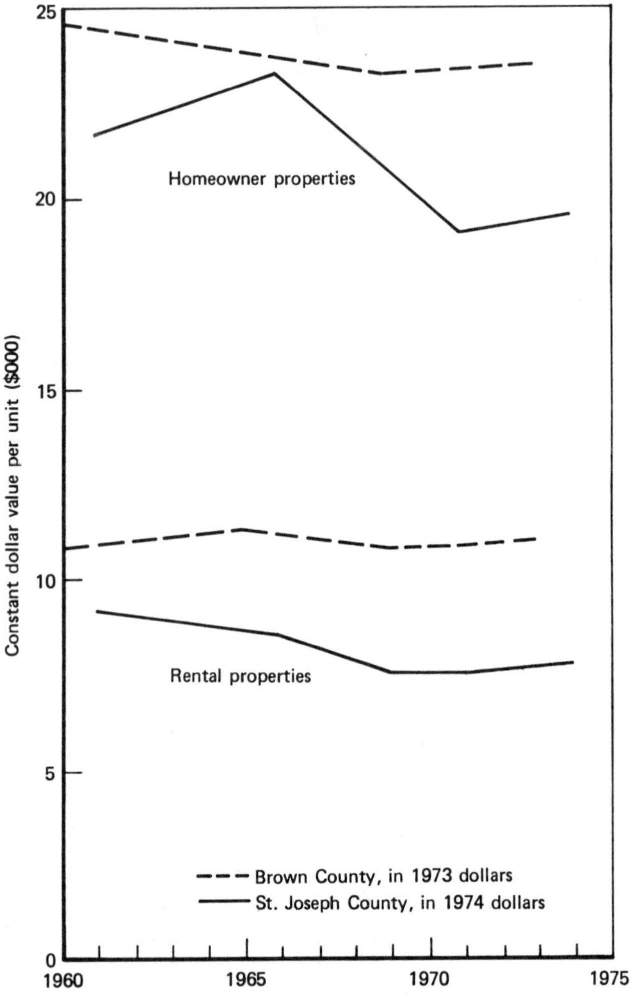

SOURCE: Baseline surveys of landlords and homeowners.
Note: Current values were deflated by the Consumer Price Index.

Fig. 2.6—Trends in average market values of residential properties: Brown and St. Joseph counties, 1960-74

Rents

The sharply different market values of rental properties in Brown and St. Joseph counties led us to expect that rents would also differ substantially. They do not. This discovery led us to reconsider accepted theories of housing market adjustment, with important consequences for our analysis of allowance-program effects (Rydell, 1979b).

Table 2.7 compares monthly gross rents for rental units in the two communities, including vacant units. Because the responsibility for fuel and utility payments is differently assigned to tenants and landlords of different properties, comparing contract rents (the amounts that tenants pay their landlords) can easily mislead. Here, we compare gross rents, which include all fuel and utility expenses, by whomever paid.[12]

Some individual entries in the table are unreliable because they are based on small samples, but the detailed decomposition of the inventory enables us to standardize gross rents for differences in inventory composition between sites. That standardization yields an average monthly gross rent in 1974 of $147 for Brown County and $144 for both central South Bend and the rest of St. Joseph County. Thus, St. Joseph County's higher vacancy rates and low property values barely reflect in rents for comparable properties. (Without standardization, central South Bend's rents are about 9 percent below those elsewhere in the county.)

The market adjustment theory that accounts for this outcome simply notes that when demand is slack, landlords can either cut rents to attract other landlords' tenants, or accept longer vacancies. In either case, their revenues will diminish; but, even without collusion, most landlords will risk longer vacancies rather than reduce rents. Since the market value of a rental property depends on its earning capacity, the diminished revenue tends to cause property values to fall, as they have done in central South Bend.

CONTRASTS IN CONSUMER CHOICES

Given the different market conditions in Brown and St. Joseph counties, one might expect the consumers of housing to behave differently in the two sites. At baseline, they clearly differed in their tenure

---

[12]About a third of the gross rent for single-family dwellings consists of direct tenant payments for fuel and utilities. For apartments in large buildings, such payments account for less than a tenth of gross rent, because the landlord usually supplies central heating.

Table 2.7

GROSS RENT BY SIZE OF PROPERTY AND YEAR BUILT: BROWN COUNTY AND PARTS OF ST. JOSEPH COUNTY, 1974

Size of Property and Year Built	Monthly Gross Rent ($) per Unit: Brown County	Central South Bend	Rest of St. Joseph County
1 Unit			
Post-1944	179	149	158
1915-1944	159	168	149
Pre-1915	142	153	161
2-4 Units			
Post-1944	181	129	151
1915-1944	129	122	128
Pre-1915	121	115	108
5+ Units			
Post-1944	165	236	214
1915-1944	120	111	120
Pre-1915	126	112	110
Average[a]	149	136	150
Adjusted Average[b]	147	144	144

SOURCE: Adapted from Rydell, 1979b, Table A.2. Entries are derived from weighted records of the baseline surveys of landlords in each site.

NOTE: Both occupied and vacant dwellings are included. Mobile homes, rooming houses, farmhouses, and federally subsidized dwellings are excluded. Gross rent consists of contract rent (the amount paid to the landlord) plus fuel and utility expenses paid by the tenant. Brown County rents for 1973 were increased by 6.4 percent to make them comparable to St. Joseph County rents in 1974.

[a] Average of column entries, each weighted by the number of dwellings of the indicated type.

[b] Average of column entries, each weighted equally.

choices and probably differed in their housing expenditures per dollar of income.

Owning versus Renting

We have seen that an excess supply of dwellings drove the market values of single-family dwellings in St. Joseph County well below the values of their counterparts in Brown County, but rents in the two places were nearly the same for comparable dwellings. Compared with renting in either place, home purchase was therefore more of a bargain in St. Joseph than in Brown County.[13] Consequently, many St. Joseph County households that would normally be renters had instead purchased homes by the time of our baseline survey there.

Figure 2.7 shows how households in each life-cycle stage were distributed by tenure and type of dwelling (single-family vs. apartment).[14] As is typically the case, the incidence of homeownership first rises then falls as households move through life-cycle stages. Although at baseline only 70 to 75 percent of all households in our sites were homeowners, nearly all those who had married and raised children became homeowners during that part of their lives. Upon the death of a marriage partner, or after a divorce or separation, many had returned to renting.

In the middle stages of the household life cycle, tenure choices were about the same in the two counties—that is, nearly all were owners. But at the extremes, tenure choices were quite different. In Brown County, only 6.5 percent of all young single household heads (Stage 1) were homeowners, but over 39 percent of the corresponding group in St. Joseph County owned their homes. In Brown County, two-fifths of all elderly single heads (Stage 7) were renters; in St. Joseph County, only a fifth were renters. The relatively favorable terms on which homes could be bought (and the relatively unfavorable terms on which they could be sold) in St. Joseph County caused many households at the margin between owning and renting to choose the former.

[13]In both counties, owning a home was typically more expensive in current outlays than renting. Helbers, 1980, Table 4.10, estimates that low-income elderly homeowners in Brown County spent 25 to 50 percent more for housing than low-income elderly renters; the corresponding range for St. Joseph County was 14 to 28 percent. However, the dwellings of owners and renters were not comparable, and the owners were also benefiting from the general appreciation of property values.

[14]For St. Joseph County, the ownership category includes some units in multiple dwellings. Occupants of mobile homes are excluded in both sites because of their complex tenure. For consistency with the preceding tables, occupants of subsidized housing units are also excluded. Including them would shift the distributions in both sites toward rental units, mostly for families with children (Stages 3, 4, 5, and 8) and elderly persons (Stages 6 and 7), but would not much change the differences between sites.

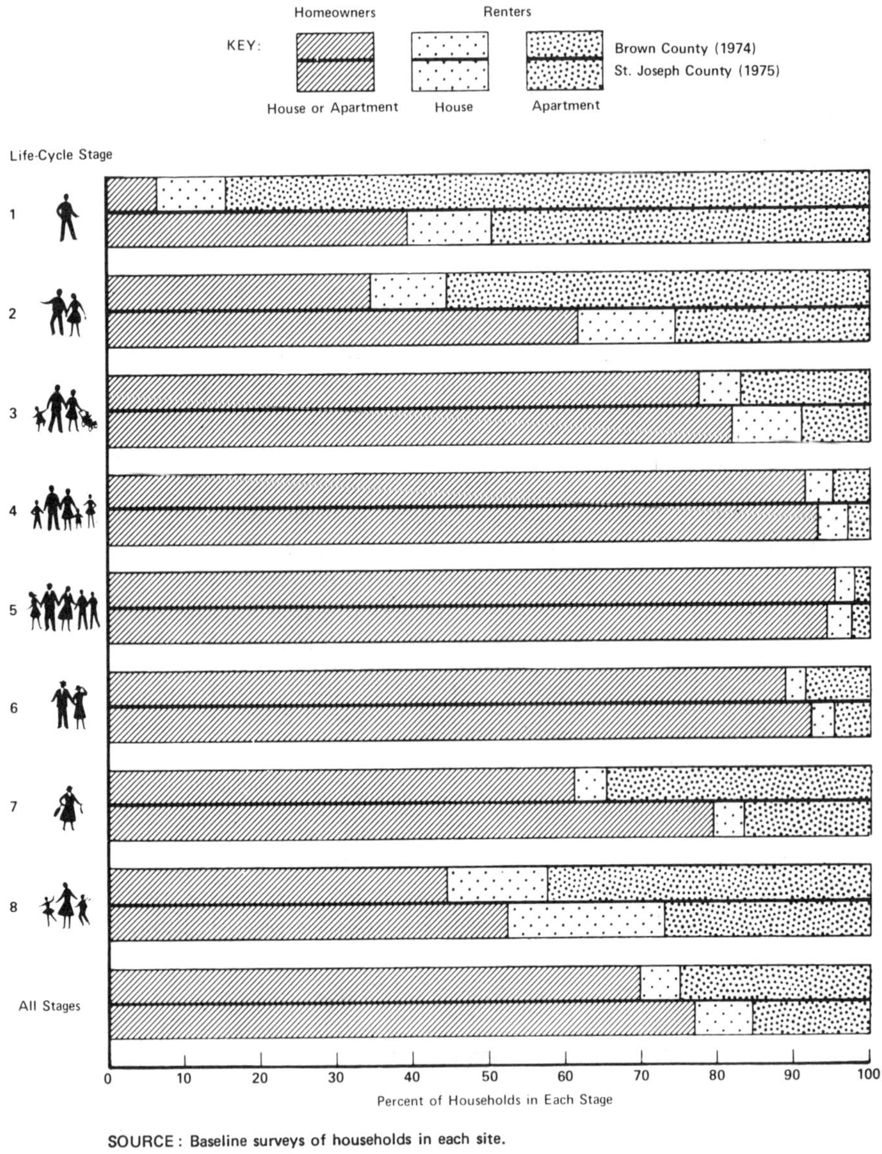

Fig. 2.7—Distribution of households by housing tenure and type of dwelling: Brown County (1974) and St. Joseph County (1975)

Single-family houses are nearly always built for owner occupancy. They enter the rental market only when the first owner dies or moves away, and even then usually because they are of a type or in a location that makes them hard to sell. Figure 2.7 shows that a measurably greater portion of St. Joseph County's single-family homes were occupied by renters and a much greater proportion of all rental units were single-family homes. In every life-cycle stage except Stage 7, renters in St. Joseph County were more likely to live in single-family houses than were renters in Brown County.

Housing Expenditures

Although analysts have never been able to account for even half of the variance among households in their housing expenditures, income has consistently been an important predictor. Regression analysis of housing expenditures by renters and homeowners in Brown and St. Joseph counties yields similar conclusions, but the effect of income is less than was estimated by earlier studies and may differ between sites.[15]

Table 2.8 reports our estimates of the income elasticity of housing expenditures in the two counties, for both current and "permanent" income. The latter is a three-year average of annually reported incomes, believed by most economists to reflect the income expectations of households when they decide on major purchases. The housing expenditures for renters are monthly gross rents; for owners, we estimated the rental values of their homes by comparing them with similar rented single-family houses. The income elasticity of expenditures is the percentage change in expenditure for each 1-percent change in income.

Comparing elasticities based on current and permanent income, we see that households are reluctant to change their housing expenditures because of short-run fluctuations in their incomes; since any substantial change in consumption would usually require a change of residence, that response is not surprising. The comparisons between renters and homeowners indicate that owners are much more inclined than renters to spend extra income on housing, perhaps because homeownership has investment as well as consumption rewards.

The point estimates of elasticity differ between the sites, suggesting

[15]The regression analysis tested the influence of income and many other household characteristics on housing expenditures. Only income and, for renters, household size were statistically significant despite current-income samples of 400 to 500 cases for owners and 1,400 to 1,900 cases for renters. Permanent-income samples were smaller. See Mulford, 1979, for details.

Table 2.8

INCOME ELASTICITY OF HOUSING EXPENDITURES: RENTERS AND HOMEOWNERS IN BROWN AND ST. JOSEPH COUNTIES

Area	Estimated Income Elasticity			
	Renters		Owners	
	Current Income	Permanent Income	Current Income	Permanent Income
Brown County (1973-76)	.12 (.01)	.22 (.03)	.38 (.03)	.51 (.06)
St. Joseph County (1974-77)	.11 (.01)	.15 (.04)	.28 (.04)	.40 (.07)

SOURCE: Adapted from Mulford, 1979, Table 5; based on records of the surveys of households in each site.

NOTE: Entries indicate the typical percentage increase in housing expenditures for a 1-percent increase in income, based on cross-sectional comparisons of households with different incomes, and controlling on other household characteristics. Housing expenditures are gross rent for renters, and equivalent rents for owner-occupied homes. Current income is income for the calendar year preceding an interview; permanent income is a 3-year average of annually reported incomes. Standard errors are shown in parentheses below each estimate.

that both renters and owners in St. Joseph County are less inclined than their counterparts in Brown County to allocate extra income to housing. However, as the standard errors of estimate show, the inter-county differences could easily have resulted by chance. The difference, if genuine, is not readily accountable to market conditions; whereas homeowners in St. Joseph County may have been reluctant to invest extra income in a declining market, renters would not face that impediment. A possible explanation is that the greater irregularity of incomes in St. Joseph County makes its citizens more cautious about large financial commitments.

Most important from the standpoint of the Supply Experiment is our finding that all these elasticities are lower than prior estimates based on other data.[16] According to the conventional wisdom, low incomes account for low housing expenditures and poor housing

[16]When the Supply Experiment began in 1972, the income elasticity of housing demand was generally thought to be close to unity, implying that expenditures would increase proportionally with income. The main reason for such high estimates appears to have been the use of inappropriate data; see Mulford, 1979, Sec. I, for a review and

quality. If so, a program of cash transfers should cause recipients to increase their housing consumption substantially. At least for renters, our data cast doubt on that scenario. Even doubling a typical renter's income in our sites would cause him to increase his housing expenditures by only a seventh.

A low income elasticity of housing demand does not necessarily imply low levels of housing expenditure, only that expenditures do not change much when income moves up or down; Fig. 2.8 illustrates for current incomes at baseline. Brown County renters with incomes under $5,000 at baseline typically spent 35 to 45 percent of their incomes for housing; those in St. Joseph County spent 40 to 55 percent. As income rises, housing expenditures do not increase much; instead, the rent/income ratio falls sharply.

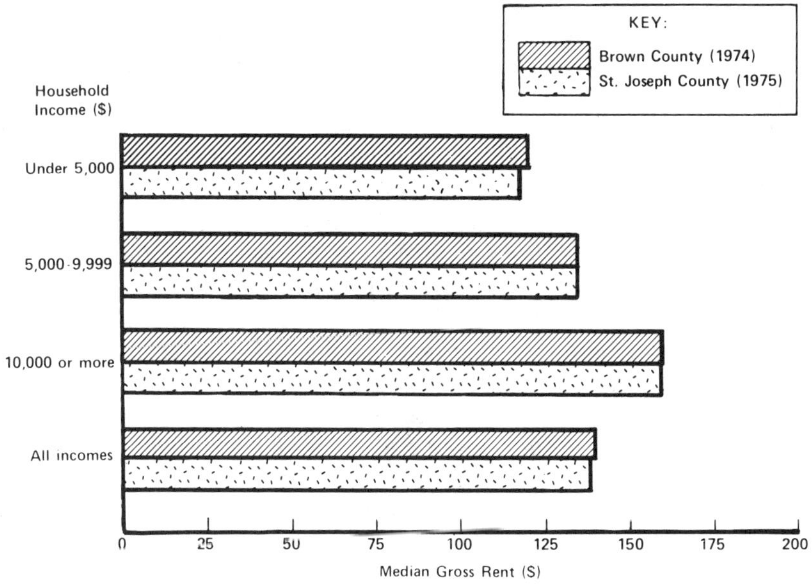

SOURCE: Baseline surveys of households in each site.

Fig. 2.8—Median gross rent paid by renter households, by income: Brown County (1974) and St. Joseph County (1975)

critique of prior studies. Comparable estimates from the Demand Experiment were 0.33 for Pittsburgh and 0.44 for Phoenix (Friedman and Weinberg, 1980, Table 4.1).

IMPLICATIONS FOR THE SUPPLY EXPERIMENT

Brown and St. Joseph counties were chosen as sites for the Supply Experiment after careful study of the available information about each—primarily 1970 census reports. As demonstrated in the preceding pages, our baseline survey data powerfully confirmed the conclusions we reached about housing market and community characteristics and showed that the sites met our selection criteria not only in 1970 but also in mid-decade, when the allowance programs began.

In short, Brown County did have a growing population and a flourishing economy, which combined to keep vacancy rates low and housing prices high despite the substantial amounts of new residential construction over the past 25 years. St. Joseph County's population was decreasing, especially in its urban core, and there was a price-depressing surplus of older homes in the central city. By 1975, suburban vacancy rates were also high.

Neither systematic data nor reports from local observers gave salience to racial or neighborhood differences as factors in Brown County's housing market. The county's racial homogeneity virtually eliminates the possibility of residential segregation by race, and ethnic differences among the white residents were not much reflected in neighborhood settlement patterns. Urban neighborhoods were unusually well mixed as to age, cost, and condition of dwellings, so that only a few of the oldest areas seemed at all endangered by a general loss of amenity. Housing problems tended to be those of specific dwellings and specific households, not neighborhoods.

St. Joseph County, on the other hand, combined the problems of racial segregation and neighborhood decline. Its substantial minority of low-income blacks lived almost entirely in South Bend, most of them in a few neighborhoods whose housing was generally deteriorated or worse. White ethnic groups also formed neighborhood settlements, so that the housing market was sharply divided along racial lines and, less strongly, along ethnic lines. Recent residential construction has been mostly on the urban fringe—very large developments of dwellings that are uniform in age, cost, and condition; the older neighborhoods have changed mostly by demolition of dilapidated houses. Thus, housing problems in St. Joseph County tended to be associated with specific neighborhoods and definable types of households.

As will be seen, these differences between Brown County and St. Joseph County were reflected in program development. Because property values were lower in St. Joseph County, more of its low-income households were homeowners, and homeowners made up a larger share of program participants than in Brown County. Because St. Joseph County's blacks had much lower incomes than whites, they were heavily represented among enrollees. Because St. Joseph County's housing was in worse condition, applicants' dwellings more often needed repairs to qualify for occupancy by allowance recipients. Because there were more vacant dwellings in St. Joseph County, program participants did more moving than in Brown County. Again, because property values were lower in St. Joseph County, more program participants there changed from renting to owning homes.

Finally, our analysis of baseline housing markets in both sites casts doubt on two widely accepted scenarios of allowance program effects. On the one hand, it appeared unlikely that the income transferred through a housing allowance program would stimulate housing demand to the extent that some observers predicted. On the other, it appeared unlikely that even a substantial program-induced shift in demand for rental housing would much affect rents. These findings, of course, were not available until well after the program was under way, and in any case warranted experimental confirmation.

REFERENCES

Bala, John E., *Neighborhoods in St. Joseph County, Indiana,* The Rand Corporation, N-1205-HUD, September 1979.

Dubinsky, Robert, *Collected Site Selection Documents: Housing Assistance Supply Experiment,* The Rand Corporation, N-1041-HUD, July 1980.

Ellickson, Bryan C., *Neighborhoods in Brown County,* The Rand Corporation, N-1055-HUD, December 1980.

Ellickson, Phyllis L., and David E. Kanouse, *Public Perceptions of Housing Allowances: The First Two Years,* The Rand Corporation, R-2259-HUD, September 1979.

Friedman, Joseph, and Daniel H. Weinberg, *The Demand for Rental Housing: Evidence from a Percent of Rent Housing Allowance,* Abt Associates, Cambridge, Mass., June 1980.

HASE Staff, *Site Selection for the Housing Assistance Supply Experiment: SMSAs Proposed for Site Visits (a Briefing),* The Rand Corporation, N-1033-HUD, July 1980a.

——, *Site Selection for the Housing Assistance Supply Experiment: Stage I,* The Rand Corporation, N-1026-HUD, July 1980b.

Helbers, Lawrence, *Measuring Homeowner Needs for Housing Assistance,* The Rand Corporation, N-1094-HUD, October 1980.

McCarthy, Kevin F., *Housing Choices and Residential Mobility in Site*

I at Baseline, The Rand Corporation, N-1091-HUD, October 1979a.

——, *Housing Choices and Residential Mobility in Site II at Baseline,* The Rand Corporation, N-1119-HUD, October 1979b.

Mulford, John E., *Income Elasticity of Housing Demand,* The Rand Corporation, R-2449-HUD, July 1979.

Rydell, C. Peter, *Rental Housing in Site I: Characteristics of the Capital Stock at Baseline,* The Rand Corporation, N-1082-HUD, November 1979a.

——, *Shortrun Response of Housing Markets to Demand Shifts,* The Rand Corporation, R-2453-HUD, September 1979b.

——, *Vacancy Duration and Housing Market Condition,* The Rand Corporation, N-1135-HUD, October 1979c.

Rydell, C. Peter, and Joseph Friedman, *Rental Housing in Site I: Market Structure and Conditions at Baseline,* The Rand Corporation, N-1083-HUD, October 1979.

Third Annual Report of the Housing Assistance Supply Experiment, The Rand Corporation, R-2151-HUD, February 1977.

U.S. Bureau of the Census, *Census of Housing: 1970,* Final Reports HC(1)-A51 and -B51 (Wisconsin); and HC(1)-A16 and -B16 (Indiana), U.S. Government Printing Office, Washington, D.C., various dates.

——, *Census of Population: 1970,* Final Reports PC(1)-A51, -B51, -C51, and -D51 (Wisconsin); and PC(1)-A16, -B16, -C16, and -D16 (Indiana), U.S. Government Printing Office, Washington, D.C., various dates.

——, *Current Population Reports,* "Estimates of the Population of Indiana Counties and Metropolitan Areas: July 1, 1974 and 1975," Series P-26, No. 75-14, U.S. Government Printing Office, Washington, D.C., 1976.

III. THE HOUSING ALLOWANCE PROGRAMS

The experimental housing allowance programs were administered in the two sites by nonprofit corporations called housing allowance offices (HAOs). As explained in Ch. I, the programs were funded by annual contributions contracts between HUD and a local housing authority in each county; the local authority delegated operating responsibility for the program to the HAO. Each HAO was governed by a board of trustees that included both members of The Rand Corporation and local citizens; the chairman of each board was also Rand's site manager for the experiment.

HASE staff and newly hired HAO staff collaborated in developing the program rules and administrative procedures documented in the *Housing Allowance Office Handbook* (Katagiri and Kingsley, 1980). After all the needed intergovernmental agreements had been secured, offices had been leased and furnished, HAO staffs had been hired and trained, and HUD had approved the *Handbook,* low-income households in each site were publicly invited to apply for assistance. Enrollment began on 20 June 1974 in Brown County and 27 December 1974 in St. Joseph County.

Through the first five program years (ending June 1979 in Brown County and December 1979 in St. Joseph County), over 25,000 households enrolled and over 20,000 received one or more allowance payments. At the end of year 5, about 11,500 households were enrolled and nearly 9,500 were receiving monthly payments.

During those five years, the program provided financial assistance to 11,350 renters and 8,650 homeowners. At the end of year 5, the average monthly payment was $97, augmenting the average recipient's gross income by 25 percent. The annual equivalent of all payments made in the first month of the sixth program year was $4.0 million in Brown County and $7.2 million in St. Joseph County, or about $11 million in all.

Nearly half of all enrollees joined the program while living in dwellings that met program standards; thus, their allowances mainly helped them meet existing housing expenses (which usually greatly exceeded the legislative norm of one-fourth of adjusted gross income). But nearly 11,000 different dwellings were repaired or improved to meet program standards, and about 5,000 households improved their housing circumstances by moving. Over 300 renters bought homes after enrolling in the program.

The following pages review key program statistics for each site, drawing mostly on monthly reports prepared by the HAOs. Our purpose here is to orient the reader by providing a brief account of program growth, characteristics of the population served, benefit standards and payments, and the condition of enrollees' and recipients' housing. Much of the data pertains to the end of the fifth program year in each site, when Rand completed its monitoring responsibilities and withdrew from governing the HAOs. Since then, the HAOs have continued to operate the programs without significant change in rules or procedures, and presumably will do so until 1984, when the annual contributions contracts expire.

ENROLLMENT AND PAYMENT AUTHORIZATIONS

Table 3.1 summarizes the status of all applications for assistance received by each HAO through year 5. The cumulative number of applications equals a third of all households in Brown County and 45 percent of all households in St. Joseph County.[1] In Brown County, 55 percent of all applicants were eventually enrolled and 84 percent of those enrolled eventually met the program's housing requirements and thereby qualified for payments. In St. Joseph County, the corresponding figures were 47 and 77 percent.

By the fifth program year, over half of those ever enrolled in each site were no longer in the program. Fourteen percent of all enrollees in Brown County and 18 percent in St. Joseph County dropped out without ever receiving a payment; their enrollment dwellings failed to meet program standards, and they were unable or unwilling to repair those dwellings or move to acceptable housing. The other terminees (41 percent of enrollees in Brown County, 36 percent in St. Joseph County) received at least one payment before leaving the program; most had become ineligible because their incomes increased after they enrolled.

At the end of the fifth year, both HAOs were well past the start-up phase of rapid enrollment in a new program but they nonetheless received a steady flow of applications from new residents and newly formed or newly eligible households. During the fifth year the Brown County HAO processed 2,272 applications, enrolled 1,354 households,

[1]From household survey data, we estimate that in 1978 there were 49,600 households in Brown County and 75,200 households in St. Joseph County. Because households formed and dissolved, and others moved into or out of the two counties, these populations are inappropriate as denominators for cumulative program statistics but do provide rough benchmarks. See Ch. IV for consistent estimates of all households, eligible households, and participating households.

Table 3.1

SELECTED ENROLLMENT AND PAYMENT AUTHORIZATION STATISTICS: HOUSING ALLOWANCE PROGRAMS IN BROWN AND ST. JOSEPH COUNTIES THROUGH YEAR 5

Item	Brown County		St. Joseph County	
	Number of Cases	Percent of Total	Number of Cases	Percent of Total
Enrollment				
All applicants	16,602	100	34,474	100
Screened out before interview[a]	4,603	28	10,019	29
Screened out by interview[b]	2,669	16	6,861	20
Awaiting interview or processing	197	1	1,501	4
Eligible and enrolled	9,133	55	16,093	47
Payment Authorization				
All enrollees	9,133	100	16,093	100
Authorized for payments	7,681	84	12,337	77
Currently receiving payments	3,563	39	5,891	37
Payments suspended[c]	356	4	673	4
Enrollment terminated[d]	3,762	41	5,773	36
Never authorized for payments	1,452	16	3,756	23
Authorization pending[e]	217	2	755	5
Enrollment terminated[d]	1,235	14	3,001	18

SOURCE: HAO management information reports for 29 June 1979 in Brown County and 28 December 1979 in St. Joseph County.

NOTE: Payments are not authorized until the housing unit chosen by an enrollee has been evaluated by the HAO and certified for occupancy; and, for a rental unit, until an executed copy of an acceptable lease agreement has been filed with the HAO.

[a]Applicant ineligible or declined to be interviewed.

[b]Applicant ineligible, declined to complete interview, or declined enrollment.

[c]Current housing is not certified, or enrollee has violated reporting requirements or other program rules.

[d]Voluntary or involuntary. Involuntary terminations usually result from change in income or family circumstances that affect eligibility.

[e]Awaiting housing certification or lease agreement. See Note above.

and reinstated 337 households whose enrollments had previously been terminated. In St. Joseph County, 6,361 households applied, 2,912 were enrolled, and 955 were reinstated.

During program years 1 through 3, the allowance program grew steadily in terms of both households enrolled and households receiving payments (see Fig. 3.1). In the fourth year, intake (new enrollments plus reinstatements) was roughly balanced by terminations in both sites. In the fifth year, the number of active enrollments and the number of households receiving payments grew by over 6 percent in both counties. Although the management information reports from which we draw these statistics are not well-enough detailed to explain why the growth occurred, it appears to reflect rising unemployment in both sites.

Figure 3.1 shows that a plateau of participation was reached during the fourth program year in each site. We have interpreted that plateau as an approximation to the long-run steady state of participation, supposing that enrollment thereafter would perhaps fluctuate from year to year in response to short-term demographic and economic forces. However, that interpretation is strained by subsequent events. During the sixth and seventh program years, the slight growth noted in year 5 accelerated. By June 1981, current enrollment and recipiency had both increased by 21 percent over end-of-year-5 levels in Brown County and by 34 percent in St. Joseph County.[2]

Table 3.2 shows the composition of new enrollment in each site—by housing tenure, age and race of household head, and household size—and how it changed over the years. In general, differences between enrollees in the two sites reflect differences in the eligible populations. As indicated in the last column of each panel in the table, cumulative enrollment data show a larger fraction of renters in Brown than in St. Joseph County (68 vs. 56 percent), relatively fewer elderly household heads (27 vs. 31 percent), but similar proportions of single-person households. Reflecting the county's racial homogeneity, Brown County's enrollment of nonwhites is only 4 percent of the total; St. Joseph County's is 28 percent.

Over time, the characteristics of newly enrolled households shifted similarly in the two sites. The percentages that were renters and sin-

[2]Because Rand no longer monitors either the allowance program or the local housing market, we can only speculate about the causes of recent increases in participation. HAO staff believe that much of the growth is because of increased unemployment in the sites, which temporarily increases the number of eligibles. The income limits for participation and the benefits at each level of income have been increased regularly to keep up with inflation, and these changes may have inadvertently widened eligibility. Possibly, longer exposure to the program has increased the propensity of eligible households to enroll.

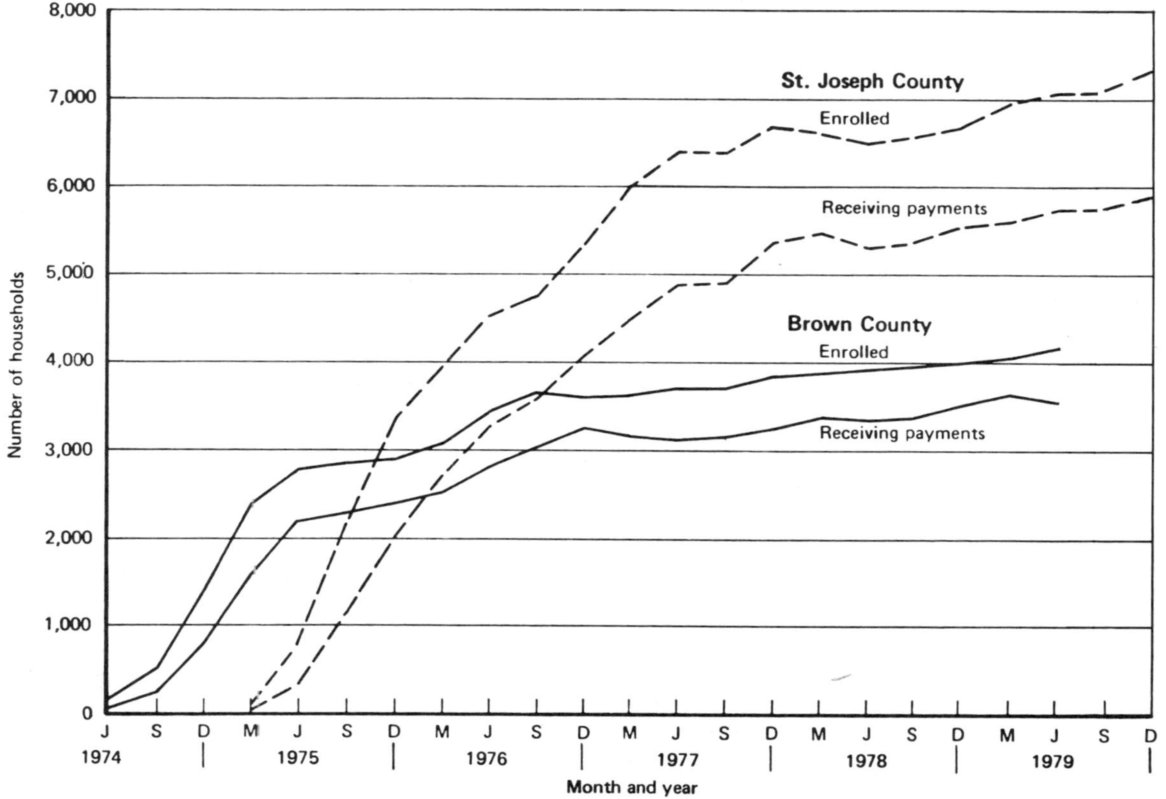

SOURCE: HAO management information reports through year 5.

Fig. 3.1—Households enrolled and receiving payments: housing allowance programs in Brown and St. Joseph counties through year 5

Table 3.2

SELECTED CHARACTERISTICS OF ENROLLEES BY ENROLLMENT PERIOD: HOUSING ALLOWANCE PROGRAMS IN BROWN AND ST. JOSEPH COUNTIES, YEARS 1-5

Household Characteristic	Percent of All Households Enrolling during Indicated Period					
	Year 1	Year 2	Year 3	Year 4	Year 5	Years 1-5
Brown County						
All enrollees	100	100	100	100	100	100
Renter	59	64	69	81	82	68
Elderly head[a]	33	28	29	23	17	27
Nonwhite head[b]	4	4	4	5	5	4
Single person[c]	28	28	24	44	45	32
St. Joseph County						
All enrollees	100	100	100	100	100	100
Renter	49	51	54	65	67	56
Elderly head[a]	30	37	37	28	21	31
Nonwhite head[b]	43	23	21	26	25	28
Single person[c]	23	30	38	39	41	33

SOURCE: HAO management information reports for the end of each program year indicated.

[a]Household head 62+ years of age.

[b]Black, Latin, American Indian, or Oriental. In Brown County, mostly American Indian; in St. Joseph County, mostly black.

[c]One person living alone or with nonrelatives. Before August 1977 (program year 4 in Brown County, year 3 in St. Joseph County), only elderly single persons could enroll.

gle persons increased, and the percentages that were elderly decreased. In St. Joseph County, the percentage that was nonwhite dropped sharply after year 1.

Because eligible homeowners were usually elderly persons, the first three changes are interrelated. The declining proportion of elderly homeowners among new enrollees is partly explained by a program change in August 1977 that permitted the HAOs to enroll nonelderly single persons, most of whom were renters. During years 4 and 5, a fourth (Brown County) to a third (St. Joseph County) of the new enrollments were of this type. However, even without the program change, nonelderly renters would have formed an increasing share of new enrollments because membership in that pool of eligibles turned over rapidly; more newly eligible households of that type were available to enroll each year than was the case for elderly homeowners.

The other compositional change was for racial minorities in St. Joseph County. Blacks and Latins comprised over two-fifths of the first year's enrollment, but only a fifth to a fourth of each subsequent year's enrollment. Minority enrollment was initially high because the program was at first limited to South Bend, where nearly all of the county's racial minorities live; the outlying areas included many eligible whites, but few blacks or Latins.[3]

Because turnover was high and termination rates varied with household characteristics, the composition of current enrollment differed from that of cumulative enrollment. Table 3.3 describes the households enrolled in the program at the end of year 5. In both sites, households headed by elderly persons and single-person households account for larger shares of those then enrolled than of those ever enrolled. Whereas the high proportion of single persons among year 5 clients mostly reflects the recent enrollment of nonelderly singles, the high proportion of elderly household heads reflects their relatively low termination rates. Also in St. Joseph County, racial minorities account for a slightly smaller share of year 5 than of cumulative enrollment, reflecting more turnover for them than for whites. The patterns for tenure (see the Note to Table 3.3) were mixed; renters accounted for a larger share of year 5 than of cumulative enrollment in Brown County and a smaller share in St. Joseph County.

BENEFIT STANDARDS AND PAYMENTS

Each enrollee's allowance entitlement was scaled to his income and to the standard cost of adequate housing (called R^*) in his community. If he were able to find certifiable housing whose cost exactly equaled R^*, his housing expenses would amount to his allowance payment plus 25 percent of his adjusted gross income. If he spent more than R^* for housing, the excess would come from his nonallowance income; if he spent less, a larger fraction of his nonallowance income would be available for other consumption. (The allowance formula is given in Ch. I, "Program Design.")

The standard cost of adequate housing for households of different sizes was estimated for each site before program operations began.[4]

[3]However, blacks and Latins were more likely than whites to be eligible and, if eligible, to enroll. Both effects were due primarily to the relatively low incomes of blacks and Latins; see Ch. IV for more details.

[4]For explanation of the principles underlying the R^* schedule and details of how

Table 3.3

SELECTED CHARACTERISTICS OF CURRENTLY ENROLLED HOUSEHOLDS: HOUSING ALLOWANCE PROGRAMS IN BROWN AND ST. JOSEPH COUNTIES, YEAR 5

Client Characteristic	Percent of All Currently Enrolled Households					
	Brown County			St. Joseph County		
	Renters	Owners	Total	Renters	Owners	Total
Age of Head						
Under 62 years	78	43	68	83	38	61
62+ years	22	57	32	17	62	39
Total	100	100	100	100	100	100
Race of Head						
White non-Latin	95	99	96	65	85	75
Other	5	1	4	35	15	25
Total	100	100	100	100	100	100
Household Size						
1 person	40	41	40	40	47	43
2 persons	26	29	27	25	30	28
3-4 persons	26	21	25	28	17	23
5-6 persons	6	7	6	6	5	5
7+ persons	2	2	2	1	1	1
Total	100	100	100	100	100	100

SOURCE: Tabulated by HASE staff from HAO records for Brown and St. Joseph counties.

NOTE: Entries include all households enrolled at the end of year 5 in each site: in Brown County, 2,934 renters and 1,202 owners; in St. Joseph County, 3,709 renters and 3,658 owners. Not all were currently receiving payments.

The figure included the full costs of shelter and utilities and was the same for renters and homeowners. In Table 3.4, the first column for each county shows the initial R^* schedules, based on field surveys conducted in September 1973 in Brown County and August 1974 in St. Joseph County. Although the costs of small units were then estimated to be the same in both sites, the larger units—mostly single-family houses—were less expensive in St. Joseph County.

Subsequent increases in contract rents and in fuel and utility prices

initial values were determined, see Lowry, Woodfill, and Repnau, 1981, and Lowry, Woodfill, and Dade, 1981. For the application of these principles to homeowners, see Lowry, 1981. Empirical analyses underlying the periodic changes in R^* are reported in Lowry, 1979; Stucker, 1979 and 1981; and Lindsay and Lowry, 1980.

Table 3.4

STANDARD COST OF ADEQUATE HOUSING BY SIZE OF HOUSEHOLD: HOUSING ALLOWANCE PROGRAMS IN BROWN AND ST. JOSEPH COUNTIES, 1974-80

Number of Persons	Number of Rooms[b]	Standard Monthly Cost ($)[a]									
		Brown County					St. Joseph County				
		June 1974	April 1976	May 1977	May 1978	July 1979	Dec 1974	Sep 1976	Sep 1977	Jan 1979	Jan 1980
1	1-2	100	125	130	140	155	100	115	120	130	155
2	1-3	125	145	155	170	180	125	140	150	160	175
3-4	4	155	175	185	200	220	145	160	175	190	200
5-6	5	170	195	205	235	255	160	175	185	195	235
7-8	6	190	210	220	265	280	170	185	190	205	260
9+	6	220	230	245	300	320	170	185	190	205	260

SOURCE: FPOG Policy Clarification Memoranda Nos. 141, 158, 186, 193, 209, 218, 221, and 224.

NOTE: Standard costs were initially estimated from preprogram field surveys of rental dwellings in each site; they were subsequently increased to reflect measured inflation, nearly all of which was in fuel and utility prices. The effective date of each schedule is shown in the table; the measurement dates were several months earlier: September 1973, January 1976, January 1977, March 1978, and January 1979 for Brown County; and August 1974, July 1976, August 1977, October 1978, and November 1979 for St. Joseph County.

[a]Estimated monthly cost of shelter and utilities for a dwelling of the indicated size that meets specified quality standards.

[b]Minimum number of rooms for household of indicated size. For one and two persons, rooming units are acceptable.

led us to increase the scheduled values of R^*, and thus the benefit levels. Table 3.4 shows the revised schedules and their effective dates. The increases cumulate to about 47 percent in Brown County and 48 percent in St. Joseph County.[5]

Increasing R^* also increased the upper income limit for enrollment. If incomes were fixed, raising the limit would also increase the number of eligible households. But because incomes were in fact rising in both sites, the number of eligible households changed comparatively

[5]These are unweighted averages of percentage increases for each size of dwelling, which range from 42 to 55 percent in Brown County and 38 to 55 percent in St. Joseph County. Note also that the last schedules shown for each site went into effect at the beginning of the sixth program year.

little during the first four program years.[6] For the same reason, benefits did not increase by as much as the indicated changes in R^*.

Table 3.5 shows average incomes and allowance payments for recipients in each site at the end of program years 2 through 5. Gross income included transfer payments such as Aid to Families with Dependent Children (AFDC) and unemployment compensation. Adjustments required by law generally reduced gross income by $300 to $3,000, the amount increasing with household size and age of head. Annual benefits were calculated by subtracting a fourth of adjusted gross income from the appropriate annualized value of R^*; the monthly payment was one-twelfth of that amount.

In both sites, the average gross incomes of allowance recipients increased between years 2 and 5—by 10 percent in Brown County and by 12 percent in St. Joseph County. The increases reflect both general inflation and changes in the client mix. Partly because most of the adjustments to gross income were specified in dollars rather than as percentages of income, average adjusted gross income rose faster than gross income—by 13 percent in Brown County and 15 percent in St. Joseph County.

In Brown County, the 13-percent increase in average adjusted gross income combined with the 47-percent increase in R^* to yield a 26-percent increase in the average allowance payment between years 2 and 5. In St. Joseph County, the 15-percent increase in income combined with the 48-percent increase in R^* to yield an average allowance increase of 31 percent.

Table 3.5 also shows that client incomes differed in the two sites. At the end of year 5, the average adjusted gross income for recipient homeowners in Brown County was 14 percent greater than for their counterparts in St. Joseph County; for participating renters, the differential was 39 percent, again favoring Brown County. For the renters, one might expect much lower allowance entitlements in Brown County; but entitlement falls by only a dollar for every four-dollar increase in income.

Because few participants had zero incomes, the average allowance payment was well below the standard cost of adequate housing. But in relation to gross income, the average payment was substantial, ranging from 18 percent for Brown County homeowners to 39 percent for St. Joseph County renters. Overall, payments in year 5 averaged 25 percent of gross income (31 percent of adjusted gross income).

Through year 5, the Brown County HAO disbursed $11.9 million in allowance payments, and the HAO in St. Joseph County disbursed $18.3 million. At the rate of disbursement for the first month of year

[6]Estimates of the eligible population are based on household surveys, the last of which were conducted during program year 4 in each site. However, the number of eligibles may subsequently have increased; see note 2, above.

Table 3.5

PARTICIPANTS' INCOMES AND ALLOWANCE PAYMENTS: HOUSING ALLOWANCE PROGRAMS IN BROWN AND ST. JOSEPH COUNTIES THROUGH YEAR 5

Item	Average Amount ($) at End of Program Year[a]							
	Brown County				St. Joseph County			
	Year 2	Year 3	Year 4	Year 5	Year 2	Year 3	Year 4	Year 5
Renters								
Annual gross income	4,311	4,493	4,602	4,708	3,266	3,380	3,453	3,542
After adjustment	3,551	3,709	3,841	3,942	2,491	2,660	2,744	2,827
Monthly allowance payment	77	80	87	97	91	92	98	114
Annual equivalent	924	960	1,044	1,164	1,092	1,104	1,176	1,368
Homeowners								
Annual gross income	4,910	5,206	5,494	5,697	4,403	4,534	4,679	5,068
After adjustment	3,824	4,150	4,447	4,619	3,457	3,636	3,738	4,040
Monthly allowance payment	70	69	75	84	63	63	71	85
Annual equivalent	840	828	900	1,008	756	756	852	1,020
All Participants								
Annual gross income	4,569	4,777	4,901	5,020	3,931	4,080	4,172	4,415
After adjustment	3,668	3,885	4,044	4,155	3,056	3,252	3,326	3,521
Monthly allowance payment	74	76	83	93	75	74	82	98
Annual equivalent	888	912	996	1,116	900	888	984	1,176

SOURCE: HAO management information reports for the end of each program year indicated.

NOTE: Gross income for a homeowner includes an imputed amount equal to 5 percent of equity in the home. Adjustments are those required by law and vary with age of head, number of dependents, and number of secondary wage earners. The monthly allowance payment is based on adjusted gross income and the standard cost of adequate housing (see Table 3.4).

[a] Comparable detail is not available for program year 1.

6, the annual outlay would be $4.0 million in Brown County and $7.1 million in St. Joseph County, an overall average of $1,168 per year for each of 9,454 households.

ENFORCING HOUSING STANDARDS

Shortly after a household enrolled in the program, the HAO evaluated its dwelling against program standards for living space, essential facilities, and health or safety hazards (see Appendix C). Through year 5, 48 percent of all enrollment dwellings in Brown County and 55 percent in St. Joseph County failed such evaluations.

The occupant of a defective dwelling had to take one of two actions to qualify for payments—either arrange for the dwelling's repair,[7] or move to another that met program standards. In the former case, he requested a reevaluation when repairs were completed. In the latter, he was supposed to request an evaluation of a prospective residence before he committed himself to it; but some clients moved, then called for a housing evaluation.

Table 3.6 shows the outcome of housing evaluations and reevaluations in each site that were associated with an enrollee's attempts to qualify for payment. (It does not include the annual evaluations for those whose housing qualified initially, nor any evaluations related to subsequent moves.) In every category, the failure rate was higher in St. Joseph County, reflecting the generally worse condition of housing there.

In both sites, just over half of all owners failed initial evaluations; but among renters, 46 percent failed in Brown County and 57 percent failed in St. Joseph County. Between a tenth and a fifth of all enrollees—nearly all renters—explored alternatives to their enrollment dwellings, some calling for evaluations of several potential residences before deciding to move or stay. In Brown County, failure rates on those evaluations were lower than for enrollment dwellings, but they were higher in St. Joseph County. Cumulatively, about two-thirds of all initially defective dwellings (those occupied at enrollment plus the prospective residences evaluated at enrollees' requests) were successfully repaired by the occupant or his landlord.

During the first five program years in Brown County, over 3,700 initially defective dwellings (including those to which enrollees moved) were repaired at the instance of enrollees seeking to qualify for payments, and over 1,000 enrollees moved before qualifying for payments. In St. Joseph County, over 6,900 dwellings were repaired and nearly 2,000 enrollees moved before qualifying for payments.

For those whose housing was initially certifiable, neither repairing nor moving was required to qualify for allowance payments. Rather, payments alleviated budgetary stresses likely to lead to nonpayment of rent or utility bills or to undermaintenance of homes. About 2,000 recipients in Brown County and 2,300 in St. Joseph County moved *after* qualifying for payments, presumably having reconsidered their housing alternatives in the light of their increased resources.[8]

The repairs needed to bring a dwelling up to program standards

---

[7]A renter may either persuade his landlord to make needed repairs or undertake them himself. Both are common practices.

[8]Moves are not reported directly as dated events, but must be inferred from transactions between clients and the HAO—usually housing evaluations conducted at different addresses. Among recipient-movers, between two-thirds and three-fourths qualified for payments in their new homes, often after repairing them.

Table 3.6

RESULTS OF HOUSING EVALUATIONS FOR NEWLY ENROLLED AND REINSTATED HOUSEHOLDS: HOUSING ALLOWANCE PROGRAMS IN BROWN AND ST. JOSEPH COUNTIES THROUGH YEAR 5

Evaluation Result	Brown County			St. Joseph County		
	Renter	Owner	Total	Renter	Owner	Total
Initial Evaluation of Enrollment Residence						
Number of cases	5,559	2,850	8,409	6,464	6,835	13,299
Percentage distribution:						
Acceptable	54.3	48.7	52.4	42.9	47.3	45.2
Not acceptable	45.7	51.3	47.6	57.1	52.7	54.8
Initial Evaluation of Other Enrollee-Nominated Dwelling						
Number of cases	2,575	127	2,702	3,302	228	3,530
Percentage distribution:						
Acceptable	57.2	49.6	56.9	30.8	35.5	31.1
Not acceptable	42.8	50.4	43.1	69.2	64.5	68.9
Evaluation for Reinstated Household						
Number of cases	716	223	939	941	664	1,605
Percentage distribution:						
Acceptable	59.2	67.7	61.2	41.2	52.7	46.0
Not acceptable	40.8	32.3	38.8	58.8	47.3	54.0
Reevaluation of Failed Dwelling						
Number of cases	2,765	1,278	4,043	4,752	3,350	8,102
Percentage distribution:						
Acceptable	89.6	96.2	91.7	80.4	92.1	85.3
Not acceptable	10.4	3.8	8.3	19.6	7.8	14.7

SOURCE: HAO management information reports for 29 June 1979 in Brown County and 28 December 1979 in St. Joseph County.

NOTE: If feasible, each enrollee's preenrollment dwelling is evaluated even though the enrollee may plan to move. Prospective residences are evaluated only at the enrollee's request; often, several such evaluations are conducted on behalf of the same enrollee. Households reinstated after an earlier termination of enrollment must have their dwellings evaluated as though they were new enrollees. Failed units are reevaluated (presumably after being repaired) at the enrollee's request.

were rarely expensive, even though genuine hazards to the occupants were often remedied. Most repairs were done by the occupant himself or his landlord; out-of-pocket expenses for materials and hired labor seldom exceeded $100; in three-fourths of the cases, cash expenses were under $30, and the median was about $10.[9]

Each dwelling occupied by an allowance recipient was evaluated annually to ensure that it continued to meet program standards. Table 3.7 reports the results of all such evaluations conducted through year 5—about 9,200 in Brown County and 14,100 in St. Joseph County. A fifth of the dwellings occupied by Brown County recipients and a third of those occupied by St. Joseph County recipients drifted below standard during the year preceding their annual evaluations. Most of those whose dwellings failed promptly repaired the new defects; some subsequently moved; and payments were suspended for those who did neither. It is thus clear that the program's housing objectives would not be met solely by initial evaluations. Periodic rechecks of the condition of recipients' dwellings are needed to ensure that they remain free of hazards to health and safety.

The housing standards on which both initial and annual evaluations were based have been amended from time to time as field experience revealed weaknesses of specification or inequities in enforcement. The most important change, prompted by federal legislation, pertains to lead-based paint hazards. The HAOs had from the start failed dwellings in which the hazard was unmistakable, but a more stringent standard was adopted in January 1977. Thereafter, the existence of any cracking, scaling, chipping, peeling, or loose paint, whether it contained lead or not, was grounds for failure if children under seven years old were residents or frequent visitors.

The new standard significantly affected subsequent evaluation results. Four percent of the dwellings evaluated in Brown County and 8 percent in St. Joseph County failed only because of lead-based paint hazards. Another 8 percent (Brown County) and 22 percent (St. Joseph County) were failed for lead-based paint hazards in combination with other defects. Actually, evaluators' reports indicated paint defects in about 45 percent of the dwellings evaluated in Brown County and 60 percent in St. Joseph County, but children were present in only a minority of the cases.

Most paint defects required scaling and repainting selected exterior

---

[9]See McDowell, 1979, for details. We have estimated the costs of repairing dwellings whose occupants instead move or drop out of the program; these unrepaired dwellings have higher average repair costs than the repaired dwellings, but not enough higher to seriously constrain the clients' decisions. The underlying fact is that even in St. Joseph County, housing defects tend to be easily remediable health or safety hazards rather than fundamental structural flaws.

Table 3.7

RESULTS OF HOUSING EVALUATIONS FOR RECIPIENT HOUSEHOLDS: HOUSING ALLOWANCE PROGRAMS IN BROWN AND ST. JOSEPH COUNTIES THROUGH YEAR 5

Evaluation Result	Brown County			St. Joseph County		
	Renter	Owner	Total	Renter	Owner	Total
Annual Evaluation of Recipient's Dwelling[a]						
Number of cases	5,466	3,726	9,192	5,366	8,769	14,135
Percentage distribution:						
Acceptable	77.3	84.2	80.1	56.4	73.7	67.1
Not acceptable	22.7	15.8	19.9	43.6	26.3	32.9
Evaluation of Other Recipient-Nominated Dwelling						
Number of cases	1,411	92	1,503	1,561	143	1,704
Percentage distribution:						
Acceptable	57.7	59.8	57.8	36.3	46.9	37.1
Not acceptable	42.3	40.2	42.2	63.7	53.1	62.9
Reevaluation of Failed Dwelling						
Number of cases	1,158	490	1,648	2,481	2,015	4,496
Percentage distribution:						
Acceptable	91.2	95.5	92.5	81.3	91.8	86.0
Not acceptable	8.8	4.5	7.5	18.7	8.2	14.0

SOURCE: HAO management information reports for 29 June 1979 in Brown County and 28 December 1979 in St. Joseph County.

NOTE: Recipients' dwellings are reevaluated annually; if defects found by these evaluations are not promptly remedied, allowance payments are suspended. When a recipient moves, the new dwelling must be evaluated and certified for occupancy to avoid payment suspension. Failed units are reevaluated (presumably after being repaired) at the recipient's request.

[a]Data on annual evaluations include a few in each site for enrollees who never qualified for payments but maintained their enrollments by completing semiannual and annual eligibility recertification requirements.

surfaces, over 100 square feet in a fourth of all such cases. Because paid labor was rarely used, the repair costs were modest, averaging $20 to $30 for single-family houses, less for apartments. In aggregate, however, correcting lead-based paint hazards accounted for a fourth of initial repair costs.[10]

Except for the paint-related rise in failure rates in 1977, housing evaluation failures generally declined over time, both for new enrollees and recipients (see Table 3.8). Several factors could account for

Table 3.8

TRENDS IN HOUSING EVALUATION FAILURES AND REPAIRS: HOUSING ALLOWANCE PROGRAMS IN BROWN AND ST. JOSEPH COUNTIES THROUGH YEAR 5

Result, by Participant's Tenure	Percent of All Evaluated or Failed Dwellings, by Program Year[a]							
	Brown County				St. Joseph County			
	Year 2	Year 3	Year 4	Year 5	Year 2	Year 3	Year 4	Year 5
Newly Enrolled and Reinstated Households								
Evaluated dwelling failed:								
Renter	48	43	44	41	61	67	58	58
Owner	51	48	51	45	54	53	50	50
Failed dwelling repaired:								
Renter	52	70	69	71	52	62	66	61
Owner	68	89	100[b]	86	67	89	82	80
Recipient Households								
Evaluated dwelling failed:								
Renter	27	32	28	21	48	56	44	45
Owner	22	18	16	10	34	32	23	23
Failed dwelling repaired:								
Renter	67	53	53	60	45	53	67	69
Owner	75	80	68	79	56	72	85	89

SOURCE: HAO management information reports for the indicated periods.

NOTE: For newly enrolled and reinstated households, the failure rate combines initial evaluations of both enrollment and reinstatement residences with initial evaluations of other enrollee-nominated dwellings, whether or not the latter were ever occupied by the enrollees. The repair rate is the total number of "acceptable" reevaluations divided by the numerator of the failure rate.

For recipients, the failure rate combines annual reevaluations of their dwellings with evaluations of other recipient-nominated dwellings, whether or not the latter were ever occupied by the recipients. The repair rate is the total number of "acceptable" reevaluations divided by the numerator of the failure rate.

[a]Comparable detail is not available for program year 1.

[b]Probably overstated because of multiple reevaluations of failed dwellings or lags in data entry.

[10]For more detail, see McDowell, 1980.

that decline: a change in enrollment patterns that brought better dwellings into the program, dwellings already evaluated and repaired by one enrollee reentering the program when they were occupied by another enrollee, and anticipatory repairs made prior to evaluation. The HAOs' housing evaluators report that as program information spread, both new enrollees and recipients often repaired obvious defects before the evaluator arrived. Probably, these anticipatory repairs account for much of the time-trend in failure rates.

For those dwellings that did fail, repair rates show no clear trend. Among new enrollees in both sites, the repair rate was distinctly lower in year 2 than subsequently. Among recipients in St. Joseph County, but not in Brown County, the repair rate climbed spectacularly. From year 3 on, required repair costs dropped, particularly in St. Joseph County. Higher repair rates and lower repair costs suggest that enrollees' dwellings were failed because of less serious or extensive defects in later program years. As before, changes in enrollment patterns, or recycling of dwellings through the evaluation system could account for those trends in repair activity.

REFERENCES

Dubinsky, Robert, William G. Grigsby, and Karen G. Watson, *Review of the Relationship between the Housing Assistance Supply Experiment and Other Types of Assisted Housing Programs,* The Rand Corporation, N-1100-HUD, March 1981.

Katagiri, Iao, and G. Thomas Kingsley, eds., *The Housing Allowance Office Handbook,* The Rand Corporation, N-1491-HUD, July 1980.

Lamar, Bruce W., and Ira S. Lowry, *Client Responses to Housing Requirements: The First Two Years,* The Rand Corporation, N-1124-HUD, May 1981.

Lindsay, David Scott, and Ira S. Lowry, *Rent Inflation in St. Joseph County, Indiana, 1974-78,* The Rand Corporation, N-1468-HUD, November 1980.

Lowry, Ira S., *Inflation in the Standard Cost of Adequate Housing: Site I, 1973-1976,* The Rand Corporation, N-1102-HUD, October 1979.

——, *Equity and Housing Objectives in Homeowner Assistance,* The Rand Corporation, N-1073-HUD, March 1981.

Lowry, Ira S., Barbara M. Woodfill, and Marsha A. Dade, *Program Standards for Site II,* The Rand Corporation, N-1079-HUD, April 1981.

Lowry, Ira S., Barbara M. Woodfill, and Tiina Repnau, *Program Standards for Site I,* The Rand Corporation, N-1058-HUD, January 1981.

McDowell, James L., *Housing Allowances and Housing Improvement: Early Findings,* The Rand Corporation, N-1198-HUD, September 1979.

——, *The Effects of the HAO Lead-Based Paint Hazard Standard,* The Rand Corporation, N-1306-1-HUD, June 1980.

Stucker, James P., *Rent Inflation in St. Joseph County, Indiana: 1974-77,* The Rand Corporation, N-1116-HUD, November 1979.

——, *Rent Inflation in Brown County, Wisconsin: 1973-78,* The Rand Corporation, N-1134-HUD, March 1981.

IV. ELIGIBILITY AND PARTICIPATION

Enrollment in the experimental housing allowance program was continuously open to all households in Brown and St. Joseph counties that met the program's standards as to income, assets, and family composition; and allowances averaging 25 percent of gross income were paid to enrollees whose dwellings had passed their most recent housing evaluations. As we had expected from preexperimental analysis, about a fifth of all households were eligible for enrollment at any given time. Participation grew rapidly during the first two program years, but abruptly leveled off in year 3. To our surprise, only a third of those eligible in year 3 were then receiving payments.

That a low-income housing assistance program would benefit only a third of the eligible population is disquieting. Although no national housing assistance program has ever approached that much participation, the obvious reason has been that appropriations were never adequate to help more than a small fraction of those nominally eligible. The HASE program broke new ground in several respects. First, it was open to both renters and homeowners on the same terms, whereas national programs have always been designed for only one or the other tenure group. Second, although the annual contribution contracts that financed the two experimental programs did limit their sizes, the limits were purposely set high enough to allow open enrollment during all of the five-year experimental period. Third, HASE was less restrictive as to participants' housing choices than any preceding national program. We expected all these factors to raise participation to perhaps 60 percent of all eligibles (Lowry, 1980, pp. 67-75).

Analysis of the participation process reveals five factors that together screened out two-thirds of the eligibles from participation; they are listed below in rough order of quantitative importance:

- Small allowance entitlements for marginally eligible households, which discouraged them from enrolling or, if enrolled, from meeting housing requirements.
- The program's housing standards, which discouraged some eligibles from enrolling and some enrollees from qualifying for payments.
- Brief durations of eligibility, so that some became ineligible before they applied, or did not apply because their benefits would be brief.

- Lack of information about the program, which forestalled enrollment.
- Reluctance to accept assistance from government, which inhibited some eligibles from applying.

These barriers to participation are not necessarily program defects. That those who are marginally or briefly eligible screen themselves out may be a program virtue rather than a defect; enrolling them would entail substantial administrative cost but would yield meager benefits. Without housing standards, the program would be indistinguishable from a negative income tax, and would result in little housing improvement; however, we learned that the exact specifications of housing standards could be startlingly important in their effect on participation. Not many eligibles were uninformed about the program, and most who applied quickly completed the steps needed to become recipients; substantial improvements in outreach or processing are neither feasible nor very beneficial to program purposes. Whether those who are reluctant to accept help should be persuaded otherwise is certainly open to argument.

Although the overall participation rate was low, we find that the poorest households and those with the longest expected duration of eligibility were, other things equal, more likely than their opposites to enroll and qualify for payments. On the other hand, those in the worst housing were, other things equal, less likely than others to receive payments. Because prosperity and housing quality were inversely correlated, these factors were partially offsetting; but the net result was that program benefits did clearly focus on lower-income eligibles. Other things equal, the program served owners as well as it did renters, and blacks as well as it did whites; however, households that include children participated more than childless households whose circumstances were otherwise similar.

The following pages offer evidence in support of these conclusions. After briefly explaining our data and analytical methods, we describe the eligible population of each site and how it changed over time. Then we show which members of that population were enrolled and receiving payments at the end of program year 3.

Because eligibility and participation are transient statuses for households, we constructed a model of participation in a mature program that takes account of turnover. In that context, we show how program features interact with household and housing characteristics to determine participation rates for various types of households. We also examine site differences and review measures that might increase participation in an allowance program. Finally, we compare the HASE participation rates with those reported by the Housing Allowance Demand Experiment.

DATA SOURCES AND ANALYTICAL METHODS

The data presented in this chapter are drawn from two sources: the countywide surveys of households conducted annually in each site; and administrative records of the housing allowance offices in each site. The survey data were used to estimate the number and characteristics of eligible households and to analyze their knowledge of the program and their decisions to enroll. The HAO records were used to analyze the outcomes of enrollees' housing evaluations and their responses to evaluation failures. For some special purposes, we linked HAO records for applicants or enrollees to survey records for the same households, but most analyses were conducted on data from only one of the two sources.

The analysis was conducted in stages corresponding to major steps in the participation process; then the findings of the several steps were analytically integrated. A series of topical reports provides full technical detail on each stage and on the integration.[1] Below, we comment only on features of the analytical methods that affect the interpretation of findings.

The Household Surveys

Analysis of participation in public programs is usually hampered by lack of information about the population that is eligible to participate. Our annual countywide surveys of households gathered data on household composition, income, and assets that enabled us to estimate the number and characteristics of households eligible to participate at the time of each survey.[2] The first survey in each site was conducted just before the allowance program began enrollment; the last was conducted near the end of program year 3 (see Appendix B, Fig. B.1).

Survey records included a detailed account of each respondent's knowledge of the program and his dealings with the HAO. We used

[1]Methods used to estimate the eligible population of each site are presented in Carter and Balch, 1981. Wendt, 1982, analyzes the acquisition of program knowledge and the decision to enroll. Coleman, 1982, analyzes housing evaluation failures and responses to failure. Carter and Wendt, 1982, integrate the findings of the three topical studies.

[2]The surveys did not elicit all of the information used by the HAOs in applying the asset limit; we used what we had, including the values of homeowners' equities. To match the HAOs' income test, we estimated each respondent's current monthly income rather than using the income he reported for the preceding calendar year. To offset general price inflation, the HAOs periodically revised the schedule of R^* and the corresponding income limits for enrollment. Because survey dates did not match the dates of schedule revisions, we interpolated between schedule changes to obtain income limits for each annual survey. Thus, some of our "eligibles" would not in fact have been permitted to enroll until the next schedule revision.

records for eligible households to model the acquisition of program knowledge, and records for eligible, informed households to model the decision to enroll. In the process, we learned that interviewing eligible households significantly increased their propensities to enroll. Fortunately, the interview effect was systematic enough so that we could correct for it in estimating enrollment probabilities.

The HAO Records

To analyze the factors associated with passing or failing housing evaluations, we used HAO records that described both enrollees' characteristics and evaluation outcomes. The analysis was not designed to determine why a dwelling failed (that information was on record) or why a household was living in a substandard dwelling, but merely to estimate the probability that a household of a specific type would encounter evaluation failure as a barrier to participation.

Responses to evaluation failures and the probability of qualifying for payments were modeled from the same HAO records used to analyze the pattern of failure. The HAO data were also used to analyze durations of recipiency for those who did qualify for payments.

Analytical Integration

Analysis of sequential steps in the participation process yielded estimates of transition probabilities between statuses, probabilities that varied with household characteristics and housing circumstances. Compounding these transition probabilities tells us the likelihood that a given household will ever reach a given step in the participation process. However, at any given time, the number of households occupying a particular status (such as receiving payments) will be less than the number that will ever occupy that status. Taking into account the average elapsed time associated with each transition, we were able to estimate the distribution of households by participation status at any given time.

We chose program year 3 in each site as the period of greatest interest because the parameters of the participation process seem by then to have stabilized. Estimates of steady-state distributions by program status closely approximate the year 3 outcomes directly observable from HAO records. Unless otherwise noted, the participation statistics in this chapter refer to year 3, representing a mature program rather than the earlier phases of rapid growth in enrollment and recipiency. However, we remind the reader that enrollment and recipiency began to grow again in program year 5; the reasons, if known, might modify some of our conclusions here (see Ch. III, "Enrollment and Payment Authorizations").

Households Excluded from Analysis

When the allowance program began, single persons under age 62 who lived alone or with nonrelatives were categorically excluded from participation unless they were handicapped, disabled, or had been residentially displaced by public action. After 1 August 1977, all nonelderly singles who met income and asset tests were eligible to enroll, but the number receiving payments could not exceed 10 percent of all recipients.

Because we monitored only a brief period during which nonelderly singles were eligible, we did not have enough data to analyze their participatory behavior. Consequently, all single persons under 62 were excluded from the eligibility estimates presented here. Those who were enrolled were excluded from our analysis of HAO records.

The analysis also excludes occupants of federally subsidized dwellings such as public housing. Such households could enroll in the allowance program but could not qualify for payments unless they moved to unsubsidized dwellings or arranged to pay full market rents for their subsidized dwellings. At the end of program year 3, there were about 930 subsidized rental units and 660 subsidized owner-occupied homes in Brown County; St. Joseph County had about 2,500 subsidized rental dwellings and 890 subsidized owner-occupied homes. The majority of these dwellings were occupied by allowance-eligible households, but very few changed to the allowance program.[3]

Finally, we excluded resident landlords (1,540 in Brown County and 750 in St. Joseph County), some of whom were eligible for assistance. Because they were surveyed only in their capacities as landlords, we lacked the data to determine their eligibility statuses; but HAO records show that a few enrolled in the allowance program, and they are counted here as participants.

THE ELIGIBLE POPULATIONS

The housing allowance program sought to reduce the burden of housing expenditures borne by the needy and to improve the quality

---

[3]During the first 18 months of program operations in St. Joseph County, 26 residents of public housing in South Bend transferred to the allowance program. These transfers amounted to 3 percent of the South Bend Housing Authority's tenant population.

of their housing. To achieve these ends, the program offered cash grants to low-income households provided that the recipients' housing met minimum standards for space, facilities, and condition. The grants varied with household size and income.

Roughly one-fifth of the households at the two sites met the income and asset requirements. The proportion was lower in Brown County (16.5 percent) than in St. Joseph County (21.4 percent). As can be seen in Table 4.1, both single-parent households and the elderly were greatly overrepresented among eligible households at both sites; in St. Joseph County, where there is a substantial black population, blacks were also greatly overrepresented.

The higher eligibility rates of single parents, the elderly, and racial minorities are in large part attributable to their especially low incomes, typical not only of the experimental sites but of the nation as a whole. The higher eligibility rate of the elderly is attributable also in part to their smaller household sizes. The housing allowance program set the income eligibility cutoff at four times the cost of adequate housing, but housing typically comprises a larger budget share for smaller households. Thus, relative to total budgets, the income eligibility limit is more generous for smaller households.[4]

The income and asset eligibility rules were more effective at identifying households with excessive housing expenditure burdens than households living in substandard dwellings. About three-fourths of the eligibles reported housing expenditure burdens in excess of 25 percent of gross income, whereas only a fourth of the ineligibles did. We estimate that 46 percent of the eligible households and 33 percent of the ineligible households in St. Joseph County lived in dwellings that would have failed an HAO evaluation.[5]

During the years covered by our surveys, the overall size of the eligible population in each site changed very little (see Table 4.2), but some components increased or decreased substantially. In both sites, the number of eligible single parents grew by over 10 percent annually, reflecting a corresponding increase in all single-parent households.

---

[4]For example, federal poverty statistics for 1977 (U.S. Bureau of the Census, 1979, Table 756) indicate that the national average cost of a minimally adequate diet for one person was then about half the cost in our sites of adequate housing for one person; for a household of 5 persons, such a diet would have cost about 78 percent of housing cost.

[5]Housing expense burdens by eligibility status are tabulated from wave 1 household survey data; see Helbers, 1980, for analysis of the hard-to-measure housing expenses of homeowners. Housing quality by eligibility status is estimated for St. Joseph County by Yildiz and Mulford, 1982; the figures cited are for program year 3. The implied county-wide failure rate of 35 percent is much higher than estimates of substandard housing based on decennial census data because HAO evaluations are both broader in scope and more rigorous than census-based evaluations. Partial analysis indicates that the comparable failure rate for Brown County would be about 30 percent.

Among the elderly, patterns were mixed. In both sites, the *proportion* of elderly single persons who were eligible declined because their social security benefits rose faster than housing costs; however, in St. Joseph County, the population of elderly singles grew enough to offset the lower eligibility rate. Also in St. Joseph County, the eligibility rate for nonelderly couples dropped sharply when employment improved in 1975-76.

The small net changes in the size of the eligible population mask frequent changes in the eligibility statuses of individual households. Each year, about 30 percent of the eligible households became ineligible and 6 percent of the ineligible households became eligible (see Fig. 4.1). The causes of these fluctuations in eligibility status were rather evenly divided between changes in income and changes in marital status.

PARTICIPATION IN A MATURE PROGRAM

Participation in the program grew rapidly during the first three years of operation (see Ch. III, Fig. 3.1). Initially, few households knew about the program; but in both communities, publicity and advertising were used during the first two years to generate as many applications as the HAOs were able to process. Although the program was larger in St. Joseph County, the enrollment rate was higher in Brown County at each stage of program development.

Excluding nonelderly singles, who first became eligible in August 1977, enrollment in both sites stabilized during the third year of program operations.[6] The experimental data from the third program year seem to reflect the operation of a "mature" housing allowance program, and therefore are informative about the long-run participation rates that would be experienced in a national program.

Participation in the Housing Allowance Program

At the end of the third program year in Brown County, 3,351 households were enrolled in the allowance program, of which 2,849 were receiving payments. In St. Joseph County, 5,820 households were enrolled, of which 4,718 were receiving payments. Enrollees not receiving payments included some who had only recently enrolled and

[6]Enrollment of nonelderly singles continued to grow during the third program year, so that Fig. 3.1 shows enrollment leveling off only during year 4. Moreover, total enrollment began growing again late in year 5. See Ch. III, "Enrollment and Payment Authorizations," for details.

Table 4.1

ALL HOUSEHOLDS AND ELIGIBLE HOUSEHOLDS IN 1977, BY SITE AND SELECTED CHARACTERISTICS

Characteristic	Number of Households		Percentage Distribution	
	All Households	Eligible Households	All Households	Eligible Households
Brown County				
Housing Tenure				
Renter	14,342	3,689	29.8	46.6
Owner	33,730	4,223	70.2	53.4
Total	48,072	7,912	100.0	100.0
Household Composition[a]				
Single parent	3,471	1,973	7.2	24.9
Other nonelderly single person	8,079	(*b*)	16.8	(*b*)
Elderly single person	3,841	1,778	8.0	22.5
Young couple, young children	12,344	1,703	25.7	21.5
Other nonelderly couple	16,458	1,105	34.2	14.0
Elderly couple	3,879	1,353	8.1	17.1
Total	48,072	7,912	100.0	100.0

St. Joseph County

Housing Tenure				
Renter	15,619	4,644[c]	21.7	30.2[c]
Owner	56,267	10,755	78.3	69.8
Total	71,886	15,399	100.0	100.0
Household Composition[a]				
Single parent	6,141	3,801	8.5	24.7
Other nonelderly single person	12,508	(*b*)	17.4	(*b*)
Elderly single person	8,589	5,464	11.9	35.5
Young couple, young children	15,279	1,878	21.2	12.2
Other nonelderly couple	20,633	1,580	28.7	10.3
Elderly couple	8,736	2,676	12.2	17.4
Total	71,886	15,399	100.0	100.0
Race of Head				
White non-Latin	64,336	12,508	89.5	81.2
Other	7,550	2,891	10.5	18.8
Total	71,886	15,399	100.0	100.0

SOURCE: Estimated by HASE staff from household survey records for wave 4 in Brown County and wave 3 in St. Joseph County. See Carter and Balch, 1981, for estimating methods.

NOTE: Resident landlords and occupants of subsidized housing are excluded from both the total and eligible populations. Distribution by race of head was not estimated for Brown County, where over 98 percent of all household heads were non-Latin whites. Distributions may not add exactly to totals because of rounding.

[a] Compositional categories are derived from life-cycle stages defined in Sec. II, Table 2.2.

[b] Single persons under 62 are all classified as ineligible, although a few were eligible because of handicaps, disabilities, or residential displacement. See text for explanation.

[c] This figure would be substantially larger if renters in federally subsidized housing units had been counted as eligible. See text for explanation.

Table 4.2

CHANGES IN THE ELIGIBLE POPULATION, BY SITE AND SELECTED HOUSEHOLD CHARACTERISTICS: 1974-77

Characteristic	Eligible Households		Average Annual Change (%)
	1974 or 1975	1977	
Brown County, 1974-77			
Housing Tenure			
Renter	3,313	3,689	3.6
Owner	4,090	4,223	1.1
Total	7,403	7,912	2.2
Household Composition			
Single parent	1,423	1,973	11.5
Elderly single person	2,380	1,778	- 9.3
Young couple, young children	1,411	1,703	6.5
Other nonelderly couple	865	1,105	8.5
Elderly couple	1,325	1,353	.7
Total	7,403	7,912	2.2
St. Joseph County, 1975-77			
Housing Tenure			
Renter	4,400	4,644	2.7
Owner	10,707	10,755	.2
Total	15,107	15,399	1.0
Household Composition			
Single parent	2,828	3,801	15.9
Elderly single person	5,487	5,464	- .2
Young couple, young children	2,041	1,878	- 4.1
Other nonelderly couple	2,260	1,580	-16.4
Elderly couple	2,491	2,676	3.6
Total	15,107	15,399	1.0
Race of Head			
White non-Latin	12,668	12,507	- .6
Other	2,439	2,891	8.9
Total	15,107	15,399	1.0

SOURCE: Estimated by HASE staff from records of the surveys of households, waves 1 and 4 in Brown County and waves 2 and 4 in St. Joseph County. See Carter and Balch, 1981, for details of estimation procedures.

NOTE: Distribution by race of head was not estimated for Brown County, where over 98 percent of all household heads were non-Latin whites.

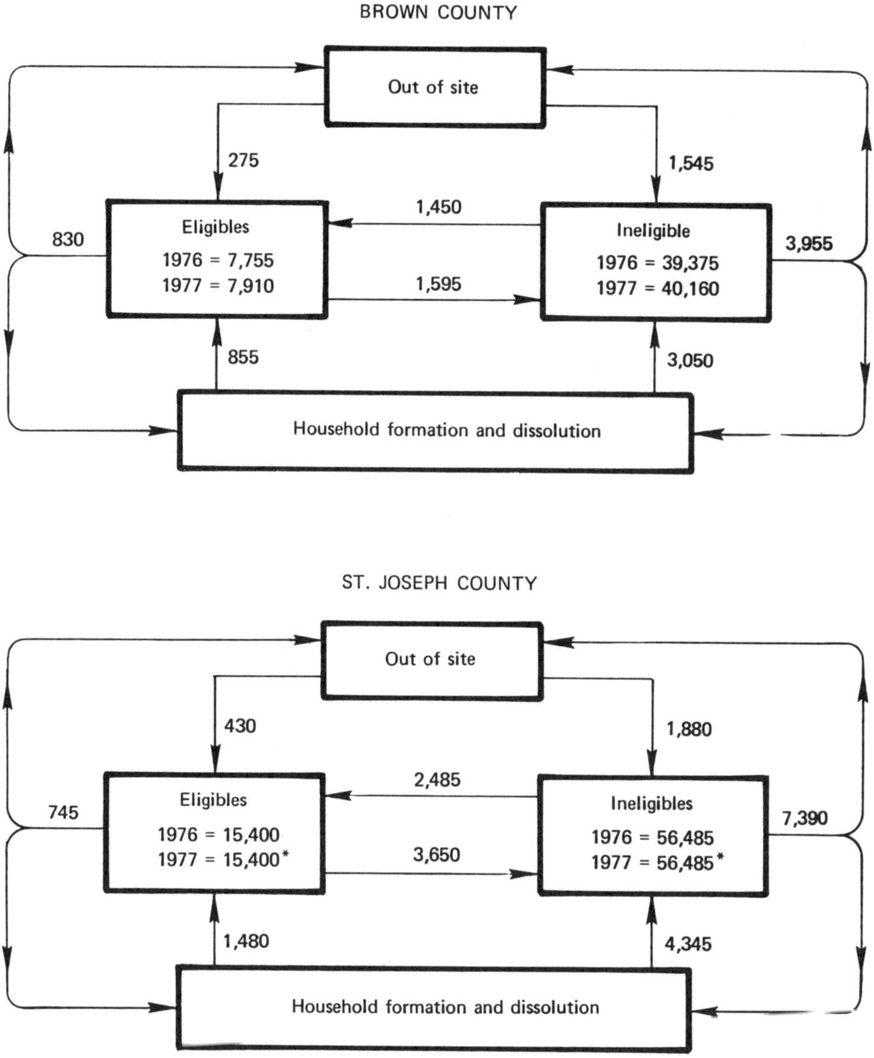

SOURCE: Estimated from household survey and HAO records.
Flow rates for Brown County are 2-year averages.

*Observed changes, 1976–77, were statistically insignificant.

Fig. 4.1—Annual changes in eligibility status of households, by site

had yet to obtain the HAOs' approval of their dwellings, and others whose dwellings had failed and who would eventually drop out of the program.

Table 4.3 shows how the recipients in each site were distributed by household composition and (in St. Joseph County) by race of head. In both sites, about a third were single parents and roughly half were elderly single persons or couples; the remainder were couples under 62 years of age, with or without children. In St. Joseph County, over a fifth were members of racial minorities.

The most striking difference between the programs in Brown and St. Joseph counties was with respect to the housing tenure of recipients. In Brown County, 58 percent were renters and 42 percent were homeowners; in St. Joseph County, 38 percent were renters and 62 percent were homeowners. This difference reflects several factors: the greater incidence of homeownership in St. Joseph County, the relatively low incomes of many homeowners there, and the greater availability there of alternative assistance programs for renters (see below, "Participation in All Low-Income Housing Programs").

Table 4.4 shows recipiency rates at the end of year 3 for renters and owners, by type of household. In nearly every comparable category, a larger proportion of eligible households were recipients in Brown County than in St. Joseph County. (The exception is elderly couples who owned their homes; their recipiency rates are about the same in the two counties.) Overall, 36 percent of the eligibles in Brown County and 31 percent in St. Joseph County were receiving payments at the end of year 3; the comparable figures for renters are 45 and 38 percent; for owners, 28 and 27 percent.

Participation in All Low-Income Housing Programs

The participation rates in Table 4.4 pertain to households that were eligible for allowances, excluding those already receiving assistance under other housing programs. In both counties, allowance recipients accounted for about two-thirds of all low-income recipients of housing assistance; presumably, the allowance programs would have been larger by about 50 percent in the absence of such alternatives. Including all recipients of low-income housing assistance in both the eligible and recipient groups,[7] the recipiency rates given in Table 4.4 would change as follows:

---

[7]When other programs are included, the recipiency rate does not increase by 50 percent because the denominator (number of eligibles) increases by the same amount as does the numerator (number of recipients).

In addition to allowance recipients, the estimates for all low-income housing programs include all renters in public housing and half of all renters in projects assisted

Table 4.3

COMPOSITION OF RECIPIENT POPULATION AT THE END OF PROGRAM YEAR 3, BY SITE AND SELECTED HOUSEHOLD CHARACTERISTICS

Characteristic[a]	Percentage Distribution of Recipients: Renter	Owner	All
Brown County			
Household Composition			
Single parent	42.2	18.1	32.2
Elderly single person	29.9	41.3	34.7
Young couple, young children	14.1	9.8	12.3
Other nonelderly couple	8.7	11.3	9.8
Elderly couple	5.1	19.5	11.1
Total	100.0	100.0	100.0
St. Joseph County			
Household Composition			
Single parent	53.5	18.1	31.4
Elderly single person	28.5	51.4	42.8
Young couple, young children	7.5	3.1	4.7
Other nonelderly couple	6.8	7.6	7.3
Elderly couple	3.7	19.8	13.8
Total	100.0	100.0	100.0
Race of Head			
White non-Latin	69.3	83.5	78.2
Other	30.7	16.5	21.8
Total	100.0	100.0	100.0

SOURCE: Computed by HASE staff from HAO records for June 1977 in Brown County and December 1977 in St. Joseph County. See Carter and Balch, 1981, Sec. IV, for additional details.

NOTE: Distributions may not add exactly to totals because of rounding.

[a]Distribution by race of head not shown for Brown County, where 96 percent of all recipients were non-Latin whites.

Table 4.4

Recipiency Rates for Households Eligible at the End of Program Year 3, by Site and Selected Household Characteristics

Characteristic[a]	Recipiency Rate (%) Renter	Owner	All Eligibles
Brown County			
Household Composition			
Single parent	54	32	46
Elderly single person	64	49	56
Young couple, young children	28	14	21
Other nonelderly couple	28	23	25
Elderly couple	32	21	23
All eligibles	45	28	36
St. Joseph County			
Household Composition			
Single parent	49	29	39
Elderly single person	40	36	37
Young couple, young children	21	7	12
Other nonelderly couple	23	21	22
Elderly couple	23	22	24
All eligibles	38	27	31
Race of Head			
White non-Latin	38	26	29
Other	38	33	36
All eligibles	38	27	31

SOURCE: Computed by HASE staff from household survey data for each site (estimated numbers of households eligible in 1977) and from HAO records for June 1977 in Brown County and December 1977 for St. Joseph County. See Carter and Balch, 1981, Sec. IV, for additional detail.

NOTE: The recipiency rate is the percentage of all currently eligible households that are currently receiving payments.

[a]Participation by race of head was not estimated for Brown County, where over 98 percent of all household heads were non-Latin whites.

	Percent of Eligibles Receiving Payments	
	Housing Allowance Program	All Low-Income Housing Assistance Programs
Brown County		
Renter	45	53
Owner	28	37
All eligibles	36	44
St. Joseph County		
Renter	38	55
Owner	27	31
All eligibles	31	39

Including the other programs naturally increases all recipiency rates, but affects renters and owners differently. The reason is simply that other housing assistance programs in Brown County were, in 1977, about equally divided between renters and owners; whereas in St. Joseph County, three-fourths of those assisted were renters.

Although it might have been analytically neater to conduct the allowance experiment in markets that had no competing assistance programs, that option was not practically available; virtually every community of any size participates in one or more of the many federal housing assistance programs. For the participation analysis in the remainder of this chapter, our strategy is to exclude participants in other programs from the population eligible for housing allowances. Thus, the participation rates given in Table 4.4 are the ones we will endeavor to explain.

under Secs. 221(d)(3) and 236 of the National Housing Act; all homeowners assisted under Sec. 235 and half of those living in cooperatives who were assisted under Sec. 221(d)(3); and a few renters and owners in Brown County assisted by the Farmers Home Administration. Estimates of the number of households assisted under other programs are based on the administrative records of those programs rather than on our household surveys; we found that survey respondents were often unclear about the help they got from government programs when it was channeled through banks or private developers. See Ch. III, "Contrasts in Housing Market Characteristics," for an account of other housing assistance programs in each site.

Eligibility tests for Secs. 221(d)(3) and Sec. 236 were more liberal than for public housing or housing allowances, so we assumed that only half of those enrolled in the former two programs would have been eligible for housing allowances. (Among survey respondents identified as living in any type of assisted housing in St. Joseph County, the allowance eligibility rate was 56 percent for renters and 76 percent for owners.) The computations in the text table above also include 10 percent of all resident landlords among the eligibles; resident landlords were not surveyed as households, so we could not test their eligibility for housing allowances. HAO records show that a few enrollees in each site were resident landlords, usually renting out rooms or otherwise subdividing a single-family house.

Determinants of Participation in the Allowance Program

The participation rates themselves tell us little about the functional determinants of participation. For example, do owners participate less frequently because they receive lower benefits? Because they are less needy? Because they find it more difficult to meet program standards? Or simply because they are less willing to accept aid? Below, we first discuss the paths that an eligible household must follow in order to become a recipient, then explain what influenced households' decisions at each step, and then speculate on the various possibilities for increasing participation rates.

THE PATH TO PARTICIPATION

Before a household can qualify for allowance payments, it must (a) become eligible, (b) learn about the program, (c) enroll, and (d) pass a housing evaluation. Figure 4.2 indicates generally what proportion of households at each stage passed on to the next and how much time elapsed between steps. Table 4.5 provides more detail about the major steps, showing how transition rates varied by site and household characteristics. The discussion below provides an overview of these transitions.

The first two steps toward receiving allowance payments are becoming eligible and learning about the program. Either may come first, but until both occur there is no chance that a household will receive payments.

Becoming Eligible

When the housing allowance program began, about 20 percent of the households in the two sites immediately became eligible for allowances. But even in a mature housing allowance program, changes in marital status, household composition, and employment status cause a steady flow of households into and out of eligibility. In our two sites, about 6 percent of the ineligibles became newly eligible each year; this annual influx equaled about 30 percent of the eligible population.

Learning about the Program

Sources of information about the program were plentiful. The HAOs conducted aggressive publicity campaigns to inform potentially eligi-

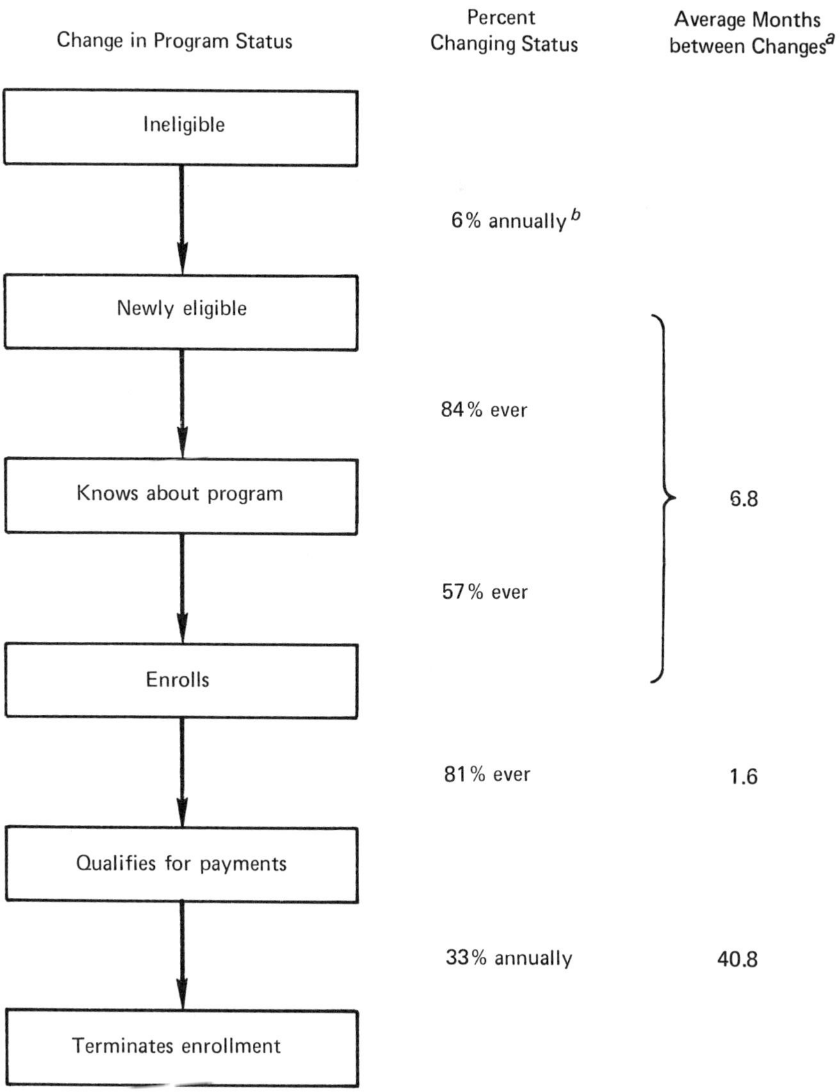

SOURCE: Household surveys and HAO records for Brown and St. Joseph counties.

[a] Based on households that made the indicated change.

[b] When the program began, about 20% of all households became eligible.

Fig. 4.2—Overview of the participation process

Table 4.5

TRANSITION RATES BETWEEN MAJOR PROGRAM STATUSES, BY SITE AND SELECTED HOUSEHOLD CHARACTERISTICS

Characteristic	Transition Rate (%)				
	Eligibles Who Learn about the Program	Informed Eligibles Who Enroll	Enrollees Whose Dwellings Pass Initial Evaluations[a]	Enrollees Whose Dwellings Fail[b], but Who Later Qualify	Enrollees Who Ever Qualify for Payments
			Brown County		
Housing Tenure					
Renter	85	77	48	74	84
Owner	78	50	48	77	88
Age of Head					
Under 62 years	88	66	43	74	84
62 or over	71	60	59	77	89
All cases	81	64	48	75	85

St. Joseph County

Housing Tenure					
Renter	85	75	31	63	72
Owner	85	43	47	75	87
Age of Head					
Under 62 years	86	52	31	63	72
62 or over	85	56	52	82	91
Race of Head					
White non-Latin	85	51	44	70	82
Other	88	62	26	64	72
All cases	85	53	39	68	79

SOURCE: Knowledge and enrollment entries were estimated by HASE staff from wave 4 household surveys in each site: see Carter and Wendt, 1982, Appendix A, for details. Remaining entries were tabulated from HAO records for households that had enrolled before the end of program year 4 in each site.

[a] About 2.5 percent of all renter enrollees passed initial evaluations but did not submit a lease agreement, so did not qualify for payments.

[b] Includes enrollees who never requested initial evaluations or whose initial evaluations were not completed. Most were renters who planned to move after enrolling.

ble households about the program, the local news media heralded the program and its operations, social workers told their clients about it, and potential recipients could learn about it indirectly through family or friends. The first column of Table 4.5 shows that over four-fifths of the eligible households in each site knew about the program after three years.

Enrolling in the Program

The third step toward receiving payments is enrolling in the program. Overall, about 57 percent of the eligibles who knew about the program eventually enrolled, but the proportions differed substantially between sites. Table 4.5 shows that in St. Joseph County about half of the eligible households that knew about the program enrolled, whereas in Brown County the proportion was nearer two-thirds.

Meeting the Housing Requirements

The fourth step toward receiving allowance payments is housing certification. Each enrollee's dwelling was evaluated to determine whether or not it met the program's requirements for space, domestic facilities, and condition. If the dwelling passed, the household immediately qualified for allowance payments. If the dwelling failed, the household had three options: to improve the failed dwelling so that it met HAO standards, to move to another dwelling that met those standards, or to forgo allowance payments. Those who chose the third option usually terminated their enrollments, but a household could continue indefinitely as an enrollee without qualifying for payments.

Table 4.5 shows that about four-fifths of all enrollees ultimately qualified for payments. However, only about half in Brown County and two-fifths in St. Joseph County passed their initial housing evaluations and thereby qualified immediately for payments. The others had first to repair or move. Both the pass rate and the repair-or-move rate were higher in Brown County.[8]

[8]About 6 percent of all enrollees in Brown County and 14 percent in St. Joseph County did not obtain housing evaluations on their enrollment dwellings. Nearly all were renters who contemplated moving after enrolling, so did not see any reason to have their enrollment dwellings evaluated. Many were living rent-free when they enrolled, usually in dwellings owned or also occupied by relatives. Of those without initial evaluations on their enrollment dwellings, about half in each site eventually qualified for payments in some other dwelling.

Termination

Once a household qualified for allowance payments it continued to receive them until either it failed an annual housing evaluation, moved to an unacceptable dwelling, or became ineligible. Although about a quarter of all recipients in Brown County and more than a third in St. Joseph County failed their first annual evaluations, few left the program because of those failures; nearly all repaired their dwellings or moved.[9] Consequently, nearly all households that qualified for allowance payments continued to receive them until they became ineligible because of changes in their incomes, assets, or family composition, or because they moved outside the county. Each year, enrollments were terminated for about 33 percent of all recipients.

Delays

Because there were delays between the steps toward receiving payments, and because there was a constant flow of households in and out of eligibility, the proportion of eligible households that ever completed a given step on the way to recipiency was greater than the proportion that had done so at any given moment. Hence, although the entries in Fig. 4.2 imply that 39 percent of all who became eligible would eventually receive payments, only 32 percent of all eligibles were receiving payments at the end of program year 3.

In addition to postponing recipiency for about 7 percent of all eligibles, the delays between steps prevented some participation. About 4 percent of eligible households that would otherwise have enrolled and qualified for payments became ineligible before they completed that process.

On average, households that enrolled in the program did so about 6.8 months after they became eligible.[10] That delay contributed substantially to the observed low participation rate, because at any moment there were many newly eligible households that would

[9]Each year, only 2 percent of all recipients in Brown County and 5 percent in St. Joseph County terminated their enrollments after failing an annual housing evaluation. Some of these terminees probably had other reasons, such as prospective loss of eligibility, for dropping out after such a failure.

[10]This estimate is based on households that were eligible when the program began in each site. Our annual surveys do not pinpoint exactly when a household becomes eligible; the data only enable us to determine whether a household was eligible at the time of the survey. For households becoming eligible after the program began, we cannot determine the elapsed time (t) until enrollment any closer than ($x \leq t \leq x + 12$) months.

someday enroll but had not yet done so. Similarly, housing evaluations and repairs following initial failure took time. The average elapsed time from enrollment to recipiency for those households that did eventually receive payments was 1.6 months.

The delay between becoming eligible and enrolling appears to be independent of a household's socioeconomic traits. Apparently, the decision to enroll was triggered by chance events that informed or reminded the household of the program's existence or prompted it to seek financial help. The delay between enrolling and receiving payments varies with the quality of enrollees' dwellings, which determines whether a dwelling passes or fails its initial evaluation. Housing quality in turn is loosely related to enrollees' incomes and household characteristics.

Summary

The programmatic outcome of the participation process sketched above is most understandable with reference to a hypothetical steady state. Table 4.6 estimates the eventual distribution of eligible households in each site by program status, assuming that the population that was actually eligible during the third program year was thereafter fixed as to size and composition (though changing in membership), and that year 3 responses to program incentives (transition rates and delays) were typical of a permanent program.

Under those conditions, we would expect to find that about a third of all currently eligible households would be receiving payments; another 6 to 7 percent would be enrolled but not receiving payments, and about three-fifths would not be enrolled. The last group includes previous participants who are again eligible but have not enrolled, newly eligible households that will subsequently enroll, some who know about the program but choose not to participate, and some who will never learn about the program. This steady-state distribution is quite close to the actual distribution observed in program year 3.

DETERMINANTS OF PARTICIPATION STATUS

Table 4.5 showed "transition probabilities" for various groups of eligible households at each step along the path to receiving payments. It is clear from the table that some types of households were more likely

Table 4.6

STEADY-STATE DISTRIBUTION OF ELIGIBLE HOUSEHOLDS IN EACH SITE BY CURRENT PROGRAM STATUS

Current Program Status	Percent of All Eligible Households		
	Renter	Owner	All
Brown County			
Receiving payments	45	28	36
Enrolled but not receiving payments	10	3	6
Not enrolled	45	69	58
All eligible households	100	100	100
St. Joseph County			
Receiving payments	38	27	31
Enrolled but not receiving payments	17	3	7
Not enrolled	45	70	62
All eligible households	100	100	100
Unweighted Average			
Receiving payments	42	28	33
Enrolled but not receiving payments	14	3	6
Not enrolled	45	70	60
All eligible households	100	100	100

SOURCE: Estimated by HASE staff from household survey and HAO records. See Carter and Wendt, 1982, Sec. V, for additional details.

NOTE: The steady-state distribution assumes an eligible population of fixed size and composition (modeled on those eligible during program year 3 in each site) but changing membership; and indefinite continuation of participation responses observed for program year 3. Percentages may not add exactly to 100 because of rounding.

than others to make the transition from one step to the next. We find that four functional factors were important in determining such transition probabilities:

- Income and assets.
- The amount and expected duration of payments.
- Housing cost and condition.
- Attitudes toward government assistance.

Below, we discuss the effects of these determinants on the progress of eligible households toward recipiency; Table 4.7 summarizes the findings that are discussed in more detail in the text. Then, we show the extent to which these determinants explain the different participation rates of the various demographic groups.

Learning about the Program

At the end of the third program year, over four-fifths of the currently eligible households in each site knew about the program. Households with lower incomes, and hence larger allowance entitlements, were more likely than others to have learned about the program, as were households with greater housing expenses (see Table 4.7, first column). Presumably, these households' greater sense of need for assistance made them more alert to the HAOs' publicity. However, neither duration of eligibility, asset holdings, nor attitudes toward government assistance significantly affected the acquisition of program knowledge.

The separate effects of lower income and higher entitlement are indistinguishable in our analysis. Every dollar increase in income was accompanied by a 25-cent drop in allowance entitlement, and at each site all households of a given size faced the same payment schedule. Consequently, we cannot disentangle the separate effects of a sense of need arising from low income (relative to household size) and an inducement arising from higher allowance payments.[11]

Deciding to Enroll

For an eligible household, the decision to enroll was complex. First, the household had to believe that it might be eligible. Many

[11]Separating these two effects was one of the fundamental purposes of the Housing Allowance Demand Experiment. The interested reader should consult Kennedy and MacMillan, 1980.

households were unclear about the program's eligibility requirements (evidenced by the large number of ineligible households that applied), so it is likely that some eligibles failed to enroll because they believed they were ineligible. Second, an eligible household had to weigh its expected economic benefits from the program against the anticipated costs of participating. Here, too, imperfect knowledge of program rules and requirements must have contributed to nonparticipation; some who judged correctly that they were eligible may not have applied because they misassessed their prospective benefits or costs. Indeed, some who enrolled and thereby learned their exact entitlements terminated without ever trying to qualify for payments, apparently because they judged that the game was not worth the candle.

However, many eligible households did have general notions about both the levels of allowance payments and the HAOs' housing requirements. Consequently, a household's allowance entitlement and the quality of its dwelling should affect its probability of enrollment. Additionally, its expected duration of eligibility should figure in the household's assessment of benefits. A household's asset holdings, as distinct from current income, might well affect its sense of need for assistance.

A third element in the decision to enroll was the household's attitude toward seeking assistance from the government. Some eligible households were against government housing subsidies; although they might find reasons why this one was more acceptable, such negative predispositions should discourage enrollment.

The second column of Table 4.7 shows that households with lower incomes and larger entitlements, longer expected durations of eligibility, and fewer assets were more likely to enroll than their opposites. On the other hand, households living in better or less crowded housing were more likely to enroll than those in worse or more crowded dwellings. These results are consistent with the notion that a greater sense of need and a larger entitlement spurred enrollment, whereas expected costs of meeting the program's housing standards deterred enrollment. Finally, those who favored government housing programs were more likely to enroll than those who opposed them.

Housing Evaluation Outcomes

Among enrollees who obtained initial housing evaluations, 53 percent in Brown County and 45 percent in St. Joseph County passed and thus immediately qualified for payments.[12] The circumstances of

[12]These figures are larger than the apparently corresponding entries in Table 4.5 (48 and 39 percent for the two counties, respectively) because the base for these figures

Table 4.7

EFFECTS OF FUNCTIONAL VARIABLES ON PARTICIPATION PROBABILITIES FOR ELIGIBLE HOUSEHOLDS: SUMMARY BY PROGRAM STEP

	Direction of Change in:				
		Conditional Probability[a] of:			
Variable Affecting Outcome	Probability of Knowing about Program	Enrolling	Passing Initial Housing Evaluation	Repairing or Moving After Failure	Probability of Ever Receiving Payments
Lower income, larger entitlement	+	+	-	+	+
Longer expected eligibility	0	+	-	+	+
Fewer assets	0	+	-	-	+
Greater housing expense, better housing, less crowding[b]	+	+	(*c*)	+	+
Less aversion to assistance	0	+	(*d*)	(*d*)	+

SOURCE: Estimated by HASE staff from household survey and HAO records. See Wendt, 1982; Coleman, 1982; and Carter and Wendt, 1982, for additional details.

NOTE: Each entry shows the direction of change in the indicated probability that is associated with the variable change shown in the stub, controlling on other functional variables as well as on housing tenure and demographic characteristics. All nonzero entries in the first four columns represent findings that were statistically significant at the 95-percent confidence level or better; statistical tests were not feasible for the results shown in the last column.

[a] Probability of enrolling, given knowledge; probability of passing initial evaluation, given enrollment; and probability of either repairing or moving, given evaluation failure.

[b] Different measures of housing circumstances were used at each stage of analysis. In the knowledge model, "housing cost/income" was included as a variable, but so was allowance entitlement, so the partial coefficient should reflect only housing cost. In the enrollment model, rent per room and persons per room were included, and their coefficients had the same signs. In the response-to-failure model, estimated cost of repair and indicators for occupancy and condition failures were included.

[c] Inappropriate for probability-of-failure model.

[d] These models were estimated from HAO records that did not include attitudinal information.

those who failed are detailed in Table 4.8. Most failures were for inoperable facilities or health or safety hazards; but a fourth of initial failures in Brown County and a fifth in St. Joseph County entailed overcrowding, sometimes remediable by making existing space usable as bedrooms but often impractical to remedy except by moving.

Owners' failure rates in the two sites were nearly identical both as to frequency (52 percent) and causes of failure. Renters failed less often (45 percent) than owners in Brown County, because their dwellings were in better condition. Renters failed more often (59 percent) than owners in St. Joseph County, both because their dwellings were in worse condition and because more renters were overcrowded.

The third column of Table 4.7 shows that poorer enrollees (larger entitlements, longer expected durations of eligibility, fewer assets) were less likely than others to pass their initial housing evaluations. Consequently, poorer enrollees typically had to exert themselves more to qualify for payments; on the other hand, their larger entitlements provided a stronger incentive to meet the housing requirements.

Responding to Evaluation Failures

For enrollees in failed dwellings, the decision to stay in the program had the same determinants as the enrollment decision. The chief difference was that the benefits and costs of participation were clarified. At the enrollment interview the household learned exactly what its allowance payments would be for the next six months. After the housing evaluation the household knew just what repairs were needed to remedy the reported defects, and could even obtain estimates of repair or moving costs before deciding on its course of action.

Overall, about a fifth of those whose enrollment dwellings failed their initial evaluations dropped out of the program without qualifying for payments (Table 4.9). Those who chose not to terminate had to decide whether to repair their dwellings or move. For owners, the transaction costs of selling a home nearly always made repairing the more economical option. For renters, decisions were more complex and outcomes less certain; moving costs had to be weighed against both the difficulty of getting landlords to repair the reported defects and the alternative of paying for repairs to the landlords' property themselves. Whether landlords or tenants made repairs, rents might be raised—though landlords sometimes grant rent concessions to tenants who systematically improve their dwellings.

includes only enrollees who obtained initial housing evaluations on their enrollment dwellings. (See note 8, above, for further explanation.) Because the records of those who never arranged initial evaluations are incomplete, we did not model their decisions.

Table 4.8

FAILURE RATES FOR INITIAL AND ANNUAL HOUSING EVALUATIONS, BY SITE, TENURE, AND CAUSE OF FAILURE

Type of Evaluation and Enrollee's Tenure	Failure Rate (%) Condition Failure[a]	Occupancy Failure[b]	Any Failure[c]
Brown County			
Initial			
Renter	37	12	45
Owner	45	11	51
Total	40	12	47
Annual			
Renter	22	3	24
Owner	17	2	19
Total	20	3	23
St. Joseph County			
Initial			
Renter	52	15	59
Owner	46	8	52
Total	49	11	55
Annual			
Renter	39	5	42
Owner	24	3	28
Total	30	4	34

SOURCE: Tabulated by HASE staff from HAO records through June 1979 in Brown County and December 1978 in St. Joseph County. See Coleman, 1982, for details.

NOTE: Failure rates are based only on complete evaluation records. About 6 percent of all enrollees in Brown County and 14 percent in St. Joseph County did not complete initial evaluations, and many recipients terminated their enrollments before completing annual evaluations. Housing standards are detailed in Appendix C.

[a] Dwelling lacked essential domestic facilities in operable condition or contained health or safety hazards.

[b] Dwelling lacked enough habitable rooms for the participant's household.

[c] Condition failure, occupancy failure, or both.

Table 4.9

Responses to Failure of Initial and Annual Housing Evaluations, by Site and Tenure

Type of Evaluation and Enrollee's Tenure	Percentage Distribution of Responses			
	Repair	Move	Terminate Enrollment	Total
Brown County				
Initial				
Renter	59	21	20	100
Owner	78	3	19	100
Total	66	14	19	100
Annual				
Renter	76	17	7	100
Owner	89	3	8	100
Total	80	12	8	100
St. Joseph County				
Initial				
Renter	56	17	27	100
Owner	78	2	20	100
Total	68	9	23	100
Annual				
Renter	71	12	16	100
Owner	87	2	11	100
Total	80	7	14	100

SOURCE: Tabulated by HASE staff from HAO records through June 1979 in Brown County and December 1978 in St. Joseph County. See Coleman, 1982, for details.

NOTE: Response distributions are based on records for those who completed the indicated type of evaluation but whose dwellings failed. About 6 percent of all enrollees in Brown County and 14 percent in St. Joseph County did not complete initial evaluations, and many recipients terminated their enrollments before completing annual evaluations.

Because their options differed, renters and owners differed in their responses to initial failures. About a fifth of the renters, but few of the owners, moved; nearly three-fifths of the renters and four-fifths of the owners repaired their enrollment dwellings.

Although it was generally the cost and number of defects that influenced households' choices when their housing failed an initial inspection, two items on the housing standards checklist were, when failed, especially likely to bring about termination—the occupancy standard and the paint standard. Occupancy failures were of varying severity: Some only required improvements to make an existing room habitable, but others required adding a room because the dwelling was overcrowded. Paint failures were for loose, chipped, or peeling paint in areas young children might reach, if young children were present; that standard was designed to prevent children from eating lead-based paint.

Given an initial failure, specific failure of the occupancy standard raised the probability that an owner would terminate by over 20 percentage points. The same circumstances raised the probability that a renter would terminate by only about 12 percentage points. Few owners, but many renters who failed the occupancy standard chose to move in order to qualify for payments; we found, however, that renters who had recently moved were more inclined than long-term residents to choose this way of qualifying for payments.

Given an initial failure, specific failure of the paint standard raised the probability of termination by about 10 percentage points for all except renters in St. Joseph County. Among those renters, failing the paint standard caused terminations to increase by 24 percentage points. Curiously, St. Joseph County renters were unlikely to move in order to remedy paint failures, although they often moved to remedy occupancy failures. In Brown County, renters often moved for both reasons.

Qualifying for Payments

As Table 4.7 shows, the same functional factor (economic or attitudinal variable) may increase the probability that an eligible household will surmount one barrier to recipiency but decrease the probability that it will surmount another. Below, we discuss the net effect of each factor, as displayed in the last column of the table. Briefly, the probability that an eligible household will eventually qualify for payments is increased (holding other factors equal) by:

- Lower income and larger allowance entitlement.
- Longer expected eligibility.

- Fewer assets.
- Greater housing expenditure, better housing, and less crowding.
- Less aversion to assistance.

These outcomes are all consistent with a model of household decisions driven by expected real costs and benefits but subject to certain attitudinal constraints. Other things equal, those who expect larger benefits or benefits for a longer time are more likely than others to persist through all the steps leading to recipiency. In addition to foreseeing greater rewards from participation, these households may also feel more pinched financially, so may value a given amount of assistance more than other eligibles who are more prosperous or whose futures look brighter. Those without accumulated assets lack a cushion for emergencies; controlling on entitlement and expected duration of eligibility, they still value assistance more highly than others who expect equal benefits but who have some savings to tide them over hard times.

The several measures of housing quality used at different stages of our analysis all indicate that occupying better and therefore more expensive housing encourages participation. Eligibles whose dwellings are large enough for their families, well-equipped, and in good condition need not move or make expensive repairs in order to qualify for payments, so the cost of participating is less for them than it is for those who are overcrowded or living in dilapidated dwellings. Moreover, the preenrollment housing choices of those in better, more expensive dwellings indicates an attentiveness to housing that may legitimize participation in a "housing program" for some who would disdain other kinds of financial assistance.

Other things equal, those who generally disapprove of housing subsidies clearly are more reluctant to enroll than those who favor such programs in principle; we were unable to test whether those who enrolled despite ideological reservations were subsequently more likely to drop out, but we suspect so.

Joint Effects of Poverty and Housing Quality

The allowance program aims to help both those who because of low incomes cannot afford adequate housing, and those who despite low incomes spend heavily in order to get adequate housing. The entries in Table 4.7 show that, other things equal, larger allowance entitlements (reflecting lower incomes relative to family size) encourage participation at each step except the initial housing evaluation, where the poorer households are more likely to fail. The entries also show that, other things equal, worse housing discourages participation at every step, not just at initial evaluations.

However, the two factors produce their main effects at different steps in the participation process. Allowance entitlement strongly influences the decision to enroll but only weakly influences postenrollment decisions. Housing quality only weakly influences the decision to enroll, but powerfully influences postenrollment decisions. As a further complication, allowance entitlement and housing quality are inversely (though weakly) correlated, so that the effects are partly offsetting. Nonetheless, we conclude that the program's benefits are more efficiently targeted on poverty than on substandard housing.

The targeting on poverty is clearly shown in the figures below, estimated from household survey data for eligible households in both sites:

Estimated Monthly Entitlement ($)	Eligibles who Enroll and Qualify for Payments (%)
10-19	17.5
20-39	21.2
40-79	36.5
80-119	46.1
120 or more	44.4

The targeting on housing quality is less clear because no single measure of quality is available for all stages of the process. But Table 4.10 shows that among enrollees, the probability of qualifying for payments drops sharply as repair costs rise—even though the average allowance payment also rises.

The strong negative correlation between repair costs and participation is curious, inasmuch as these one-time outlays would soon be compensated by allowance payments. Among enrolled owners in both sites who terminated after an initial dwelling failure, we estimate that repair outlays would typically have been compensated by less than two months' allowance; for renters, the corresponding recapture times were six months in Brown County and three months in St. Joseph County (Shanley and Hotchkiss, 1980, Table 3.11). It appears that low-income households did not much value the housing improvements required by the HAOs, considering them a cost, not a benefit, of

Table 4.10

REPAIR COST, ALLOWANCE ENTITLEMENT, AND RECIPIENCY RATE FOR ENROLLED HOUSEHOLDS, BY TENURE AND SITE

Initial Repair Cost ($)	Average Monthly Allowance Entitlement ($)		Percentage Qualifying for Payments	
	Renters	Owners	Renters	Owners
Brown County				
Under $10	75	69	96	97
10-24	85	77	84	73
25-49	86	84	73	79
50-99	88	85	67	76
100 or more	91	(*a*)	80	(*a*)
St. Joseph County				
Under $10	78	55	97	98
10-24	94	61	81	89
25-49	95	66	71	84
50-99	98	71	63	78
100-249	110	73	56	64
250 or more	89	92	56	58

SOURCE: Tabulated by HASE staff from HAO records for all households that enrolled in 1977 and completed an initial housing evaluation.

NOTE: Repair costs were estimated for each evaluated dwelling using standard cost figures for each type of housing defect reported for the dwelling. Overcrowding was not considered a housing defect. Dwellings that passed initial evaluations are included in the category of repair costs under $10.

[a]Too few cases for reliable estimation.

participating. It also appears that they heavily discounted future benefits as recompense for current outlays.[13]

Joint Effects of Household Size and Housing Quality

Larger enrollee households lived in worse housing than smaller ones, so were less likely to qualify for payments. For example, when all factors in Table 4.7 except housing quality are held constant, five-person eligible households were about 13 percentage points less likely to receive payments than two-person households. No other demographic groups were differentially disadvantaged by the housing standards. However, it should be noted that only about 16 percent of all eligible households and 12 percent of all households that ever enrolled had five or more members.

Large households faced two difficulties in qualifying for payments. Their enrollment dwellings were more likely to fail the occupancy standard, usually remediable only if they moved to larger dwellings. Second, large dwellings in our sites were more likely than small ones to be substandard as to facilities or condition. With more rooms, there is more chance for random defects; and with more occupants (especially more children), more wear and tear is expectable.

Residual Effects of Tenure, Household Composition, and Race

The economic and attitudinal variables listed in Table 4.7 explain much of the variation in participation rates by tenure, household composition, and race that was reported in Table 4.4. As between renters and owners, old and young, blacks and whites, there are differences in average income and household size (thus, in allowance entitlement), expected duration of eligibility, assets, housing quality, and attitudes toward government assistance. When these variables are controlled by regression analysis, the residual participation effects of tenure, household composition, and race change dramatically.

Table 4.11 shows in its first column the observed variation in recipiency rates for households eligible in year 3; the variations are

[13]Over three-fourths of the enrolled owners who terminated rather than repair or move said they could not pay repair costs that averaged about $125, including unpaid labor valued at the minimum wage. Only about 15 percent of these terminees actively sought credit. Among renter terminees, facing average repair costs of $350, most blamed their landlords for not repairing. See Shanley and Hotchkiss, 1980, pp. 29-42, for a full discussion of these issues.

Table 4.11

RESIDUAL VARIATION OF PARTICIPATION WITH TENURE AND SELECTED HOUSEHOLD CHARACTERISTICS

Characteristic	Deviation from Mean Recipiency Rate (%)	
	Observed	Controlled
Housing Tenure		
Renter	+ 8	(*a*)
Owner	- 6	(*a*)
Household Composition		
Single parent	+ 9	+ 8
Couple with children[b]	-17	+18
Other nonelderly couple[b]	-10	-12
Elderly single person	+13	-10
Elderly couple	-10	-14
Race of Head		
White non-Latin	- 1	(*a*)
Other	+ 5	(*a*)

SOURCE: Estimated by HASE staff from household survey and HAO records. For additional detail, see Carter and Wendt, 1982, Sec. VI.

NOTE: Observed deviations are cross-site averages for program year 3. Controlled deviations indicate the (partial) effect on the recipiency rate of each characteristic shown in the stub, setting other characteristics and the functional variables discussed earlier equal to their mean values for the entire population of eligibles. The control variables are fully specified in Carter and Wendt, Table 5.4. Deviations are measured in percentage points from the overall mean recipiency rate, 33 percent.

[a]Not significantly different from zero. The estimation model also established that there were no significant interactions between tenure, household composition, and race.

[b]Note difference from earlier tables. Here, *all* couples with children are grouped, whereas earlier tables grouped all *young* couples with *young* children.

expressed as deviations from the overall mean recipiency rate (33 percent). As we saw earlier, participation was more likely for renters than owners, for single persons than couples, and for racial minorities than whites.

The second column of the table shows our estimates of the partial participation effects of each characteristic, controlling on other characteristics (e.g., for renters, controlling on household composition and race) and also on the economic and attitudinal variables mentioned above. We find that neither tenure nor race *in themselves* affect the probability of becoming an allowance recipient; the apparent effects were all due to other variables correlated with tenure and race. In fact, the only household characteristic that affects participation strongly is the presence of children in the household: Parents, whether single or couples, are much more likely to participate than nonparents. (The stub of the table has been reorganized from that of earlier tables to highlight this finding.)

The presence of children in a household affected outcomes at each step in the participation process, but the direction of influence varied. Parents were much more likely than others to know of the program and to enroll given knowledge, but they were also more likely to fail initial inspections and to terminate after failing.

We suspect that children drew their parents into contact with public institutions that disseminated program information, and that parents were more willing to accept government aid for the sake of their children than they would have been for themselves. Probably, children also contributed disproportionately to dwelling deterioration, accounting for the above-average failure rates of households with children.

Summary

Within the eligible population, participation rates differed substantially for renters and owners, for whites and nonwhites; and for households headed by couples and single persons, by old and young persons, and by parents and childless persons. However, we find that most of these differences are explained by underlying differences between the groups either as to benefits and costs of participation or attitudes toward assistance. The principal functional determinants of participation turn out to be the amount and expected duration of allowance payments, asset holdings that provide an economic cushion, the cost of meeting the program's housing standards, and general attitudes toward government assistance. Once these variables are controlled, the only statistically significant status difference is between households with and without children: The former are more likely to participate than the latter.

The functional determinants suggest a model of generally rational choice in which housing improvements are not much valued. Eligibles and enrollees seem to balance the expected stream of cash payments against the expected trouble and out-of-pocket costs of meeting housing standards. Their decisions may also be influenced by perceptions of need that covary with expected benefits and are clearly affected by predispositions concerning the proper role of government.

SITE DIFFERENCES

At the end of program year 3, 36 percent of the eligible households in Brown County and 31 percent in St. Joseph County were receiving payments. Given the many differences in population characteristics between the sites, some difference in overall recipiency rates is expectable. However, as shown earlier (Table 4.4), recipiency rates for comparable demographic subgroups differed more between counties than did the overall rate. For example, the recipiency rate for eligible elderly single persons was 56 percent in Brown County but only 37 percent in St. Joseph County.

Much of the intercounty difference in participation by comparable demographic subgroups is accounted for by different values for the functional determinants of participation (allowance entitlements, expected durations of eligibility, expected cost of repairs, and so on) that reflect household circumstances and predispositions. Controlling on tenure and demographic status, as well as on functional factors, we estimate that truly comparable populations would have about the same recipiency rate in the two sites. With one minor exception, our data do not indicate any substantial intersite difference in the behavior of comparable and comparably situated eligible households.[14]

However, one difference in household circumstances is worth highlighting because of its implications for a national program: We find both direct and indirect evidence that recipiency rates in the two counties were substantially affected by differences in housing quality. Controlling on tenure, demographic characteristics and all functional determinants of participation *except* housing quality, we estimate that comparable eligible households were on the average 8 percentage points more likely to qualify for payments in Brown than in St. Joseph County.

---

[14]The exception is renter enrollees' responses to failing the paint standard; see above, "Responding to Evaluation Failures."

Because the HAOs did not evaluate the dwellings of unenrolled eligibles, our evidence on the enrollment effects of housing quality is weak, depending as it does on indirect measures of housing quality. However, among eligible nonapplicants who knew about the program, 6 percent in Brown County and 13 percent in St. Joseph County told interviewers that the housing standards were obstacles to their enrollment.[15] After enrollment, the site differences focus on renters. In both sites, about 52 percent of the owner enrollees whose dwellings were evaluated failed those evaluations; but among renter enrollees, the corresponding failure rates were 45 percent in Brown County and 59 percent in St. Joseph County.

Comparable households in the two sites responded similarly to failure; whether they repaired, moved, or terminated depended on the type of defect and estimated cost of repair and the inducement provided by their allowance entitlements. The single exception was the anomalous response of St. Joseph County's renters to paint failures, discussed earlier.

COULD PARTICIPATION BE INCREASED?

Eligible households failed to participate in the program because they did not know about it, because of reluctance to accept government aid, because the housing standards were too much of a burden, or because their allowance entitlements were too small. Moreover, households that did eventually participate did not usually enroll and qualify for payments as soon as they became eligible. Below, we examine how much each of these factors contributed to nonparticipation, and what might be done to alleviate their effects.

Improving Outreach

At the time of the wave 4 survey of households, 81 percent of all eligible households in Brown County and 85 percent in St. Joseph County knew about the program. If all eligibles had known, more would have enrolled and qualified for payments. From the characteristics of the uninformed, we estimate that universal knowledge would

---

[15]Eligibles' attitudes toward housing standards are tabulated from the wave 4 survey of households in each site. The figures cited include those who mentioned housing standards as a cause of nonenrollment, as a program feature that should be changed, or as a reason for objecting to the program.

have increased the recipiency rate by 8 percentage points in Brown County and 5 percentage points in St. Joseph County (Table 4.12).

Although these are substantial increases, they could not easily be achieved. The HAOs conducted energetic and imaginative outreach campaigns to inform the public about the program, distributing posters and brochures, talking to civic and fraternal groups, advertising in newspapers and on radio and television broadcasts, and mailing program information directly to populations thought to include many eligibles. Because the St. Joseph County HAO used television advertising and direct mailings much more than did the Brown County HAO, it spent nine times as much on outreach per new recipient ($46 vs. $5; see Ch. VIII for details). Yet, by survey wave 4 only 4 percent more eligible households knew about the program in St. Joseph County than in Brown County.

Modifying Attitudes toward Assistance

Many people dislike the idea of accepting any kind of charity and others specifically object to tax-funded charity. In our study, we did not explore the roots of such predispositions, but we did find that, other circumstances equal, eligibles who said they disapproved of government housing assistance were less likely than others to participate.

Such attitudes are certainly modifiable in specific cases. Even those who disapprove of government assistance programs distinguish some as more worthwhile or legitimate than others: Many more people approve of Medicare than of AFDC. So public perceptions of the purposes and integrity of a housing allowance program would certainly affect the willingness of eligibles to participate. Generally, the allowance program had an exceptionally favorable image among both recipients and the general public. Substantial majorities approved its purposes and those who had some experience with the program approved its management (see Ch. VII).

Although we think it would be easy for a national program to lose the favorable image of the experimental one, improving on that image would be difficult. In any event, further improvements would not much affect participation. If all eligibles who expressed opposition to government assistance programs had changed their views, we estimate that participation would have increased by about 2 percentage points in Brown County and 1 percentage point in St. Joseph County (Table 4.12).

Table 4.12

ESTIMATED EFFECT OF SELECTED PROGRAM CHANGES ON PARTICIPATION BY ELIGIBLE RENTERS AND OWNERS, BY SITE

Assumption	Percent of Eligibles Receiving Payments		
	Renters	Owners	All Eligibles
Brown County			
Observed outcome	45	28	36
Estimated outcome:			
With universal knowledge[a]	52	36	44
Absent negative attitudes[b]	46	30	38
Absent enrollment delays[c]	53	38	44
Absent housing standards[d]	59	41	50
Combined effect[e]	81	63	71
St. Joseph County			
Observed outcome	38	27	31
Estimated outcome:			
With universal knowledge[a]	44	31	36
Absent negative attitudes[b]	39	28	32
Absent enrollment delays[c]	35	37	39
Absent housing standards[d]	65	52	56
Combined effect[e]	88	70	75

SOURCE: Estimated by HASE staff from HAO records for program year 3 in each site and from records of the survey of households, wave 4, in each site. See Carter and Wendt, 1982, Sec. V, for details of the underlying models of household decisions.

[a]Assumes that households learn about the program as soon as they become eligible.

[b]Assumes that all eligible households think that the government should provide housing assistance to those with low or moderate incomes.

[c]Assumes that all households that would eventually apply do so as soon as they become eligible, and are immediately enrolled.

[d]Assumes that enrollment is not deterred by poor housing quality and that all enrollees immediately qualify for payments.

[e]Does not include effect of negative attitudes.

Expediting Enrollment

Few households apply for enrollment immediately upon becoming eligible, and enrollment procedures (screening applications and scheduling and conducting enrollment interviews) were designed to occupy about six weeks on average. When application backlogs developed, as they did during the first months after the program began, more time might elapse between application and formal enrollment. However, among eligibles who applied during program year 3, two-thirds in Brown County and three-fourths in St. Joseph County signed participation agreements within 30 days after they applied.[16]

If households had applied immediately after they become eligible and had been enrolled immediately after applying, a larger proportion of those currently eligible would have been enrolled at any given time, and some who became ineligible before enrolling would have been in the program at least briefly. We estimate that instantaneous application and enrollment would have increased the average recipiency rate by 8 percentage points in each county.

These prospective gains are optimistic. Although enrollment processing could have been expedited, most of the elapsed time between becoming eligible and enrolling was because of delayed application, a responsibility of the prospective applicant, not the HAO. The data do not suggest easy ways to expedite the transition from eligibility to enrollment except eliminating the means test, which would clearly be inconsistent with program purposes.

Relaxing Housing Standards

By far, the most important factor in the low participation rate was the housing standards. Table 4.12 presents estimates of participation in the absence of housing standards. The estimated participation rate would have risen to 50 percent in Brown County and 56 percent in St. Joseph County.

[16]Applicants were interviewed by appointment, and most of the delay was in scheduling appointments, including rescheduling for those who failed to appear at the appointed time. At the end of the enrollment interview, an applicant was either told he was ineligible or else invited to sign a participation agreement. The interview record and entitlement computations were subsequently reviewed for errors and the applicant's undocumented income estimates were verified for a sample of cases. If problems arose, an enrollee would be later informed that he was not eligible after all; or that his allowance entitlement had been changed. Only if the interviewer was uncertain about eligibility or entitlement, or if the applicant wanted time to reflect on the participation agreement was enrollment delayed beyond the interview date.

Those increases would arise mainly from the fact that without housing standards no enrollees would terminate because of housing evaluation failures. The rest of the increases would stem from the elimination of delays between enrollment and receiving payments, and from slightly higher enrollment rates among households in low-quality housing. The estimated increase in St. Joseph County (25 percentage points) is much larger than that in Brown County (14 percentage points) because many more eligible households in St. Joseph County lived in substandard housing. Without housing standards, renters in both sites would still participate more than owners; the difference is largely because owners had lower allowance entitlements and more of them had very short expected durations of eligibility.

Although participation could be substantially increased by eliminating housing standards, doing so would also reduce the program's effectiveness as a means of improving housing conditions; as shown in Ch. V, unrestricted cash transfers would induce only half the increase in housing consumption that was achieved by conditional transfers, and voluntary consumption increases would rarely include remedies for the health and safety hazards that were found in so many enrollees' dwellings. However, it is worth asking whether *specific* housing standards could have been modified to yield higher participation rates without prejudice to the program's housing improvement goals.

The most likely candidates for change are the occupancy and paint standards. The latter, especially, induced terminations that did not seem to us justified by either the degree of hazard or the cost of repair.[17] However, dropping either standard would not have increased participation by more than 2 percent overall. Dropping any one of the other 36 standards in the HAOs' housing code would have similarly small effects on participation. Some specific changes in housing standards may be desirable on other grounds, but more than piecemeal concessions would be needed to substantially increase program participation.

Increasing Allowance Entitlements

During program year 3, the average monthly allowance payment was about \$86 for renters and \$66 for homeowners. For eligibles not receiving payments, we estimate that the corresponding averages

---

[17]The present paint standard was not initially part of the HAOs' housing code. It was added in 1977 pursuant to federal legislation that imposed on HUD the specific obligation to remedy lead-based paint hazards in all assisted housing. There is considerable evidence that lead-based paint has been erroneously blamed for lead actually ingested from quite different sources. See McDowell, 1980, for details.

were $71 and $62. Would larger entitlements have increased participation substantially?

Our data show a strong correlation between participation and allowance entitlement, but its interpretation is confounded by the fact that entitlements decrease as income rises. The low participation rate (17.5 percent) for eligibles with monthly entitlements under $20 undoubtedly reflects their disdain of such small sums, but surely also reflects less urgent need for any benefits at all. Increasing the allowance entitlement at every level of income would affect the perceived benefits of participating but not the felt need for assistance.

There is also a link between allowance entitlement and duration of eligibility. Whether entitlements were increased by arbitrarily raising the standard cost of adequate housing R^*, or by lowering the implicit household contribution rate (say, from 25 to 20 percent of adjusted gross income), the effect would be not only to increase entitlements but to raise the income limit for eligibility. With higher income limits, eligible households could reasonably expect to stay eligible longer, and longer expected durations of eligibility also are correlated with higher participation rates.

Because of these complications, we do not think that data from the Supply Experiment are well suited to quantifying the effect of larger entitlements on participation. The Housing Allowance Demand Experiment was designed explicitly to test the effects of alternative benefit levels, and we must defer to their findings that a $50 increase in all monthly entitlements would have raised the participation rate from 37 to 51 percent.[18]

However, it is worth noting that increasing participation by raising allowance entitlements would be (a) quite expensive per added participant, and (b) might not raise the participation *rate* by much despite increasing the number of participants.

The expense arises from the fact that entitlements would have to be increased for the third of all eligibles who already participate as well as for the target group, nonparticipating eligibles. Thus, if (as the Demand Experiment's findings suggest) a $10 increase in monthly benefits were needed to increase the recipiency rate by 3 percentage points, the marginal cost per new recipient would be nearly $200 per month, based on the Supply Experiment's year 3 experience.[19]

---

[18]Kennedy and MacMillan, 1980, p. 132. The estimate refers to the Demand Experiment's program (Housing Gap with Minimum Standards) that was similar to the Supply Experiment's program, but which entailed a 63-percent failure rate on initial housing evaluations. The average entitlement among the renters to whom enrollment was offered was $56 in Pittsburgh and $73 in Phoenix.

[19]Assuming an average monthly entitlement of $75, raising benefits by $10 would entail paying 3 new recipients $85 and 33 prior recipients an extra $10 each.

Even though the number of participants increased, the participation rate might not, because higher income limits would extend eligibility into more densely populated regions of the income distribution. At the margin, there would always be eligible households whose entitlements were too small to induce participation. In the Supply Experiment about 10 percent of all eligibles were entitled to less than $20 and 30 percent were entitled to less than $40 monthly. Moreover, 15 percent of the eligible households in Brown County and 28 percent in St. Joseph County could expect their eligibility to last for less than a year—and these were the very households whose entitlements were smallest.

Summary

To summarize, the housing standards were the greatest impediment to participation in the housing allowance program; but program benefits, duration of eligibility, lack of program knowledge, and personal attitudes also influenced households in their decisions. Further, delays in enrolling and receiving payments also reduced the number of households receiving allowance payments at any given moment during the program. Table 4.13 incorporates these insights into the description of the steady-state distribution of eligible households given earlier in Table 4.6. Averaging across sites, we find that 33 percent of eligible households would be currently receiving payments; 6 percent more would subsequently receive payments; 20 percent would never participate because of the housing standards; 24 percent would never participate because of low benefits, short duration of eligibility, or reluctance to accept aid; and 17 percent would never learn about the program. The table also shows what would have happened to the unaware households had they known of the program.

COMPARISON WITH THE DEMAND EXPERIMENT

The Housing Allowance Demand Experiment conducted by Abt Associates also analyzed participation in housing allowance programs (Kennedy and MacMillan, 1980). In that experiment, samples of eligible renter households in Pittsburgh, Pennsylvania, and Phoenix, Arizona, were invited to enroll in one of several allowance programs that differed as to benefit standards and housing requirements. One program closely resembled that used in the Supply Experiment both as to benefit levels and housing requirements; another was similar as to benefits but had no housing requirements. Still others offered

Table 4.13

Steady-State Distribution of Eligible Households in Each Site by Current and Prospective Program Status

Current and Prospective Program Status	Percent of All Eligible Households		
	Renter	Owner	All
Brown County			
Receiving payments	45	28	36
Will eventually receive payments[a]	9	6	8
Informed, but will never receive payments:[b]			
Because of housing standards	14	13	14
For other reasons[c]	17	31	23
Not informed, but if informed:			
Would eventually receive payments	10	10	10
Would never receive payments:			
Because of housing standards	2	4	3
For other reasons[c]	3	8	6
All eligible households	100	100	100
St. Joseph County			
Receiving payments	38	27	31
Will eventually receive payments[a]	8	4	5
Informed, but will never receive payments:[b]			
Because of housing standards	27	24	25
For other reasons[c]	12	30	24
Not informed, but if informed:			
Would eventually receive payments	8	6	6
Would never receive payments:			
Because of housing standards	4	4	4
For other reasons[c]	3	5	5
All eligible households	100	100	100

Table 4.13—continued

Current and Prospective Program Status	Percent of All Eligible Households		
	Renter	Owner	All
Unweighted Average			
Receiving payments	42	28	33
Will eventually receive payments[a]	8	5	6
Informed, but will never receive payments:[b]			
Because of housing standards	20	18	20
For other reasons[c]	14	30	24
Not informed, but if informed:			
Would eventually receive payments	9	8	8
Would never receive payments:			
Because of housing standards	3	4	4
For other reasons[c]	3	6	5
All eligible households	100	100	100

SOURCE: Estimated by HASE staff from household survey and HAO records. See Carter and Wendt, 1982, Sec. V, for additional detail.

NOTE: The steady-state distribution assumes an eligible population of fixed size and composition (modeled on those eligible during program year 3 in each site) but changing membership. Prospective responses of uninformed households assumes no correlation between lack of information and willingness to participate if informed. Percentages may not add exactly to 100 because of rounding.

[a]Households that are enrolled but have not yet qualified for payments and informed households that will subsequently enroll and qualify.

[b]Includes some former enrollees who are again eligible, but will not reenroll.

[c]Primarily small entitlement, short expected duration of eligibility or aversion to government programs.

higher or lower benefits. Homeowners were excluded from all programs, and participation was limited to three years.

Program variation in the Demand Experiment allowed the use of analytical methods not available to the Supply Experiment, whereas the Supply Experiment's household surveys, open enrollment policy, and longer duration provided better evidence of participatory behavior in an operational program as distinguished from an experiment. The findings of the two experiments agree on several important points; and apparent disagreements are usually traceable to differences in program design.

Analysts of both experiments agree that larger expected benefits and longer expected durations of eligibility encourage participation, whereas failing or expecting to fail an initial housing evaluation discourages participation. They also agree that housing quality (thus likelihood of passing an initial evaluation) was lower for those with larger allowance entitlements (thus smaller incomes).

However, for the most nearly comparable allowance programs, the Demand Experiment indicates that with respect to participation decisions, poor housing quality outweighed larger entitlements; whereas the Supply Experiment indicates the reverse. Thus, in the Demand Experiment, the recipiency rate rose with income, but in the Supply Experiment the rate fell as income rose. Moreover, the overall recipiency rate was much lower in the Demand Experiment (38 percent of those invited to enroll) than in the Supply Experiment (50 percent of renters eligible to enroll).

Differences in outreach and housing standards clearly account for much of the difference in experimental outcomes, although differences in the populations and housing stocks of the experimental sites were also important. Table 4.14 compares outcomes in the four sites of the two experiments, showing the attrition of eligibles in each site at each major step in the participation process.

In the Demand Experiment, enrollers visited eligible renters in their homes, explained the program, and provided each household with an estimate of its allowance entitlement. Thus, all those "eligible" (invited) to enroll were well informed about the program. In the Supply Experiment, about 15 percent of all eligible renters never learned about the program. Enrollment rates for *informed* eligibles in the two experiments are quite similar. In both experiments, those who failed to enroll were predominantly households whose entitlements were small or who were reluctant to accept aid from a government program. In neither experiment did housing characteristics much affect enrollment decisions.

Among those whose enrollment dwellings were evaluated, initial evaluation failures were much higher in the Demand Experiment.[20] This outcome was partly because of differences in housing stocks and partly because of differences in housing standards. According to a field study conducted by The Urban Institute (Valenza, 1977, Table 4), about a third of the average difference in failure rates between experiments is due to the lower quality of the dwellings occupied by enrollees in the Demand Experiment, and two-thirds to differences in the standards by which dwellings were evaluated in the two experiments.

Although the designers of the two experiments did not intend to apply radically different standards, they did choose somewhat different operational tests for decent, safe, and sanitary housing. For example, the Demand Experiment's standards required a minimum ratio of window area to room size, whereas the Supply Experiment required enough natural light to permit "normal domestic activities" during daylight hours. The Supply Experiment required handrails on stairways of six or more steps, whereas the Demand Experiment did not. Thus, some dwellings that passed one set of standards would fail the other, and the reverse. Below, we estimate the net effects of applying each experiment's housing standards to each site's initial enrollment dwellings:[21]

Source of Housing Standard	Failure Rate (%) Brown County	St. Joseph County	Pittsburgh	Phoenix
Supply Experiment	45	59	61	65
Demand Experiment	68	88	67	71

Finally, among renters who failed initial evaluations, those in the Supply Experiment were much more likely to repair and somewhat more likely to move than those in the Demand Experiment. This outcome may partly reflect differences in average entitlement or ex-

[20]Among renters in the Supply Experiment whose enrollment dwellings were evaluated, failure rates were 45 percent in Brown County and 59 percent in St. Joseph County. For purposes of the discussion immediately following, these figures are more pertinent than the entries in Table 4.14 (54 and 72 percent), which include enrollees whose enrollment dwellings were not evaluated (see note 8, above). However, in a broader context, the entries in Table 4.14 are more pertinent; they distinguish enrollees who had to move or repair in order to qualify for payments from those who qualified without further effort.

[21]The estimates were derived by applying ratios from Valenza, 1977, Table 3, to the failure rates reported for renter enrollees in each experiment.

Table 4.14

Comparison of Participation Rates in the Supply and Demand Experiments: Renter Households Offered "Housing-Gap," Minimum Housing Standards Program, by Site

Eligibility Status and Outcome	Percent of Indicated Total			
	Supply Experiment		Demand Experiment	
	Brown County	St. Joseph County	Pittsburgh	Phoenix
Summary				
Eligible to enroll	100	100	100	100
Ever enrolled	65	64	75	84
Ever qualified for payments	55	46	30	45
Detail				
Eligible to enroll	100	100	100	100
Informed about program	85	85	100	100
Not informed	15	15	--	--
Informed eligible	100	100	100	100
Ever enrolled	77	75	75	84
Never enrolled	23	25	25	16

Enrollee	100	100	100	100
Qualified for payments[a]	46	28	33	29
Had to repair or move[b]	54	72	67	71
Had to repair or move[b]	100	100	100	100
Ever qualified for payments	71	61	34	42
Never qualified for payments	29	39	66	58

SOURCES: For Supply Experiment, Table 4.5, above, and additional detail from HAO records; for Demand Experiment, Kennedy and MacMillan, 1980, Tables 2-4 and 2-9.

NOTE: Differences between experiments in program design and record systems qualify the parallelism of entries. Difference in outcomes reflects both differences in program design and differences in the eligible populations. See text for discussion.

[a] Qualified immediately after enrolling and completing an initial housing evaluation.

[b] For the Supply Experiment, this group includes enrollees who did not complete an initial evaluation on the enrollment dwelling, failed such an evaluation, or passed the evaluation but did not submit a lease agreement. In the Demand Experiment, all were evaluation failures.

pected duration of recipiency, but appears mostly attributable to the kinds of repairs that were required to meet standards in each experiment. In particular, a large fraction of failed dwellings in the Demand Experiment could have been made acceptable only by increasing the window areas of one or more rooms—an expensive undertaking requiring professional skills.

Program differences aside, Table 4.14 reminds us of site variability: The outcome differences between sites in each experiment are often greater than the average difference between experiments. In the Supply Experiment, regression analysis has traced nearly all intersite differences essentially to variations in income and housing quality rather than demographic characteristics. The Demand Experiment found that demographic variables contributed little to the explanation of response patterns within each site once income, housing quality, and prior mobility were taken into account, but the effects of the latter group of variables differed across sites.[22]

We conclude that both experiments observed the same underlying response to the incentives offered by an allowance program; the different outcomes in the four sites reflect not only the differences in program design that distinguish the experiments, but differences in each site's eligible population and their housing.

CONCLUSIONS

In a national housing allowance program, we would expect to find substantial local variation in population characteristics that bear on eligibility, and in housing characteristics that bear on participation. But the similarity of outcomes in our two very different experimental sites, and the similarity of behavioral responses in the Demand and Supply Experiments support some general conclusions about the national outcome of a permanent, full-scale program that followed the design of the Supply Experiment.[23]

---

[22]The Demand Experiment's analysis of the determinants of participation status is detailed in Kennedy and MacMillan, 1980, Chs. 3 and 4. There were some demographic differences (controlling on other variables) in enrollment rates but none in responses to dwelling failure. The site differences show up mostly in the response to dwelling failure, as an unexplained intercept shift rather than as a different marginal response to the amount of the allowance or the cost of repairs.

[23]The generalizations below apply to households not currently served by other low-income housing assistance programs; and they assume that the program growth after year 5 (that we have noted but not analyzed) was due to an increase in the number of eligible households rather than to a change in household responses to program incentives.

- About a fifth of all households would be eligible for assistance. The membership of this group would change rapidly, but its aggregate size would not.
- About two-fifths of those who were ever eligible would ever qualify for payments, and about a third would be receiving payments at any given time.
- The program would target assistance more efficiently on lower-income eligibles than on eligibles in the worst housing. The latter tend to drop out even though their expected cash benefits exceed the direct costs of meeting housing requirements.

We see no way of substantially increasing the participation rate among eligibles without undermining program purposes. The elimination of housing requirements would increase participation substantially, but would not yield much housing improvement. Arbitrarily raising benefits beyond what is implied by the "housing gap" principle would increase the number of participants but also the number of eligibles; it would diminish the efficiency of program dollars relative to other means of securing improved housing for low-income families (see Ch. V).

However, we do think that housing standards for a national program should be specified with great care. We find that minor differences in specification can greatly affect participation. Participants in the program did not seem to value the health and safety features that accounted for so many evaluation failures; rather they seemed to view these requirements merely as obstacles to the receipt of cash transfers. There has been little scientific effort to determine whether the health and safety requirements adapted for the Supply Experiment from national model housing codes are genuinely important either for the welfare of a dwelling's occupants or that of their neighbors. Thus, a key program element is based on a professional consensus whose premises are largely unexamined.

REFERENCES

Carter, Grace M., and Steven L. Balch, *Measuring Eligibility and Participation in the Housing Assistance Supply Experiment,* The Rand Corporation, R-2780-HUD, September 1981.

Carter, Grace M., and James C. Wendt, *Participation in an Open Enrollment Housing Allowance Program: Evidence from the Housing Assistance Supply Experiment,* The Rand Corporation, R-2783-HUD, June 1982.

Coleman, Sinclair B., *How Housing Evaluations Affect Participation in a Housing Allowance Program,* The Rand Corporation, R-2781-HUD, April 1982.

Ellickson, Phyllis L., *Who Applies for Housing Allowances? Early Lessons from the Housing Assistance Supply Experiment,* The Rand Corporation, R-2632-HUD, August 1981.

Helbers, Lawrence, *Measuring Homeowner Needs for Housing Assistance,* The Rand Corporation, N-1094-HUD, October 1980.

Kennedy, Stephen D., and Jean MacMillan, *Participation under Alternative Housing Allowance Programs: Evidence from the Housing Allowance Demand Experiment,* Abt Associates, Inc., Cambridge, Mass., June 1980.

Kozimor, Lawrence W., *Eligibility and Enrollment in the Housing Allowance Program: Brown and St. Joseph Counties through Year 2,* The Rand Corporation, N-1125-HUD, January 1981.

Lamar, Bruce W., and Ira S. Lowry, *Client Responses to Housing Requirements: The First Two Years,* The Rand Corporation, N-1124-HUD, May 1981.

Lowry, Ira S., ed., *The Design of the Housing Assistance Supply Experiment,* The Rand Corporation, R-2630-HUD, June 1980.

McDowell, James L., *Effects of the HAO Lead-Based Paint Hazard Standard,* The Rand Corporation, N-1306-1-HUD, June 1980.

Rydell, C. Peter, John E. Mulford, and Lawrence Kozimor, *Dynamics of Participation in a Housing Allowance Program,* The Rand Corporation, N-1137-HUD, February 1981.

Shanley, Michael G., and Charles M. Hotchkiss, *The Role of Market Intermediaries in a Housing Allowance Program,* The Rand Corporation, R-2659-HUD, December 1980.

U.S. Bureau of the Census, *Statistical Abstract of the United States: 1979,* U.S. Government Printing Office, Washington, D.C., 1979.

Valenza, Joseph J., *Program Standards in the Experimental Housing Allowance Program: Analyzing Differences in the Demand and Supply Experiments,* UI-19300, The Urban Institute, Washington, D.C., July 1977.

Wendt, James C., *Why Households Apply for Housing Allowances,* The Rand Corporation, R-2782-HUD, forthcoming, 1982.

Yildiz, Orhan, and John E. Mulford, *Measuring Housing Quality: Evidence from St. Joseph County,* The Rand Corporation, N-1774-HUD, forthcoming, 1982.

V. EFFECTS ON PARTICIPANTS

Those who enrolled in the experimental allowance program were offered monthly cash payments that began as soon as their eligibility was certified and their dwellings met the HAOs' housing standards; those payments continued as long as enrollees passed regular eligibility and housing recertifications. As explained in Ch. IV, about 80 percent of all enrollees eventually qualified for payments. In the two sites combined, more than 20,000 households became allowance recipients during the first five program years. Drawing on their participation records and on our countywide surveys of households, this chapter estimates how the program affected those who were recipients at the end of the third program year, a group that we think fairly represents the characteristic mix of participants in a mature, permanent program.

Our assessment of program effects focuses on changes in housing consumption and changes in household budgets. That focus reflects the program's dual purposes: (a) to improve the housing of low-income households and (b) to ease their housing expense burdens (or equivalently, increase their nonhousing consumption). The HAOs' housing standards and recipients' housing preferences together determine the balance that was achieved between the two functions.

Briefly, we found that the housing allowance program affected recipients' consumption and budgets in the following ways:

- As measured by expenditures, both renters and owners increased their housing consumption by about 8 percent. Nearly a third of each group who would otherwise have occupied substandard housing instead occupied dwellings that met generally accepted standards for space and privacy, domestic equipment, and safety and sanitation.
- Renters increased their housing consumption mainly by moving to better dwellings or not moving to worse ones; homeowners increased their housing consumption mainly by repairing and improving their homes.
- Renter recipients spent about a sixth, and owner recipients a fifth of their allowances to increase their housing consumption; the remainder went to increase their consumption of other goods and services.

- Allowance payments caused about half of the increased housing consumption by renters and an eighth of the increase by homeowners; housing standards and other program features caused the remainder.

The implications of these findings for federal housing policy are illuminated by comparing the consumption and housing-quality effects of housing allowances with the corresponding effects of public housing and of unrestricted cash grants to low-income families:

- Although housing allowances cause only modest increases in recipients' housing consumption, the increase per program dollar is twice that caused by either public housing or unrestricted cash grants.
- Both public housing and housing allowances dramatically upgrade recipients' housing when quality is measured by housing-code standards. Unrestricted grants have virtually no effect on that measure of quality because they are not contingent on the recipient's compliance with such standards.
- Per program dollar, recipients of housing allowances get twice the benefit (increased total consumption) that accrues to occupants of public housing, but slightly less than accrues to recipients of unrestricted grants. The relative inefficiency of public housing results mainly from its above-market development costs; the relative efficiency of unrestricted grants results mainly from their administrative simplicity.

In short, housing allowances are much more efficient than public housing in using public funds to benefit low-income families and, specifically, improve their housing circumstances. Unrestricted grants are even more efficient as income transfers, but are less efficient at increasing housing consumption and only negligibly affect housing quality.

Below, we briefly explain how we estimated program effects; then we report how participation in the program affected housing consumption and budget allocation; finally, we compare the effects of the housing allowance program with the effects of alternative programs of public housing and unrestricted cash grants.[1]

---

[1]For a full account of the analytical methods and results summarized in this section, see Mulford et al., 1982.

ESTIMATING PROGRAM EFFECTS WITHOUT A FORMAL CONTROL GROUP

The program's effect on recipients' housing consumption equals their consumption while in the program[2] minus what their consumption would have been without the program. We can observe recipients' consumption while they are in the program; we must estimate what it would have been without the program.

Typically, one estimates without-program behavior by observing a control group: subjects who receive no experimental treatment, but whose characteristics are identical to those of the treated subjects. Because open enrollment was important to other HASE research objectives, the experimental design did not designate a group of eligible households to serve as a formal control group. However, by using household survey data that span the period from before the program began through program year 3 (see Fig. 5.1), we constructed a control model for recipients.

Control households must behave the same as recipient households (or display measurable differences that can be corrected for); and they must be observed while the program is operating, yet not be affected by it. From baseline survey data, which predates the allowance program, we learned that households that never enrolled in the allowance program during the five years we monitored it—including both ineligibles and eligibles who chose not to enroll—responded to the determinants of housing consumption in nearly the same way as did future allowance recipients. Speaking technically, the two groups had statistically indistinguishable coefficients (except for an intercept shift) in a log-linear regression of housing expenditures on income and demographic characteristics. Given identical incomes and demographic characteristics, we estimate that future recipients would have spent 1 to 3 percent (depending on site) more for housing than the never-enrolled.

We did not use the baseline housing consumption of future recipients as an estimate of recipients' without-program consumption, because it was not contemporaneous with observed program behavior and could therefore be in error by the amount of any general trend in housing consumption between baseline and program year 3, the year in which we measured recipients' consumption. Instead, we used contemporaneous wave 4 survey data for households that never enrolled in the program as a benchmark for recipients' without-program hous-

[2]The program may also affect housing consumption for those who expect to become recipients or who formerly were recipients. Effects on these nonrecipients are included in our comparison of alternative assistance programs.

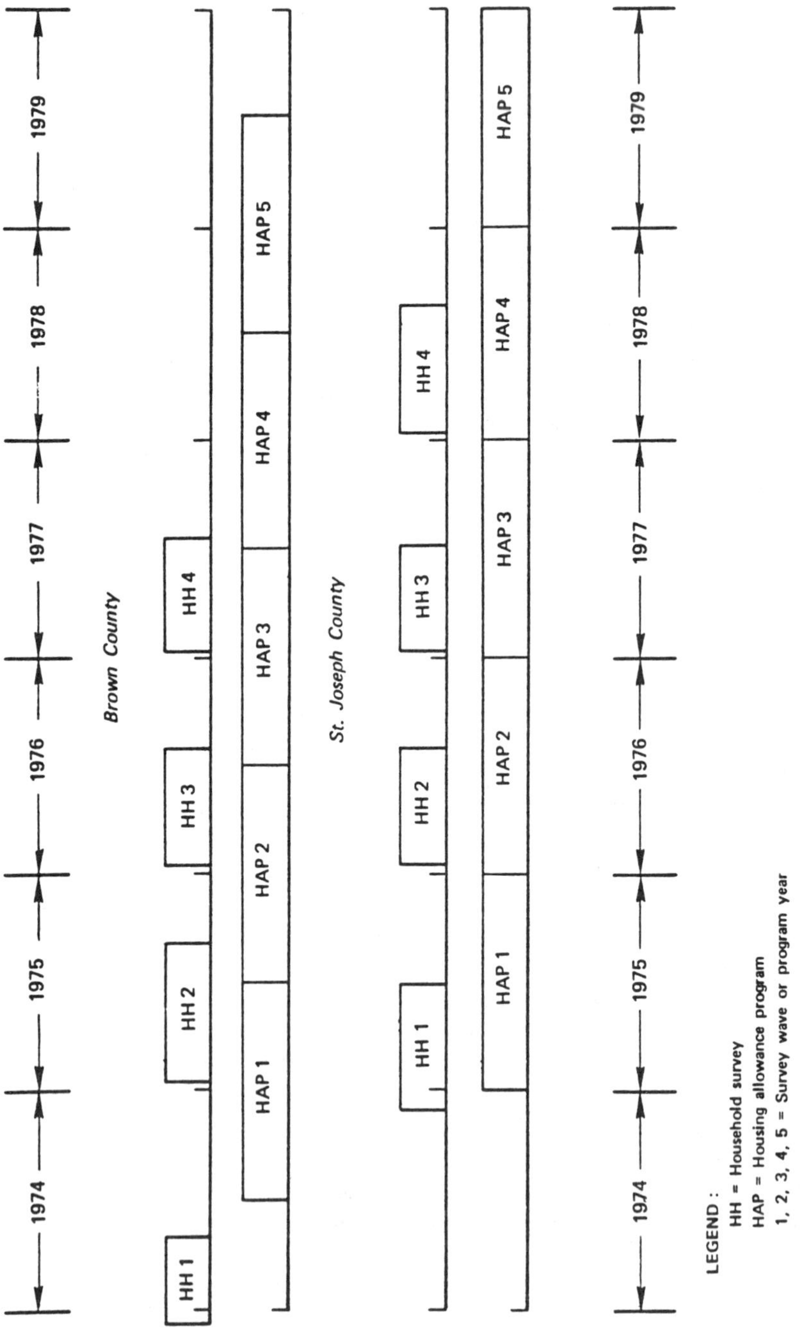

Fig. 5.1—Relationship between household surveys and allowance program years, by site

ing behavior. The never-enrolled are unaffected by the allowance program because the program gives them no money, has virtually no effect on the price they pay for housing (see Ch. VI), and has very little effect on the kinds or quality of housing available to them (see Hillestad and McDowell, 1982).

To adjust for the income and demographic differences between recipients and those who never enrolled, we fitted a regression model to wave 4 survey data for the never-enrolled. It yielded estimates of the determinants of their housing expenditures at the end of program year 3. We evaluated that model at the income (excluding the allowance) and demographic characteristics of each year 3 recipient, then adjusted the result to account for the difference observed at baseline between the consumption behavior of recipients and the never-enrolled. The result is our estimate of recipients' housing expenditures in year 3 had there been no program. Table 5.1 shows the average incomes and housing expenditures absent the program. The difference in expenditures is our estimate of the program's effect on housing consumption. As explained below, we also used program data to estimate the change in housing quality (measured by program standards) that resulted from participation in the program.

HOUSING CONSUMPTION CHANGES

We find that the allowance program caused recipients to consume about 8 percent more housing than they would have consumed without the program, and that the proportion living in dwellings of standard quality increased from about half to over four-fifths. Renters achieved their housing improvements partly by repairing and partly by moving; owners achieved theirs almost entirely by repairing their homes.

Consumption Increases

Table 5.2 reports estimates of the program-induced increase in housing consumption separately for renters and owners in each county. Although the point estimates differ slightly, none of the differences is statistically significant; a rounded average of 8 percent reasonably summarizes the evidence.

The estimates are similar for owners and renters, although different measures of housing consumption changes were used for the two groups. For renters, we measured housing consumption changes by comparing gross rent expenditure without and with the program. For

Table 5.1

INCOME AND HOUSING EXPENDITURE WITHOUT AND WITH HOUSING ALLOWANCES: YEAR 3 RECIPIENTS, BY SITE AND TENURE

Item	Year 3 Average Annual Amount ($)			
	Brown County		St. Joseph County	
	Renter	Owner	Renter	Owner
Gross Income				
Without program	4,569	5,081	3,632	4,198
With program	5,530	5,877	4,698	4,965
Difference (housing allowance)	961	796	1,066	767
Housing Expenditure[a]				
Without program	2,053	2,004	1,975	1,944
With program	2,212	2,182	2,137	2,097
Difference (program effect)	159	178	162	153

SOURCE: Estimated by HASE staff from HAO records for households receiving payments at the end of program year 3 in each site and from housing expenditure models fit to household survey data for each site.

NOTE: "With program" entries for housing expenditure are averages based on HAO records for each recipient. "Without program" entries are averages of estimates for the same recipients, based on nonallowance income and household characteristics. See text for explanation of estimating methods.

[a]For renters, gross rent expenditure; for owners, gross rent equivalent of property value. Because renter recipients paid a small premium over market price for their housing, their with-program gross rents have been adjusted downward to reflect the market value of the housing services they consumed.

homeowners, we compared only repair and improvement expenditure, assuming that other housing expenses were the same without and with the program.

The average program-induced gross rent increase for renter recipients measures the program's effect on their consumption of housing services, because rent equals the market price per unit of housing service times the quantity purchased. Without the program, recipients would have paid the normal market price for their housing; when they joined the program, they paid a slight premium (see Ch. VI). We corrected our estimate of program-induced expenditure to compensate for that premium (see Mulford et al., 1982, Appendix A), thus obtaining an estimate of the real change in housing consumption due to the program.

Table 5.2

PROGRAM-INDUCED HOUSING CONSUMPTION INCREASE: ALLOWANCE RECIPIENTS, BY TENURE AND SITE

Site	Percent Increase in Housing Consumption			
	Renter		Owner	
	Point Estimate	Standard Error	Point Estimate	Standard Error
Brown County	7.8	3.1	8.9	4.0
St. Joseph County	8.2	4.3	7.9	5.0
Average	8.0	2.7	8.4	3.2

SOURCE: Estimated by HASE staff from HAO records and models fit to countywide household survey data. For details, see Mulford et al., 1982, Appendixes A and B.

NOTE: Estimates are based on the characteristics of those receiving payments at the end of program year 3 in each site.

Homeowners' housing expenses are hard to measure directly because some expenses (opportunity cost of equity investment, unpaid labor devoted to home maintenance) must be imputed. To estimate without-program housing expense for an owner recipient, we transformed the market value of his home, using relationships estimated by regressing the sum of cash and imputed expenses on property values and dwelling characteristics for all homeowners in the two sites (Helbers, 1980, pp. 36-40). However, to estimate the *change* in an owner's housing expense attributable to the program, we compared only his annual cash expense for repairs and improvements without and with the program. Repairs and improvements are the major input to the production of housing services that owners can and likely will change in response to an allowance program.[3]

[3]Using the repair data as a measure of consumption change implicitly assumes (a) that a dollar of repair expenditure yields a dollar's worth of housing service in the year the expenditure was made, and none thereafter; (b) that owners never change housing consumption by moving or by nonrepair expenditures; and (c) that the owners' labor applied to repairs and improvements has no value. None of these assumptions is strictly

Quality Improvements

The modest program-induced increase in housing consumption evaluated in terms of market rents and repair expenditures contrasts sharply with the 30-point increase in the percentage of recipients occupying dwellings that would pass the HAOs' housing evaluation standards (Table 5.3). The large increase in standard housing for recipients was possible without a large increase in their housing consumption because many violations of housing codes were inexpensive to remedy. With housing allowances as an incentive, enrollees fixed many such defects that they would otherwise have ignored. Not all recipients lived continuously in standard housing. Even though recipients had to occupy standard housing in order to begin receiving payments, defects appeared in their dwellings between annual inspections; consequently, at any given time about a fifth of all recipients were living in dwellings that had fallen below standard.

REPAIRING AND MOVING

The allowance program affected recipients' housing consumption by altering both their repair and moving behavior. Moving offers much wider possibilities for housing change than does repairing. When a household moves, it can change all the attributes of its housing—space, quality, and location. Repairs, on the other hand, address primarily dwelling quality. Adding rooms is expensive and often inefficient, and a repair cannot change the location of a dwelling.

Because their characteristics and circumstances differed greatly, owners and renters used much different combinations of moving and repairing to change their housing consumption. Because owners controlled their own repair policies, and because moving would entail selling one house and buying another, they nearly always made program-induced housing adjustments by repairing their dwellings rather than by moving. Renters had less control over repair policies, and moves were less expensive for them. Landlords usually maintain their properties with the *expected* tenant in mind; if a current tenant

---

true, but the biases work in opposing directions. Repairs made in one year are partly consumed in later years, so current repair expenses overestimate current consumption. Some owners may have moved or changed nonrepair outlays in response to the allowance program; omitting those changes underestimates the program-induced housing consumption increase. Omitting unpaid labor causes us to underestimate the value of program-induced repairs by 7 to 12 percent, depending on site, if the unpaid labor is valued at the minimum wage.

Table 5.3

EFFECT OF THE ALLOWANCE PROGRAM ON HOUSING QUALITY: ALLOWANCE RECIPIENTS, BY TENURE AND SITE

Site	Percent Occupying Standard Housing			
	Renter		Owner	
	Without Program[a]	With Program[b]	Without Program[a]	With Program[b]
Brown County	50	87	56	91
St. Joseph County	47	70	58	84
Average	48	78	57	87

SOURCE: Estimated by HASE staff from HAO housing evaluation records and a housing deterioration model fit to HAO data. For details, see Mulford et al., 1982, Appendix D.

NOTE: Estimates are based on the characteristics of those receiving payments at the end of program year 3 in each site.

[a]Percent of year 3 recipients whose enrollment dwellings passed their initial evaluations.

[b]Percent of year 3 recipients whose dwellings would pass evaluations administered at random dates between regularly scheduled evaluations.

wants much different housing, he is more likely to move than to persuade his landlord to repair or remodel the dwelling. However, the expense of many HAO-required repairs was so low that renters often repaired their dwellings without consulting their landlords.

Program-Induced Repairs

Both owners and renters made some repairs in response to the program. Violations of HAO housing standards were so often easy and inexpensive to remedy, that virtually all owner recipients and three-quarters of the renter recipients repaired the defects rather than move. We call such repairs *required* because they remedied violations of the housing standards that were explicitly cited by the HAOs' evaluators.

Both owners and renters made other repairs while receiving payments, but only owners clearly did more than they would have done absent the allowance program. We call those repairs *voluntary* because they were not prompted by a housing evaluation—they occurred during the year between evaluations—and they did not affect allowance payment status during the periods in which they occurred.

Required Repairs. Housing defects were measured by the HAOs' housing standards, which were derived from the current housing codes in the two sites, the Building Officials and Code Administrators model code, and minimum housing standards developed by organizations such as the American Public Health Association. The standards consist of a 38-item checklist (see Appendix C) that requires each dwelling to:

- Provide essential space and privacy.
- Contain specified domestic equipment in good working order.
- Be free of hazards to health or safety.

At enrollment, future recipients in Brown County had almost 80 defects per 100 dwellings evaluated, and even more in St. Joseph County (89 per 100 homeowners and 127 per 100 renters). The most common reasons for failure were interior stairway hazards, lead-based paint hazards, and broken or damaged windows. Missing or inoperable toilets, washbasins, and bathing facilities, and unsafe plumbing, heating, and electrical systems were also common. Various other hazardous conditions, inadequate kitchen facilities, and inadequate living space or lack of privacy comprised the remaining defects found in recipients' dwellings at enrollment.

Fixing defects once does not guarantee standard housing in perpetuity; many recipients failed their annual housing evaluations:[4]

	Percent Failing Annual Evaluations	
	Brown County	St. Joseph County
Homeowners	15.8	26.2
Renters	22.7	43.2

[4]Recipients usually fail not because previously repaired defects recurred but because new defects appeared as a result of general deterioration. Annual failures happened despite voluntary repairs and improvements during the year because little of the voluntary activity was aimed at the health and safety hazards that accounted for most failures.

Consequently, those already receiving payments as well as new enrollees faced repair requirements.

Required repairs that were completed by enrollees and recipients (itemized in Table 5.4) ranged from clearing unsanitary debris to residing or reroofing entire buildings. To qualify for allowance payments, enrollees and recipients installed stairway handrails, replaced broken windows, sealed leaky vent pipes, fixed plumbing leaks, and repaired walls and roofs. A few installed kitchen or bathroom facilities, added fire exits, or rewired their dwellings. Some undertook several such actions, and a few virtually rehabilitated an entire dwelling.

Table 5.4

REPAIRS MADE BY ENROLLEES AND RECIPIENTS IN RESPONSE TO EVALUATION FAILURES, BY TENURE, SITE, AND TYPE OF REPAIR

Item Repaired	Percent of All Repair Actions			
	Brown County		St. Joseph County	
	Renter	Owner	Renter	Owner
Handrail, steps	16	25	12	20
Window, door	37	31	37	34
Structure	16	16	19	16
Plumbing system	11	12	13	14
Heating system	2	2	4	3
Electrical system	4	4	4	3
Refrigerator, range	2	(*a*)	2	1
Outbuildings, grounds	6	6	4	5
Other	6	4	5	4
All repair actions	100	100	100	100

SOURCE: Tabulated by HASE staff from HAO housing evaluation records for January 1976 through June 1979 in Brown County and through December 1979 in St. Joseph County.

NOTE: Data include both repairs made by enrollees seeking to qualify for payments and those made by recipients in response to subsequent annual evaluation failures. For renters, entries include repairs undertaken by either the landlord or the tenant. Percentages may not add exactly to 100 because of rounding.

[a]Less than 0.5 percent.

Nonprofessionals—owners, occupants, and their friends—made most of the required repairs (see Ch. VI, Fig. 6.5). Averaging across sites, we estimate that owners and their friends did about 80 percent of the work on owner-occupied homes. Tenants and their friends did about 50 percent of the work on rental dwellings, and their landlords nearly 40 percent. Less than 16 percent of the required repairs for owners and less than 10 percent for renters were made by professional contractors.

About a third of the households receiving payments in a mature program did some required repairs during the course of a year, either in connection with their initial qualification for payments or in order to avoid suspension (Table 5.5). Those required repairs cost nearly

Table 5.5

COST OF REPAIRS MADE BY ENROLLEES AND RECIPIENTS IN RESPONSE TO EVALUATION FAILURES, BY TENURE AND SITE

Site	Percent Repairing during a Year	Average Cost ($/year)	
		Per Recipient Making Repairs	All Recipients
Renter			
Brown County	24	111	27
St. Joseph County	40	95	38
Average	32	103	33
Owner			
Brown County	24	95	23
St. Joseph County	35	77	27
Average	29	86	25

SOURCE: Estimated by HASE staff from HAO housing evaluation records for January 1976 through June 1979 in Brown County and through December 1979 in St. Joseph County, and from records of a special survey of recipients' landlords, conducted in 1979.

NOTE: Data include both repairs made by enrollees seeking to qualify for payments and those made by recipients in response to subsequent annual evaluation failures. Repair costs include unpaid labor evaluated at the minimum wage, as well as cash expenditures. For renters, both landlord and tenant expenses and labor are included.

$100 on the average, which comes to about $30 per recipient when averaged over both repairers and nonrepairers.

Voluntary Repairs. Because only owners did a measurable amount of voluntary repairs in response to the allowance program, we exclude renters from the discussion of voluntary repairs below.[5] Owners' voluntary repairs often dealt with structural problems that posed no immediate hazard, or added amenities that were not required by the HAOs.

As Table 5.6 shows, about half of the voluntary repair actions dealt with components of the dwelling's structure—walls, floors, ceilings, roofs, and foundations. The largest category—wall repairs—included patching holes, painting, wallpapering, paneling, and installing aluminum siding. About half of the structural repairs were painting jobs that averaged about $80 per action, or about 20 percent of the annual voluntary repair bill. The remaining voluntary repairs distribute fairly evenly over the range of housing components.

Almost three-quarters of the owners did some voluntary repairs each year. Averaged over all owner recipients, the annual cash expense was $403 per recipient (Table 5.7). This figure includes both repairs they would have made even without the program ($263 average for the two sites) and the voluntary repairs that were caused by the program ($140 average), but not the required repairs ($25 average).

Comparing owners' total annual repair expenses while in the program with our estimate of their expenses without the program, we conclude that the program caused them to increase their cash outlays for repairs and improvements by $165 annually.

Program-Induced Moves

The allowance program affected both the timing of recipients' moves and the amount of their housing changes when they moved. It caused some households to cancel or delay moves that would have decreased their housing consumption, and it caused others to speed up moves that increased their housing consumption. When recipients

[5]Regressions of annual repair expenditures for rental properties on property and occupant characteristics indicate a positive program effect, but the data are so "noisy" that even a large average effect might be attributable to sampling variability. One reason for the "noise" is that the several tenants on a given multi-unit property were not usually all recipients or all nonrecipients; and repair expenses could not be associated with specific units on such properties.

Table 5.6

VOLUNTARY REPAIRS MADE BY OWNER RECIPIENTS, BY SITE AND TYPE OF REPAIR

Item Repaired	Percent of All Voluntary Repair Actions	
	Brown County	St. Joseph County
Handrail, steps	3	3
Window, door	12	11
Structure:		
Walls	27	25
Floor, ceiling	14	10
Roof	8	11
Foundation	2	2
Plumbing system	14	19
Heating system	4	5
Electrical system	3	3
Refrigerator, range	2	2
Outbuildings, grounds	8	7
Other	4	2
All repair actions	100	100

SOURCE: Tabulated by HASE staff from HAO housing evaluation records for January 1976 through June 1979 in Brown County and through December 1979 in St. Joseph County.

NOTE: Data include repairs made by recipients during the year preceding an annual housing evaluation except for repairs required by the last prior evaluation. Percentages may not add exactly to 100 because of rounding.

moved, the program caused them to increase housing consumption by more than they would have done in its absence.

Renters' Moves. With normal mobility rates (i.e., without a program), we estimate that 54 percent of the renter recipients would have moved within the 18-month average period from their enrollment to end of year 3. However, only 40 percent actually moved, implying that the program's net effect was to delay moves.

Once an enrollee's dwelling had been certified as acceptable, the program's housing standards should have deterred moving, because

Table 5.7

COST OF ALL PROGRAM-INDUCED REPAIRS MADE BY OWNER RECIPIENTS, BY SITE

Site	Average Annual Repair Expense ($)				
	Total Without Program[a]	With Program			Program-Induced Repairs[d]
		Required Repairs[b]	Voluntary Repairs[c]	Total	
Brown County	236	23	391	414	178
St. Joseph County	290	27	416	443	153
Average	263	25	403	428	165

SOURCE: Estimated by HASE staff from HAO housing evaluation records for January 1976 through June 1979 in Brown County and through December 1979 in St. Joseph County; and from repair expenditure models fit to household survey data for each site.

NOTE: Except as indicated, repair costs reported in this table do not include any allowance for unpaid labor. When valued at the minimum wage, such labor adds about 12 percent to repair costs in Brown County, 7 percent in St. Joseph County.

[a]Estimated without-program repair expenses of year 3 owner recipients.

[b]From Table 5.5; includes a small amount of unpaid labor, valued at the minimum wage.

[c]Voluntary repairs equals total minus required repairs.

[d]Total with-program minus total without-program repairs.

another dwelling might fail the standards, causing suspension of payments until repairs were made.[6] The average housing change for those who moved while receiving payments was greater than it was for similar households observed before the program started, suggesting that the program delayed moves that decreased housing consumption more than it delayed moves that increased consumption. Therefore, delayed moves contribute positively to the program's effect on current recipients' housing.

Although the program appears to have reduced the overall mobility of renter recipients, the 40 percent who did move after enrolling accounted for most of the increased housing consumption attributable to the program. As shown in Table 5.8, the typical year 3 recipient who

[6]When a recipient's dwelling failed an annual evaluation, or when a recipient moved to a dwelling that failed its initial evaluation, he was allowed 60 days for repairs before payments were suspended.

Table 5.8

PROGRAM-INDUCED HOUSING CONSUMPTION INCREASES BEFORE AND AFTER ENROLLMENT BY MOBILITY STATUS: RENTER RECIPIENTS, BY SITE

Site	Percent Increase in Housing Consumption				
	Total	Before Enrolling[a]	After Enrolling[b]		
			Total	Nonmover	Mover
Brown County	7.8	.4	7.4	1.7	16.4
St. Joseph County	8.2	2.6	5.6	.5	16.6
Average	8.0	1.5	6.5	1.1	16.5

SOURCE: Estimated by HASE staff from HAO records for households receiving payments at the end of program year 3 and from models fit to household survey data for each site.

[a]Ratio of average gross rent at enrollment to average gross rent without the program, expressed as a percentage. Both rent variables were adjusted to year 3 dollars.

[b]Ratio of average gross rent at the end of year 3 to average gross rent at enrollment, expressed as a percentage. Both rent variables were adjusted to year 3 dollars. Mobility status indicates whether or not a recipient moved between enrollment and the end of year 3.

moved after enrolling increased his gross rent expenditure (in constant dollars) by about 16 percent, whereas those who did not move increased their expenditures by only 1 percent, presumably because of repairs. (Both figures are based on enrollment rather than without-program rents.)

Table 5.8 also suggests that renter recipients altered their moving behavior before enrolling because they anticipated receiving allowance payments: Recipients' enrollment rents exceeded their predicted without-program rents by about 2 percent. Households that were having trouble making ends meet might have moved to less expensive housing if housing allowances had not been available. It appears that some of those households remained in their dwellings, factoring anticipated allowance payments into their preenrollment housing decisions. Households that moved for nonprogram reasons before enrolling (e.g., job change, troubles with landlord, wanted larger or smaller house) may have factored anticipated allowances into their decisions; by choosing more housing than they otherwise would have, they could avoid moving again after enrolling. Finally, some households may have moved from dwellings that they thought would fail the housing standards to dwellings they thought would pass to avoid the embarrassment of being told they lived in substandard housing.

Housing evaluation data lend support to the hypothesis that the program affected renter recipients' housing consumption before they enrolled. Initial housing evaluation failure rates for those who became recipients declined over program time—from 45 to 29 percent in Brown County and from 59 to 41 percent in St. Joseph County between program years 1 and 5—suggesting that as knowledge of program standards spread, households began considering the standards in their preenrollment housing decisions.[7]

Even though moves offer more opportunity for housing change than do repairs, renter recipients who moved did not much change the attributes unique to moving—total space and location. Movers' destination dwellings had the same number of rooms (on average) as their origin dwellings, and the small fraction of movers who changed neighborhoods—a third in Brown County and a fifth in St. Joseph County—chose destination neighborhoods that resembled origin neighborhoods in terms of quality of buildings and landscaping, general cleanliness, and access to employment. Instead, movers' changes concentrated on habitable space (rooms meeting HAO standards) and dwelling quality (high ratings on HAO checklist items).[8]

Owners' Moves. The program affected owners' moves much less than it did renters' moves. Few homeowners increased their housing consumption by making unscheduled (program-induced) moves to better houses, because transaction costs for owners are high. The program might have caused some to delay moving to less expensive housing (e.g., from single-family homes to apartments), but because

---

[7]An alternative interpretation of these data is that, over program time, renter enrollees whose dwellings failed were less likely to repair or move, so fewer became recipients. That interpretation is refuted by Table 3.8 in Ch. III, which reports the trends of initial failures and repairs for all enrollees, not just those who became recipients. The table shows that failure rates decreased and repair rates increased in the later years of the program.

There remains the possibility that as eligible renter households learned more about program standards, their enrollment decisions took more account of the expected outcomes of housing evaluations, so that fewer enrollees (and fewer eventual recipients) failed initial evaluations. Although Wendt, 1982, does not test for time trends, he does show that poor housing quality discouraged enrollment by renters who had not recently moved (Sec. V, Table 12). It is certainly plausible that better information about the costs of participating would alter decisions at the margin, with respect *both* to enrolling and to preenrollment moves or repairs. Anecdotal evidence from the HAOs indicates that a significant number of preenrollment moves and preenrollment repairs explicitly took account of program standards.

[8]Details are given in Mulford, Weiner, and McDowell, 1980, Sec. IV.

homeowners move infrequently (fewer than 10 percent of all homeowners in our sites normally move each year), there were few moves to be delayed. Controlling for life-cycle stage, homeowner recipients in program year 3 moved slightly less frequently than homeowners surveyed at baseline (preprogram), suggesting that the program delayed moves for perhaps 2 percent of the year 3 recipients.

Assuming that the program caused no unscheduled moves by owners, that it delayed moves for roughly 2 percent, and that it had some effect on housing choice among the 4 percent who moved after enrollment, the program affected the moving behavior of 6 percent of the owner recipients in year 3. We cannot accurately estimate how much housing consumption changed for these cases because our data on pre- and post-move housing consumption for homeowners is less precise than for renters. But on the average the moving effect must be quite small, since it involves only 6 percent of recipients. Therefore, we ignore move-related consumption changes for homeowner recipients in our final accounting.

HOUSEHOLD BUDGET ALLOCATION

On average, housing allowances added about 25 percent to the gross incomes of renter recipients in year 3 and about 17 percent to the incomes of homeowner recipients. Before the experiment, most observers expected recipients to increase their housing expenditures by about the same percentage as their incomes were increased. As we have seen, housing consumption actually rose by only 8 percent for both renters and owners, much less than the percentage increase in gross incomes.

Put another way, renter recipients allocated about 16 percent of their allowances to additional housing consumption and owners allocated about 21 percent; the remainder of allowance income was used to augment nonhousing consumption. Because of the modest program-induced change in expenditures, allowance recipients were able to reduce their housing expense burdens (the ratio of housing expense to income), but the size of the reduction depends very much on the choice of accounting conventions.

Budget Allocation without the Program

Both renters and homeowners in our sites gave housing consumption a high budgetary priority; but once they had achieved a certain level of housing consumption, additional housing had a low priority relative to other forms of consumption. Households with low incomes spent nearly as much for housing as did middle-income households, but the budget share of housing dropped sharply as income rose. This pattern is observable in national data as well as in our sites.

Allowance recipients, of course, had low incomes relative to the general populations of our sites. Table 5.9 shows that the average renter recipient, with a gross income of only $4,101, would have spent about half that income for housing in the absence of an allowance program. The average owner recipient, with a gross income of $4,640, would have spent 42 percent for housing. These estimates are based on the control model for without-program expenditures described earlier; but they are also very close to actual preprogram expenditures, expressed in year 3 dollars.

How Allowances Were Allocated

Table 5.10 shows how year 3 recipients spent their allowances. The average renter received an annual allowance of $1,014, which he divided 16 percent for additional housing consumption and 84 percent for other consumption. The average owner received $781, dividing it 21 percent for housing and 79 percent for other consumption.

Housing Expense Burdens

The allowance program's benefit schedule was designed so that a participant who spent exactly R^*—the standard cost of adequate housing—for his dwelling would need to devote only a fourth of his adjusted gross income to housing; the allowance would make up the difference. However, participants were not required to spend exactly R^*, so some ended with higher and some with lower expense burdens. For year 3 recipients, the average burden thus calculated was about 35 percent for renters and 37 percent for owners, indicating that most participants spent more than R^* for their housing.[9]

It should be noted that this ratio is not at all comparable to the "without program" budget share for housing that is reported in Table 5.9. There, total housing expense is compared with gross income.

[9]A tabulation of program records covering the first three years of enrollment in each site indicates that the average renter enrollee was spending 3 to 8 percent more and the average owner enrollee was spending 25 to 42 percent more than the current R^* for households of the appropriate size (the ranges reflect variation between sites). For both groups, some of the excess reflects lags in the adjustment of R^* schedules to current market conditions; the owners' large excess expenditures were clearly related to the fact that their dwellings were larger than required by program standards.

Table 5.9

HOW ALLOWANCE RECIPIENTS WOULD HAVE ALLOCATED THEIR INCOMES WITHOUT THE PROGRAM, BY TENURE AND SITE

Site	Year 3 Average Annual Amount ($)			Percentage Distribution		
	Nonallowance Income	Expenditure		Nonallowance Income	Expenditure	
		Housing	Other		Housing	Other
Renter						
Brown County	4,569	2,053	2,516	100	45	55
St. Joseph County	3,632	1,975	1,657	100	54	46
Average	4,101	2,014	2,087	100	49	51
Owner						
Brown County	5,081	2,004	3,077	100	39	61
St. Joseph County	4,198	1,944	2,254	100	46	54
Average	4,640	1,974	2,666	100	42	58

SOURCE: Estimated by HASE staff from HAO records for households receiving payments at the end of program year 3 in each site and from housing expenditure models fit to household survey data for each site.

NOTE: The HAO recorded only income and housing expenses, so expenditure for "Other" items is a residual that could include savings or omit dissavings.

Table 5.10

HOW RECIPIENTS ALLOCATED THEIR ALLOWANCES, BY TENURE AND SITE

Site	Year 3 Average Annual Amount ($)			Percentage Distribution		
		Marginal Expenditure			Marginal Expenditure	
	Allowance	Housing	Other	Allowance	Housing	Other
Renter						
Brown County	961	159	802	100	17	83
St. Joseph County	1,066	162	904	100	15	85
Average	1,014	161	853	100	16	84
Owner						
Brown County	796	178	618	100	22	78
St. Joseph County	767	153	614	100	20	80
Average	781	165	616	100	21	79

SOURCE: Estimated by HASE staff from HAO records for households receiving payments at the end of program year 3 in each site and from housing expenditure models fit to household survey data for each site.

NOTE: Each recipient's allowance payment and housing expenditure for year 3 were recorded by the HAO. For renters, marginal housing expenditure is the difference between the observed expenditure and the estimated without-program expenditure reported in Table 5.9. For owners, marginal expenditure equals estimated program-induced repairs and improvements. "Other" expenditure is a residual that could include savings or omit dissavings.

Here, total housing expense *minus the housing allowance* is compared with *adjusted* gross income. The adjustments typically reduce gross income by about 20 percent, though the effect varies with the level of gross income, age of head, and household composition.

Although the 25-percent-of-income standard for housing affordability is widely used, the method of calculation varies with context so that the standard is not uniformly applied. The calculation embodied in the "housing-gap" allowance formula came directly from the federal public housing program, where the housing authority supplied each participating household with a dwelling and charged rent equal to 25 percent of the household's adjusted gross income. However, in the experimental allowance program, the participant's income was augmented by an allowance and participants paid full market prices for their housing; the more natural computation of expense burden in this case is the ratio of total housing expense to gross income, which is comparable to the rent-income ratios published by the Bureau of the Census for the general population of renters.

Table 5.11 shows housing expense burdens for year 3 recipients without and with housing allowances, computed by the different methods that are in common use. Under all computations, the effect of the program was to reduce the typical expense burden, but both the without-program burden and the amount of the reduction varies greatly depending on the computational method. The important message of the table is that program effects on expense burdens must be consistently computed and compared only with similarly computed external data.

ACCOUNTING FOR INCREASED HOUSING CONSUMPTION

Had the allowance been an unrestricted cash grant, even less would have been spent for housing—probably about 8 percent of renters' allowances and perhaps as little as 3 percent of owners' allowances, as compared with the actual 16 and 21 percent for the two groups, respectively. Other program features, in particular housing standards, caused recipients to spend more on housing than they would have done, given unrestricted grants.

The Effect of Allowance Payments

We estimated the effect of allowance payments on recipients' housing consumption by computing the ratio of allowance-augmented in-

Table 5.11

EFFECT OF ALLOWANCE PROGRAM ON HOUSING EXPENSE BURDENS, BY SITE AND TENURE

Program Status and Accounting Method	Brown County		St. Joseph County	
	Renter	Owner	Renter	Owner
Housing Expense/Gross Income (%)				
Without program[a]	45	39	54	46
With program				
Allowance added to income[b]	40	37	46	42
Allowance subtracted from housing expense[c]	27	27	30	32
Housing Expense/Adjusted Gross Income (%)				
Without program[a]	54	49	70	58
With program				
Allowance added to income[b]	47	45	55	51
Allowance subtracted from housing expense[c]	33	34	38	40

SOURCE: Estimated by HASE staff from HAO records for households receiving payments at the end of year 3 in each site and from housing expenditure models fit to household survey data for each site.

NOTE: For each column, housing expense burdens have been calculated by several methods that are in common use. In all cases, the entries are ratios of average dollar amounts, not averages of ratios.

[a]Estimated without-program average housing expense of year 3 recipients divided by their average nonallowance gross income (adjusted gross income in lower panel).

[b]Average year 3 housing expense, divided by average nonallowance gross income (adjusted gross income in lower panel) plus average year 3 housing allowance.

[c]Average year 3 housing expense minus average allowance, divided by average nonallowance gross income (adjusted gross income in lower panel).

come to nonallowance income and raising that ratio to the power of an appropriate income elasticity. Table 5.12 shows the numbers for that calculation.

The income elasticities used for renter recipients were those for "permanent" income, estimated on the general population of renters at baseline (Mulford, 1979); they are discussed in Ch. II, above. The elasticities used for owners pertain not to total housing expenditures

Table 5.12

INCOME AND HOUSING EXPENDITURE EFFECTS OF ALLOWANCE PAYMENTS, BY TENURE AND SITE

Site	Increase in Gross Income[a] (%)	Estimated Income Elasticity[b]	Allowance-Induced Expenditure Increase	
			%[c]	\$/yr[d]
Renter				
Brown County	21.0	.22	4.3	88
St. Joseph County	29.4	.15	3.9	78
Average	(*e*)	(*e*)	4.1	83
Owner				
Brown County	15.7	.49	7.4	17
St. Joseph County	18.3	.52	9.1	26
Average	(*e*)	(*e*)	8.4	22

SOURCE: Estimated by HASE staff from HAO records for households receiving payments at the end of year 3 in each site and from housing expenditure models fit to household survey data for each site.

[a] Average allowance payment as a percentage of nonallowance gross income at the end of year 3; see Table 5.1.

[b] Elasticity of gross rent expenditure for renters, as estimated by Mulford, 1979, Table 5; elasticity of repair and improvement expenditures for owners, as estimated by Helbers and McDowell, 1982, Table 5.

[c] Percent of without-program gross rent for renters (Table 5.9), without-program repair expenditures for homeowners (Table 5.7). Computed from entries in the first two columns.

[d] Percentage increase applied to base as specified in note *c*.

[e] Not applicable.

but to expenditures for repairs and improvements (Helbers and McDowell, 1982); we used these more specific parameters for owners because our analysis of program effects for owners takes account only of the changes in their repair and improvement outlays.

The dollar amounts attributed to allowance payments are compared in Table 5.13 with the total program-induced changes in housing consumption whose derivations were explained at the beginning of this chapter (see Table 5.1). For renters, we attribute an average $83 consumption increase specifically to allowances, leaving $78 of program-induced consumption to be otherwise explained. For owners, we attribute an average $22 consumption increase to allowances, leaving $143 of program-induced consumption to be otherwise explained.

The Effect of Housing Standards

We expected housing standards, which distinguish housing allowances from unrestricted cash transfers, to cause most of the increased housing consumption not attributable to the allowance payments themselves. That expectation was fulfilled for renters; but for owners, other factors are more important.

We judge that housing standards caused virtually all required repairs made by recipients, their friends, and their landlords.[10] But the required repairs, which amounted to $33 per recipient-year for renters and $25 for owners (see Table 5.5), account for only a small fraction of the consumption increase caused by the program. However, housing standards also affected consumption through moves and voluntary repairs.

About 17 percent of all renter recipients moved after failing an initial housing evaluation; as a consequence of those moves, the movers' housing expenditures rose by an average of 21 percent. Renter recipients who voluntarily moved from HAO-approved dwellings averaged only a 9-percent expenditure increase. The difference, 12 percent of preenrollment gross rent, is mostly attributable to the former group's attempt to meet program standards, though those who moved after failing also had slightly larger average allowance entitlements than those who moved voluntarily. Averaged over all renter recipients, the housing standards' effect on moving amounts to about $40 annually per household. Adding this figure to the one for renters' required repairs ($33) yields a total of $73 for increased housing consumption

[10]Although some of those repairs might have been done eventually without the program, most of them remedied defects such as stairway hazards, electrical hazards, poor ventilation, or lead-based paint hazards that did not much concern either enrollees or their landlords.

Table 5.13

INCREASED HOUSING CONSUMPTION BY CAUSE OF INCREASE: ALLOWANCE RECIPIENTS, BY TENURE AND SITE

Site	Year 3 Average Amount ($)			Percentage Distribution		
	Housing Consumption Increase	Attributed Cause		Housing Consumption Increase	Attributed Cause	
		Allowance Payments	Other[a]		Allowance Payments	Other[a]
Renter						
Brown County	159	88	71	100	55	45
St. Joseph County	162	78	84	100	48	52
Average	161	83	78	100	52	48
Owner						
Brown County	178	17	161	100	10	90
St. Joseph County	153	26	127	100	17	83
Average	165	22	143	100	13	87

SOURCE: Estimated by HASE staff from HAO records for households receiving payments at the end of program year 3 in each site and from housing expenditure models fit to household survey data for each site.

[a] Possible causes include the HAOs' housing standards, "Hawthorne effect" of participating in an experiment, housing inspections that call attention to incipient problems, and the moral pressure of receiving a *housing* allowance.

because of the program's housing standards. All but \$5 of the \$161 of renters' program-induced housing consumption is thus attributable to either allowances (\$83) or housing standards (\$73).

Whatever the outcomes of their initial housing evaluations, owners rarely moved. However, some of their voluntary repairs may have been prompted by the housing standards. In Table 5.14, we estimate lower and upper bounds for how much of the program-induced consumption increase was caused by housing standards.

Assuming that no voluntary repairs were standards-induced gives the lower-bound estimates, which indicate that only 15 percent of program-induced repairs were attributable to housing standards. But recipients probably did some voluntary repairs to prevent dwelling failures in the future. Comparing deficiency and voluntary repairs by type, McDowell estimates that up to 15 percent of voluntary repairs may have fixed items that would have failed at the next annual evaluation.[11] Under the upper-bound assumption, housing standards caused half of the housing consumption increase for owners.

Other Program Effects

Even the upper-bound estimate leaves a third of the owners' housing consumption increase unaccounted for. The HAOs' data-collection activities and advertising that stressed the *housing* objectives of the program may explain the residual increase in owners' consumption. Regular housing evaluations and questions about repairs may have stimulated recipients to do more repairs so that they would "look good" at the next evaluation. Calling the program the *Housing* Allowance Program and advertising it heavily as a means to help people with their housing might also have increased repair expenditures. Many recipients (particularly elderly homeowners) who would never have joined a welfare program joined the housing allowance program because its advertising convinced them that the money was for a socially acceptable purpose—improved housing. After joining the program, they may have felt morally obligated to spend their allowances on housing even though they had already met the program's housing standards.

[11]See McDowell, 1979, p. 46. Even if that 15 percent of voluntary repairs would have been required by the HAOs had they not been done voluntarily, attributing all of them to housing standards probably overstates causality: Recipients would have made some of those repairs without standards. Considering that 15 percent is the upper bound for voluntary repairs that fix items similar to ones fixed in response to failing an evaluation, and that housing standards probably did not cause all of those "similar" voluntary repairs, the standards-induced upper bound in Table 5.12 clearly is an upper bound.

Table 5.14

INCREASED REPAIR EXPENDITURES BY CAUSE OF INCREASE: OWNER RECIPIENTS, BY SITE

Attributed Cause of Increase	Increase in Annual Repair Expenditures					
	Brown County		St. Joseph County		Average	
	$	%	$	%	$	%
At Lower Bound for Housing Standards Effect[a]						
Allowance payments	17	10	26	17	22	13
Housing standards	23	13	27	18	25	15
Other[c]	138	78	100	65	118	72
All causes	178	100	153	100	165	100
At Upper Bound for Housing Standards Effect[b]						
Allowance payments	17	10	26	17	22	13
Housing standards	82	46	89	58	86	52
Other[c]	79	44	38	25	58	35
All causes	178	100	153	100	165	100

SOURCE: Estimated by HASE staff from HAO housing evaluation records for January 1976 through June 1979 in Brown County and through December 1979 in St. Joseph County; and from repair expenditure models fit to household survey data for each site.

NOTE: Repair expenditures include both voluntary repairs and those required by the HAOs. Estimates are for owners receiving payments at the end of year 3. Increases by cause may not add to entries for "All causes" because of rounding.

[a]Assumes that no voluntary repairs were caused indirectly by housing standards.

[b]Assumes that 15 percent of all voluntary repairs were caused indirectly by housing standards.

[c]Possible causes include "Hawthorne effect" of participating in an experiment, housing inspections that call attention to incipient problems, and the moral pressure of receiving a *housing* allowance.

PROGRAM EVALUATION

As shown above, those who participated in the experimental housing allowance program benefited both with respect to housing consumption and budgetary relief. Their overall housing consumption increased by about 8 percent; nearly a third shifted from substandard to standard dwellings; and the funds available to recipients for nonhousing consumption increased by 41 percent for renters and 23 percent for homeowners. These are measures of program *effectiveness,* but they must be qualified by the fact that benefits were received by less than half of all eligibles and 80 percent of all enrollees (see Ch. IV).

The *efficiency* of the program can be measured by comparing benefits actually bestowed with the program's cost. We have excellent data on program costs, and the benefits of housing allowances to participants are readily measured. We are confident that the incidental costs and benefits to nonparticipants are small, but we could estimate them only indirectly.

Because housing allowances are of interest as an alternative to other policy instruments, we present parallel assessments of the efficiency of the public housing program, whose low-income participants live in dwellings that are owned and operated by local housing authorities but are federally subsidized; and of a hypothetical program of unrestricted cash grants to low-income households, such as has been studied by the Office of Economic Opportunity and the Department of Health, Education and Welfare.

Program Costs and Benefits to Participants

The public housing program fully specifies its participants' housing consumption, the housing allowance program merely sets minimum standards for housing consumption, and the unrestricted-grant program leaves consumption choices entirely to recipients. These are the essential differences between the three policy instruments, although other differences can be created by varying eligibility or entitlement standards.

To understand how program structure affects efficiency, we must apply all three programs to a standard case even though they may actually serve somewhat different populations and have somewhat different benefit schedules. We have designed a standard case (see Table 5.15) such that each program delivers approximately the same amount of benefit ($73.50 per month) to a typical renter participant with an income of $4,000. We use data from HASE and from a concurrent study of public housing in the two sites of the Demand Experi-

Table 5.15

PROGRAM COSTS AND PARTICIPANT BENEFITS FOR ALTERNATIVE ASSISTANCE PROGRAMS

Item	Monthly Costs and Benefits per Standard Case ($)		
	Public Housing	Housing Allowances	Unrestricted Grants
Program Cost to Deliver Equal Participant Benefit			
Benefit to participant	73.55	73.55	73.55
Administration and other	141.60	13.55	9.22
Total	215.15	87.10	82.77
End Use of Benefit by Standard Participant			
Housing consumption	11.68[a]	11.68[a]	6.04
Other consumption	61.87	61.87	67.51
Total	73.55	73.55	73.55

SOURCES: All entries were estimated by HASE staff. Entries for public housing are based on data in Mayo et al., 1980; entries for housing allowances and unrestricted grants are based on HAO records and models of housing expenditure fit to household survey data, averaged across HASE sites.

NOTE: The standard case is a renter participant whose adjusted gross income is $4,000 annually. Without the program, he would spend $144.16 monthly for housing. The public housing authority provides him with a dwelling whose market rental value is $155.67, the amount he would choose to spend if given a housing allowance. With an unrestricted grant, he chooses to spend $150.09. In fact, the typical public housing tenant has a lower income and is provided with a dwelling whose market rental value is $145.00.

[a] Participants in the public housing and housing allowance programs would evaluate this portion of the benefit at less than $11.68 because of constraints on its use.

ment (Mayo et al., 1980) to estimate (a) the total program cost entailed in supplying the benefit, (b) how the participant divides the benefit between housing and other consumption, and (c) how households not in the program are affected. Implicitly, we assume that all three programs were operated in the HASE sites, and that they were open only to the renters eligible for assistance under HAO rules.[12]

The upper panel of Table 5.15 reveals the main consequence of the differences between the programs: To deliver the specified benefit, the public housing program incurs 2.5 times the cost incurred by the housing allowance or unrestricted grant program. The main reason, according to Mayo, is that public housing authorities are inefficient real-estate developers; they pay about $2 for every $1 of housing service they produce. The housing allowance program spends about $14 per recipient-month to administer means tests and housing evaluations, whereas the unrestricted transfer program would only need the means test, estimated at $9 per recipient-month.

The lower panel of the table shows how the participant would use his benefit. In order to make the programs comparable, we assumed that the public housing program provided somewhat better dwellings than they actually do, so that both the public housing and housing allowance programs caused participants to increase their housing consumption by about $12, taking the rest of their benefit in cash. The recipient of an unrestricted grant would choose to spend about $6 extra on housing, using the rest for other purposes.

Marketwide Consumption Changes

The costs and benefits of these programs are not necessarily limited to those participating in them; they may affect the housing choices available to others in the same marketplace. Below, we compare the marketwide consumption changes caused by the three programs. We divide consumption into housing and other goods because we are evaluating the housing allowance program. We consider housing consumption changes first from society's perspective—that is, in terms of housing quality standards—and then from the individual's perspective—that is, in terms of his total housing consumption. We also distinguish consumption changes for program participants from those for nonparticipants, who are affected through market mechanisms.

Housing Quality. In the HASE sites, about 59 percent of all renter

[12]The models and assumptions underlying our comparisons of alternative programs are detailed in Rydell and Mulford, 1982.

households lived in standard dwellings (as judged by HAO standards) when the allowance program began (Table 5.16).[13] Among those who later became recipients, less than half lived in standard dwellings. Among nonrecipients, who account for nearly 90 percent of all renter households, about 61 percent lived in standard dwellings.

Table 5.16

HOUSING QUALITY CHANGES CAUSED BY ALTERNATIVE ASSISTANCE PROGRAMS, BY PARTICIPATION STATUS

Participation Status	Percent Occupying Standard Housing			
	No Program	Public Housing	Housing Allowances	Unrestricted Grants
Participants[a]	48	78	78	50
Nonparticipants	61	61	62	61
All households	59	64	64	59

SOURCE: Estimated by HASE staff from HAO records for Brown and St. Joseph counties and from models of market effects fit to household survey data and HAO data for both sites.

NOTE: Program assumptions are the same as in Table 5.15. Housing standards for all programs are those used by the HAOs; the incidence of standard housing for participants is based on HASE experience.

[a]In the "no program" case, prospective participants.

Both public housing and housing allowances cause a 30-point increase in the percentage of participants who occupy standard housing.[14] Under housing allowances, nonparticipant housing improves slightly—from 61 to 62 percent standard—as participants transfer their standard dwellings to the nonparticipant market either

[13]The estimate for all renters is based on a study by Yildiz and Mulford, 1982, that applied HAO standards to a marketwide sample of rental dwellings in St. Joseph County. Census-based estimates of the incidence of standard housing are much higher because the HAO standards are both broader in scope and more rigorous in detail than census standards.

[14]Because we standardized the two housing programs to supply dwellings with equal market rents, we assume that they impose the same housing standards in the same way. However, even with the same housing standards, different inspection policies could lead to different housing quality improvements.

by moving while in the program or by terminating from the program and becoming nonparticipants themselves. The effect is small because participants turn only a few upgraded dwellings onto the nonparticipant market each year (relative to the size of the latter market) and the effects do not accumulate much over time because those upgraded dwellings deteriorate quite rapidly to substandard (see Mulford et al., 1982, Appendix D). Public housing causes no improvement in nonparticipants' housing quality, because no public housing units are turned over to nonparticipants. Marketwide, both programs cause about a 5-point increase in the percent of households occupying standard housing.

In contrast to the housing programs, unrestricted cash grants do little for housing quality, even for participants. The percentage of participants occupying standard housing increases by only 2 points, as a consequence of their increased housing expenditures. Without the housing standards requirement and recurrent inspections, participants do not attend to many violations of HAO standards. Marketwide, the increase in percent substandard is less than one-half of one percentage point.

Below, we normalize dollar increases in housing and other consumption by program costs (in dollars) to facilitate interprogram comparisons. Because it is difficult to attribute a dollar value to improvements in substandard housing, we did not normalize here. However, housing allowances are clearly more efficient than public housing at improving housing quality because they effect slightly more improvement for less than half the cost. For almost any value one might attribute to substandard dwellings made standard, housing allowances are also more efficient than unrestricted grants, because allowances do much more for only slightly greater cost.

Consumption Changes per Program Dollar. Table 5.17 shows how both housing and other consumption are changed by each program. It includes separate accounts for participants and nonparticipants.

Participants' consumption increases per program dollar are always less than 1.0 because of the administrative and other nonsubsidy program costs. Delivering unrestricted cash grants entails the least administrative cost; therefore, they provide the greatest consumption increase per program dollar—89 cents for participants. Housing allowances, which require modest housing standards enforcement costs, deliver almost as much subsidy to participants as do unrestricted cash grants. Public housing's high development costs combine with administrative expense to absorb nearly two-thirds of the federal subsidy without benefit to participants; only 34 cents of each program dollar went for participants' consumption increases.

Table 5.17

CONSUMPTION CHANGES CAUSED BY ALTERNATIVE ASSISTANCE PROGRAMS, BY PARTICIPATION STATUS AND TYPE OF CONSUMPTION

Type of Consumption	Consumption Change per Assistance Program Dollar ($)		
	Public Housing	Housing Allowances	Unrestricted Grants
Participants			
Housing	.05	.13	.07
Other	.29	.71	.82
Total	.34	.84	.89
Nonparticipants			
Housing	.03	.01	(*a*)
Other	.03	-.02	-.01
Total	.06	-.01	-.01
All Households			
Housing	.08	.15	.07
Other	.32	.68	.81
Total	.40	.83	.88

SOURCE: Rydell and Mulford, 1982, Table 4.1.

NOTE: Population characteristics for all programs are averages across HASE sites.

[a] Rounds to zero; calculated value is -.002.

The high development costs of public housing have been well-known for years (see Rydell and Mulford, 1982, pp. 1-2). But supporters of public housing have argued that the addition of public housing units benefited nonparticipants as well as participants. If an increased supply of housing leads to lower marketwide prices, nonparticipants' benefits could outweigh the higher cost per participant of the supply-side strategy. In contrast, housing allowances and unrestricted cash grants stimulate demand, possibly pushing up prices for nonparticipants.

We have modeled the market effects of each program, using HASE and other data (Rydell and Mulford, 1982). We conclude that none of the programs has much effect on nonparticipants' consumption of housing or other goods. In response to supply programs, the market response offsets most of the new public housing units; either private new construction is deferred or demolitions increase. In response to demand programs, housing prices increase only slightly, causing only a small reduction in nonparticipant demand.[15] Nonparticipant housing consumption actually increases with housing allowances because future participants increase their consumption in anticipation of joining the program, and former participants continue to consume above-normal housing for a while after they leave the program.

Altogether, housing allowances cause about twice as much increase in marketwide housing consumption per program dollar as do either of the other programs. As compared with public housing, housing allowances cause both more housing consumption increase and more nonhousing consumption increase per program dollar.

The comparison between the demand programs does not yield a clear winner. Housing allowances cause more housing-consumption increase than unrestricted cash grants, but less increase in the consumption of other goods, and less total consumption increase. Because increased housing consumption, particularly if it rids dwellings of health and safety hazards, has social as well as individual value, the extra housing consumption caused by housing allowances might outweigh the cost of the housing standards enforcement that distinguishes housing allowances from unrestricted cash grants.

REFERENCES

Barnett, C. Lance, *Using Hedonic Indexes to Measure Housing Quantity,* The Rand Corporation, R-2450-HUD, October 1979.

Helbers, Lawrence, *Estimated Effects of Increased Income on Homeowner Repair Expenditures,* The Rand Corporation, N-1192-HUD, November 1979.

——, *Measuring Homeowner Needs for Housing Assistance,* The Rand Corporation, N-1094-HUD, October 1980.

Helbers, Lawrence, and James L. McDowell, *Determinants of Housing*

[15]Housing prices rise only slightly because supply increases quickly in response to the extra demand. See Ch. VI for details.

Repair and Improvement, The Rand Corporation, R-2777-HUD, forthcoming, 1982.

Hillestad, Carol E., and James L. McDowell, *Measuring Neighborhood Change Due to Housing Allowances,* The Rand Corporation, R-2776-HUD, forthcoming, 1982.

Mayo, Stephen K., Shirley Mansfield, David Warner, and Richard Zwetchkenbaum, *Housing Allowances and Other Rental Housing Assistance Programs—A Comparison Based on the Housing Allowance Demand Experiment*; Part 1: *Participation, Housing Consumption, Location, and Satisfaction*; Part 2: *Costs and Efficiency,* Abt Associates, Inc., Cambridge, Mass., 1980.

McDowell, James L., *Effects of the HAO Lead-Based Paint Hazard Standard,* The Rand Corporation, N-1306-1-HUD, June 1980.

——, *Housing Allowances and Housing Improvement: Early Findings,* The Rand Corporation, N-1198-HUD, September 1979.

Menchik, Mark D., *Residential Mobility of Housing Allowance Recipients,* The Rand Corporation, N-1144-HUD, October 1979.

Mulford, John E., *Income Elasticity of Housing Demand,* The Rand Corporation, R-2449-HUD, July 1979.

Mulford, John E., James L. McDowell, Lawrence Helbers, Michael P. Murray, and Orhan M. Yildiz, *Housing Consumption in a Housing Allowance Program,* The Rand Corporation, R-2779-HUD, forthcoming, 1982.

Mulford, John E., George D. Weiner, and James L. McDowell, *How Allowance Recipients Adjust Housing Consumption,* The Rand Corporation, N-1456-HUD, August 1980.

Noland, Charles W., *Assessing Hedonic Indexes for Housing,* The Rand Corporation, N-1305-HUD, May 1980.

Rydell, C. Peter, and John E. Mulford, *Consumption Increases Caused by Housing Assistance Programs,* The Rand Corporation, R-2809-HUD, April 1982.

Shanley, Michael G., and Charles M. Hotchkiss, *How Low-Income Renters Buy Homes,* The Rand Corporation, N-1208-HUD, August 1979.

Yildiz, Orhan M., and John Mulford, *Measuring Housing Quality: Evidence from St. Joseph County,* The Rand Corporation, N-1774-HUD, forthcoming, 1982.

VI. MARKET EFFECTS

The primary purpose of the Supply Experiment was to learn how a full-scale housing allowance program would affect local housing markets. This chapter summarizes what we learned about the program's effect on housing prices, neighborhood conditions, and the policies of market intermediaries (such as mortgage lenders) and indirect suppliers (such as repair contractors). We conclude that all three market effects were negligibly small, and we judge that a full-scale national program of similar design would also only slightly affect housing markets. With minor qualifications, only participants and their dwellings are affected by the program.

Before the experiment, many people thought differently. There was general agreement that disbursing housing allowances would increase low-income families' purchasing power and that the program's housing standards would focus their increased spending on housing. Because the allowances would be portable, the increased demand for housing services would not necessarily be confined to participants' preenrollment dwellings or neighborhoods, but might spill over into other parts of the housing market. Whether participants were in fact able to move or change tenure would depend partly on the policies of market intermediaries such as rental agents, real-estate brokers, and mortgage lenders. Regardless of whether they moved, participants' attempts to upgrade their dwellings would require the services of home improvement contractors and perhaps lending institutions. However, observers disagreed among themselves about the most probable market responses to such demand pressures and how those responses would vary with market structure and initial market conditions (Barnett and Lowry, 1979, Sec. I).

The optimistic scenario was that to avoid losing tenants landlords would respond promptly to renter participants' demands for repairs and improvements. Homeowner participants would bring their dwellings up to standard by an efficient combination of do-it-yourself and contracted repairs. In neighborhoods where recipients were concentrated, the visible improvements to their dwellings would motivate others, not in the program, to improve their own homes. Black residents of segregated neighborhoods might choose to stay and participate in neighborhood improvement; but those who chose otherwise could, with the aid of their allowances, afford housing in white neighborhoods. Dilapidated dwellings would become hard to rent, so would either be withdrawn from the market or rehabilitated to compete for allowance recipients' rents. The steady income provided by allowances would enable some low-income renters to qualify for mortgage credit and become homeowners. Housing conditions would improve generally, low-income families would have more housing choices, deteriorating neighborhoods would improve, and all would be accomplished without significant price increases.

The pessimistic scenario stressed other possibilities, in particular, the prospect of initial market disturbances and neighborhood destabilization. The most widely voiced concern echoed that of the Kaiser Committee, quoted in Ch. I: that in a tight housing market, program-induced demand would drive up the price of housing services not just for participants but for others as well. One analysis, based on a computer simulation of the program, reached the opposite conclusion: Price increases would be greater in a loose than in a tight market (Vanski and Ozanne, 1978).

Others were concerned that program-induced demand would concentrate in a few high-enrollment neighborhoods, driving up housing prices there even though the rest of the market was unaffected. A contrary, yet also pessimistic, view was that participants in such neighborhoods would use their allowances to find better housing elsewhere, causing prices to fall precipitously in the depopulated neighborhoods; in the neighborhoods to which participants moved, prices would rise and so might social tensions.

The policies of market intermediaries could affect such outcomes. Racial steering by real-estate brokers or redlining by mortgage lenders might restrict the alternatives available to program participants. Whether or not lenders viewed the allowance as a reliable source of income would affect the ability of renter participants to buy homes. Experience in earlier federal programs led some to predict that participants trying to improve their homes would need protection against unscrupulous contractors and lenders.

Five years of program operations in two metropolitan housing markets provide conclusive evidence that both optimists and pessimists greatly overestimated the market stimulus that would result from an open-enrollment program. Although about a fifth of all households in each site were eligible for assistance, only about 8 percent were enrolled at any given time and only about 7 percent were actually receiving payments. Even in neighborhoods where enrollees were concentrated (e.g., central South Bend), allowance payments added less than 1 percent to neighborhood income. Moreover, only a fraction of the added income was spent for housing. In Brown County's rental market, where over a fifth of all renters were enrolled, increased spending by participants added less than 2 percent to total rent expenditures. Although thousands of dwellings in each site were repaired, program-related repair expenditures added less than 3 percent to preprogram residential repair outlays in each community.

Although one could devise a housing program that would yield a greater market stimulus, it would not resemble housing allowances as to target population (low-income households) or housing improvement goals (decent, safe, and sanitary dwellings). As shown in Ch. IV, enrollment in the allowance program is self-limiting because of the inverse relationship between benefits and income. As shown in Ch. V, the program's housing standards could be met by most participants without much increasing expenditures, and expensive repair requirements discouraged participation; requirements aside, few voluntarily spent more than a fifth of their allowances for additional housing consumption. We conclude that a full-scale national program of housing allowances would provide a market stimulus comparable to that of the experimental program.

Given the modest demand stimulus provided by the allowance program, it is not surprising that market effects were mild, but it is worth noting that the housing market responded more efficiently to the program than many observers expected. For example, although renter participants increased their consumption of housing services by about 8 percent on the average, the price of those services increased by about 2 percent for allowance recipients and not at all for others. The increased demand was met initially by improving existing dwellings and redistributing vacancies, and subsequently by modest changes in the housing inventory.

Other market effects were similarly mild. Although thousands of recipients moved in each site, their moves were too diffuse both as to origins and destinations to measurably alter the composition of neighborhood populations or to cause new social tensions. Although thousands of dwellings were repaired because of the program, we found no evidence of strain on either the resources or ethics of the home repair industry. Although commercial banks and thrift institutions were conspicuously uninterested in mortgage loans on low-valued properties, several hundred low-income renters in the program nonetheless found lenders willing to finance home purchases for them.

When we compare the characteristics of the experimental sites with those of a national sample of metropolitan housing markets, we do not find any persuasive reason to suppose that the experimental outcomes are aberrant. We conclude that the effects of a national housing allowance program would be limited to participants and their dwellings; the broader community would be virtually unaffected for good or ill. Although that outcome is less than the optimists hoped for, it is far better than the pessimists feared. In any case, it does simplify the assessment of allowances as an instrument of federal policy to know that spillover effects are negligible.

In the following pages, we summarize the evidence in support of these conclusions. The first topic, price effects, is treated at greatest length because it has been the persistent focus of policy concern and theoretical speculation. We first present our estimates of rent increases in each site during the first three program years and apportion the total increase between "cost-push" and "demand-pull," the former reflecting general price inflation and the latter including possible program effects. To explain the observed outcome, we model the demand "shock" caused by the program and the supply "response" to it; and from the model we estimate the probable time paths for program-induced price increases. The observed and modeled outcomes do not match perfectly, but they are close enough to yield the same messages for housing policy.

The analysis just described applies only to the market for rental housing in each site. Although about half of all program participants were homeowners, these homeowners were housing suppliers as well as demanders; no one has seriously suggested that their attempts to increase their housing consumption by repairing or improving their homes would significantly affect the market *price* of homeowner housing services, although those who substantially improved their dwellings would thereby increase the market *values* of their properties. Because very few homeowners in the program moved and fewer changed tenure, their program-induced housing behavior was virtually insulated from the general market.

In the subsequent discussions of neighborhood effects and the policies of the various market intermediaries and indirect suppliers, both renters and homeowners are considered. Neighborhood effects could result from housing improvement actions of either renter or owner participants, though only the renters were likely to move. Some market intermediaries and suppliers deal only with renters and their landlords, some only with owners or prospective owners, and some with both tenure groups.

The chapter ends by comparing the two experimental sites with a national array of metropolitan housing markets surveyed by the Bureau of the Census during the experimental period. Those comparisons are intended to help the reader judge the relevance of the experimental findings to a national allowance program. Although no two experimental sites could statistically represent all metropolitan housing markets, we have formally tested the generality of the experimental outcomes by applying the market model described above to a national sample of metropolitan housing markets; and have less formally considered whether peculiarities of the experimental sites might have been important in shaping aberrant outcomes.

PRICE EFFECTS IN THE RENTAL MARKET

To learn how the allowance program affected the price of rental housing services in each site, we measured rent changes within a marketwide panel of rental properties during the first three program years—the period of rapid enrollment growth. We also analyzed landlords' revenue and expense accounts for the same years.

Although rents rose rapidly in both sites, the rent-change data, examined both marketwide and for special groups of dwellings, shows no evidence of *marketwide* increases that could reasonably be attributed to the program; participants, however, apparently paid a small premium upon entering the program. The landlord accounts imply that the observed marketwide rent increases were driven by the rising costs of supplying housing services; their expenses rose faster than their revenues, the opposite of what one would expect had the observed rent increases been driven by excess demand for housing.

The direct evidence described above establishes that no *major* price disturbance was caused by the introduction of the program in either Brown County's tight housing market or St. Joseph County's loose market, but does not rule out *small* program-induced effects, which would be hard to distinguish against a statistically "noisy" background. To estimate those effects, we modeled market prices in each site: how the allowance program affected the demand for rental housing, how landlords responded to demand signals, and how prices changed consequently. Given the initial market conditions in each site and the characteristics of its allowance program, the model predicts virtually no effect on the marketwide price of rental housing services and only a small and temporary effect on price within the sector of the market patronized by program participants.

Rent Changes during the First Three Program Years

The four annual surveys of households in each site obtained information on the rents paid by the occupants of a marketwide sample of about 2,300 dwellings; the surveys span roughly the first three years of program operations.[1] We linked records for individual dwellings whose occupants responded in two or more annual surveys, and calculated the annualized percentage change in rent for each pair of linked records. Because few dwellings are physically altered each

[1]Taking into account nonresponse and vacancies, we obtained rent information each year for about 1,800 dwellings in Brown County and 1,500 in St. Joseph County. See Appendix B, Fig. B.1, for a comparative chronology of the survey fieldwork and the allowance program in each site.

year, the average percentage change in rent should approximate the average percentage change in the price paid per unit of housing service.[2]

Table 6.1 presents the principal findings. The upper panel reports average annual changes in gross rent, which measures the tenant's total housing cost, including fuel and utilities for which he pays directly. The lower panel reports similarly on contract rent, the amount that a tenant agrees to pay his landlord. Annualized changes are reported for three periods. Period 1 begins about six months before the allowance program started enrolling renters and ends late in the first program year. Period 2 is exactly one year, during which the program was still growing rapidly. Period 3 takes the program to its year 3 plateau of enrollment. The calendar dates associated with each period differ in the two sites, lagging by about a year in St. Joseph County.

Throughout all three periods, rent increases were larger in Brown County's tight market than in St. Joseph County's loose market (see Ch. II, Table 2.6, for evidence on initial market conditions). In both sites, gross rent increased more rapidly than contract rent, indicating that tenants' fuel and utility bills were rising faster than their payments to landlords.[3]

Since the allowance program did not affect fuel prices, it is perhaps most instructive to focus on the contract rent increases. They averaged about 5.6 percent annually in Brown County and 4.4 percent in St. Joseph County, but in both counties the rate of increase rose over time.

We expected rents to rise during the experimental period because of general price inflation that would affect both tenants' incomes and landlords' costs. Nationally, contract rents rose by about 5.8 percent annually during the period covered by our experimental data; in the north-central region, where the experimental sites are located, the annual rate of increase was 5.2 percent.[4] Thus, external comparisons do not signal any unusual rent increase in the experimental sites.

---

[2]The rent-change analysis for St. Joseph County is documented in Lindsay and Lowry, 1980. An exactly parallel analysis for Brown County was not published, but its results are summarized in Rydell, Neels, and Barnett, 1982, Sec. II. The latter report also examines the biases in our rent-change data when they are used to estimate price changes.

[3]In Brown County, tenants paid two-thirds of the total fuel bill; in St. Joseph County, they paid three-fifths. Fuel and utilities not included in contract rent amounted to about 18 percent of gross rent in each county (Neels, 1982b). The largest jump in fuel prices occurred in the fall of 1973, but its full effect was not felt until the next calendar year.

[4]These figures are based on the Bureau of Labor Statistics' index of residential rent for 1974 through mid-1978. The Bureau does not index gross rent, but we estimate (Lowry, 1982) that gross rents increased nationally during this period at an annual rate

Table 6.1

MARKETWIDE RENT CHANGES DURING THE FIRST THREE PROGRAM YEARS, BY SITE

Period[a]	Brown County		St. Joseph County	
	Average Annual Change (%)	Standard Error of Estimate	Average Annual Change (%)	Standard Error of Estimate
Gross Rent				
Period 1	5.98	.39	4.61	.66
Period 2	9.98	.39	7.73	.60
Period 3	7.47	.35	5.26	.47
All periods	7.70	.20	5.71	.27
Contract Rent				
Period 1	5.34	.38	3.11	.60
Period 2	5.53	.37	4.32	.54
Period 3	5.89	.34	5.44	.44
All periods	5.63	.19	4.41	.24

SOURCE: Estimated by HASE staff from linked records of the annual surveys of households in each site. For additional detail on St. Joseph County, see Lindsay and Lowry, 1980, Tables 3.1 and 3.2. Parallel tables for Brown County are available but unpublished.

NOTE: Gross rent consists of a tenant's payment to his landlord (contract rent) plus the cost of fuel and utilities for which the tenant paid directly.

[a]In Brown County, where program enrollment began in June 1974: Period 1 = December 1973-December 1974; Period 2 = January 1975-December 1975; Period 3 = January 1976-July 1977. In St. Joseph County, where program enrollment began in April 1975: Period 1 = November 1974-December 1975; Period 2 = January 1976-December 1976; Period 3 = January 1977-July 1978.

Absent the allowance program, of course, rents might have risen even less than they did with the program because of local market conditions that prevented landlords from passing on cost increases resulting from general price inflation. Even with the program, the data suggest that St. Joseph County's loose market restrained rent increases. We therefore looked *within* each housing market for evidence of program effects.

We would expect the largest program effects to occur among dwellings currently occupied by program participants. The landlords of those dwellings knew that their tenants received housing allowances and in many cases had to make repairs so that the dwelling would be acceptable to the HAO. They were also asked to sign one-year leases, a practice not common for low-rent housing in either site. Of course, a tenant could move (without losing his allowance entitlement) if his rent was increased excessively, so the landlord's leverage was limited.

Direct evidence from HAO records shows that few landlords chose to raise rents when their tenants entered the allowance program. The HAOs recorded the rents paid by applicants at the time of their enrollment interviews and again about two months later when their dwellings had been evaluated, repaired if need be, and certified for occupancy. Table 6.2 shows that the rents entered on the lease agreements averaged less than 2 percent more than the preenrollment rents of tenants who did not move. The increase was even smaller among dwellings that did not need repairs in order to meet program standards.

Our marketwide survey data enable us to identify dwellings occupied by program participants and compare their annual gross rent increases with those for all other dwellings (Table 6.3).[5] We find that during Period 1, participants' rents rose by about 3 percent more per year than nonparticipants' rents, but the difference subsequently diminished.

The interpretation of Table 6.3 carries two important qualifications. First, the participation effect it shows includes the effect of other characteristics of participants' housing that distinguish it (on average) from nonparticipants' housing. In St. Joseph County, for example, we found that rents rose most for very small and very large dwellings, least for those of intermediate size; that low rents in-

of 7.1 percent, as compared with 7.7 percent in Brown County and 5.7 percent in St. Joseph County. All the rent-increase figures cited above, including those in Table 6.1, understate price changes by about 0.7 percentage points annually because of age-related deterioration in the dwelling samples used to measure rent changes.

[5]Because the division of responsibility for fuel and utility payments differs in various sectors of the market, this comparison is better made in terms of gross rather than contract rent.

Table 6.2

RENT CHANGES FOR DWELLINGS WHOSE OCCUPANTS ENROLLED IN THE ALLOWANCE PROGRAM, BY SITE

Repair Status	Average Monthly Gross Rent ($)		Average Increase (%)
	Enrollment Interview	Certification for Payments	
Brown County			
No repair required	164	167	1.6
Repair required	151	155	2.5
All cases	159	162	1.9
St. Joseph County			
No repair required	157	158	.7
Repair required	152	155	1.7
All cases	155	156	1.2

SOURCE: Tabulated by HASE staff from HAO records through program year 3 in each site.

NOTE: Entries are for renter enrollees who did not move when they entered the program. They reported their contract rents when they enrolled and again when their dwellings were certified for occupancy; the HAO estimated the value of tenant-paid utilities in each case from standard tables. The average interval between the enrollment interview and first certification was 1.6 months in Brown County and 2.1 months in St. Joseph County.

creased faster than high rents; and that rents for single-family dwellings increased faster than rents for multiple dwellings. From regression analysis controlling on dwelling characteristics, we estimate that the pure participation effect (covering all three periods) was 1.4 percent in Brown County and 2.1 percent in St. Joseph County, as compared with the estimates shown in Table 6.3 (2.5 and 2.0 percent for the counties, respectively).

The other and more important qualification is that the participation effect does not appear to be cumulative. Diagnostics on the data indicate fairly clearly that participants' extra rent increases occur when or shortly after they enter the program or move into a dwelling not

Table 6.3

RENT CHANGES FOR PARTICIPANTS' AND NONPARTICIPANTS' DWELLINGS DURING THE FIRST THREE PROGRAM YEARS, BY SITE

Period[a]	Average Annual Change (%) in Gross Rent			
	Participants' Dwellings	Nonparticipants' Dwellings	Difference	
			Amount	Standard Error
Brown County				
Period 1	8.8	5.6	3.2	1.7
Period 2	12.2	9.6	2.6	1.3
Period 3	9.2	7.2	2.0	1.1
All periods	9.9	7.4	2.5	.8
St. Joseph County				
Period 1	7.4	4.3	3.1	2.5
Period 2	9.5	7.4	2.1	2.1
Period 3	6.3	5.3	1.0	1.5
All periods	7.5	5.5	2.0	.9

SOURCE: Estimated by HASE staff from linked records of the annual surveys of households in each site. For additional detail on St. Joseph County, see Lindsay and Lowry, 1980, Tables 4.1 and 4.2. Parallel tables for Brown County are available but unpublished.

NOTE: Entries in the first column are estimates of average rent changes for dwellings occupied by participants during at least part of the observation interval. Entries in the second column are for dwellings not occupied bv participants during the interval of observation. A given dwelling could appear in both columns but for different periods. Annual differences between participants' and nonparticipants' rent increases are not cumulative; see text for explanation.

[a]Periods correspond roughly to program years; calendar intervals differ by site.

previously occupied by a participant. As continuing tenants, their subsequent rent increases are only slightly if at all affected by their status as participants. The decline over time in the participation effect is thus mostly attributable to the fact that later rent-change observations pertain to relatively fewer newly participating tenants and relatively more continuing participants.

We analyzed the rent-change data in many different ways, looking for evidence of program effects in various sectors of the market. Although quantitative results varied with specification of the models, all yielded essentially the same message: Program effects were small, and limited to the dwellings occupied by participants.

Trends in Operating Income and Expense

The four annual surveys of landlords in each site obtained information on the rental income and operating expenses of each sampled property during the preceding calendar year; the data cover 1973-76 for Brown County and 1974-77 for St. Joseph County. From these data, we constructed annual marketwide operating statements for rental properties that indicate their average profitability.[6] Trends in income, expenses, and profits help us assess the causes of the rent increases discussed above.

We find that operating expenses rose much faster than rents in Brown County and slightly faster in St. Joseph County. Although net operating income, measured in current dollars, increased in both counties, its purchasing power declined in Brown County and rose only slightly in St. Joseph County. The data strongly imply that rent increases in both counties reflect cost-push rather than demand-pull inflation, exacerbated in Brown County by a softening market and moderated in St. Joseph County by improved occupancy rates as surplus rental dwellings were removed from the market.

Table 6.4 compares first- and fourth-year operating statements in each site. In Brown County, the average gross rent per dwelling rose by about 28 percent, almost exactly the rate of increase in the national consumer price index for the same interval.[7] However,

---

[6]Although the annual surveys were addressed to a panel of about 1,300 rental properties, not all landlords responded fully each year. The marketwide accounts for the first year are based on 928 properties in Brown County and 904 in St. Joseph County; those for the fourth year are based on 412 and 361 properties in the two counties, respectively. Although we can link annual records for individual properties, the analysis that follows is based on comparison of marketwide average values. See Neels, 1982b, for details on the construction of the accounts, sample weighting, and accounts for selected submarkets. The accounts include data from tenants as to their labor and cash expenses in connection with property maintenance and operation.

[7]The equivalent average annual increase in gross rent is 8.7 percent, somewhat higher than the Brown County estimate of 7.7 percent derived from linked household records (Table 6.1). However, the two estimates are not comparable, for several reasons. First, they pertain to overlapping but different periods. Second, the linked household records do not, but the landlord accounts do, reflect inventory changes between baseline and wave 4. Third, the entries in Table 6.1 are averages in which individual dwellings are equally weighted, whereas the entries in Table 6.4 are averages in which individual properties are equally weighted.

The same qualifications apply to estimates of gross-rent change for St. Joseph County, discussed below.

Table 6.4

TRENDS IN RENTAL PROPERTY OPERATING EXPENSE AND INCOME DURING THE FIRST THREE PROGRAM YEARS, BY SITE

Item	Annual Amount ($) per Dwelling: Year 1[a]	Annual Amount ($) per Dwelling: Year 4[b]	Ratio (Year 4: Year 1)	Price Index (Year 1 = 1.000)	Real Change (%)
Brown County					
Operating expense[c]	1,063	1,482	1.394	1.348	3.4
Vacancy loss and related items[d]	121	142	1.174	1.285	- 8.6
Net operating income[e]	576	638	1.108	1.281	-13.5
Gross rent[f]	1,760	2,262	1.285	1.281	.3
St. Joseph County					
Operating expense[c]	1,323	1,696	1.282	1.332	- 3.8
Vacancy loss and related items[d]	216	244	1.130	1.265	-10.6
Net operating income[e]	228	296	1.298	1.229	5.6
Gross rent[f]	1,767	2,236	1.265	1.229	2.9

SOURCE: Estimated by HASE staff from records of the surveys of rental properties in each site and from price indexes constructed by HASE staff for each site. See Neels, 1982a and 1982b, for details of property accounts; and Noland, 1981 and 1982, for details of price indexes.

NOTE: Entries are averages for regular rental properties (excluding farms, mobile-home parks, rooming houses, and properties with commercial space) operating in each site for the full calendar year preceding the baseline and wave 4 surveys respectively. To make the accounts comparable between properties, all expenses are included whether paid directly by the tenant or included in contract rent. The entries were formed by computing average values per dwelling on each sampled property, then weighting the properties to reflect their sampling probabilities.

[a]For Brown County, 1973; for St. Joseph County, 1974.

[b]For Brown County, 1976; for St. Joseph County, 1977.

[c]Includes fuel and utilities, maintenance, janitorial service, management, property tax, and insurance. Excludes capital improvements.

[d]Vacancy rent-loss, including an allowance for utilities that would have been paid by the tenant; uncollectable rent; and the rental value of appliances supplied by the tenant. The corresponding price index is the rate of increase in gross rent.

[e]Income available to the landlord for debt service and equity return; the corresponding price index is the national consumer price index.

[f]Gross rent, assuming 100-percent occupancy; the corresponding price index is the national consumer price index.

operating expense rose by 39 percent and vacancy loss and related items increased by 17 percent, so that net operating income rose by only 11 percent. When converted to constant dollars, the 11-percent increase in operating income becomes a 14-percent decrease in real income from the property.

The trend for St. Joseph County's rental properties is somewhat different. Gross rent increased slightly faster than the consumer price index; neither operating expense nor vacancy loss increased as rapidly as in Brown County.[8] Consequently, net operating income increased by nearly a third in current dollars, or by about 6 percent in constant dollars.

At first glance, it is surprising to see that the real net income from rental properties declined in Brown County's tight market but rose in St. Joseph County's loose market. Although our estimates from sample data are imprecise, it appears that Brown County's tight market was loosening and St. Joseph County's loose market was tightening during the years in question.[9] Rydell, Neels, and Barnett, 1982, Appendix C, estimate that the supply of rental housing services increased by nearly 6 percent in Brown County and decreased by 3 percent in St. Joseph County. Although these changes were at least partly offset by population growth (Brown County) and decline (St. Joseph County), the rent-loss data cited in note 8 do imply opposite shifts in the counties' market conditions.

The net operating income from a rental property is divided between debt service and return to the landlords' equity.[10] Table 6.5 subtracts out the mortgage interest payments[11] to obtain an estimate of current

---

[8]Because the Brown County data cover 1973-76, the change in operating expense includes the full effect of the late-1973 jump in fuel prices. The data for St. Joseph County cover 1974-77, so reflect only the subsequent smaller fuel-price increases. "Vacancy loss and related items" includes some elements (see Table 6.4, note *d*) not usually found in rental property financial statements. Those items were added to our accounts to improve the comparability of gross rents across properties with different vacancy experience and different landlord policies concerning appliances.

We estimate that the amount of current-dollar gross rent lost because of vacancies increased by 26 percent in Brown County, 1973-76; and did not change significantly in St. Joseph County, 1974-77. However, the St. Joseph County average for 1977 (about $175) was twice the Brown County average ($84) for 1976.

[9]An additional factor in Brown County was the weather. If the winter of 1976 had been as mild as that of 1973, we estimate that fuel expenses in 1976 would have been lower by 12 percent, and net operating income would have been higher by 3 percent (based on unpublished calculations by K. Neels).

[10]The value of the landlord's labor, for both management and maintenance, is accounted for as operating expenses, so is not included in net operating income. For resident landlords, the rental value of their dwellings is counted as operating income.

[11]Interest *rates* rose in both counties during the years covered by the data, but mortgage interest *payments* did not increase in St. Joseph County between 1974 and 1977 because landlords were rapidly retiring mortgage debt (see the middle panel of the table). In neither county were investors highly leveraged.

Table 6.5

Trends in Rental Property Return on Equity during the First Three Program Years, by Site

Item	Brown County 1973	Brown County 1976	St. Joseph County 1974	St. Joseph County 1977
Annual Amount ($) per Dwelling				
Current Equity Income				
Net operating income	576	638	228	296
Less: Mortgage interest payments	341	453	143	147
Equals: Current equity income	235	185	85	149
Total Equity Income				
Current equity income	235	185	85	149
Plus: Property value appreciation	919	1,129	512	488
Less: Capital additions	-69	-36	-67	-28
Equals: Total equity income	1,085	1,278	530	609
Midyear Amount ($) per Dwelling				
Landlord's Equity				
Property value[a]	12,220	15,822	8,888	10,680
Less: Outstanding mortgage debt	-3,790	-3,846	-1,831	-1,248
Equals: Landlord's equity	8,430	11,976	7,057	9,432
Annual Rate of Return (%)				
Current equity return[b]	2.8	1.5	1.2	1.6
Total equity return[c]	12.9	10.7	7.5	6.5

SOURCE: Tabulated by HASE staff from records of the surveys of rental properties in each site. For additional detail, see Neels, 1982a and 1982b.

NOTE: See Table 6.4 for general qualifications.

[a] Average of estimates made by three alternative methods. Excludes value of tenant-owned appliances.

[b] Current equity income divided by landlord's equity.

[c] Total equity income divided by landlord's equity.

equity income (before taxes). The table also shows our estimate of the market value per dwelling on the average property, and also the annual rate of appreciation of market value. These data are used in the bottom panel of the table to calculate investment performance measures (pretax rates of return) for the average property in each county.

In both sites and both years, the current equity return was trivial; in neither Brown nor St. Joseph County were landlords earning enough from current operations to warrant holding the average property as an investment. However, value appreciation brought the total equity return in Brown County to nearly 13 percent in 1973. In St. Joseph County, current return was smaller and property values were rising less rapidly; total equity return was only about 7.5 percent in 1974. In both sites, the total rate of return on equity declined over the period covered by our data.

If the rent increases in either site were caused by excess demand for housing services (whether created by the allowance program or other factors), we would expect to find rents rising faster than costs, and net operating incomes increasing faster than rents. The opposite occurred in Brown County; and in St. Joseph County, the rapid increase in net operating income from its very low level in 1973 was mostly due to higher occupancy rates; gross rents increased slightly less than operating costs. Although the allowance program may have contributed to landlords' revenues in both sites, they still were unable to pass on all operating cost increases to their tenants, much less pass on rising mortgage interest rates.

Why property values should continue to rise in the face of such miserable operating experience is an interesting question. It helps, however, to distinguish nominal from real increases. In Brown County, rental property values rose over the three-year period by 29.5 percent in current dollars, but by only 1.4 percent in constant dollars. In St. Joseph County, property values rose by 20.2 percent in current dollars, but fell by 2.7 percent in constant dollars. Thus, the real value of rental property changed very little in either site during those three years.

A Model of Program Effects

Although our data on rent changes by market sector show that program participants' rents increased only slightly more than nonparticipants' rents, and our data on rental property incomes and expenses show that landlords were not able to raise rents enough in either site to fully compensate for increases in their costs during the first three program years, the data do not tell us directly what would have happened in either market absent the program.

We need such a benchmark to derive a quantitative estimate of program effects. By taking the initial condition of each market as a benchmark and assuming that the only change in those conditions was in program-induced demand, we can model the ensuing market processes to derive estimates of program effects absent extraneous changes such as general price inflation or local population growth. Such a model is presented below.[12]

Briefly, we use program data to model the time-path of program-induced demand changes, and data mostly from the national Annual Housing Survey to model the time-path of suppliers' aggregate responses to market signals of excess demand. Then, we estimate the time-path of price changes that would be needed to continuously balance the shifting demand for housing services against the available supply. All changes (in demand, supply, and prices) are expressed relative to initial market conditions, and abstract entirely from the effects of national price inflation on incomes and housing prices.

Below, we explain the demand and supply components of the model; readers not interested in technical detail may prefer to skip to "The Time-Path of Short-Run Prices," especially Figs. 6.1 and 6.2, to learn what the model predicted for each site.

Program-Induced Demand Changes

The allowance program increased participants' demands for housing services in two ways: by setting minimum housing standards for them, and by augmenting their incomes by more than was needed to meet those standards. The analysis summarized in Ch. V indicates that renter recipients increased their housing consumption by about 8 percent (Table 5.2). About half that increase was due to housing standards, half to increased income (Table 5.13).

We used site-specific estimates of average consumption change per recipient and the average number of recipients during each program year to estimate the amount of program-induced demand. To model the consequences of that demand, it is important to know whether it was distributed randomly over the entire rental market, or was focused on a limited part of that market. We therefore divided the rental market into a *recipient submarket* and a *nonrecipient submarket* and modeled demand changes in each submarket as described below.

---

[12]The model is a simplified version of the more comprehensive market model presented in Rydell, Neels, and Barnett, 1982, Secs. III and IV.

The Recipient Submarket. We define the recipient submarket as the set of dwellings that recipients can afford and that either meet program standards as to quality or could inexpensively be brought up to standard. Because neither element of that definition is precise, we cannot precisely bound the recipient submarket. Generally, it would encompass the middle range of dwelling quality, excluding high-quality but high-rent dwellings and also excluding low-rent but dilapidated dwellings.

We estimated the size of the recipient submarket in each site from records of housing evaluations conducted by the HAOs. Such evaluations were conducted not only for dwellings already occupied by program participants but for dwellings they considered as possible residences. During the first five program years, 68 percent of all rental dwellings in Brown County and 51 percent in St. Joseph County were evaluated at least once.[13]

As estimates of submarket size, these figures reflect two offsetting biases. On the one hand, some dwellings that recipients could afford and that would meet program standards may never have been evaluated. On the other hand, some dwellings that were evaluated failed and were not repaired, possibly because repairing was too expensive. We judge that these biases roughly cancel each other; in any case, the recipient submarket clearly contained several times more rental dwellings than were currently occupied by recipients.[14]

The Nonrecipient Submarket. The remainder of the rental inventory in each site constitutes the nonrecipient submarket: 32 percent of all rental dwellings in Brown County and 49 percent in St. Joseph County.

The Incidence of Demand Shifts by Submarket. Among those allowance recipients who occupied standard housing when they enrolled, the program-induced demand increase averaged about 4 percent and resulted entirely from the income effect. For those whose enrollment dwellings were substandard but were repaired, the demand increase was about 9 percent, partly because of increased income but mostly because of the program's housing standards. Others

[13]The HAOs periodically evaluated each participant's dwelling to determine whether it met program standards for space, facilities, and condition. When a participant contemplated moving, he might request evaluations of several prospective dwellings before choosing one. We sorted the evaluation reports by address to determine the number of *different* dwellings ever evaluated during the first five program years.

[14]At peak, about 17 percent of the recipient submarket's dwellings were occupied by current recipients in Brown County, and about 22 percent were so occupied in St. Joseph County. The remainder, though once evaluated by the HAOs, were currently occupied by nonrecipients, including both former recipients and others who were never enrolled or never eligible to enroll.

who moved from standard dwellings after enrolling also increased their consumption by about 9 percent, choosing larger or better dwellings. All this increased demand originated and ended in the recipient submarket.

Those whose enrollment dwellings were irremediably substandard had to move in order to qualify for payments. Not only did they increase their housing consumption by 21 percent, they also transferred their augmented demand from the nonrecipient to the recipient submarket. Thus, they caused demand to increase in the recipient submarket and decrease in the nonrecipient submarket.

A limitation of the model is that it does not provide for a reverse flow of nonrecipient demand from the recipient to the nonrecipient submarket when relative prices change in the two submarkets. For this reason, the model tends to overstate price changes in both submarkets.

The Time-Path of Demand Change. We have estimated each component of the demand shift for each submarket and for the rental market as a whole. The estimates are summarized in Table 6.6 for both Brown and St. Joseph counties. Because the cumulative demand shift increased as participation grew, we show estimates for each of the first five program years, based on actual participation data; and a tenth-year estimate, based on our projected steady-state level of participation.

Taking into account both the annual numbers of allowance recipients and their initial submarket locations, we estimate that the demand for rental housing service grew in the recipient submarket by 4.4 percent during the first five program years in Brown County and 5.5 percent in St. Joseph County (upper panel of Table 6.6). Most of that growth was due to the minority of recipients who shifted their housing demand from the nonrecipient to the recipient submarket because their enrollment dwellings were unacceptable and possibly unrepairable. The much larger number of recipients who did not change submarkets contributed only their modest program-induced demand increases to the recipient submarket total.

Demand in the nonrecipient submarket decreased as enrollees moved to the recipient submarket (middle panel of Table 6.6). The percentage decrease was greater in Brown County because the nonrecipient submarket there is relatively smaller than in St. Joseph County.

The lower panel of the table shows that the marketwide demand increases were negligible—about 1.2 percent—in each site. (The marketwide change is the weighted sum of the submarket changes, which have opposing signs.) Although the allowance programs at peak

Table 6.6

Estimated Demand Changes Caused by the Housing Allowance Programs in Recipient and Nonrecipient Submarkets, by Site

Program Year	Percentage Change[a] in Rental Housing Demand by Submarket Location of Enrollment Dwelling					
	Brown County			St. Joseph County		
	Recipient Submarket	Nonrecipient Submarket	Total Change	Recipient Submarket	Nonrecipient Submarket	Total Change
	Recipient Submarket					
1	.76	1.66	2.42	.97	1.96	2.93
2	1.12	2.44	3.55	1.43	2.90	4.34
3	1.29	2.80	4.09	1.66	3.35	5.01
4	1.36	2.97	4.34	1.76	3.57	5.33
5	1.40	3.05	4.45	1.81	3.68	5.49
.	.	.	.	.	.	.
10	1.43	3.12	4.55	1.86	3.77	5.63
	Nonrecipient Submarket					
1	--	-3.17	-3.17	--	-1.82	-1.82
2	--	-4.65	-4.65	--	-2.70	-2.70
3	--	-5.35	-5.35	--	-3.12	-3.12
4	--	-5.67	-5.67	--	-3.32	-3.32
5	--	-5.83	-5.83	--	-3.42	-3.42
.	.	.	.	.	.	.
10	--	-5.96	-5.96	--	-3.50	-3.50
	Entire Market					
1	.52	.11	.63	.49	.11	.60
2	.76	.17	.93	.73	.16	.89
3	.87	.19	1.07	.84	.18	1.03
4	.93	.21	1.13	.90	.19	1.09
5	.95	.21	1.16	.93	.20	1.13
.	.	.	.	.	.	.
10	.97	.22	1.19	.95	.21	1.15

SOURCE: Estimated by HASE staff from the demand model described in the text, using participation data from HAO records through year 5. For additional details, see Rydell, Neels, and Barnett, 1982.

NOTE: Entries reflect only demand changes for renters who enroll and qualify for payments. Those who move from substandard to standard dwellings shift their housing demand from the nonrecipient to the recipient submarket. Others increase their demands within the recipient submarket. The three panels of the table describe the effects of these actions on aggregate demand within the indicated market sectors. The recipient submarket constitutes 68 percent of all rental dwellings in Brown County and 51 percent in St. Joseph County.

[a] Change relative to preprogram demand; entries are cumulative.

served about 15 percent of all renters in each site, those in the program increased their housing consumption by only 8 percent on average—not enough to substantially change marketwide totals.

Supply Response

Our model of supply response assumes that when the aggregate demand for housing service in a market or submarket increases, the price per unit of that service is bid up enough to reduce the quantity demanded and so clear the market during the short run, while the supply is fixed. However, landlords soon notice such price increases and find it profitable to expand the occupied supply in one of the three ways described below. As the supply expands, prices are bid downward and consumption increases until the market again clears.

Of course, if demand changes continuously, the supply response may never quite catch up. In our model, the demand shift approaches a limit as the allowance program stops growing, and the market does approach a new equilibrium of demand and supply at a price per unit of housing service that is close to the preprogram price.[15] The sizes of the intervening short-run price increases depend on the promptness of supply response; if there were no response over the first five program years, the cumulative demand change (4.4 to 5.5 percent in our sites) would cause larger short-run price increases than if supply were increased each year.

Response Modes. We distinguish three ways in which the supply of rental housing services could respond to the demand shifts described above. First, some existing rental dwellings could be repaired or improved so as to increase the services they provide; or allowed to deteriorate, with the opposite effect. Second, the occupancy rate within the existing rental inventory could rise or fall. Third, the inventory itself could change, by new construction, demolition, or conversion, including shifting dwellings between the rental and ownership markets.

Because the response lags will differ for each of the three supply response modes, we have estimated the time-path of each response mode separately and summed them. Below, we briefly explain how the components were estimated.

Repairs and Improvements. Our estimate of the repair response has two components: required and voluntary repairs. We have reliable

[15]Given the relatively small size of the demand shifts caused by the allowance program, there is no reason to expect a long-run increase in the average cost of supplying the additional housing services, so the long-run equilibrium price should not rise significantly.

data on the required repairs, but are only able to place upper and lower bounds on the voluntary repairs.

We know from program records how many rental dwellings were repaired each year after failing initial or annual housing evaluations. For all rental dwellings occupied by allowance recipients, the average annual deficiency repair bill was $33 per dwelling (see Ch. V, Table 5.5). However, even at maximum program size, only a fifth of the dwellings in the recipient submarket were currently occupied by recipients, so the total annual bill for required repairs in that submarket never exceeded about 0.5 percent of the preprogram value of housing services produced in that submarket. By definition, no required repairs were made in the nonrecipient submarket.

The data in Ch. V indicate that renter recipients increased their housing consumption by about 4 percentage points beyond the amount represented by required repairs. Some of that increase was accommodated by repairs and improvements that landlords voluntarily made to recipients' dwellings, but annual repair expenses for individual dwellings are so variable that we have been unable to demonstrate a significant difference in voluntary repair expenses between recipients' and nonrecipients' dwellings.[16] In fact, most of the increased consumption by program participants is associated with post-enrollment moves to better dwellings, so the voluntary repair effect, if it exists, might well have concentrated on dwellings not occupied by recipients, or even in dwellings outside the recipient submarket.[17]

Fortunately, our model of supply response can deal with this uncertainty about program-induced repairs. We estimated alternative outcomes assuming that (a) only required repairs were made because of the program, and (b) the landlords of recipients who did not move further improved their properties enough to add 4 percent to the flow of services from each recipient-occupied dwelling. In both cases, we assumed that there was no program-induced repair response in the nonrecipient submarket.

Stock Utilization. The general effect of the allowance program was to increase demand in the recipient submarket and decrease demand

---

[16]Estimates based on a special survey of the landlords of program participants indicate that they spent 8 to 11 percent more on voluntary repairs than did landlords generally (Helbers and McDowell, 1982, Table 2); however, the results are sensitive to both errors in the repair data and repair price indexes required to make the two data sources comparable. A regression analysis based on data from the general landlord survey yields point-estimates that indicate a similar participation effect, but the estimated effect is not statistically significant (ibid., Appendix A).

[17]When recipients increase their housing consumption by moving, they occupy dwellings that would otherwise be used by nonrecipients. To meet the continuing nonrecipients' demand for housing of that size and quality, landlords might voluntarily improve dwellings not occupied by recipients.

in the nonrecipient submarket. Specifically, about 10 percent of all renter enrollees moved from the nonrecipient to the recipient submarket. The immediate effect of such moves was to raise both the occupancy rate and the price of housing service in the recipient submarket and to lower both in the nonrecipient submarket.

We have used data from both the HASE surveys and the national Annual Housing Survey to estimate how occupancy rates and prices adjust to demand shifts in the short run, and find that the adjustment depends on initial market conditions (Rydell, 1980). The tighter the market, the smaller is the fraction of a given demand shift that is accommodated by changes in occupancy rates and the larger is the fraction that is absorbed by price changes.[18]

Applying our findings to HASE sites, we estimate that a 1-percent increase in submarket demand would cause the occupancy rate in that submarket to rise by 0.35 percent in Brown County and 0.61 percent in St. Joseph County. The effect is symmetrical for a demand decrease. (These estimates reflect initial marketwide occupancy rates of 96 percent in Brown County and 91 percent in St. Joseph County.) Those parameters were applied to program-induced moves from the nonrecipient to the recipient submarkets, to estimate the changes in stock utilization for each submarket; the price effects are discussed later in this chapter.

Stock Adjustment. The short-run repair and occupancy-rate adjustments discussed above are sufficient to moderate price changes in both the recipient and nonrecipient submarkets, but do not eliminate them. With uneven price changes in the two submarkets, landlords are encouraged to shift capital from the less profitable to the more profitable submarket; and with an aggregate (marketwide) increase in demand, to augment the total stock of rental housing.

However, demolishing redundant dwellings, building new ones, converting large homes to small apartments, and so on, take time. Various studies have shown that the rate of stock adjustment varies with the relative size of the gap to be filled. We combined time-series and cross-sectional data from the Annual Housing Survey to estimate the rate of change in the number of rental dwellings as a function of the rental occupancy rate, and found that stock adjustments (the net result of new construction, demolition, conversion, and tenure change) typically close 17 percent of the gap between the current and equilibrium occupancy rate each year (Rydell, Neels, and Barnett, 1982). At

[18]A *shift* in demand means that at every alternative price, consumers would be willing to purchase (more/less) of the commodity in question, e.g., because they are (more/less) numerous, or because their incomes are (higher/lower). The *amount* demanded depends on the price that clears the market.

that speed, more than 15 years would pass before stock adjustments alone could restore a market to equilibrium after a one-time demand shift.[19]

The Time-Path of Supply Response. Using the parameters described above, we have estimated each component of the supply response for each submarket and for the market as a whole. The estimates are summarized in Table 6.7 for Brown County and Table 6.8 for St. Joseph County. Again, we detail annual values for the first five program years and for year 10. The first four columns of the table report outcomes under the assumption that the program induced only required, not voluntary repairs; the fifth column shows how the aggregate supply response differs if we assume that some voluntary repairs were program-induced.

The response pattern is similar in the two counties. In the recipient submarket, the repair response is small but grows as the program grows; the occupancy rate rises during the first three program years, but then declines because the inventory is by then growing faster than program-induced demand. At the end of five years, supply response has closed two-thirds of the gap between supply and demand in Brown County's tight market, and four-fifths in St. Joseph County's loose market.

The marketwide changes in supply are negligible, like the corresponding changes in demand. The increased supply of rental housing in the recipient submarket is mostly offset by a decreased supply in the nonrecipient market.

In both submarkets, the supply responses set in motion by the allowance program continue to operate for at least ten years, by which time the supply-demand gaps are all nearly closed at occupancy rates that are within one percentage point of their initial values in each submarket.

The final column of each table shows that the outcomes are not much affected by our alternative assumptions about voluntary repairs; the total supply response in the recipient submarket increases by at most a third of one percentage point (Brown County, year 5) if we allow for voluntary repairs to accommodate recipients' voluntary increased housing consumption, rather than depending on occupancy and inventory changes.

---

[19]More precisely, 95 percent of the initial gap would be closed in 15 years. Our estimate of the annual rate of stock adjustment is about half the rate (32 percent) estimated by Muth in 1960 from aggregate national data. We cannot presently account for the difference; but substituting Muth's parameter for our own would only reduce the range of price fluctuations yielded by the model.

Table 6.7

Estimated Supply Response to the Demand Changes Caused by the Housing Allowance Program in Brown County

Program Year	Percentage Change[a] in Rental Housing Supply				
	Response Mode, Assuming No Voluntary Repair[b]				Total Change, Assuming Some Voluntary Repair[c]
	Required Repair	Occupancy Change	Inventory Change	Total Change	
	Recipient Submarket				
1	.24	.69	.19	1.12	1.39
2	.35	.91	.57	1.83	2.19
3	.41	.93	1.00	2.33	2.69
4	.43	.86	1.41	2.71	3.04
5	.44	.77	1.79	3.00	3.30
.	.	.	.	.	.
10	.45	.36	3.05	3.87	4.01
	Nonrecipient Submarket				
1	--	-1.02	- .27	-1.29	-1.29
2	--	-1.35	- .82	-2.18	-2.18
3	--	-1.38	-1.45	-2.83	-2.83
4	--	-1.28	-2.05	-3.33	-3.33
5	--	-1.14	-2.60	-3.74	-3.74
.	.	.	.	.	.
10	--	- .53	-4.44	-4.97	-4.97
	Entire Market				
1	.16	.14	.04	.35	.53
2	.24	.19	.12	.55	.79
3	.28	.19	.21	.68	.93
4	.29	.18	.30	.77	1.00
5	.30	.16	.38	.85	1.05
.	.	.	.	.	.
10	.31	.08	.66	1.04	1.14

SOURCE: Estimated by HASE staff from the supply response model described in the text, using demand estimates from Table 6.6. For additonal details, see Rydell, Neels, and Barnett, 1982.

NOTE: Entries refer only to the rental market of Brown County, of which the recipient submarket constitutes 68 percent. The model assumes no changes in market conditions except those caused by the allowance program.

[a] Change relative to preprogram supply; entries are cumulative.

[b] All voluntary increases in recipients' housing consumption are accomplished by moving. Landlords improve dwellings only as required to meet program standards.

[c] All voluntary increases in recipients' housing consumption are accommodated directly or indirectly by voluntary repairs.

Table 6.8

Estimated Supply Response to the Demand Changes Caused by the Housing Allowance Program in St. Joseph County

Program Year	Percentage Change[a] in Rental Housing Supply				
	Response Mode, Assuming No Voluntary Repair[b]				Total Change, Assuming Some Voluntary Repair[c]
	Required Repair	Occupancy Change	Inventory Change	Total Change	
	Recipient Submarket				
1	.28	1.55	.23	2.05	2.21
2	.41	2.06	.69	3.16	3.38
3	.47	2.11	1.22	3.80	4.03
4	.50	1.97	1.74	4.21	4.42
5	.52	1.76	2.21	4.48	4.67
.	.	.	.	.	.
10	.53	.84	3.79	5.15	5.24
	Nonrecipient Submarket				
1	--	-1.07	- .15	-1.23	-1.23
2	--	-1.43	- .48	-1.90	-1.90
3	--	-1.46	- .84	-2.30	-2.30
4	--	-1.36	-1.19	-2.56	-2.56
5	--	-1.22	-1.52	-2.74	-2.74
.	.	.	.	.	.
10	--	- .58	-2.60	-3.18	-3.18
	Entire Market				
1	.14	.26	.04	.44	.53
2	.21	.35	.12	.68	.79
3	.24	.36	.21	.81	.93
4	.26	.34	.30	.89	1.00
5	.26	.30	.38	.95	1.04
.	.	.	.	.	.
10	.27	.14	.66	1.07	1.12

SOURCE: Estimated by HASE staff from the supply response model described in the text, using demand estimates from Table 6.7. For additional details, see Rydell, Neels, and Barnett, 1982.

NOTE: Entries refer only to the rental market of St. Joseph County, of which the recipient submarket constitutes 51 percent. The model assumes no changes in market conditions except those caused by the allowance program.

[a]Change relative to preprogram supply; entries are cumulative.

[b]All voluntary increases in recipients' housing consumption are accomplished by moving. Landlords improve dwellings only as required to meet program standards.

[c]All voluntary increases in recipients' housing consumption are accommodated directly or indirectly by voluntary repairs.

The Time-Path of Short-Run Prices

We have shown how the allowance program caused the demand for rental housing services to increase in the recipient submarket, and have estimated the amounts and timing of supply responses to the resulting market signals. Those signals were short-run price changes; in the recipient submarket, excess demand for housing service would bid up its price; in the nonrecipient submarket, excess supply would encourage price-cutting.

The supply response in our model persistently lags the demand changes. Consequently, clearing the market at any particular time would require a short-run price per unit of housing service that was above (recipient submarket) or below (nonrecipient submarket) the initial price. How large would these price changes be?

With excess demand, the short-run price increase needed to clear the market (by reducing the amount demanded) is the product of two numbers: the inverse of the price elasticity of demand,[20] and the proportion of total demand that exceeds the available supply.

Estimates of price elasticity of the demand for rental housing service vary considerably, ranging from 0.17 to 1.28 (Mayo, 1978). However, most of the estimates lie between 0.3 and 0.7, and their central tendency is 0.5. In our model, we use a value of 0.5, implying that a 10-percent increase in market price would cause a 5-percent reduction in consumption.[21]

We multiplied the inverse (2.0) of that elasticity by the annual difference between supply and demand in each submarket of our two experimental sites as calculated from Tables 6.6 and 6.7 for Brown County and Tables 6.6 and 6.8 for St. Joseph County. For example, in the recipient submarket of Brown County during program year 1, we estimated that demand increased (relative to year 0) by 2.42 percent and supply increased by 1.12 percent (no voluntary repair). The price increase (relative to year 0) needed to clear the market is

$$2.0(2.42 - 1.12) = 2.6 \text{ percent.}$$

The results are plotted as index numbers by program year in Figs. 6.1

[20]The price elasticity of demand is the percentage change in quantity demanded for a given percentage change in the unit price of the commodity in question. It is ordinarily a negative number; but to simplify exposition, we present it here as an absolute number, the minus sign understood.

[21]Varying this parameter between 0.3 and 0.7 alters the price-change estimates from our model within reasonable limits. For example, we estimate that the program-induced price change for year 3 in Brown County's recipient submarket would be 3.5 percent if the price elasticity were 0.5. An elasticity of 0.3 would increase the price change to 5.9 percent; an elasticity of 0.7 would decrease the price change to 2.5 percent. See Rydell, Neels, and Barnett, 1982, for a full sensitivity test on price elasticity.

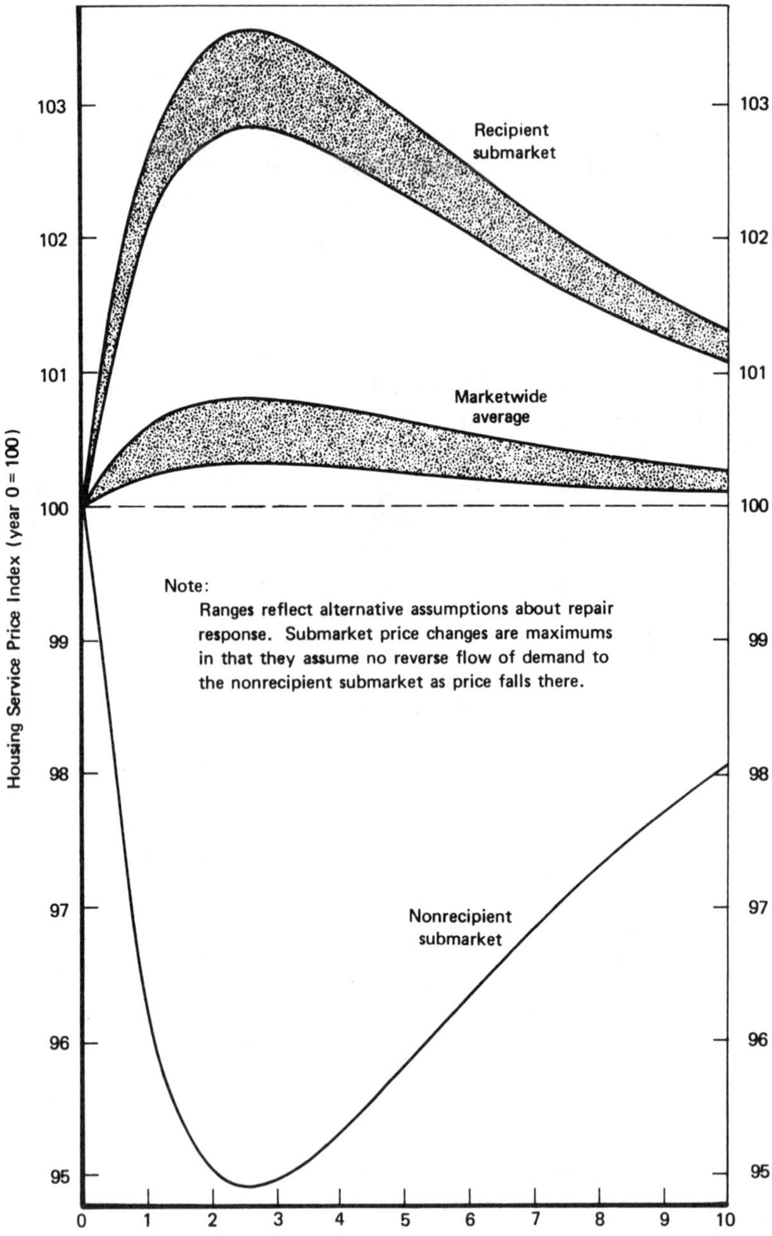

SOURCE: Tables 6.6 and 6.7.

Fig. 6.1—Price changes caused by the allowance program: a model of the rental housing market in Brown County

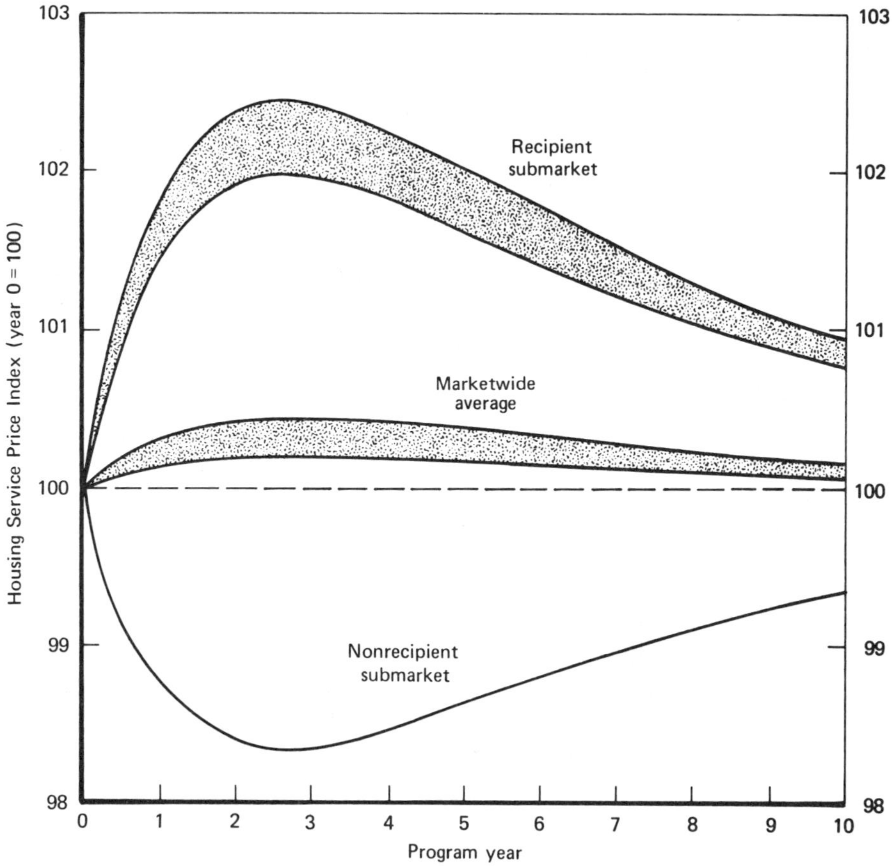

SOURCE: Tables 6.6 and 6.8.

Note: Ranges reflect alternative assumptions about repair response. Submarket price changes are maximums in that they assume no reverse flow of demand to the nonrecipient submarket as price falls there.

Fig 6.2—Pricc changes caused by the allowance program: a model of the rental housing market in St. Joseph County

and 6.2. To accommodate our uncertainty about the voluntary repair response, we show upper and lower bounds of price increase for each submarket and the market as a whole.

The results for the two counties are similar. In each submarket, the maximum price disturbance occurs between program years 2 and 3; thereafter, prices gradually converge on their preprogram values as long-run supply adjustments are made.

However, the maximum disturbances are small. In the recipient submarkets, we estimate a short-run increase of up to 3.5 percent for Brown County and 2.5 percent for St. Joseph County. In the nonrecipient submarkets, we estimate price decreases of up to 5.0 percent in Brown County and 2.4 percent in St. Joseph County. Marketwide, price changes never exceed 0.8 percent in Brown County and 0.5 percent in St. Joseph County. If we assume some program-induced voluntary repairs, all these maximums are smaller.

The model results are generally consistent with the empirical evidence as to the size of price increases in the recipient submarket and in the market as a whole, but imply larger price reductions in the nonrecipient market than we found in fact.[22]

We think that the main reason for this discrepancy is that our model does not allow the nonrecipient occupants of dwellings in the recipient submarket to move to the nonrecipient submarket when they notice falling prices there. If they did so, prices would not rise by as much in the recipient submarket and would not fall by as much in the nonrecipient submarket. Thus, the main inference from the model —that the allowance programs operated in our experimental sites caused only small price increases in the recipient submarket—would be strengthened had the model incorporated that reverse flow across submarket boundaries.

Summary

We have presented three kinds of evidence bearing on the price effects of the allowance program: measurements of rent changes during the program, analyses of landlords' financial statements, and estimates from a model of market processes calibrated to conditions in each site. Each source of information entails ambiguities and approximations that allow reasonable people to disagree somewhat in their interpretations of the evidence. But the only conclusion that is consistent with all three kinds of evidence is that the housing allowance

[22]The rent-increase measurements presented in Tables 6.1, 6.2, and 6.3 must of course be adjusted for background inflation to be comparable to the model's results. However, the difference in rent changes between participants' and nonparticipants' dwellings should be comparable to the submarket differences estimated by the model.

program had very little effect on the price of rental housing service in either Brown County's tight market or St. Joseph County's loose market.

The reasons for this outcome are also clear: The program generated only a modest increase in the marketwide demand for rental housing service, and (because the allowances were portable) that demand did not focus narrowly on specific dwellings or small submarkets. Consequently, the suppliers of rental housing were never in a position to raise recipients' rents much above the general price set by marketwide forces.

NEIGHBORHOOD EFFECTS

Housing assistance programs have often been designed to focus on specific neighborhoods that need preservation or renewal, and usually provide assistance only to the occupants of selected dwellings. In contrast, the experimental housing allowance program was open to low-income households throughout Brown and St. Joseph counties, and the allowances were portable in the sense that enrollees could move without losing their entitlements. One purpose of the experiment was to learn how a program with those features would affect deteriorated neighborhoods. A related purpose was to learn how such a program would affect existing patterns of residential segregation that tend to concentrate both low-income households and racial minorities in deteriorated neighborhoods.

Briefly, we find that because of such segregation, allowance payments did focus on deteriorated low-income neighborhoods, especially those predominantly occupied by blacks. Although the allowances augmented the incomes of participants and caused many to repair their homes, we are unable to discern spillover effects in the form of general neighborhood improvement. Although many participants moved, their moves did not significantly alter the economic or ethnic composition of neighborhood populations. Below, we summarize the evidence and explore the reasons for this outcome.

Program Activity and Neighborhood Characteristics

To assess the spatial distribution of assistance, we divided each county into small, residentially homogeneous neighborhoods (108 in Brown County and 86 in St. Joseph County), and classified each according to its level of program activity. We measured program activity by average allowance payments per resident household, cumulating the payments made to neighborhood residents during the first three program years. The classification by activity level yielded five groups of neighborhoods, roughly equal in population, within each site (Table 6.9).

Although the program did not have explicit neighborhood targets, the pattern of participation did cause payments to concentrate in certain neighborhoods. The 23 most active neighborhoods in Brown County, containing less than a fifth of all households in the county, jointly received over two-fifths of all allowance payments. In St. Joseph County, nearly half of all payments went to the residents of the 21 most active neighborhoods. At the other extreme, the least active group of neighborhoods in each county received about 5 percent of all payments.

The spatial distribution of program activity differed in the two sites. In Brown County, the incidence of allowance payments was highest in the older urban neighborhoods along the Fox River and parallel to but not on the lakeshore (see Ch. II, Fig. 2.1, for a map of Brown County). Participation was low in most suburban neighborhoods but rose in the outlying rural townships. In St. Joseph County, participation was highest in central South Bend and on the southwestern fringe of the city; moderate in the older neighborhoods along the St. Joseph River, and very low in rural townships (see map, Fig. 2.2). Generally, the pattern in Brown County reflects concentrations of households headed either by elderly persons or single parents; in St. Joseph County, the pattern also reflects concentrations of black households.

Although the neighborhoods with high levels of program activity do not form a single geographic cluster in either county, they are distinguishable from inactive neighborhoods in several respects. Table 6.10 shows that they have on average the lowest incomes and property values and the lowest incidence of homeowners. Our neighborhood surveys also indicate that the residential properties in the most active neighborhoods are below average in quality and maintenance. Thus, by most standards, the housing allowance program focused on the neighborhoods as well as on the individual households that most needed help.

Program-Induced Neighborhood Change

We find very little evidence that the program altered even the most active neighborhoods. In both counties, the greatest increases in population and income occurred in the least active neighborhoods; the

Table 6.9

CLASSIFICATION OF NEIGHBORHOODS IN EACH SITE, BY LEVEL OF PROGRAM ACTIVITY

Neighborhood Group		Resident Population[b]		Cumulative Allowance Payments, Years 1-3	
Program Activity Level[a]	Number of Neighbor-hoods	Number of Households	Percent Enrolled (Year 3)	Total ($000)	Per Resident Household ($)[c]
Brown County					
1 (high)	23	8,231	13	2,074	252
2	21	9,017	9	1,362	151
3	14	8,578	6	832	97
4	20	9,084	4	500	55
5 (low)	18	8,868	2	328	37
St. Joseph County					
1 (high)	21	14,113	21	3,105	220
2	12	14,780	10	1,759	119
3	16	13,886	6	847	61
4	15	15,786	4	695	44
5 (low)	18	16,254	2	260	16

SOURCES: Tabulated by HASE staff from records of the survey of households, waves 1 and 4, in each site; and from HAO records through program year 3. See Hillestad and McDowell, 1982, for details.

NOTE: Population statistics are based on samples of about 2,600 households in Brown County and 2,100 in St. Joseph County. Neighborhood groups exclude 12 thinly populated neighborhoods in Brown County and 4 in St. Joseph County because sample sizes were too small for reliable classification by level of program activity.

[a] Neighborhoods were grouped according to cumulative allowance payments per resident household.

[b] Population data are from survey wave 1, conducted just before the allowance program began. Participation rate is based on the resident population at survey wave 4, corresponding to the end of program year 3.

[c] Resident households at survey wave 1.

Table 6.10

SELECTED CHARACTERISTICS OF NEIGHBORHOODS IN EACH SITE, GROUPED BY LEVEL OF PROGRAM ACTIVITY

Neighborhoods, by Program Activity Level	Annual Income ($) per Household	Property Value ($) per Dwelling	Index of Dwelling Quality[a]	Incidence (%) of Owner Occupancy
Brown County				
1 (high)	9,534	16,141	1.00	50
2	10,761	20,862	1.06	63
3	12,393	22,005	1.05	72
4	14,067	25,320	1.15	79
5 (low)	15,330	24,928	1.17	87
St. Joseph County				
1 (high)	8,758	8,613	1.00	63
2	10,431	9,266	.99	59
3	11,566	11,601	1.04	76
4	13,264	14,382	1.09	81
5 (low)	14,015	20,127	1.11	88

SOURCE: Tabulated by HASE staff from records of the surveys of households, landlords, and neighborhoods, wave 1, in each site. See Hillestad and McDowell, 1982, for details.

NOTE: All data refer to neighborhood conditions at the time of survey wave 1, just before the allowance program began. Data for individual neighborhoods within each group were pooled to calculate the measures shown.

[a]Based on observer ratings of residential quality on a scale of 1 (poor) to 4 (good), divided by the average rating for neighborhood group 1.

greatest increases in property value and dwelling quality occurred in neighborhoods with intermediate levels of program activity (Table 6.11). Although these results do not preclude program effects, they certainly do not signal them.

Considered in context, the program stimulus even in the most active neighborhood was simply not great enough to generate observable neighborhood change. In the neighborhoods of group 1, allowance payments augmented neighborhood income by less than one percent, so that the general standard of living in such neighborhoods could not have been visibly affected. About a fifth of the allowance payments received by residents of these neighborhoods were used to increase

Table 6.11

SELECTED MEASURES OF NEIGHBORHOOD CHANGE IN EACH SITE, BY LEVEL OF PROGRAM ACTIVITY

Neighborhoods, by Program Activity Level	Percentage Change, Wave 1 to Wave 4			
	Resident Households	Average Income	Property Value	Dwelling Quality
Brown County				
1 (high)	3	18	27	2
2	2	25	34	-2
3	4	25	31	4
4	7	28	30	(*a*)
5 (low)	9	25	30	-4
St. Joseph County				
1 (high)	-6	12	9	-1
2	-4	21	16	(*a*)
3	6	24	24	3
4	7	37	11	1
5 (low)	2	32	49	-4

SOURCE: Tabulated by HASE staff from records of the surveys of households, landlords, and neighborhoods, waves 1 and 4, for each site. See Hillestad and McDowell, 1982, for details.

NOTE: Average incomes and property values were computed in current dollars for resident households and dwellings at survey wave 1 and again at wave 4. Thus, percentage changes reflect changes in the resident population and housing inventory of each neighborhood as well as changes for households and dwellings present on both occasions.

[a] 0.5 percent or less.

housing consumption; but when averaged over all neighborhood residents, program-induced consumption amounts to only $15 annually per household. The program caused many participants to repair their dwellings, but when program-induced repair expenditures are averaged over all neighborhood residents, they amount to only a few extra repair dollars annually.

Perceived Change

Besides searching for objective evidence of neighborhood change that could be linked to the allowance program, we asked household heads how they thought their neighborhoods had been affected by the program. Interestingly, they perceived effects we were unable to measure directly.

Table 6.12 shows how household heads responded to a series of questions asked at survey wave 4 in St. Joseph County, after three years of program operations.[23] The first two columns pertain to respondents from groups 1 and 2 (high activity) neighborhoods; the third column pertains to respondents from groups 3, 4, and 5 (low activity) neighborhoods; and the last column pertains to all respondents.

Countywide, about half of all household heads thought that the allowance program had caused property values to rise, improved property upkeep, and increased the amount of residential repair, even though less than a fifth acknowledged any direct effect on their own households. The proportion perceiving positive neighborhood effects was substantially greater where the program was active than where it was inactive, and was naturally greatest among participants in the active neighborhoods.

In part, these perceptions can be attributed to what attitude researchers call the "positivity bias"—in this case, a general tendency to respond favorably to questions about efforts at civic betterment. But the differences between high-activity and low-activity neighborhoods indicate that respondents in the former group were at least more aware of program activity, even if their own households were not directly involved. We doubt that their responses were prompted by systematic evidence of neighborhood-wide improvements, but suspect that they were generalizing from particular instances: friends or

[23]Responses from Brown County households were quite similar, so are not reproduced here. See Ch. VII for a full analysis of community attitudes toward the allowance program.

Table 6.12

PERCEIVED NEIGHBORHOOD CHANGE BY LEVEL OF PROGRAM ACTIVITY: ST. JOSEPH COUNTY

Perceived Program Effect	Percentage Distribution of Responses by Level of Program Activity in Respondent's Neighborhood			
	Groups 1 and 2 (High)		Groups 3-5 (Low)[a]	All Neighborhoods
	Recipients	Nonrecipients		
Effect of Program on Neighborhood Property Values?				
Increased	67	45	38	45
No effect	32	49	57	50
Decreased	1	6	5	5
Effect of Program on Neighborhood Property Upkeep?				
Increased	84	50	48	54
No effect	16	46	49	43
Decreased	--	4	3	3
Effect of Program on Repairs?				
Increased	67	55	40	50
No effect	32	42	53	46
Decreased	1	3	7	4
Has the Program Affected Your Household?				
A lot	75	3	4	9
Somewhat	15	2	5	5
Very little	4	4	4	4
Not at all	6	91	87	82

SOURCE: Tabulated by HASE staff from records of the survey of households, wave 4, for St. Joseph County. See Hillestad and McDowell, 1982, for additional details.

NOTE: Entries are based on responses from 1,665 household heads who were familiar with program details. Except for rounding error, all distributions should add to 100 percent.

[a]About 88 percent of the residents of these neighborhoods were nonrecipients.

neighbors (in the case of participants, themselves) whose homes had visibly benefited from the program.

That interpretation does not make their testimony unimportant. How the residents of a neighborhood feel about its characteristics and especially its probable future has considerable influence on what actually happens. If the one dilapidated or illkept house on a block is spruced up, the whole blockface takes on a different appearance. The neighbors benefit both tangibly (property values increase) and intangibly (the view is improved). However, at the end of three program years, the tangible changes resulting from the program, if any, were too small to be distinguished by the tools at our disposal.

Residential Mobility and Neighborhood Change

The portability of housing allowances led some observers to speculate that a full-scale program would result in substantial spatial rearrangements of low-income households, particularly those belonging to racial minorities. Some thought that the program would help achieve a desirable pattern of residential integration, dispersing low-income and minority households among more prosperous white neighborhoods. Others worried that participants would abandon deteriorating neighborhoods and move in unwelcome numbers to a few better neighborhoods. Still others were skeptical that the program would much alter the residential distribution of participants.

We find that about 40 percent of all renter recipients and 4 percent of all homeowner recipients moved after enrolling in the program: About half of those who moved did so in order to qualify for payments; the others moved voluntarily after they were receiving payments. The annualized mobility rate for renter participants is distinctly lower than the rate for comparable nonparticipants. We think that participation dampens mobility by enabling some renters to stay in dwellings they could not otherwise afford; and possibly by deterring others from moving, because they do not understand that their allowance entitlements are portable, or worry about possible repair requirements that might be imposed by the HAOs on a new residence.[24]

To learn how program-related moves affected residential neighborhoods, we compared the origins and destinations of all postenrollment moves made by allowance recipients during the first five program

[24]See Mulford and others, 1982, Sec. II, for further details on mobility rates and reasons for them. The mobility rates for renters and owners cited above are for the 18-month average duration of participation between enrollment and the end of year 3. From the preprogram behavior of future allowance recipients, the authors estimate that, absent the program, 54 percent of the renter participants would have moved during any 18-month interval.

years in each site. Below, we present the findings for St. Joseph County, where interest in the issue is sharpened by the fact that a fifth of all allowance recipients were members of a racial minority. Nearly all were blacks who, when they enrolled, were living in segregated neighborhoods in South Bend; a few were Latins or Orientals.

To assess the effects of moves on the racial balance of neighborhood populations, we assigned each neighborhood in St. Joseph County to one of three groups:

- Nonwhite: 50 percent or more nonwhite households.
- Integrated: 5 to 49 percent nonwhite households.
- White: Less than 5 percent nonwhite households.

Figure 6.3 shows the resulting configuration of neighborhoods: nonwhite or integrated in central South Bend, integrated or white elsewhere in the city and on its fringes, and nearly all white in the rest of the county.

These three groups of neighborhoods differ in expectable ways (Table 6.13). Enrollment was highest in the nonwhite neighborhoods, and incomes and property values were lowest. We estimate that 58 percent of the dwellings in the nonwhite neighborhoods would have failed an HAO housing evaluation, as compared with about 45 percent in the integrated and white neighborhoods. Whatever attitudes the residents of nonwhite neighborhoods had toward integration, a search for better housing might well have led them to look elsewhere.

During the first five program years, enrolled households who ever qualified for payments changed their residences 3,641 times, an average of 0.3 moves per household. However, nearly two-thirds of those moves were between addresses within the same group of neighborhoods; the average distance moved was less than one mile. Figure 6.4 shows the origins and destinations of the remaining, cross-neighborhood moves. The larger flows either began or ended in integrated neighborhoods; the interchange between nonwhite and white neighborhoods amounted to only 15 percent of all cross-neighborhood moves and 5 percent of all moves.

Moreover, the flows and counterflows between paired groups of neighborhoods very nearly balanced. Nonwhite neighborhoods lost a net of only 52 households because of moves by program participants over a five-year period. Integrated neighborhoods gained 41 households from nonwhite and lost 46 to white neighborhoods. White neighborhoods gained 57 households, mostly from integrated neighborhoods.

Manifestly, these flows are insufficient to significantly alter housing-market conditions in either the sending or receiving neighborhoods. And, as Table 6.14 shows, they also had little effect on the

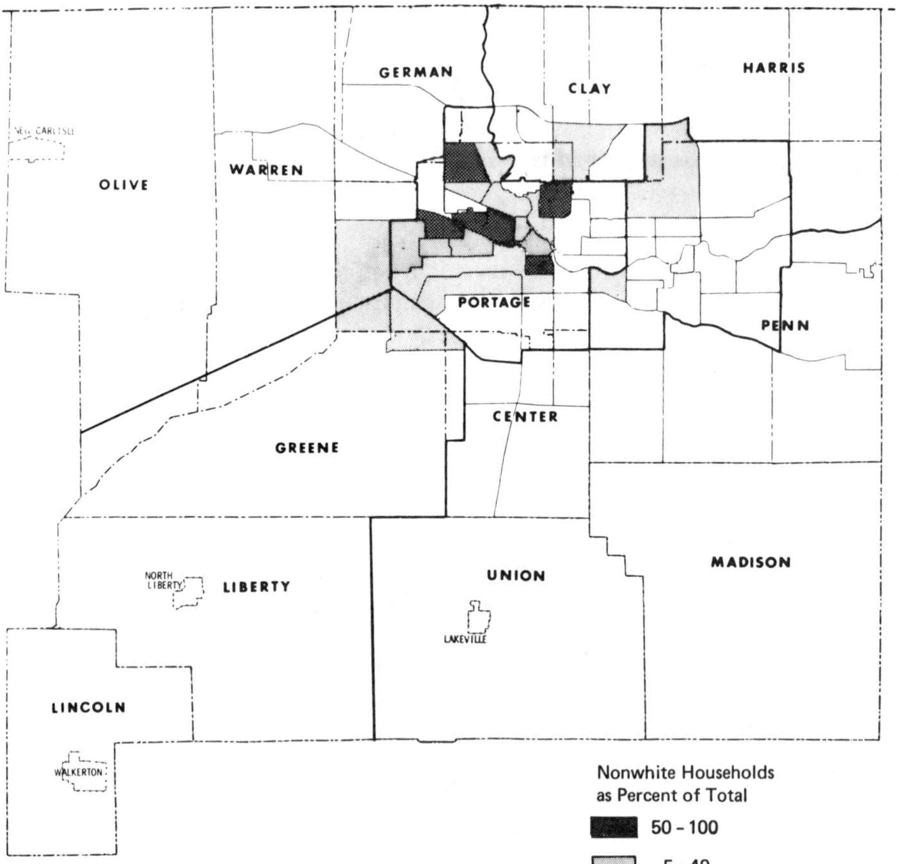

SOURCE: Records of the survey of households, wave 1.

Fig. 6.3—Racial balance of neighborhoods in St. Joseph County

composition of neighborhood populations. Those who moved from and to each group of neighborhoods differed demographically: The nonwhite neighborhoods were net exporters (to integrated neighborhoods) of nonwhites and single parents, and net importers of elderly persons. But all such flows were small relative to the aggregate populations of each neighborhood group. Because all were low-income program participants, their incomes and housing expenses were similar.

Table 6.13

SELECTED CHARACTERISTICS OF NEIGHBORHOODS GROUPED BY RACIAL COMPOSITION OF RESIDENTS: ST. JOSEPH COUNTY

Neighborhood Group		Resident Population				
Racial Composition[a]	Number of Neighborhoods	Number of Households	Percent Enrolled (Year 3)	Annual Income ($) per Household	Property Value ($) per Dwelling	Incidence (%) of Substandard Dwellings[b]
Nonwhite	6	7,719	32	7,973	8,104	58
Integrated	16	21,158	17	8,446	8,856	45
White	59	45,721	10	10,362	12,825	44
All neighborhoods	81[c]	74,598	14	9,702	11,613	46

SOURCE: Tabulated by HASE staff from records of the surveys of households, landlords, and neighborhoods, waves 1 and 4, for St. Joseph County; and from HAO records for St. Joseph County through program year 3.

NOTE: All entries except percent enrolled are based on data from survey wave 1, conducted just before the allowance program began. The participation rate is based on the resident population at survey wave 4, corresponding to the end of program year 3.

[a]Nonwhite = 50 percent or more nonwhite households; integrated = 5 to 49 percent nonwhite households; white = less than 5 percent nonwhite households. Nearly all nonwhites are blacks; a few are Latins or Orientals.

[b]Estimated from a failure model based on HAO housing standards. See Yildiz and Mulford, 1982, for details.

[c]Excludes 5 neighborhoods because sample sizes were too small for reliable classification by racial composition.

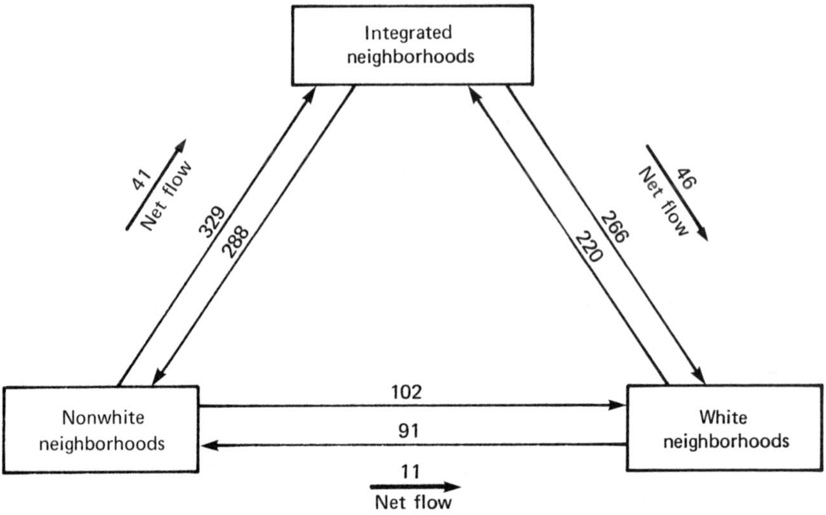

SOURCE: Compiled by HASE staff from HAO records through program year 5.

Note: Entries are based on 3,641 moves made by households while enrolled, of which 1,296 were between the different types of neighborhoods described in the text.

Fig. 6.4—Moves by program participants between nonwhite, integrated, and white neighborhoods in St. Joseph County, 1974-79

Brown County's population is nearly all white, so racial segregation is not an issue in its housing market. There, we examined moves between central Green Bay, where enrollment was highest, and the rest of the county. Of 2,700 program-related moves, only 794 crossed the boundary of central Green Bay; the net flow of program participants was outward, but amounted to only 106 households. As in St. Joseph County, moves by program participants did not visibly affect either neighborhood housing markets or the composition of neighborhood populations.

Summary

Although housing allowances were not explicitly targeted on particular neighborhoods, the pattern of participation caused payments to focus on the low-income neighborhoods where housing conditions were worst; in St. Joseph County, the residents of such neighborhoods included most of the county's nonwhites.

However, even when thus focused, the program was not enough to

Table 6.14

SELECTED CHARACTERISTICS OF PROGRAM PARTICIPANTS WHO MOVED BETWEEN NONWHITE, INTEGRATED, AND WHITE NEIGHBORHOODS: ST. JOSEPH COUNTY

Type of Neighborhood and Direction of Move	Characteristics of Movers: Household Head (% of all Movers)				
	Nonwhite	Single Parent	Elderly	Average Annual Income ($)	Average[a] Monthly Gross Rent ($)
Nonwhite					
Moved to	58	58	8	3,600	200
Moved from	68	67	5	3,500	210
Integrated					
Moved to	53	60	7	3,400	200
Moved from	44	56	10	3,700	210
White					
Moved to	15	55	13	4,000	230
Moved from	12	52	13	3,800	210

SOURCE: Tabulated by HASE staff from HAO records for St. Joseph County through program year 5. See Hillestad and McDowell, 1982, for additional details.

NOTE: Entries are based on all moves between the types of neighborhoods described in Table 6.13; see Fig. 6.4 for numbers of moves corresponding to each stub entry.

[a]Excludes a few movers who purchased homes.

make a substantial difference in average neighborhood income or housing quality. Within one group of neighborhoods in St. Joseph County, over a fifth of all households were enrolled at the end of the third program year; but we estimate that allowances paid to that neighborhood raised the average income there by less than 1 percent, and program-induced housing expenditures amounted to about $15 annually per resident household.

Residents of neighborhoods in which the program was especially active, however, did perceive positive consequences for property values, as well as increased levels of residential maintenance and repair. We think they were responding to conspicuous instances rather than to systematic evidence; but their impressions are nonetheless important insofar as they lead to individual actions that do improve the neighborhood.

About 40 percent of the renters in the program moved after enrolling, substantially fewer than the 54 percent who would have moved absent the program. We think that the program enables some renters to stay in dwellings they could not otherwise afford, and discourages others from changing a certified dwelling for an alternative that might not be acceptable to the HAO. Moves by program participants were mostly to nearby dwellings, and the longer moves were too diverse as to origins and destinations to perceptibly affect the spatial distribution of low-income households or, in St. Joseph County, nonwhites.

In short, the allowance program's benefits are virtually limited to participants. Their neighbors may notice and approve participants' housing improvements, but the program does not physically transform even high-enrollment neighborhoods; nor does it alter preexisting patterns of residential segregation by income and race. Although the absence of neighborhood effects will doubtless disappoint some proponents of the allowance concept, it is worth noting that some well-intentioned programs that focused on particular neighborhoods have been accused of destroying them, and other programs have been accused of promoting economic and racial segregation by concentrating participants in "project" housing. Housing allowances do neither.

THE ROLE OF MARKET INTERMEDIARIES

Because the housing allowance program relies on the private market, program outcomes could be affected by the policies or practices of a variety of market intermediaries and indirect suppliers of housing services. The former include mortgage and home improvement lenders, insurance underwriters, real-estate brokers, rental agents, and property management firms; the latter include residential repair and improvement contractors and providers of janitorial and maintenance services.

We investigated how these industries were organized in Brown and St. Joseph counties, who used their services, and how their policies affected participants in the allowance program.[25] Briefly, we found that the industries were amorphous, that some were seldom used by either landlords or homeowners, and that program-related housing transactions did not account for a substantial share of any

[25]The results of these investigations are presented in more detail in Shanley and Hotchkiss, 1980. They are based on periodic interviews with a sample of intermediaries (industry organization and policies), annual surveys of households and landlords (use of intermediary services), and HAO records (interactions with participants).

intermediary's or supplier's activity. Consequently, few firms in any of the industries ever articulated special policies toward program participants who might deal with them, or actively sought participants' business.

Nearly all landlords in both sites managed, maintained, and rented their properties without the aid of property management firms, maintenance firms, or rental agents. Throughout both counties, property owners could readily obtain insurance at standard rates. We therefore focused on the four remaining industries that might affect or be affected by program-related transactions: residential repair and improvement contractors, home improvement lenders, real-estate brokers, and mortgage lenders. The first two were potentially important resources for program participants seeking to repair their dwellings, and the latter two for participants seeking to buy homes. Below, we summarize our findings.

The Intermediary Role in Home Improvement

Enrollees whose dwellings failed initial or annual evaluations had to repair or move in order to qualify for payments. Complicated repairs might require the skills of professional contractors and expensive repairs might require credit. Some observers of the experiment worried that program-generated demands for home repairs would strain the capacity of the industry, drive up the prices of repair services, and encourage shoddy work. Others worried that homeowner enrollees lacked the cash to pay for major repairs and would be unable to obtain credit.

We found that about a third of all enrollees repaired their dwellings in order to qualify for payments, and about the same proportion of recipients made additional repairs each year to avoid suspension of payments. In addition, about two-fifths of all recipient renters and nearly three-fourths of all recipient homeowners made voluntary repairs to their dwellings each year. However, nearly all the required repairs and most of the voluntary repairs were made by the recipients themselves, their friends, or their landlords (see Fig. 6.5).

Although no more than a fourth of all repair "jobs" done on participants' dwellings were delegated to professional contractors, these were the larger and more expensive jobs, accounting for over half of all program-related repair expenditures. Table 6.15 shows the total program-related expenditure on contracted repairs for a typical year,

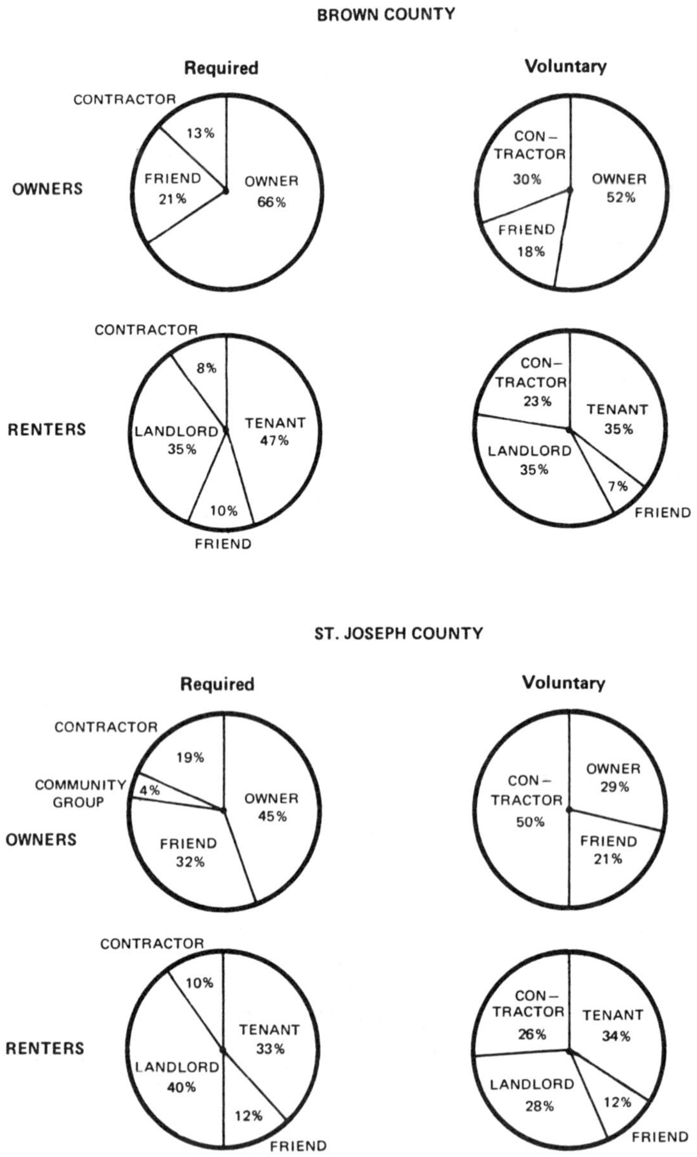

SOURCE: HAO Records from January 1976 through June 1977.

Fig. 6.5—Sources of labor for required and voluntary repairs: enrolled renters and owners in each site

Table 6.15

PROGRAM-RELATED CONTRACT REPAIR EXPENDITURES IN EACH SITE, JULY 1977-JUNE 1978

Site and Type of Repair	Number of Repair Reports	Cost of Contracted Repairs	
		Average ($) per Report	Total ($000)
Brown County			
Required	1,146	10	11
Voluntary	2,417	93	225
Total	3,563	66	236
St. Joseph County			
Required	3,004	24	72
Voluntary	4,208	164	686
Total	7,212	105	757

SOURCE: Estimated by HASE staff from HAO housing evaluation records for each site. See Shanley and Hotchkiss, 1980, for additional details.

NOTE: Required repairs were reported when a failed dwelling was reevaluated at the client's request. Voluntary repairs made during the preceding year were reported during the dwelling's annual evaluation. The estimate of total contract repair expense for July 1977-June 1978 combines counts of repair reports filed during that period with average cost data from a special study covering an earlier period, January 1976-June 1977. Neither required nor voluntary repairs are necessarily program-induced; some would have been made in any case. See Ch. V for analysis of program-induced repairs.

about $236,000 in Brown County and $757,000 in St. Joseph County.[26] Although these are substantial sums, they are small compared with the normal volume of residential repair business done in each county. For example, repair data from our surveys of landlords and homeowners indicate that the industry's receipts in 1975 amounted to at least $13.8 million in Brown County and $22.8 million in St. Joseph County. Program-related repairs account for only 2 to 3 percent of total receipts, and program-induced repairs account for even less.

In our sites as elsewhere, the residential repair and improvement industry includes many small firms and self-employed individuals in addition to general contractors who work mostly on new construction.

---

[26]These are total expenses for contracted repairs to participants' dwellings, not extra repairs induced by the program.

The industry's capacity was too flexible to have been strained by program-induced demand, and firms were so numerous that customers could easily avoid overpriced services. Nor did we find evidence that HAO clients were victimized by shoddy work. For example, in St. Joseph County between June 1976 and December 1977, some 774 dwellings were repaired by contractors after failing HAO evaluations; all but 27 passed their reevaluations.

Because required repairs were usually inexpensive, few participants or landlords needed credit to finance them. In Brown County, lenders had so little contact with allowance recipients that few could remember even one application. In St. Joseph County, four institutional lenders reported a joint total of about 50 home repair loans to HAO clients during the first program year, but fewer thereafter. In both sites, various nonprofit organizations and public agencies offered help to those whose homes needed repairs in order to meet HAO standards. As nearly as we can judge, the handyman services they provided were more pertinent than credit to the needs of HAO clients.

We also looked for evidence that home repair problems had discouraged eligible households from applying, or had caused enrolled households to drop out of the program. We found that nonapplicants rarely (6 percent in Brown County, 13 percent in St. Joseph County) mentioned home repair problems or HAO housing standards when explaining their failure to apply; but about half of those who dropped out of the program without qualifying for payments cited problems meeting its housing requirements as one of their reasons. Analysis of their circumstances suggests to us that easier access to credit in the form of loans at the market interest rate would have enabled only a few such terminees to qualify for payments.

A well-publicized offer of interest-free loans for home improvement could increase program participation by 5 to 10 percent.[27] However, interest-free lending is clearly beyond the scope of policies to be urged on private market intermediaries. Cash advances by the HAOs for required repairs could serve the same purpose; such advances are already made to help enrollees with the security deposits required by landlords and utility companies.

---

[27]See the analysis by Shanley and Hotchkiss, 1980, pp. 38-42. They conclude that the upper bound is 9 percent in Brown County and 17 percent in St. Joseph County, but regard those figures as quite optimistic. Carter and Wendt, 1982, estimate that total elimination of housing standards from the allowance program would increase participation by 14 percent in Brown County and 25 percent in St. Joseph County (see Ch. IV, Table 4.12, above).

The Intermediary Role in Home Purchase

Renters enrolled in the allowance program could become homeowners without losing their entitlements; but aside from the monthly allowance payment, the program offered no special incentives or assistance for home purchase. The prospective buyer was responsible for finding a home that he could afford and that met HAO standards, for negotiating the sale, and for arranging mortgage or other credit to finance the purchase.

We did not expect many renter enrollees to buy homes. Less than a third in Brown County and less than a fourth in St. Joseph County were young couples, the type of household that accounts for most first purchases. Although house prices were advantageously low in St. Joseph County, enrollees' incomes were also low and their savings were meager. Even with housing allowances, we estimate that less than 1 percent of all renter enrollees in either site met prevailing standards for mortgage credit (Shanley and Hotchkiss, 1980, Appendix).

To our surprise, 2.0 percent of the renter enrollees in Brown County and 2.6 percent in St. Joseph County bought homes after enrolling. Although they were not regarded as prime prospects by either real-estate brokers or institutional lenders, program participants found various ways around these obstacles. In St. Joseph County, the Federal Housing Administration (FHA) played an important role, as will be explained later.

Participants' interest in homebuying is best gauged by their interaction with real-estate brokers. Brokers receive initial inquiries from buyers, screen out those unlikely to qualify for mortgage loans, and direct others to lending institutions likely to grant them credit.

In Brown County, brokers reported few contacts with allowance recipients, a fact that they attributed to a shortage there of low-priced homes. In St. Joseph County, where home prices were lower, brokers reported about 200 inquiries from participants during the first program year, and about 100 inquiries annually thereafter. However, few such inquiries led to home purchases. Brokers in both sites reported that most participants who inquired either lacked incomes adequate to carry mortgage loans or had unacceptable credit histories.

Residential finance was organized differently in the two sites (Table 6.16). In Brown County, 84 percent of the loans were originated by either savings and loan associations or commercial banks, and the loans were usually retained in these institutions' portfolios. In St. Joseph County, such institutions were less active than mortgage banks, which do not accept deposits and typically replenish their capital by selling the mortgages they originate (but continuing to service them). Mortgage banks deal mainly in insured mortgages and were the only

Table 6.16

SOURCES OF CREDIT FOR PURCHASING SINGLE-FAMILY OWNER-OCCUPIED HOMES: ALL PURCHASES IN EACH SITE, 1969-74

Source of Credit	Percent of All Home Purchases: Brown County (1969-73)	Percent of All Home Purchases: St. Joseph County (1970-74)
Institutional		
Savings and loan	55.3	14.5
Commercial bank	28.8	18.2
Mortgage bank	6.7	39.8
Other[a]	1.2	6.5
Noninstitutional		
Previous Owner	2.8	20.0
Friend or relative	5.1	1.0
All sources	100.0	100.0

SOURCE: Tabulated by HASE staff from records of the survey of homeowners, wave 1, in each site.

NOTE: Distributions are based on responses of 278 homeowners in Brown County and 182 in St. Joseph County who purchased homes in the years indicated. Percentages may not add exactly to 100.0 because of rounding.

[a]Credit unions, finance companies, real-estate firms, and other institutions.

institutional lenders in our sites that would accept FHA insurance; the others found the paperwork and restrictive terms oppressive. Also in St. Joseph County, about a fifth of all home purchases were financed directly by the seller, who sometimes took back a mortgage but more often made the sale under a land contract.[28] Such transactions are characteristic of weak housing markets, where institutional lenders are unwilling to write loans on low-valued properties with uncertain prospects.

[28]A land contract is an installment purchase plan; although the buyer takes possession of the property, title remains with the seller until the last installment is paid. Recovery in the event of default is thus easier than under the terms of a mortgage loan.

Institutional lending standards were similar in the two sites. As a general rule, housing costs (including amortization, interest, taxes, and insurance) could equal no more than a fourth of the borrower's total income; and all credit-based obligations could equal no more than a third of income. All lenders required borrowers to have "sound" credit histories. Down payments on uninsured loans were usually a minimum of 20 percent, but were less for insured loans; mortgage banks in St. Joseph County offered FHA-insured loans that required only 3-percent down payments.

Most commercial banks and savings and loan associations were reluctant to lend on inexpensive properties. Such loans are risky; and in any case they are relatively unprofitable because servicing a small loan is as costly as servicing a large one but yields less interest. However, the mortgage banks in St. Joseph County were willing to write such loans provided that the FHA would insure them. For program participants, the most important feature of FHA-insured loans was the FHA's treatment of allowance income in determining credit worthiness. The FHA counted allowance income as a deduction from housing expense, rather than as an addition to income, making the allowance count four times as much as ordinary income.

During the first four program years, 101 renter participants in Brown County and 185 in St. Joseph County bought homes at prices ranging from less than $5,000 to over $25,000 (see Table 6.17). The low-priced purchases in Brown County were mostly mobile homes, but in St. Joseph County a third of the conventional houses cost less than $10,000.

Table 6.18 describes the homebuyers and compares them with all renter enrollees. Although the buyers' incomes were well above average, they were nonetheless low for the homes they purchased; conventional lenders typically limit the purchase price to about twice the buyer's income, which for the typical participant-buyer implied a limit of $14,400 in Brown County and $11,000 in St. Joseph County. Nor did many have enough liquid assets to make a 20-percent down payment. In St. Joseph County, a number of buyers were single parents whose only income was from public assistance and housing allowances.

Case-by-case investigation revealed a number of home-purchase strategies. Some buyers got help from relatives to meet conventional lending standards, or made a joint purchase with another family. A few got direct loans from state agencies such as the Wisconsin Department of Veterans Affairs. Others took advantage of the FHA's favorable treatment of allowance income to obtain insured loans with 3-percent down payments. Nearly a third of the purchases were financed by the previous owner under land contracts. Mobile homes

Table 6.17

PURCHASE PRICES OF HOMES BOUGHT BY ENROLLED RENTERS IN EACH SITE THROUGH YEAR 4

Purchase Price ($)	Percentage Distribution of Dwellings			
	Brown County		St. Joseph County	
	House	Mobile Home	House	Mobile Home
Under 5,000	--	44	5	17
5,000-9,999	8	50	31	67
10,000-14,999	26	51	38	17
15,000-19,999	24	--	17	--
20,000-24,999	20	--	5	--
25,000 or more	22	--	4	--
Total	100	100	100	100
Number of purchases	83	18	173	12
Median price ($)	18,000	5,400	11,500	7,600

SOURCE: Compiled by HASE staff from HAO and public records through June 1978 in Brown County and December 1978 in St. Joseph County. See Shanley and Hotchkiss, 1980, for additional details.

NOTE: Dwellings were purchased by renters while enrolled in the allowance program. Purchase prices were on record for 92 percent of the cases in Brown County and 50 percent in St. Joseph County; the remaining purchase prices were inferred from related data (assessed value, mortgage amount). Percentages may not add exactly to 100 because of rounding.

were purchased with consumer rather than mortgage loans. A few buyers were helped by nonprofit organizations.

In short, the rigid credit standards of conventional lenders and their disinterest in low-priced properties did not prevent an unexpectedly large (though absolutely small) number of home purchases by allowance recipients. Those who used land contracts or consumer loans did pay higher interest rates and got shorter amortization periods than were typical of mortgage loans, but these terms were linked to the inherent riskiness of the loans.[29]

[29]We were unable to follow case histories for long enough to assess how well participant homebuyers met their obligations to lenders, but there were enough early defaults to signify that the loans were indeed risky (Shanley and Hotchkiss, 1980, pp. 61-2).

Table 6.18

SELECTED CHARACTERISTICS OF ENROLLED RENTERS WHO BOUGHT HOMES IN EACH SITE THROUGH YEAR 4

Site and Housing Circumstance	Median Gross Income[a] ($)	Average Household Size (persons)	Percent of All Cases		
			Single-Parent Households	No Earned Income	Liquid Assets[b] under $500
Brown County					
All enrolled renters	4,813	2.7	34	67	97
Homebuyers	7,195	3.7	31	29	72
St. Joseph County					
All enrolled renters	3,987	2.7	49	70	99
Homebuyers	5,498	3.7	67	54	94

SOURCE: Compiled by HASE staff from HAO records through June 1978 in Brown County and December 1978 in St. Joseph County. See Shanley and Hotchkiss, 1980, for additional details.

NOTE: Entries refer to houehold characteristics at time of enrollment (all enrolled renters) or at the time of purchase (homebuyers).

[a] Annualized amount, including current allowance entitlement.

[b] Cash on hand, checking and savings accounts, stocks, bonds, and other securities.

Racial Steering and Redlining

Real-estate brokers are often accused of "managing" racial segregation by steering their clients to or away from particular neighborhoods. Lenders are often accused of sealing the fates of deteriorating neighborhoods by refusing loans on properties there, regardless of the buyers' qualifications (redlining). We investigated these phenomena in our sites as they pertained to the outcome of the allowance program.

Neither steering nor redlining was an issue in Brown County, which lacks both racial minorities and seriously deteriorated neighborhoods. In St. Joseph County, anecdotes about racial steering abound, but reliable evidence on the extent of the practice is lacking. Most commercial banks and savings and loan associations avoided lending on central South Bend properties, but other lenders did not.

Racial Steering. The racial pattern of home purchases by renter enrollees is consistent with the steering hypothesis. Eighty-six percent of the black homebuyers in the program bought within central South Bend, where 82 percent of the black population lives. In contrast, only 40 percent of the white homebuyers in the program bought in central South Bend; the remainder bought in fringe areas of South Bend, Mishawaka, or other suburban areas.

However, the pattern of buying is also consistent with a theory of consumer preference and household mobility that does not involve steering. Homebuyers, like renters who move (see above, "Residential Mobility and Neighborhood Change"), often limit their housing search to nearby or similar neighborhoods, either because they prefer their accustomed environments or do not know about alternative possibilities. Once in place, a pattern of racial segregation tends to perpetuate itself even without special efforts by market intermediaries to maintain it.

Redlining. Initial interviews with lenders and brokers in St. Joseph County indicated that commercial banks and savings and loan companies were reluctant to lend on properties in the core of central South Bend; they would lend in adjoining neighborhoods, but on less favorable terms than elsewhere in the city and suburbs. Subsequently, some of these institutions adopted minimum loan policies; at one time, six of the largest were unwilling to lend on properties valued at less than $10,000. These minimums excluded many properties in central South Bend.

However, three mortgage banks and two other institutional lenders remained active in central South Bend, and their resources seemed adequate to fill the demand by conventionally qualified buyers of low-priced properties. Those not qualified for institutional loans had to seek other kinds of financing, as did most program participants who purchased homes.

Summary

Market intermediaries and indirect suppliers of housing services played only minor roles in the outcome of the experimental housing allowance programs in Brown and St. Joseph counties. The most salient services were those provided by residential repair and improvement contractors, home improvement lenders, real-estate brokers, and mortgage lenders. None of these industries had enough contact with program participants to warrant special policies or practices toward them.

Program participants and their landlords used contractors for the more difficult and expensive repair jobs, but program-induced work accounted for less than 3 percent of the normal receipts of the industry. Most repairs required by the HAOs were inexpensive, so generated little demand for home improvement loans. Easier credit would have made little difference in program outcomes.

By conventional standards, few renters who enrolled in the program were qualified for home purchase. Though absolutely small, the number who bought homes was greater than we anticipated. Commercial banks and savings and loan associations were conspicuously uninterested in financing purchases of inexpensive homes, and few participants met their standards of credit worthiness; but program participants were able to obtain credit from other sources such as mortgage banks (FHA-insured loans) and the previous owners of the properties they purchased (land contracts).

Neither racial steering nor redlining was apparent in Brown County. In St. Joseph County, nearly all the black home purchasers in the allowance program bought in black neighborhoods, where dwellings were cheapest. We are unable to tell how much that outcome was influenced by real-estate brokers (who sometimes steer their clients so as to maintain racial segregation) and how much it reflected the buyers' preferences. Some lending institutions clearly avoided lending on central South Bend properties, but others were willing and able to meet the credit needs of qualified buyers who chose properties there. Underqualified buyers were often able to find other sources of credit.

GENERALIZING FROM EXPERIMENTAL EVIDENCE

Because the Supply Experiment was conducted in two sharply contrasting housing markets, we were able to observe the market effects of a full-scale allowance program under quite different market conditions. Although the outcomes differed in detail, the differences that bear on program evaluation are modest. Furthermore, they are readily traced to measurable differences in population composition, characteristics of the housing stock, and initial market conditions.

These circumstances give us the confidence to extrapolate our findings to U.S. housing markets generally. We do not claim that our two experimental sites encompass the full range of local housing market variation, nor that the average outcome in our two sites would be the national average. We do think that the experimental findings identify the features of local markets that would most affect local outcomes and allow us to set reasonable bounds on those effects.[30]

Table 6.19 places the experimental sites in a national context. The table lists the 21 metropolitan areas that were included in the 1975 Annual Housing Survey; these areas are a randomly chosen subset of

[30]The charter of the Supply Experiment does not include systematic generalization, a task assigned by HUD to The Urban Institute. However, the Institute's work on that

Table 6.19

PROGRAM AND RENTAL MARKET CHARACTERISTICS OF 21 SMSAs COMPARED WITH BROWN AND ST. JOSEPH COUNTIES, 1975

Standard Metropolitan Statistical Area	Eligible Renters[a] (% of total)	Allowance/ Gross Income[b] (median %)	Dwellings Built before 1949 (%)	Rental Vacancy Rate (%)	Black or Latin Renters (% of total)
Atlanta, GA	22.0	22.2	27.4	15.0	31.8
Chicago, IL	26.2	23.5	66.2	6.7	34.3
Cincinnati, OH-KY-IN	19.5	22.1	58.5	7.0	20.2
Colorado Springs, CO	24.7	13.0	25.5	17.6	11.9
Columbus, OH	22.4	24.3	43.0	10.7	15.4
Hartford, CT	24.5	18.9	57.3	6.8	19.5
Kansas City, MO-KS	17.8	15.9	46.7	11.3	17.7
Madison, WI	14.3	15.2	36.1	5.2	3.2
Miami, FL	42.9	22.9	29.5	11.2	47.5
Milwaukee, WI	20.4	17.6	57.5	3.6	16.1
New Orleans, LA	20.9	22.8	59.8	7.8	43.5
Newport News, VA	17.6	15.1	36.3	13.2	34.0
Paterson-Clifton-Passaic, NJ	28.3	17.9	61.2	3.3	20.2
Philadelphia, PA-NJ	27.6	23.8	59.9	7.1	29.0
Portland, OR	20.0	17.6	41.2	7.3	3.6
Rochester, NY	26.6	19.1	58.6	8.6	16.4
San Antonio, TX	29.1	24.5	45.5	9.6	46.4

San Bernardino-Riverside -Ontario, CA	28.8	15.7	33.1	10.4	21.8
San Diego, CA	27.7	15.9	30.2	5.7	14.7
San Francisco-Oakland, CA	22.3	20.1	51.7	7.2	21.4
Springfield-Chicopee -Holyoke, MA-CT	26.8	20.7	69.7	6.5	13.4
Brown County, WI	21.9	14.9	54.7	5.1	.6
St. Joseph County, IN	24.7	23.0	67.5	11.0	17.3

SOURCE: Tabulated by HASE staff from records of the 1975 Annual Housing Survey conducted by the U.S. Bureau of the Census; and from records of the 1976 HASE surveys of households (wave 3 for Brown County, wave 2 for St. Joseph County).

NOTE: Statistics for Brown and St. Joseph counties may not agree with those elsewhere in this book because they were computed here by methods that could also be used on records of the Annual Housing Survey.

[a] Adjusted gross incomes less than 4 × standard cost of adequate housing - $120; nonelderly singles and occupants of subsidized housing are excluded.

[b] Estimated median entitlement of eligible renters, divided by median gross income of eligible renter households.

156 large SMSAs that compose a rotating panel, some of which are surveyed each year. From records for individual renter respondents in each place, we computed values for five variables that bear directly on program outcomes.[31] From our 1975 household surveys in Brown and St. Joseph counties, we computed comparable values for those five variables. The results are displayed graphically in Figs. 6.6 and 6.7.

Figure 6.6 shows how Brown and St. Joseph counties rank within the national sample as to renters' eligibility for assistance and the ratio of their allowance entitlements to their nonallowance gross incomes. These two factors are major determinants of an allowance program's effect on the demand for rental housing. Renter eligibility rates range among the 23 metropolitan areas from a low of 14 percent to a high of 43 percent; the two HASE sites closely bracket the median value. Income augmentation ranges from 13 percent to 24 percent; the HASE sites are near the opposite extremes of this distribution.

Figure 6.7 presents similar comparisons for three variables that bear on market responsiveness: the age of the rental inventory, a proxy for physical condition that indicates in a general way the difficulty of bringing dwellings up to program standards; the rental vacancy rate, an important factor in determining how landlords respond to increased housing demand; and the percent of renters who belong to racial minorities (black or Latin), an indicator of the degree of submarket segmentation and possible focusing of program effects. HASE sites span the upper half of the range of dwelling ages, most of the range of vacancy rates, and the lower half of the range on minority representation.

From all these comparisons, we judge that program outcomes in 20 of the 21 metropolitan areas would be similar to those observed in either Brown or St. Joseph County. The exception is Miami, Florida. In that metropolitan area, refugee immigration has added a large population of very poor Latins to the prior population of poor blacks; we estimate that 43 percent of Miami's renters would be eligible for assistance. However, with a relatively new housing stock and a high vacancy rate, we suspect that even Miami's rental market would absorb an allowance program without much market disturbance.

task was interrupted before the Supply Experiment was completed. The conclusions that follow reflect both our informal assessment of experimental results and systematic modeling of market outcomes for other cities, the latter conducted by HUD with technical support from Rand.

[31]We also computed similar measures for homeowner respondents, but do not present them here because the allowance program's effect on the homeowner housing market is inherently limited to program participants.

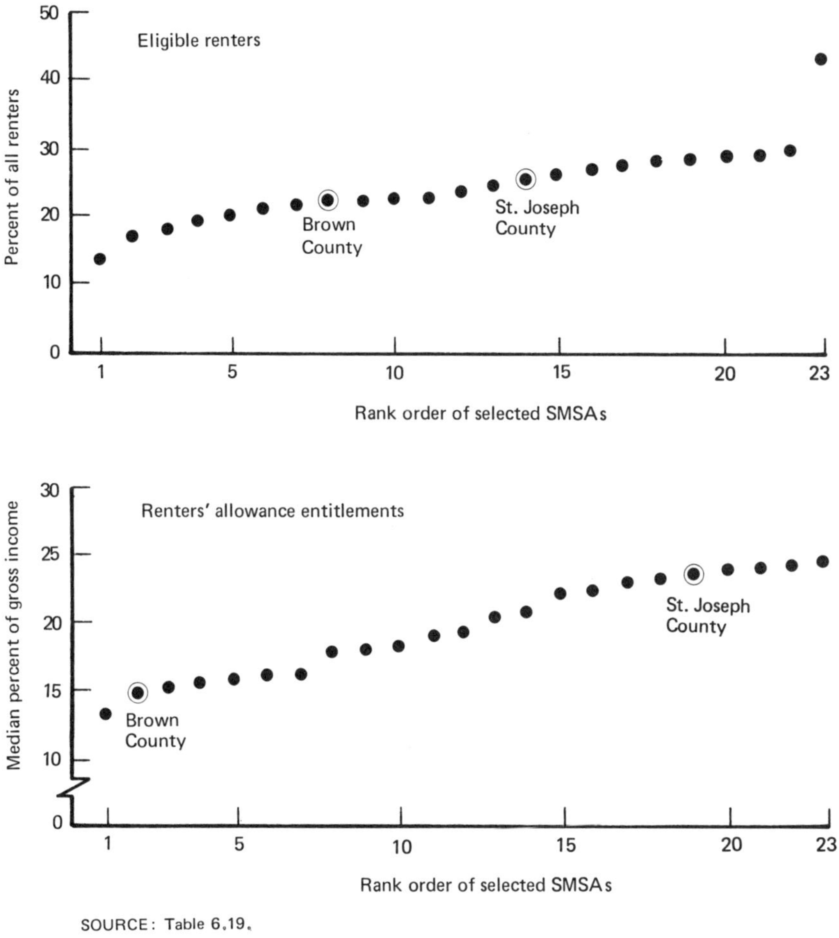

Fig. 6.6—Program characteristics for Brown and St. Joseph counties in a national context: 1975

These judgments are reinforced by a more rigorous analysis conducted by HUD staff on a different national sample of 20 metropolitan areas selected from among those surveyed in the 1976 and 1977 Annual Housing Surveys. The HUD study postulated a "housing voucher" program that differed only slightly from the HASE experimental allowance program, and simulated the voucher program's effects on rents by means of a model similar to the one presented earlier in this chapter.[32]

---

[32]The unpublished analysis was conducted in the spring of 1981 by Howard Hammerman, Office of Policy Development and Research, HUD, and is cited here with his

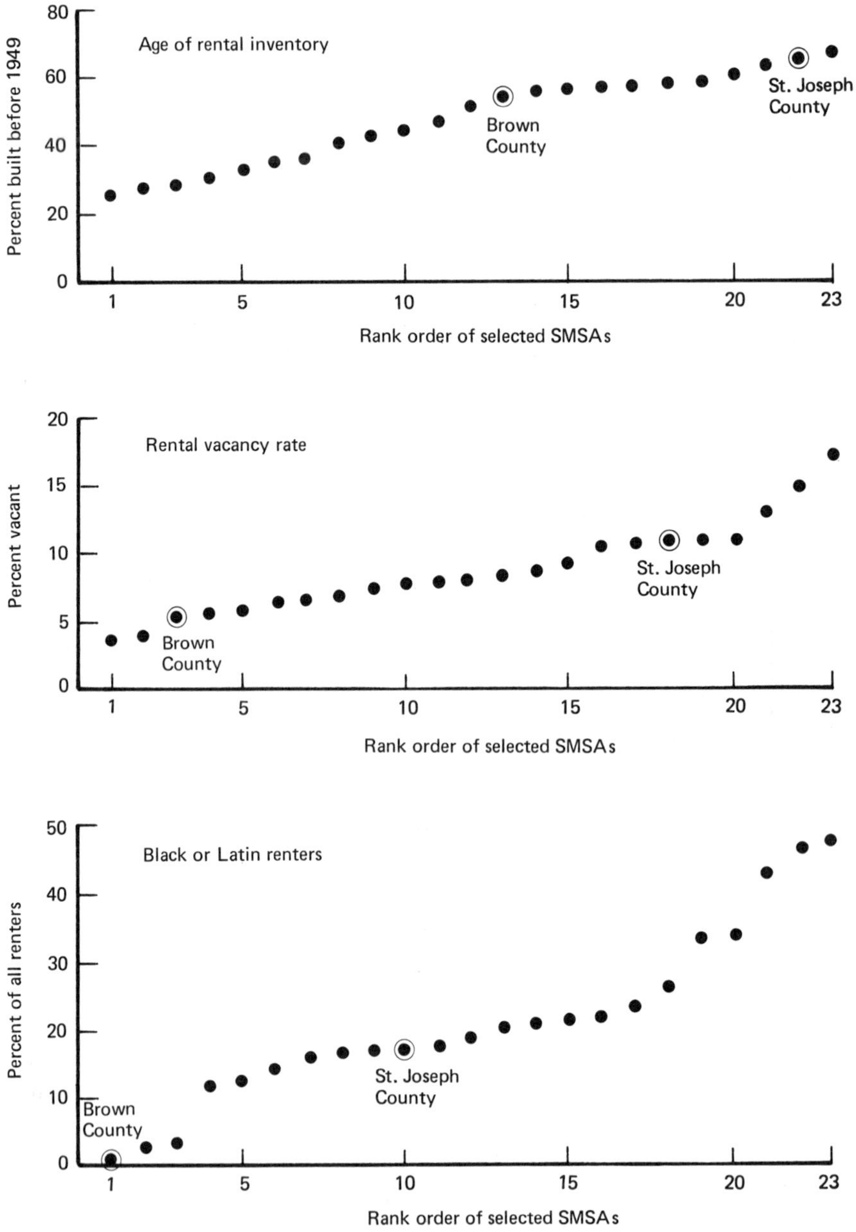

SOURCE: Table 6.19.

Fig. 6.7—Rental market characteristics for Brown and St. Joseph counties in a national context: 1975

The simulation study varied the values of three key parameters, using HASE estimates as the central reference point. In the worst-case simulations, program-induced price increases ranged from 1.4 to 11.3 percent. Using the parameters estimated from HASE experience, the range was from 0.6 to 4.8 percent. The best-case simulations yielded price increases ranging from 0.3 to 3.8 percent. The market characteristics that accounted for the largest share of the intersite variation in simulation outcomes were the proportion of rental dwellings that were substandard and the rental vacancy rate.

We conclude that a national housing allowance program patterned on the HASE experimental program would yield only a modest augmentation of housing demand even in local markets where eligibility rates are high. This fact, combined with the evident flexibility of housing supply in nearly all local markets, virtually guarantees that the price effects of the program would be small even in communities where rental vacancy rates are in the range of 3 to 5 percent.[33]

Nor would we expect the neighborhood effects of a national program to be conspicuous. Program-induced repairs fall well short of the good-as-new rehabilitation that sometimes (if only temporarily) transforms the appearance of a blockface, and we can find no reason to suppose that an allowance program would spark the redevelopment of deteriorated neighborhoods. Our findings on residential mobility are consistent with the general literature on that subject. Neighborhoods change because a minority population is growing in numbers and therefore spreads out into formerly white areas; absent such growth, the frequent moves of individual households have little net effect on the economic or racial composition of a neighborhood's population.

Finally, we would not expect market intermediaries or indirect suppliers to play important roles in a national housing allowance program, for the same reasons that they did not do so in Brown or St. Joseph County. The residential repair and improvement industry is everywhere flexible enough to accommodate the modest increase in demand for their services that an allowance program would generate. Only a small percentage of potential program participants would need home improvement loans to finance repairs, and could get such loans unless their credit records were blemished. Relatively few renter participants would want to buy homes at market prices, and fewer still

permission. The underlying model of short-run market adjustment is presented in Rydell, 1980.

[33]There are few well-documented instances of lower rental vacancy rates for either a city or metropolitan area. The only national statistical system that reliably estimates local vacancy rates is the decennial census, in which complete enumeration of dwellings and their occupancy status is attempted. Only occasionally does a local study use statistically credible methods to arrive at vacancy estimates.

would be acceptable risks for private mortgage loans; only direct government loans or government insurance of private loans would appreciably broaden the participant market for home purchases, as they appear to have done in St. Joseph County.

The most important conclusion to be drawn from our analysis of the market effects of the experimental housing allowance program is that those effects were negligible. The allowance program substantially affected only those who participated and the dwellings in which they lived. Preexperimental concerns about undesirable market disturbances were groundless, and preexperimental hopes for neighborhood rejuvenation were unfulfilled.

The absence of broader effects, either good or bad, at least simplifies the assessment of housing allowances as a tool of federal housing policy. The desirability of a national program depends on whom it serves, how and how much they benefit, and how much those benefits cost the taxpayer. Chapter IV of this book addresses the first issue, Ch. V addresses the second, and Ch. VIII addresses the third.

REFERENCES

Barnett, C. Lance, and Ira S. Lowry, *How Housing Allowances Affect Housing Prices,* The Rand Corporation, R-2452-HUD, September 1979.

Carter, Grace M., and James E. Wendt, *Participation in an Open Enrollment Housing Allowance Program: Evidence from the Housing Assistance Supply Experiment,* The Rand Corporation, R-2783-HUD, June 1982.

Helbers, Lawrence, and James L. McDowell, *Determinants of Housing Repair and Improvement,* The Rand Corporation, R-2777-HUD, forthcoming, 1982.

Hillestad, Carol E., and James L. McDowell, *Measuring Neighborhood Change due to Housing Allowances,* The Rand Corporation, R-2776-HUD, forthcoming, 1982.

Lindsay, D. Scott, and Ira S. Lowry, *Rent Inflation in St. Joseph County, Indiana, 1974-78,* The Rand Corporation, N-2468-HUD, November 1980.

Lowry, Ira S., *Inflation Indexes for Rental Housing,* The Rand Corporation, N-1832-HUD, January 1982.

Mayo, Stephen K., *Theory and Estimation in the Economics of Housing Demand,* Abt Associates Inc., paper presented at the American Economic Association meetings, Chicago, Illinois, 29-31 August 1978.

McCarthy, Kevin F., *Housing Search and Mobility,* The Rand Corporation, R-2451-HUD, September 1979.

McDowell, James L., *Housing Allowance and Housing Improvement: Early Findings,* The Rand Corporation, N-1198-HUD, September 1979.

Mulford, John E., Lawrence Helbers, James L. McDowell, Michael P. Murray, and Orhan M. Yildiz, *Housing Consumption in a Housing Allowance Program,* The Rand Corporation, R-2779-HUD, forthcoming, 1982.

Mulford, John E., George D. Weiner, and James L. McDowell, *How Housing Allowance Recipients Adjust Housing Consumption,* The Rand Corporation, N-1456-HUD, August 1980.

Muth, Richard, "The Demand for Nonfarm Housing," in Arnold C. Harberger, ed., *The Demand for Durable Goods,* University of Chicago Press, Chicago, 1960, pp. 32-52.

Neels, Kevin, *The Economics of Rental Housing,* The Rand Corporation, R-2775-HUD, forthcoming, 1982a.

——, *Revenue and Expense Accounts for Rental Properties,* The Rand Corporation, N-1704-HUD, March 1982b.

Noland, Charles W., *Indexing the Cost of Producing Rental Housing Services in Site I, 1973-76,* The Rand Corporation, N-1627-HUD, September 1981.

——, *Indexing the Cost of Producing Rental Housing Services in Site II, 1974-77,* The Rand Corporation, N-1653-HUD, February 1982.

Rydell, C. Peter, *Shortrun Response of Housing Markets to Demand Shifts,* The Rand Corporation, R-2453-HUD, September 1979.

——, *Supply Response to the Housing Allowance Program,* The Rand Corporation, N-1338-HUD, October 1980.

Rydell, C. Peter, Kevin Neels, and C. Lance Barnett, *Price Effects of a Housing Allowance Program,* The Rand Corporation, R-2720-HUD, forthcoming, 1982.

Shanley, Michael G., and Charles M. Hotchkiss, *How Low-Income Renters Buy Homes,* The Rand Corporation, N-1208-HUD, August 1979.

——, *The Role of Market Intermediaries in a Housing Allowance Program,* The Rand Corporation, R-2659-HUD, December 1980.

Vanski, Jean E., and Larry Ozanne, *Simulating the Housing Allowance Program in Green Bay and South Bend,* The Urban Institute, Working Paper 249-5, Washington, D.C., October 1978.

Yildiz, Orhan M., and John E. Mulford, *Measuring Housing Quality: Evidence from St. Joseph County*, The Rand Corporation, N-1774-HUD, forthcoming, 1982.

VII. COMMUNITY ATTITUDES

From the standpoint of public policy, how people feel about a social program may be fully as important as what it objectively does to or for them. As part of the Supply Experiment, we gathered considerable information on community attitudes toward the experimental allowance program. We sought to learn how knowledge of the program spread, how attitudes toward it were formed, what those attitudes were, and how they differed as between public officials, nonparticipating households, participants, and landlords.

The most systematic information was collected in annual communitywide surveys of households and landlords. In addition, resident observers attended public meetings at which the program was discussed, talked informally to both influential and ordinary citizens, compiled statistical reports on the content of telephone calls received by the HAOs, and monitored the treatment of program-related news by local media. We drew on observers' reports for the political history of program implementation in each site and for insights that helped us interpret the systematic data on community attitudes that were collected in the surveys.

In the following pages, we summarize our findings. First, we discuss the diffusion of program knowledge and the formation of attitudes toward the program; then we consider how attitudes varied with the respondent's relationship to or experience with the program. Briefly, we find that knowledge of the program's existence spread quite rapidly, but most people were vague about program details. Over time, both favorable and unfavorable attitudes toward the program hardened. Most household heads were favorably disposed toward the program, but only participants believed that it substantially affected the community. Landlords were less enthusiastic about the program than household heads, but landlords with participating tenants were more positive than those without such tenants.

The wide base of community support for this program and the solidification of that support as community experience accumulated are not characteristic of all new social programs. From detailed responses to our attitude questions, we conclude that this program was especially popular because (a) it was a policy experiment; (b) it was financed without local taxes; (c) it was well-designed as a housing assistance program; and (d) it was managed competently and humanely.

THE SPREAD OF PROGRAM KNOWLEDGE

The first information about the allowance program reached Brown and St. Joseph counties when HUD notified local officials that their communities were being considered as experimental sites. A long period of negotiations and planning ensued, marked first by formal designation of the sites; second, by local government approvals of the plan; and third, by the organization and staffing of the housing allowance office in each site; and ending with the opening of enrollment. In Brown County, these events occupied 22 months, from September 1972 to June 1974. In St. Joseph County, the same events covered 15 months, from January 1974 to the beginning of April 1975.

During this period, public officials were thoroughly briefed on the nature of the allowance program and how it would operate in their jurisdictions; and they debated among themselves the wisdom of accepting the program. The local news media reported these events fully, emphasizing controversy whenever it arose (see Fig. 7.1). Ordinary citizens could learn about the program either from the media or, if sufficiently interested, by attending public sessions of local councils and commissions when the subject was on the agenda.

Although public officials and leaders of civic organizations became quite familiar with the program during this period, ordinary citizens paid little attention to it until enrollment began. In our baseline surveys, conducted shortly before enrollment opened in each site, only a fourth of the household heads in Brown County and a third in St. Joseph County said that they had heard of the housing allowance program; and (in St. Joseph County) only 16 percent of all household heads could supply any accurate details. Landlords knew little more than did the general public.

Once enrollment began, knowledge spread rapidly. The publicity attendant on that event brought over 1,200 applications to the Brown County HAO within the first three months; and 1,350 applications to the St. Joseph County HAO within the first month, despite the fact that the HAO's jurisdiction was then limited to South Bend. During this early period, HAO staffs made dozens of informational presentations to local audiences, distributed brochures and application forms through many channels, and maintained a steady flow of press releases, most of which were published by the local media.

Once the first rush of applications had been processed, the HAOs kept up the flow of applicants by periodic advertising campaigns, saturating local television and radio channels as well as newspapers.[1]

[1]During the first five program years, the Brown County HAO spent $76,000 on advertising and the St. Joseph County HAO spent $357,000. (Both figures are for space

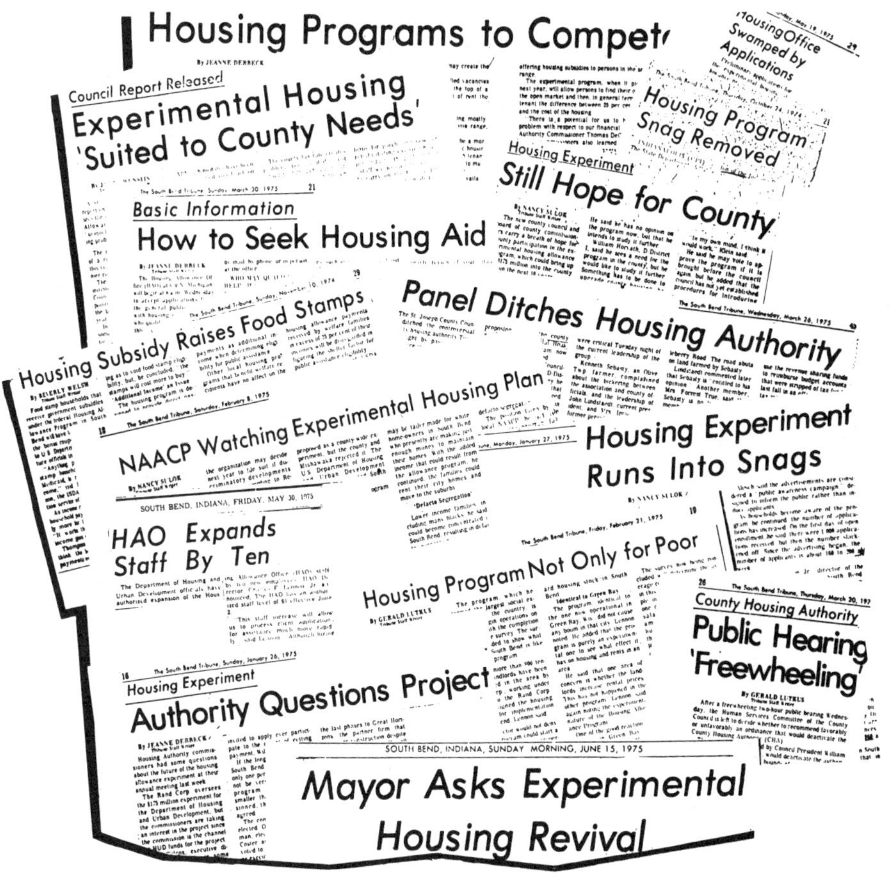

Fig. 7.1—A sample of newspaper stories on the housing allowance program in St. Joseph County

After about two years of such campaigns, paid advertising was reduced to a "maintenance" level, and the HAOs concentrated on mailings and presentations to hard-to-reach groups.

Table 7.1 shows how quickly knowledge of the program spread after

---

or broadcast time only, exclusive of professional services.) The expenditures differ between sites for two reasons. First, the Brown County HAO did little television advertising because local stations served a much larger area than the program jurisdiction; radio and newspaper advertising was both cheaper and better focused as to audience. Second, influential citizens objected to the use of public funds to advertise the program. In St. Joseph County, television broadcasting was better focused on the appropriate audience, and few citizens objected to the advertising.

Table 7.1

PROGRAM KNOWLEDGE AMONG HOUSEHOLD HEADS AND LANDLORDS: SURVEY WAVES 2 AND 4, BY SITE

Level of Program Knowledge	Percentage Distribution			
	Brown County		St. Joseph County	
	Wave 2	Wave 4	Wave 2	Wave 4
Household Heads				
None	19.7	10.7	12.6	5.6
Has heard of program	31.5	19.1	39.7	21.1
Knows some correct details	28.9	46.3	35.7	48.7
Knows some unique details	19.9	23.9	12.0	24.6
Total	100.0	100.0	100.0	100.0
Landlords				
None	24.0	5.9	10.2	2.4
Has heard of program	18.7	18.9	33.0	17.0
Knows some correct details	35.8	50.2	41.5	51.7
Knows some unique details	21.6	24.9	15.4	28.9
Total	100.0	100.0	100.0	100.0

SOURCE: Tabulated by Hase staff from weighted records of the surveys of households and landlords.

NOTE: For respondents who had heard of the program, their levels of knowledge were determined by content analysis of their verbatim program descriptions. "Correct details" characterize the allowance program but could apply equally well to other local programs. "Unique details" characterize the allowance program but no other locally active housing or welfare program. Percentages may not add exactly to 100.0 because of rounding.

Distributions are based on the following sample sizes: in Brown County, 2,468 households and 950 landlords (wave 2); 2,422 households and 782 landlords (wave 4); in St. Joseph County, 1,956 households and 792 landlords (wave 2); 2,102 households and 720 landlords (wave 4).

enrollment began. The second survey wave began seven months after enrollment opened in Brown County and ten months after enrollment opened in St. Joseph County. By wave 2, 80 percent of all household heads in Brown County and 87 percent in St. Joseph County had heard of the program. The corresponding figures for landlords are 76 and 90 percent. By wave 4, two years later, nearly everyone in both counties had heard of the program.

Although awareness of the program was widespread, knowledge of its details was limited. At wave 2, less than half the household heads in either site could supply any correct details about the program: whom it helped, what it was intended to accomplish, or how it worked. Less than 20 percent unequivocally distinguished it from other programs such as public housing or neighborhood improvement. Landlords were somewhat better informed. By wave 4, 70 to 80 percent of all household heads and landlords knew some correct details; but only 24 to 29 percent could give unique details.

From the sources of information cited by survey respondents and by applicants, it is clear that the rapid diffusion of program knowledge was attributable mainly to the HAOs' advertisements. After some early experiments, these advertisements (see Fig. 7.2) avoided specifics such as entitlement schedules or income limits in favor of general indications of who might be eligible (low-income renters and homeowners, elderly persons) and how they might benefit (help with housing expenses). Thus, only those who actually applied were likely to learn about the program in any depth, unless through friends, neighbors, or tenants who had enrolled.

ATTITUDE FORMATION

The formation of attitudes toward the allowance program began with civic leaders directly involved in the negotiations leading to site selection, then spread to organized groups that perceived potential benefits or dangers from the program. In neither county were landlords well enough organized to form a coherent interest group. The general public knew little about the program until enrollment began, so were late to form attitudes about it.

The Civic Leadership

The two counties differ markedly in political organization and political style (see Ch. II). These differences were reflected in the site-selection negotiations and subsequent organization of the HAOs.

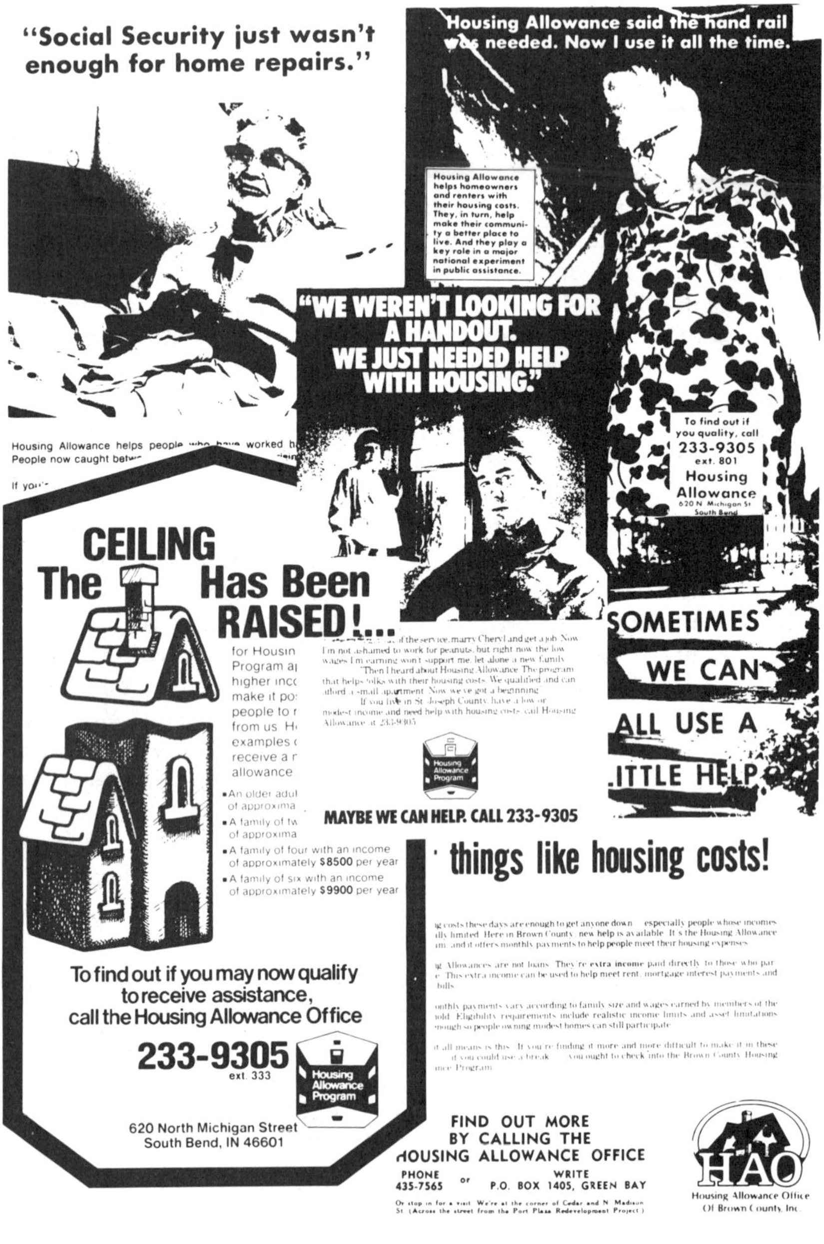

Fig. 7.2—A sample of newspaper advertisements for the housing allowance programs in Brown and St. Joseph counties

Although Brown County had hitherto virtually abstained from federal housing assistance, civic leaders quickly agreed that the allowance program was desirable. Under state law, every civil division in the county—the county itself, two cities, four villages, 18 townships, and an Indian tribal council—had to separately consider participation in the program. All but one rural township had formally agreed to participate before enrollment began, and that one joined the program about two months later.

Although the consensus on participation was prompt, it was reached only after civic leaders had probed for dangers to the community. The concerns most often voiced during negotiations were that

- The program would become a welfare magnet attracting migrants who would inflate county welfare rolls.
- The program could not adequately differentiate the needy from the undeserving.
- Program termination ten years hence would pose serious problems for participants and the community.

Commitments from HUD as to program design and transition allayed these concerns. No organized opposition to the program ever surfaced, either during negotiations or during the first five years of program operation. There were, to be sure, individual complaints about undeserving recipients or unfair program rules, and objections to the HAO using public funds to advertise the availability of income transfers. The latter objections were taken seriously by the HAO, which modified its advertising policy both as to intensity and tone.

In St. Joseph County, the city of South Bend had aggressively sought (and obtained) federal funding for housing and community development programs for at least a decade before the experimental allowance program was proposed. Both the mayor and city council of South Bend strongly endorsed the allowance program, convincing Rand and HUD that the county was viable as an experimental site despite the hesitations of other jurisdictions. Officials of Mishawaka and the county probed repeatedly into the contractual relationships that would be required for their participation, as well as into issues of program design and operation; eventually, governing bodies of both jurisdictions voted against participation.

At this stage, local supporters of the experimental program stressed the federal money it would bring into the community and its benefits to elderly persons. Opposition ranged from concern that undeserving persons would be helped to fears that the county's black population, concentrated in central South Bend, would use their allowances to relocate elsewhere—for example, in neighboring Mishawaka, whose government was often at odds with that of South Bend.

When enrollment began, the program's jurisdiction was limited to South Bend. However, local elections changed the membership of the governing bodies of both Mishawaka and the county, and the new members subsequently voted to enter the program. Outlying incorporated areas followed, but it was not until November 1976—20 months after enrollment began—that the entire county was participating.

Throughout the prolonged and often intemperate debate over the merits and control of the experimental program, press coverage was lively; but our surveys (see below) indicate that the general public paid little attention to the controversy. However, especially after enrollment began, a number of local organizations focused their attention on the program.

One civic group that provides social services to the elderly lobbied for the program; a taxpayer's association was persistently hostile, and a group that operated social programs in low-income neighborhoods was at least briefly so. Leaders of two organizations representing minorities, although not opposing the program in principle, attacked program features that they thought were adverse to the interests of their members. A local NAACP officer sought a more forceful desegregation policy; representatives of a Mexican-American organization successfully sought revision of a policy that delayed enrollment of new residents. A Mishawaka developer argued that adopting the program would cut off federal subsidies for new rental housing. And the South Bend Housing Authority charged that the allowance program drew away many of its "best" tenants.

Some objections centered on program management. For example, a labor union accused the HAO of improper conduct in soliciting non-union bids to renovate its permanent quarters. The owner of a downtown office building complained that in choosing its office space, the HAO had not supported efforts to reinvigorate the city's central business district.

The white ethnic groups that figure prominently in the social and political structure of the county did not take formal positions, although some of their leaders offered public support for the program. The exception was a group of Hungarian immigrants who persuaded a member to withdraw his application for enrollment because it required information on household composition and income.

The contrast with events in Brown County, where there was no organized criticism of the program, is striking. It is also notable that most complaints about the program in St. Joseph County were based less on objections to the concept of housing allowances than on concerns for special constituencies.

Household Heads

In neither county did the general public pay much attention to the program before enrollment began. When they subsequently learned about it, their descriptions clearly reflected the features stressed in the HAOs' advertisements: what the program was designed to do (help pay housing costs, improve housing conditions), whom it helped (low-income families, both renters and homeowners), and the form of assistance (monthly cash payments). The concerns of public officials about local control and broader community effects were not salient in the perceptions of ordinary citizens.

Early evaluations of the program were strongly positive (see Table 7.2). At survey wave 2, at least three-fifths of those in each site who knew about the program thought it was "a good idea" and only 10 to 13 percent expressed negative views. Over time, approval ratings fell slightly, either because early expectations were disappointed or because those who were slow to learn about the program were also less enthusiastic.

Brown County's inexperience with federal housing programs is reflected in the first column of the table. About half the informed household heads there were unwilling at wave 2 to judge program administration and 28 percent had no views on the appropriate federal role in housing assistance. By wave 4, Brown County households were more likely than their counterparts in St. Joseph County to have opinions on these subjects. Program administration was then more generally approved in Brown County, but the two counties' views on a national program and on the federal role in housing assistance were similar. When asked to balance the merits of a national program against its tax costs, respondents in both counties lost some of their enthusiasm for housing allowances.

Landlords

The owners of rental property—most of them owners of only one or two small properties[2]—seemed, like the general public, to have learned about the program primarily from the HAOs' advertisements, and retained the same kinds of information. However, they were noticeably less positive than household heads in their early

[2]Over 90 percent of the rental properties in Brown County and 84 percent in St. Joseph County were owned by individuals, as opposed to partnerships, corporations, or public authorities. Eighty percent of the landlords in each site owned only one rental property containing one to four dwellings. Nearly all had another source of income besides the rental property; about 84 percent in Brown County and 60 percent in St. Joseph County worked at least 30 hours weekly at another job.

Table 7.2

PROGRAM EVALUATIONS BY INFORMED HOUSEHOLD HEADS: SURVEY WAVES 2 AND 4, BY SITE

Respondent's Evaluation	Percentage Distribution			
	Brown County		St. Joseph County	
	Wave 2	Wave 4	Wave 2	Wave 4
Overall Program Evaluation[a]				
Good idea	60.0	61.6	64.4	61.8
Neutral, no opinion	29.7	21.6	22.4	25.1
Bad idea	10.4	16.9	13.2	13.2
Do HAO staff know what they are doing?				
Yes	38.9	71.5	57.5	59.9
Neutral, no opinion	48.0	15.1	21.0	18.8
No	13.0	13.3	21.5	21.2
Is the program run the way it should be?				
Yes	27.1	59.8	47.8	50.2
Neutral, no opinion	60.3	18.4	29.7	24.1
No	12.6	21.9	22.4	25.7
Would a national program be worth the taxes?				
Yes	(b)	46.9	50.8	47.8
Neutral, no opinion	(b)	10.8	11.8	13.4
No	(b)	42.1	37.4	38.9
Should the federal government help with housing costs?				
Yes	55.9	57.8	58.8	58.8
Neutral, no opinion	28.1	7.6	10.4	8.9
No	16.1	34.5	30.8	32.4

SOURCE: Tabulated by HASE staff from weighted records of the surveys of households.

NOTE: Distributions are based on records for household heads who were able to give at least some correct details about the allowance program. Sample sizes for Brown County were 1,173 (wave 2) and 1,638 (wave 4); for St. Joseph County, 944 (wave 2) and 1,522 (wave 4). Except for rounding errors, each column in each panel of the table would add to 100.0 percent.

[a] Respondents rated the program on a 7-point scale, "good idea" to "bad idea." In this panel, ratings 1-3 are coded as "good idea" and ratings of 5-7 are coded as "bad idea." Ratings of 4 are coded as "neutral" and are combined with "no opinion" and "don't know" responses.

[b] This question was not asked of respondents to the wave 2 survey in Brown County.

evaluations (see Table 7.3). At survey wave 2, about half thought the program was a good idea and a fourth thought it was a bad idea.

Those views subsequently shifted negatively in Brown County but positively in St. Joseph County. In the former case, we are not sure whether informed landlords changed their minds, or whether those who were slowest to learn about the program were also the least enthusiastic about it. Like household heads there, Brown County's landlords had little prior experience with federal housing assistance programs, so had few benchmarks against which to judge this one. By wave 4, they were clearly less enthusiastic both about the local allowance program and about federal housing assistance generally than were St. Joseph County landlords, who seem to have been pleasantly surprised by the HAO's performance there. At any rate, landlords' approval of the program and its staff increased and negative views diminished in frequency between waves 2 and 4 in St. Joseph County.

KNOWLEDGE AND ATTITUDES AFTER EXPERIENCE WITH THE PROGRAM

The final (wave 4) annual surveys of households and landlords were conducted in Brown County some 30 months after enrollment began, and in St. Joseph County, 36 months after enrollment began. By then, we think that community knowledge of and attitudes toward the program had matured and stabilized.

At the time of the wave 4 surveys, nearly everyone in both counties had at least heard of the program, and over two-thirds of the adult residents knew at least some pertinent details (see Table 7.1, above). The HAOs were no longer exotic innovations; they had become community institutions whose functions were accepted and whose officers participated fully in civic affairs. Nearly a fourth of all household heads had contacted the HAO to inquire about eligibility; 12 percent had been enrolled at some time and about 7 percent were currently receiving payments. Many others had friends or relatives in the program. About a third of all landlords recalled at least one housing evaluation conducted by the HAO for a current or prospective tenant; nearly a fifth had tenants who were then in the program.

Nonetheless, the allowance program was only a vague presence to about a fourth of the community's adult residents—mainly, those who assumed they were ineligible, who had neither friends, relatives, nor tenants in the program, and who were uninterested in civic affairs. Given that the extensive early publicity did not intrude on their awareness and that normal program operations did not directly involve

Table 7.3

PROGRAM EVALUATIONS BY INFORMED LANDLORDS: SURVEY WAVES 2 AND 4, BY SITE

Respondent's Evaluation	Percentage Distribution			
	Brown County		St. Joseph County	
	Wave 2	Wave 4	Wave 2	Wave 4
Overall Program Evaluation[a]				
Good idea	54.9	43.3	48.7	55.3
Neutral, no opinion	15.2	25.6	27.4	25.0
Bad idea	29.9	31.1	23.9	19.7
Do HAO staff know what they are doing?				
Yes	26.6	47.5	46.4	53.3
Neutral, no opinion	60.9	28.4	31.3	27.0
No	12.6	24.1	22.3	19.7
Is the program run the way it should be?				
Yes	13.0	40.7	37.3	43.7
Neutral, no opinion	71.9	26.3	34.7	31.1
No	15.0	33.0	28.0	25.2
Would a national program be worth the taxes?				
Yes	(*b*)	25.2	36.4	37.3
Neutral, no opinion	(*b*)	16.1	17.4	17.3
No	(*b*)	58.7	46.1	45.4
Should the federal government help with housing costs?				
Yes	33.1	34.7	49.0	51.9
Neutral, no opinion	28.6	10.1	16.5	10.3
No	38.2	55.3	34.4	37.8

SOURCE: Tabulated by HASE staff from weighted records of the surveys of landlords.

NOTE: Distributions are based on records for landlords who were able to give at least some correct details about the allowance program. Sample sizes for Brown County were 552 (wave 2) and 598 (wave 4); for St. Joseph County, 469 (wave 2) and 575 (wave 4). Except for rounding errors, each column in each panel of the table would add to 100.0 percent.

[a] Respondents rated the program on a 7-point scale, "good idea" to "bad idea." In this panel, ratings 1-3 are coded as "good idea" and ratings of 5-7 are coded as "bad idea." Ratings of 4 are coded as neutral and are combined with "no opinion" and "don't know" responses.

[b] This question was not asked of respondents to the wave 2 survey in Brown County.

them, we doubt that this fourth of the adult population would ever become well-informed about the program. We think that by wave 4, the residents of Brown and St. Joseph counties understood the allowance program nearly as well as they ever would, and that their attitudes toward it reflected substantial experience with its day-to-day operations. To be sure, some future change in local circumstance or in program rules might increase local awareness or change existing attitudes; but the breadth and depth of community exposure to the program at wave 4 seem to us close to what should be expected from a permanent program.

In the following pages, we examine wave 4 perceptions and attitudes first among all household heads, then among program participants, and finally among landlords. In each case, we distinguish respondents according to their degree of exposure to the program and its results for them.

HOUSEHOLD HEADS AT SURVEY WAVE 4

In their wave 4 interviews, about 23 percent of all household heads acknowledged that they had once contacted the HAO to inquire about their eligibility for assistance, and about 12 percent had actually enrolled in the program. Ten percent subsequently qualified for payments, and 7 percent were still receiving payments at the time of the interview (Table 7.4).

These different degrees of experience with the program should correlate with knowledge of program standards and administrative procedures, and possibly with attitudes toward the program. Those who never applied were either oblivious of the program, sure they were ineligible, or if eligible, not interested; with no personal stake, those who were familiar with the program would judge it in terms of its consequences for their community and, possibly, for specific friends or relatives. Most of those who inquired or applied but did not enroll were rejected as ineligible; but a few eligibles dropped out because of what they learned about the program or their own entitlements. Those who enrolled but never qualified for payments were unwilling or unable to meet the program's housing standards, and might well judge the HAO harshly for "leading them on." Finally, one would expect that the attitudes of those who did qualify for payments would be strongly influenced by the benefits they received—although they might also be able to consider the program's merits from a broader perspective.

Table 7.5 shows that perceptions of the program's effects do vary

Table 7.4

HOUSEHOLD HEADS BY PROGRAM STATUS: SURVEY WAVE 4, BY SITE

Program Status	Distribution of Household Heads			
	Brown County		St. Joseph County	
	Number	Percent	Number	Percent
All household heads	48,592	100.0	72,509	100.0
Has heard of program[a]	43,371	89.3	67,821	93.5
Knows some correct details[a]	34,639	71.3	54,270	74.8
Inquired about enrolling	10,631	21.9	17,623	24.3
Attended enrollment interview	7,009	14.4	12,481	17.2
Signed participation agreement	5,392	11.1	8,668	12.0
Received allowance payments	4,873	10.0	7,146	9.9
Currently receives payments	3,488	7.2	5,392	7.4

SOURCE: Tabulated by HASE staff from weighted records of the wave 4 survey of households.

NOTE: Population estimates are based on records for 2,422 respondents in Brown County and 2,102 in St. Joseph County.

[a]Entries do not agree exactly with those in Table 7.1 because a different test of program knowledge was applied to facilitate screening of respondents to subsequent questions.

with exposure to the program. Those who never inquired about joining (but knew about the program) were least likely to perceive either good or bad consequences for themselves or their neighborhoods, although they did vaguely imagine countywide effects. Among those who inquired or enrolled but never received payments, 14 percent in Brown County and 18 percent in St. Joseph County thought that their neighborhoods had been significantly affected ("somewhat" or "a lot") —perhaps because they were more likely than the first group to live near recipients. Among those who actually received payments, 30 and 34 percent in the counties, respectively, perceived significant neighborhood effects. Only in the latter group did many respondents perceive direct effects on their own households; but a majority of each group thought that the county had been noticeably affected.

Since few respondents had access to systematic evidence on the nature of countywide effects, we think that their perceptions of such effects were based on a priori reasoning. In their own neighborhoods, where personal observation could guide perceptions, their claims for

Table 7.5

Scope of Program Effects Perceived by Informed Household Heads, by Program Status: Survey Wave 4, by Site

Perceived Program Effect	Percentage Distribution of Households in Each Status[a]					
	Brown County			St. Joseph County		
	Informed, Never Inquired	Inquired or Enrolled, Never Paid	Received Payments	Informed, Never Inquired	Inquired or Enrolled, Never Paid	Received Payments
Has program affected respondent's household?						
A lot	.8	3.0	65.1	.4	4.4	63.6
Somewhat	4.3	4.2	22.2	1.8	4.6	17.1
Very little	6.0	5.3	8.5	3.8	2.6	5.6
Not at all, don't know	88.9	87.4	4.3	94.1	88.4	13.7
Has program affected respondent's neighborhood?						
A lot	.7	1.8	9.4	.8	7.9	15.2
Somewhat	7.9	12.3	20.8	6.1	10.3	18.4
Very little	14.3	18.2	11.5	8.6	7.6	6.4
Not at all, don't know	77.1	67.6	58.3	84.4	74.1	60.0
Has program affected respondent's county?						
A lot	13.5	15.6	45.3	13.6	27.2	46.1
Somewhat	54.2	55.4	36.3	47.6	32.6	21.4
Very little	12.7	9.6	4.2	11.0	4.8	2.1
Not at all, don't know	19.5	19.4	14.2	27.8	35.4	30.4

SOURCE: Tabulated by HASE staff from weighted records of the wave 4 surveys of households.

NOTE: Population distributions are based on records for 1,638 respondents in Brown County and 1,522 in St. Joseph County. Except for rounding error, each column in each panel would add to 100.0 percent.

[a]See Table 7.4 for details of program status.

the program were more modest. When asked about specific kinds of effects, all groups were most impressed by the program's effects on housing maintenance and property values and least impressed by its effects on rents and residential mobility (Table 7.6). As above, those with the greatest program exposure were most likely to perceive consequences, either because they better understood the cause, and so inferred an effect; or because the effects were truly more conspicuous in their neighborhoods.

When asked to evaluate the allowance program, those with greater exposure to it were, not surprisingly, more likely to have opinions (Table 7.7). They were also more likely to have favorable opinions. Over 90 percent of those who had received payments approved of the program generally and of the HAO staff's performance specifically; nearly that many thought the program was properly run (probably meaning that its rules were fair and appropriate). Those who had rejected or been rejected by the program were less inclined to think it was properly run, but over half were satisfied on that score and about two-thirds approved of staff performance.[3]

Nearly all respondents had opinions on national housing policy, as distinct from the local experiment. Only two-fifths of those most distant from the experimental program thought that a national allowance program would be worth the taxes, but over half favored some kind of federal housing assistance. Those exposed to the program but not in it were more enthusiastic both about a national program and about unspecified federal housing assistance. Among recipients, about a tenth of those who approved of the local allowance program thought a national program wouldn't be worth the taxes.

Content analysis of verbatim responses indicates that for all three groups the salient feature of the allowance program was its choice of beneficiaries. Those who approved of that choice characterized the beneficiaries as "people who need help," mentioning specifically the elderly, handicapped persons, and renters. Those who disapproved characterized the beneficiaries as "people who don't need help," but the only commonly mentioned group was "people on welfare." In both sites, allowance recipients were held in much higher esteem than welfare recipients, although in fact the two groups overlapped considerably.

[3]More detailed tabulations show that those in Brown County who attended enrollment interviews but did not enroll (usually because they were found to be ineligible) were least content with either program rules or staff. In St. Joseph County, approval ratings rise steadily with each step of exposure to the program; a majority of both those rejected at the interview stage and those who enrolled but did not qualify for payments agreed that the program was properly run; and two-thirds of each group approved of staff performance.

PROGRAM PARTICIPANTS AT SURVEY WAVE 4

We have seen that allowance recipients took much more positive views of the allowance program than did other households (Tables 7.5 to 7.7). That outcome was perhaps expectable, given that recipients were getting monthly cash payments that averaged about a fifth of their nonallowance incomes. However, the beneficiaries of federal housing programs are not always so appreciative.

Table 7.8 compares attitudes reported by current recipients of allowances in Brown and St. Joseph counties with those reported a few years earlier by a national sample of participants in three other federal housing programs (Louis Harris and Associates, 1976). Because the respondents from the various programs were not matched as to personal characteristics, and because there were minor differences in question wording and response scaling, the cross-program differences shown in the table are not conclusive. Nonetheless, the comparisons suggest that the housing allowance program better satisfied its beneficiaries than did Sec. 236 rent subsidies, Sec. 235 mortgage subsidies, or public housing.[4]

Favorable views of the allowance program were not confined to current recipients. Majorities of those who applied and were turned away, who enrolled but never received payments, or who formerly received payments but were no longer in the program also gave it high marks. The reasons appear to be that the HAOs' rules were comprehensible and the staffs were courteous. Among the wave 4 survey respondents who applied and were told that they were ineligible, only about 15 percent complained about program rules, although nearly two-fifths expressed disappointment or annoyance with the outcome.

Those who enrolled could not qualify for payments until their dwellings had been evaluated. About half the respondents in Brown County and slightly more in St. Joseph County reported that their dwellings had failed initial evaluations; but only 9 and 11 percent of those whose dwellings failed thought that the evaluations were unfair (Table 7.9). That judgment was doubtless related to the fact that 90 percent in Brown County and 71 percent in St. Joseph County thought that the required repairs were not at all difficult.

Before signing a participation agreement, each prospective enrollee was told how much his housing allowance would be, so few enrollees entered the program with false expectations. However, subsequent changes in an enrollee's income or household composition often

---

[4]Currently, the federal housing program closest to housing allowances is the Sec. 8 Existing Housing Program, with over 900,000 participants nationwide. It was enacted in 1972, but was only beginning operations in 1973 when the Harris survey was conducted, so we do not have comparable data on participants' attitudes.

Table 7.6

NEIGHBORHOOD EFFECTS PERCEIVED BY INFORMED HOUSEHOLD HEADS, BY PROGRAM STATUS: SURVEY WAVE 4, BY SITE

Perceived Program Effect	Percentage Distribution of Households in Each Status[a]					
	Brown County			St. Joseph County		
	Informed, Never Inquired	Inquired or Enrolled, Never Paid	Received Payments	Informed, Never Inquired	Inquired or Enrolled, Never Paid	Received Payments
Effect on Housing Repairs						
More repairs	8.3	11.9	28.9	6.4	15.1	26.5
No effect, mixed effect	91.3	86.3	70.7	93.0	83.8	72.9
Fewer repairs	.4	1.8	.5	.6	1.1	.7
Effect on Property Upkeep						
Better upkeep	6.6	8.1	26.6	6.5	14.2	34.3
No effect, mixed effect	92.6	91.0	73.4	93.0	85.4	65.7
Worse upkeep	.8	.8	--	.6	.4	--

Effect on Housing Rents						
Made rents rise	3.3	3.0	5.9	2.3	6.6	6.4
No effect, mixed effect	96.0	96.2	93.7	97.7	93.2	93.5
Made rents fall	.6	.7	.4	--	.2	.1
Effect on Property Values						
Increased property values	5.8	5.5	22.3	5.2	13.9	26.0
No effect, mixed effect	93.8	93.1	77.5	94.2	85.6	73.7
Decreased property values	.4	1.4	.2	.6	.5	.4
Effect on Bringing New People into the Neighborhood						
Desirable people	3.1	2.3	9.9	.8	4.9	6.8
No effect, mixed effect	95.9	95.9	89.9	98.2	94.5	92.9
Undesirable people	1.0	1.8	.2	1.0	.6	.3

SOURCE: Tabulated by HASE staff from weighted records of the wave 4 survey of households.

NOTE: Population distributions are based on records for 2,422 respondents in Brown County and 2,102 in St. Joseph County. Except for rounding error, each column in each panel would add to 100.0 percent.

[a]See Table 7.4 for details of program status.

Table 7.7

PROGRAM EVALUATIONS BY INFORMED HOUSEHOLD HEADS, BY PROGRAM STATUS: SURVEY WAVE 4, BY SITE

Respondent's Evaluation	Percentage Distribution of Households in Each Status[a]					
	Brown County			St. Joseph County		
	Informed, Never Inquired	Inquired or Enrolled, Never Paid	Received Payments	Informed Never Inquired	Inquired or Enrolled, Never Paid	Received Payments
Overall Program Evaluation[b]						
Good idea	56.1	61.4	90.0	54.3	68.5	92.0
Neutral, no opinion	25.0	18.3	7.9	30.2	20.6	3.6
Bad idea	18.9	20.3	2.2	15.4	10.9	4.4
Do HAO staff know what they are doing?						
Yes	67.7	72.4	90.4	53.0	65.0	90.0
Neutral, no opinion	18.3	10.6	4.2	23.9	8.9	5.5
No	14.0	17.0	5.4	23.0	26.2	4.5
Is the program run the way it should be?[c]						
Yes	54.8	57.1	88.9	43.9	50.2	84.0
Neutral, no opinion	23.2	10.1	3.4	28.4	19.1	8.2
No	22.1	32.8	7.8	27.7	30.6	7.9

Would a national program be worth the taxes?

Yes	40.3	49.6	78.0	37.2	64.3	82.0
Neutral, no opinion	12.0	6.9	10.5	13.9	12.8	10.6
No	47.7	43.4	11.5	48.9	23.0	7.4

Should the federal government help with housing costs?

Yes	52.2	62.4	81.8	51.4	70.7	82.3
Neutral, no opinion	8.6	6.1	4.2	9.9	9.2	2.8
No	39.2	31.4	14.0	38.8	20.2	14.8

SOURCE: Tabulated by HASE staff from weighted records of the surveys of households.

NOTE: Population distributions are based on records for 2,422 respondents in Brown County and 2,102 in St. Joseph County. Except for rounding error, each column in each panel would add to 100.0 percent.

[a]See Table 7.4 for details of program status.

[b]Respondents rated the program on a 7-point scale, "good idea" to "bad idea." In this panel, ratings 1-3 are coded as "good idea" and ratings of 5-7 are coded as "bad idea." Ratings of 4 are coded as neutral and are combined with "no opinion" and "don't know" responses.

[c]Although the instrument does not elaborate on the intent of this question, it follows the question on staff performance and thereby encourages the respondent to focus on program rules and procedures rather than personnel.

Table 7.8

RECIPIENTS' EVALUATIONS OF SELECTED FEDERAL HOUSING ASSISTANCE PROGRAMS

Respondent's Evaluation	Percentage Distribution of Households in Each Program			
	Housing Allowances (n = 381)	Sec. 236 Rent Subsidy (n = 556)	Sec. 235 Mortgage Subsidy (n = 391)	Public Housing (n = 511)
Own Experience with Program				
Satisfactory	95	84	86	77
Neutral, no opinion	3	5	3	9
Unsatisfactory	2	11	11	14
Is the program run the way it should be?				
Yes	91	69	68	63
Neutral, no opinion	5	13	16	20
No	4	18	16	17
Should the program be changed in any way?				
No	78	52	49	48
Neutral, no opinion	2	12	16	29
Yes	19	36	35	23

SOURCES: For housing allowances, tabulated by HASE staff from weighted records of the wave 4 surveys of households. For other programs, Louis Harris and Associates, 1976, pp. 1,427-31.

NOTE: HASE and Harris questions are nearly parallel in wording; however, responses to the "own experience" question were independently scaled by the two sources so may not be exactly comparable. Harris surveyed a national sample of participants in each program in 1973; the HASE data are for 1978-79.

changed his allowance entitlement; indeed, about a third of all recipients became ineligible each year. From their responses to wave 4 survey questions, it is clear that nearly all recipients understood the link between income and allowance entitlement, but nearly half supposed that their allowances would increase if their rents or property taxes increased.[5]

[5]Allowances were increased periodically for all recipients to offset average housing cost inflation (see Ch. III); however, the HAOs were careful neither to promise nor forecast such increases.

Table 7.9

Participants' Experience with Housing Evaluations and Payments: Survey Wave 4, by Site

Response	Percentage Distribution	
	Brown County	St. Joseph County
For Failed Dwellings: Do you think the evaluation was fair or unfair?		
Fair	91.3	85.6
Unfair	8.7	10.9
Don't know	--	3.5
For Failed Dwellings: How difficult (were/would be) the required repairs?		
Very difficult	2.9	7.3
Somewhat difficult	7.5	22.2
Not difficult at all	89.6	70.5
For Recipients: (Is/was) your allowance as much as you expected?		
More than expected	32.7	25.1
About the same as expected	43.6	53.3
Less than expected	14.3	13.1
Don't know	9.4	8.5
For Recipients: (Is/was) your allowance enough?		
Not enough	27.1	27.6
About right	71.0	69.6
Too much	.5	.8
Don't know	1.4	1.9
For All Applicants: Did the HAO staff spend enough time with you?		
Enough time	93.3	87.8
Not enough time	5.3	9.3
Don't know	1.3	2.9
For All Applicants: Did you need advice that the HAOs failed to give?		
Yes	5.6	7.1
No	94.3	92.6
Don't know	.1	.2

SOURCE: Tabulated by HASE staff from weighted records of the wave 4 surveys of households.

NOTE: Sample sizes for respondents whose dwellings failed their initial evaluations are 112 in Brown County, 104 in St. Joseph County; for recipients, 378 and 312; for all applicants who attended enrollment interviews, 520 and 492. Except for rounding error, each column in each panel would add to 100.0 percent.

Despite that confusion, no more than 14 percent of the wave 4 respondents who had ever qualified for payments said that their allowances were less than they had expected when they enrolled (Table 7.9). About a fourth in each site described their allowances as "not enough," but that response does not necessarily imply resentment or disappointment; it merely reflects the indisputable fact that many recipients were on tight budgets.

Thus, with respect to the two salient features of the program—housing evaluations and allowance entitlements—about four-fifths of the participants thought that the application of program rules to their cases was reasonable. An even greater proportion were satisfied with the attention and advice they got from the HAO staffs. About 90 percent of those who attended enrollment interviews (whether or not they enrolled) said that the HAO staff had spent enough time with them, and only about 6 percent said that they needed advice that they did not get from the HAOs (Table 7.9).[6] These attitudes varied little with respondents' characteristics such as age, race, or education; or with household characteristics such as family size, housing tenure, income, or location of residence.

When enrollees were asked whether anything about the allowance program should be changed, about a fifth had suggestions; but there was little consensus on desirable changes. Their responses included 50 different recommendations and criticisms, none mentioned by more than a few enrollees. Generally, critics favored more money and looser rules, but more thought that the income and asset limits were overgenerous than that they were overstrict.

Even among those who enrolled but never qualified for payments, a surprisingly small proportion wanted more help or guidance from the HAOs. In 1979, we surveyed a sample of 652 such cases in the two sites, asking why they had not become recipients (Kingsley, Kirby, and Rizor, 1982, Sec. VII). About a seventh dropped out because they thought (usually correctly) that they were no longer eligible. Another third dropped out because they thought their allowances were too small or because they found the program rules oppressive. Over a seventh were unwilling to repair their dwellings or move, and did not think the HAOs could help; essentially, their allowance entitlements

[6]Both HAOs offered voluntary classes that included sessions on program rules, tenants' rights and responsibilities, home purchase guidance, choosing an appropriate residence, and home maintenance. So few enrollees attended these sessions that they were eventually discontinued. Participants did often call or visit the HAO to clarify repair requirements, inquire about apparently overdue allowance payments, or to get help in disputes with their landlords. Although the HAOs were ready to explain and reexplain program rules and the reasons for particular administrative actions, they carefully avoided becoming parties to repair arrangements or disputes between landlords and tenants.

were inadequate inducements for an otherwise undesired change in their domestic arrangements. Only a third thought that either allowance advances or more guidance would have enabled them to complete the needed repairs or move to another dwelling. The remainder (less than 5 percent) gave no specific reason for dropping out.

LANDLORDS AT SURVEY WAVE 4

Although the HAOs did not deal directly with landlords, the allowance program was naturally a matter of interest to them inasmuch as it affected the incomes of actual or potential tenants and set standards for property maintenance. Nearly all landlords who responded to the wave 4 survey had heard of the program and at least three-fourths in each site knew some details about it (see Table 7.10). Nearly a third recalled that at least one dwelling on their property had been evaluated by the HAO[7] and nearly a fifth currently had tenants who were allowance recipients. A few landlords in each site had themselves applied for enrollment.[8]

As with household heads, landlords' perceptions of the allowance program and their attitudes toward it varied with their exposure to program operations, as those operations affected either their own or nearby properties. However, the allowance program was clearly less important to landlords than to household heads with roughly equivalent program experience, and landlords viewed the program less favorably.

Table 7.11 shows that only about a fifth of the landlords whose tenants included allowance recipients thought that the program had affected the management of their properties or nearby properties ("somewhat" or "a lot"). The table also suggests that housing evaluations were salient in these perceptions; those landlords who recalled evaluations but had no currently participating tenants perceived program effects nearly as often as those with currently participating tenants, and much more often than informed landlords who had no direct experience with the program.

Exposure to program operations generally sharpened landlords' attitudes toward the program, but made them only slightly more favorable (Table 7.12). Among those with the greatest exposure, about half

---

[7]From program records, we estimate that about two-thirds of all rental dwellings in Brown County and half in St. Joseph County were evaluated at least once during the first five program years. The wave 4 surveys occurred during the fourth program year.

[8]At the time of the survey, an estimated 94 landlords in Brown County and 248 in St. Joseph County were enrolled; most were people who had subdivided their homes in order to augment their incomes.

Table 7.10

LANDLORDS BY PROGRAM STATUS: SURVEY WAVE 4, BY SITE

Program Status[a]	Distribution of Landlords			
	Brown County		St. Joseph County	
	Number	Percent	Number	Percent
All landlords	4,775	100.0	6,031	100.0
Has heard of program[b]	4,492	94.1	5,820	96.5
Knows some correct details[b]	3,631	76.0	4,978	82.5
At least one dwelling was evaluated	1,484	31.1	1,920	31.8
Now has recipients as tenants	904	18.9	992	16.5
Landlord has applied or is enrolled	240	5.0	517	8.6

SOURCE: Tabulated by HASE staff from weighted records of the wave 4 surveys of landlords.

NOTE: Population estimates are based on records for 782 landlords in Brown County and 720 in St. Joseph County.

[a]The first three categories are nested subsets. The last three categories are overlapping subsets of those who knew some correct details. A few landlords with recipients as tenants or who were themselves recipients did not recall any housing evaluations; and landlords who had applied or were receiving payments did not necessarily have tenants who were recipients.

[b]Entries do not agree exactly with Table 7.1 because a different test of program knowledge was applied to facilitate screening of respondents for subsequent questions.

in Brown County and three-fifths in St. Joseph County thought the program was a "good idea." In Brown County, about a fourth each were neutral and negative; in St. Joseph County, about a fifth each were neutral and negative. These views carried over into attitudes toward the HAOs' staffs and policies and also toward federal housing policy generally. If put to a vote among the landlords whose current tenants included participants, a national allowance program would have lost in Brown County and won in St. Joseph County.

As the reader assesses these findings, he should keep in mind that the allowance program was not a bonanza for landlords. As was shown in Ch. VI, it did not enable them to raise rents nor did it protect them against vacancy losses. At best, it made tenants more cooperative about property maintenance (see Ch. V) and more regular in paying their rents. At worst, landlords were asked by their tenants to

Table 7.11

Scope of Program Effects Perceived by Informed Landlords, by Program Status: Survey Wave 4, by Site

Perceived Program Effect	Percentage Distribution of Landlords in Each Status[a]					
	Brown County			St. Joseph County		
	Informed, No Program Contact	Had Housing Evaluation on Property	Now Has Recipients as Tenants	Informed, No Program Contact	Had Housing Evaluation on Property	Now Has Recipients as Tenants
Has program affected management of respondent's property?						
A lot	.4	.9	3.2	.5	9.0	8.2
Somewhat	1.7	14.4	10.0	1.3	11.6	12.8
Very little	4.3	15.3	14.9	1.6	6.0	15.0
Not at all, don't know	93.6	69.3	71.9	96.6	73.4	63.9
Has program affected nearby properties?						
A lot	1.0	.6	1.6	1.2	.6	6.8
Somewhat	4.6	5.3	18.4	3.7	11.1	12.1
Very little	8.8	15.9	11.6	6.0	11.8	9.0
Not at all, don't know	85.6	78.1	68.3	89.1	76.5	72.1

SOURCE: Tabulated by HASE staff from weighted records of the wave 4 surveys of landlords.

NOTE: Distributions are based on records for 579 respondents in Brown County and 545 respondents in St. Joseph County who were informed about the program but were not themselves applicants or enrollees. Except for rounding error, each column in each panel would add to 100.0 percent.

[a] See Table 7.10 for details of program status.

Table 7.12

PROGRAM EVALUATIONS BY INFORMED LANDLORDS, BY PROGRAM STATUS: SURVEY WAVE 4, BY SITE

Respondent's Evaluation	Percentage Distribution of Landlords in Each Status[a]					
	Brown County			St. Joseph County		
	Informed, No Program Contact	Had Housing Evaluation on Property	Now Has Recipients as Tenants	Informed, No Program Contact	Had Housing Evaluation on Property	Now Has Recipients as Tenants
Overall Program Evaluation[b]						
Good idea	37.0	50.5	48.1	52.7	45.9	59.2
Neutral, no opinion	28.7	21.7	24.3	25.4	36.9	20.7
Bad idea	34.3	27.8	27.6	22.0	17.2	20.0
Do HAO staff know what they are doing?						
Yes	44.2	50.2	48.6	49.4	51.6	55.3
Neutral, no opinion	31.6	31.8	24.2	33.5	23.5	19.3
No	24.2	18.0	27.2	17.1	24.9	25.4
Is the program run the way it should be?						
Yes	38.5	39.8	42.8	39.4	39.8	49.7
Neutral, no opinion	29.7	31.3	18.6	37.4	23.1	26.2
No	31.8	28.9	38.6	23.2	37.1	24.1

Would a national program be worth the taxes?						
Yes	22.9	17.0	31.1	33.0	31.6	41.2
Neutral, no opinion	16.2	11.6	13.6	16.4	15.5	23.0
No	60.9	71.4	55.4	50.6	52.9	35.8
Should the federal government help with housing costs?						
Yes	33.5	29.2	35.5	44.8	53.3	57.8
Neutral, no opinion	10.4	8.7	6.0	9.3	12.7	14.0
No	56.1	62.2	58.5	46.0	34.0	28.2

SOURCE: Tabulated by HASE staff from weighted records of the wave 4 surveys of landlords.

NOTE: Distributions are based on records for 579 respondents in Brown County and 545 respondents in St. Joseph County who were informed about the program but were not themselves applicants or enrollees. Except for rounding error, each column in each panel would add to 100.0 percent.

[a] See Table 7.10 for details of program status.

[b] Respondents rated the program on a 7-point scale, "good idea" to "bad idea." In this panel, ratings 1-3 are coded as "good idea" and ratings of 5-7 are coded as "bad idea." Ratings of 4 are coded as "neutral" and are combined with "no opinion" and "don't know" responses.

make repairs that did not seem likely to increase the market value of the property, and to enter a lease agreement that might impede evictions.

Although a few landlords advertised that their rentals met HAO standards (presumably to attract participants), a landlord's contact with the program was usually initiated by a current or prospective tenant who sought permission to have a specific dwelling evaluated by the HAO; or, based on an evaluation report, asked for repairs that were needed to bring the dwelling up to HAO standards. After a dwelling was approved by the HAO, the enrollee would ask the landlord to sign a standard lease agreement prepared by the HAO, or to prepare a lease that incorporated the required provisions.[9]

Leases were not customary for low-rent dwellings in either site, and few landlords saw any advantage in having them. Some worried that the HAO might interpose obstacles to evictions, although any who inquired were told that the HAO's interest was limited to pre-eviction notice. A good many landlords asked whether the HAO would help them collect overdue rents or repair damage caused by tenants who were in the program; they were told that the HAO had no obligation in these matters except to make sure that allowance payments did not exceed actual housing expenses. An allowance recipient who failed to pay his rent could therefore lose his allowance.

Given these features of the program, we are surprised that the program was as popular among landlords as the survey data indicate it was. One reason for that popularity is surely that landlords, contrary to stereotype, are often concerned about the welfare of their tenants, and were glad to see them get financial help. Another is that the HAOs' housing evaluations were widely regarded as reasonable.

Housing Evaluations and Repairs

For most landlords who dealt with program participants, the salient issue was HAO-required repairs. A housing evaluation report detailing the repairs needed to make a dwelling acceptable was supplied to the enrollee, leaving him either to make the repairs himself or ask the landlord to do them. At first, there was often confusion about what repairs would suffice; but as the HAOs learned how to clarify and

[9]The standard lease was not onerous. It merely specified the amount of the rent and any deposits, indicated who was responsible for utilities, and required the landlord to notify the HAO prior to evicting the lessee. The lease had a nominal term of one year, but could be terminated sooner by either party. The resolution of landlord-tenant disputes, including evictions, remained subject only to the civil codes of each jurisdiction.

landlords became familiar with evaluation reports, such confusion became infrequent.

Most such required repairs were inexpensive remedies for health or safety hazards. According to repair logs maintained by the HAOs, landlords paid for about half of all required repairs in Brown County and a third in St. Joseph County, and personally worked on about the same proportions.[10] Tenants often made inexpensive repairs without consulting their landlords. Depending on circumstances and temperament, the landlords of HAO tenants might be pleased by the tenants' extra maintenance effort, annoyed by their requests for repairs, or grateful to the HAO for finding hitherto unnoticed hazards or incipient deterioration.

According to program records, 45 percent of all initial evaluations of rental dwellings in Brown County and 59 percent in St. Joseph County found that the dwelling was unacceptable without repairs. However, only about 40 percent of the landlords responding to the wave 4 survey in each site could recall such failures on their properties. Quite likely, there were many other cases in which both evaluation and repair were handled by tenants without even informing their landlords.

Those who recalled evaluation failures were asked about the fairness of the evaluation. As shown in Table 7.13, four-fifths in each site were satisfied that the failures were appropriate. That remarkable complacency is partly explained by the remaining entries in the table. According to the respondents, about 80 percent of the dwellings that initially failed were subsequently repaired and passed their reevaluations.[11] For this group of dwellings, the landlords nearly all said that the repairs were easy. Even for dwellings that were not repaired, repair difficulty was often not the reason.

Program Participants as Tenants

One of the major problems of rental property management is finding and keeping "good" tenants—people who pay their rents promptly, take reasonable care of the landlord's property, and don't disturb the

[10]These estimates are based on repair logs for the period January 1976-June 1979 in Brown County and January 1976-December 1979 in St. Joseph County. Figure 6.5 in Ch. VI shows related data through June 1977, which indicate more participation by landlords in St. Joseph County than do data for the longer period.

[11]Program records show that only about 60 percent of the rental dwellings that failed initial evaluations subsequently passed. Although the two figures are not directly comparable because of different units of observation (landlords vs. specific dwellings), and some evaluations and repairs were conducted without the landlords' knowledge, we think the landlords recalled more favorable outcomes than actually occurred.

Table 7.13

Landlords' Experience with Housing Evaluations and Repairs: Survey Wave 4, by Site

Response	Percentage Distribution	
	Brown County	St. Joseph County
For Failed Dwellings: Do you think the evaluations on your property were fair or unfair?		
Fair	80.3	78.7
Some fair, some unfair	5.0	4.6
Unfair	14.7	16.7
For Repaired Dwellings: How difficult were the repairs?		
Very difficult	1.6	1.7
Somewhat difficult	13.9	9.5
Not difficult at all	81.2	88.9
Some difficult, others not	3.3	--
For Unrepaired Dwellings: How difficult would repairs have been?		
Very difficult	45.6	30.9
Somewhat difficult	18.5	10.4
Not difficult at all	35.9	58.7
Some difficult, others not	--	--

SOURCE: Tabulated by HASE staff from weighted records of the wave 4 surveys of landlords.

NOTE: Distributions in the first panel are based on records for respondents who recalled at least one housing evaluation failure (111 in Brown County and 137 in St. Joseph County). Distributions in the second panel are based on records for respondents some of whose rental units were repaired to meet HAO requirements (87 in Brown County and 107 in St. Joseph County). Distributions in the third panel are based on records for respondents some of whose rental units failed evaluations but were not repaired (24 in Brown County and 30 in St. Joseph County). Except for rounding error, each column in each panel would add to 100.0 percent.

neighbors. Although some landlords check references provided by prospective tenants, the results are only occasionally informative. Consequently, most landlords form attitudes toward classes of tenants based on experience but leavened by social prejudices that have little to do with tenant performance.

Landlords in Brown and St. Joseph counties agree that the most desirable tenants are mature white childless couples. They most often object to single parents, families with many children, and families with pets. They are, however, divided in their attitudes toward single adults; some prefer them as tenants, others avoid them.[12]

By these standards, program participants are a mixed lot. At the end of the fourth program year, over a third of the current recipients were elderly single persons or couples, a favored class of tenants; but nearly half were single parents, a disfavored class. Household sizes were typically small; less than 10 percent had five or more members. In Brown County, nearly all renter recipients were white, but in St. Joseph County nearly a third belonged to racial minorities.

Landlord respondents to the wave 4 survey were asked their views of allowance recipients as tenants, whether or not they had actual experience with such tenants (Table 7.14). The general opinion was that allowance recipients were indistinguishable from other renters, although about a fifth of the landlords thought they were worse and a smaller number thought they were better. Only a tenth of the respondents were unwilling to rent to program participants.

Overall Experience with the Program

The program evaluations reported in the first panel of Table 7.12 were obtained from respondents early in the interview, when those who had heard of the program were asked to rate it on a 7-point scale running from "good idea" to "bad idea." Among those with tenants who were recipients, about half in Brown County and three-fifths in St. Joseph County rated the program positively (1 to 3 on the scale).

After responding to a series of questions about their experiences with the program, the same landlords were asked to rate their satisfaction with the program "based on your own experience with it." Almost 63 percent in each site chose positive ratings; only a fifth in Brown County and a fourth in St. Joseph County chose negative ratings. There is no necessary inconsistency between different responses

[12]Tenant characteristics preferred by St. Joseph County landlords are analyzed in Kanouse, 1980, pp. 45-52. Unpublished tabulations for Brown County show that landlords there have similar views.

Table 7.14

LANDLORDS' EXPERIENCE WITH ALLOWANCE RECIPIENTS: SURVEY WAVE 4, BY SITE

Response	Percentage Distributions	
	Brown County	St. Joseph County
Are recipients better or worse than other tenants?		
Better	11.9	18.2
About the same	66.5	62.1
Worse	21.5	19.6
Did/would you object to renting to a recipient?		
No	18.4	26.2
Recipients are like other tenants[a]	69.1	63.3
Yes	12.5	10.6

SOURCE: Tabulated by HASE staff from weighted records of the wave 4 surveys of landlords.

NOTE: Distributions in the first panel are based on records for 557 respondents in Brown County and 529 in St. Joseph County, including those who did and did not currently have tenants who were recipients. The second question was asked only of those who thought recipients were either better or worse than other tenants, to gauge the intensity of the respondent's attitude. We presume that those who did not distinguish between recipients and others would also be willing to rent to recipients. Except for rounding error, each column in each panel would add to 100.0.

[a]"About the same" respondents to preceding question.

to the differently worded questions; but it appears that the program as run in Brown and St. Joseph counties alienated fewer landlords than one might have supposed from responses to the earlier question.

CONCLUSIONS

The evidence summarized above documents the spread of knowledge about an experimental social program and the formation of attitudes toward it in two very different political and social environments. Brown County was a conservative community, remarkably free of competing interest groups and inexperienced with federal assistance programs. St. Joseph County was less a "community" than a network of overlapping interest groups—jurisdictional, political, economic, and ethnic—and had participated in similar federal programs. Although negotiations in the two sites followed very different patterns, the outcomes in terms of public knowledge and attitudes were quite similar. The evidence suggests an important distinction between the concerns of ordinary citizens and those who are politically active on their behalf.

- Before enrollment began, awareness of the program did not spread far beyond the civic leaders who participated in negotiations, despite public controversy in St. Joseph County and thorough media coverage of those negotiations in both sites.
- After enrollment began, awareness of the program and knowledge of its details spread rapidly, spurred by the HAOs' extensive outreach activities and, as enrollment grew, by word-of-mouth. After three years of enrollment, nearly everyone had at least heard of the program and over three-fourths of all household heads knew some correct details. However, only those who had dealt with the HAOs as applicants or enrollees and some whose tenants, relatives, or friends were participants, really became well-informed about program standards and procedures.
- Public officials were primarily interested in the program's potential effects on the local economy, social structure, and division of political power. Organized private interests (which in neither county included landlords) were interested in how the program would affect their particular constituencies. Ordinary citizens were mostly concerned about whether the program would help truly needy and deserving people, even if they did not count themselves as such.

These findings suggest that to gain community support, a social program must be designed with several levels of appeal. Whatever benefits it offers to ordinary citizens, it must first satisfy civic leaders both that it will improve the community and that it will not upset the established political and social order. Influential private interest groups must be persuaded that their constituencies will not be damaged. Only then does the new program have a chance to test its broader appeal.

Community Attitudes toward the Experimental Program

The experimental housing allowance program passed those initial tests easily in Brown County but with difficulty in St. Joseph County. Having done so, it quickly achieved a broad base of community approval.

- After three years of program operations, a solid majority of informed household heads approved of the program, its management, and its staff, despite the fact that less than a fourth had any direct contact with the program, and less than a tenth had benefited from it.
- Support for the program seems to reflect several beliefs about it: that it helped the right people; that it was well run; and that, as a local experiment funded by federal taxes, it yielded a net fiscal gain to the community. More people approved of the local program than thought a national program would be worth the taxes, although the latter proposition was supported by a plurality.
- After three years of program operations, its housing and neighborhood effects were barely perceptible to nonparticipants, although many assumed that such effects existed elsewhere in the county. Participants, both because of their own experiences and because they usually lived near others in the program, saw much more evidence of the program's benefits in their neighborhoods. Virtually no one perceived negative consequences such as rent increases, property deterioration, or undesirable new neighbors.

The Experiences and Attitudes of Participants

The experiences of those participating in the program were, we think, important influences on the attitudes of their friends and neighbors. Although the beneficiaries of social programs usually approve of those programs, the allowance program achieved unusually high ratings from its participants.

- Over 90 percent approved both of the program and the performance of the HAO staffs, and nearly as many approved of program rules and procedures. Approval ratings varied little with household characteristics.
- About a fifth of the recipients were willing to suggest improvements, but there was little consensus on desirable improvements. For example, those who thought that income

and eligibility rules were too strict were outnumbered by those who thought the rules were too generous.

- Those who applied but were found ineligible and those who enrolled but never qualified for payments were less enthusiastic about the program than recipients, but a majority approved of the concept, the staff, and the rules and procedures. Their highest ratings were for the staffs.

Although causal relationships are not rigorously demonstrable, we judge that the participants' high regard for the program reflected some important features of both its design and its management, further discussed in Ch. VIII. Briefly, program rules were comprehensible and fairly administered, staff training emphasized courtesy and respect for clients' privacy and dignity, bureaucratic errors were rare, and administrative procedures both forestalled and discovered attempted abuses of the program.

How Landlords Responded to the Experimental Program

Because about two-fifths of all eligible households and well over half of those who enrolled were renters, landlords were an important constituency of the program. After three years of program operations, only a third of all landlords could recall dealing with enrollees about housing evaluations and less than a fifth currently had tenants who were recipients. However, nearly all landlords knew about the program and about three-fourths were at least minimally informed.

- Few landlords, whatever their exposure to the program, thought that it had much affected the management of their own or nearby properties.
- Among those who had experience with the program, about half approved of it and its staff and about two-fifths approved of its standards and procedures. Only about a third thought that a national program would be worth the taxes.

Considering that the program could only indirectly benefit landlords and often caused them inconvenience, their approval ratings are high. We think that those who approved were often responding to a genuine concern for the welfare of their low-income tenants, and were also impressed by the reasonableness of the program's housing standards. Remarkably, 80 percent of those whose dwellings failed initial housing evaluations nonetheless thought those evaluations were fair.

Although few landlords thought that allowance recipients were better tenants than others, only about a tenth preferred not to rent to recipients. Over three-fifths of those who currently had recipients as tenants said that their own experience with the program had been satisfactory, including some who thought the program was not a good idea.

Relevance to a National Program

On the whole, the experimental allowance program was quite well received by the publics of Brown and St. Joseph counties and by its special constituencies: eligible households and landlords. Whether a national program would encounter an equally favorable response is doubtful for several reasons.

First, the program was essentially free to Brown and St. Joseph counties. The national public would be inclined to balance its benefits against the implied tax costs. Although three-fifths of the household heads in Brown and St. Joseph counties thought that the experimental program was a "good idea," less than half thought that a national program would be worth the taxes.

Second, a national program in the current fiscal environment would surely be more restrictive as to eligibility than the experimental program, which was open to nearly all low-income households. If a national program were limited to, say, renters only, an important source of its appeal would be lost. Not only are there many low-income homeowners who would then see no personal benefit, but such homeowners, usually elderly, are perceived by others as being both needy and deserving.

Finally, a substantial element in the experimental program's success was its administrative style. Although that style could easily be adapted to a national program, there are few precedents for it. A poorly managed program, one that was less considerate of its participants, or one whose housing standards were more onerous would surely be less popular.

REFERENCES

Carter, Earl, comp., *Brown County Press Coverage of the Housing Assistance Supply Experiment and the Allowance Program: December 1972-December 1974,* The Rand Corporation, N-1085-HUD, May 1981.

——, *South Bend Press Coverage of the Housing Assistance Supply*

Experiment and the Allowance Program: January 1974-December 1974, The Rand Corporation, N-1086-HUD, May 1981.

Ellickson, Phyllis L., *Public Knowledge and Evaluation of Housing Allowances: St. Joseph County, Indiana, 1975,* The Rand Corporation, R-2190-HUD, February 1978.

Ellickson, Phyllis L., and David E. Kanouse, *Public Perceptions of Housing Allowances: The First Two Years,* The Rand Corporation, R-2259-HUD, September 1979.

Gray, Kirk L., comp., *Press Coverage of the Experimental Housing Allowance Program in Site I: January-June 1975,* The Rand Corporation, N-1099-HUD, May 1981.

Harris, Louis, and Associates, "A Survey of the Attitudes and Experience of Occupants of Urban Federally Subsidized Housing," in U.S. Department of Housing and Urban Development, National Housing Policy Review, *Housing in the Seventies: Working Papers,* Vol. 2, U.S. Government Printing Office, Washington, D.C., 1976, pp. 1384-1432.

Kanouse, David E., *Landlord Knowledge and Evaluation of Housing Allowances: St. Joseph County, Indiana, 1975,* The Rand Corporation, R-2475-HUD, May 1980.

Kingsley, G. Thomas, Sheila Nataraj Kirby, and W. Eugene Rizor, *Administering a Housing Allowance Program: Findings from the Housing Assistance Supply Experiment,* The Rand Corporation, R-2718-HUD, forthcoming, 1982.

O'Nell, Nancy, and Michael G. Shanley, *Monitoring the Housing Allowance Program in St. Joseph County, Indiana: September 1974-March 1975,* The Rand Corporation, N-1221-HUD, March 1981.

——, *Monitoring the Housing Allowance Program in St. Joseph County, Indiana: April-August 1975,* The Rand Corporation, N-1222-HUD, March 1981.

——, *Monitoring the Housing Allowance Program in St. Joseph County, Indiana: September-December 1975,* The Rand Corporation, N-1223-HUD, March 1981.

——, *Monitoring the Housing Allowance Program in St. Joseph County, Indiana: January-June 1976,* The Rand Corporation, N-1224-HUD, April 1981.

O'Nell, Nancy, and Wim Wiewel, *Monitoring the Housing Allowance Program in St. Joseph County, Indiana: July-September 1976,* The Rand Corporation, N-1225-HUD, April 1981.

——, *Monitoring the Housing Allowance Program in St. Joseph County, Indiana: October-December 1976,* The Rand Corporation, N-1226-HUD, May 1981.

Shanley, Michael G., *Monitoring the Housing Allowance Program in*

St. Joseph County, Indiana: July-September 1974, The Rand Corporation, N-1220-HUD, March 1981.

Wiewel, Wim, and Nancy O'Nell, *Monitoring the Housing Allowance Program in St. Joseph County, Indiana: January-March 1977,* The Rand Corporation, N-1227-HUD, May 1981.

VIII. PROGRAM ADMINISTRATION

As compared with other methods for delivering housing assistance to low-income households, a housing allowance program has at least the virtue of administrative simplicity. In an allowance program, the administering agency does not build, buy, lease, or manage residential property; nor does it supervise, regulate, or audit private builders, owners, or managers. The agency deals only with households that apply for assistance, and those dealings are limited to two issues: determining applicants' eligibility and entitlements, and checking on the physical adequacy of their dwellings. Enrollees conduct their own housing transactions on the private market without supervision or assistance from the agency.

Earlier chapters of this book document the experimental program's degree of success in delivering assistance to those who were eligible, and explain how they used their benefits. Here, we summarize the program's administrative experience. Briefly, that experience indicates that a well-planned housing allowance office, hiring its staff locally at prevailing wages, can perform its functions promptly, equitably, and humanely at the surprisingly low cost of $163 per recipient-year (1976 dollars).

Both the structural features of the program, noted above, and its administrative procedures contributed to that result. Some of those features and procedures could be applied to other programs whose functions include income transfers or earmarked benefits. In particular, our findings are relevant to agencies that, like the HAOs, experience rapid turnover of clients.

In reviewing the HAOs' administration of the allowance program, we benefit from more comprehensive record-keeping than is usual for public programs. The data enable us not only to report administrative outcomes, but also to learn more about the determinants of variation in those outcomes than is typically possible in public management studies.

In the pages that follow, first we outline the allowance program's administrative design, explaining each of the functions performed by the HAOs. Next, we present measures of administrative effectiveness and efficiency, where possible comparing the HAOs' performance with that of other assistance programs. Third, we examine factors that influenced the HAOs' performance, and from them draw lessons relevant to national policy and to the administration of other programs.

The administrative procedures for operating the housing allowance program were designed by Rand's Field and Program Operations Group and the senior staffs of the two HAOs. They are documented in a comprehensive *Housing Allowance Office Handbook* (Katagiri and Kingsley, 1980) and in a series of more detailed manuals and operating instructions.

With a few minor exceptions, administrative procedures were the same for both HAOs, both on paper and in practice. Though rules and procedures were often amended in detail, the same basic principles governed program administration throughout the experimental period.

HAO FUNCTIONS

While the Supply Experiment was under way, the HAOs had two basic objectives: (a) to operate the housing allowance program, and (b) to support the experiment's research agenda by preparing data files for use by Rand researchers, conducting special studies, and preparing special reports and presentations. This section deals with the five major administrative functions required to accomplish the first of these objectives. Three functions—outreach, eligibility certification, and payments—are a necessary part of any income-transfer program. The fourth function, housing certification, partially earmarked the transfer for housing; and the fifth, administrative support, includes management, accounting, and other general support activities.

Outreach

The HAOs used various traditional techniques to inform eligible households about the program and encourage them to apply: distributing posters and brochures, briefing community organizations, and arranging for referrals from other social agencies. Because of the experimental interest in rapid enrollment, however, they also advertised extensively in newspapers and on local radio and television broadcasts.

Eligibility Certification

Those who applied were enrolled in the program after the HAOs had determined that they were eligible for assistance under the program's rules as to income, assets, household composition, and residence. The initial certification entailed:

- Screening applicants and scheduling enrollment interviews for those not clearly ineligible.
- Informing applicants about program rules, and interviewing them to obtain information on household status and income; determining whether each applicant was eligible; if eligible, determining the applicant's allowance entitlement; and signing participation agreements with eligibles who chose to enroll.
- Checking enrollment forms to detect and correct errors; verifying undocumented information with employers, banks, and public agencies; and creating client records in the HAO's computer system.

In the "maintenance" phase (for enrollees already receiving allowance payments), periodic eligibility recertifications were mandatory to weed out participants who subsequently became ineligible; and to adjust allowance entitlements for the others in response to changes in income or other household circumstances. Program rules called for three types of recertification:

- Semiannual. Mail-back questionnaires on household status and income were sent to each enrollee midway between enrollment anniversaries. Processing the returned questionnaires entailed asking for additional information when responses were inadequate, plus error control and data entry.
- Annual. A full recertification interview was conducted in the month of the client's enrollment anniversary. Activities were similar to those in enrollment certification: scheduling, interviewing, error control, and data entry.
- Special. Unusual circumstances such as a radical change in household composition or income led to special recertifications conducted either by telephone or interview between semiannual and annual recertifications.

Although all income-transfer programs require the administration of "means tests" like those just outlined, many handle them differently. Four features distinguish the HAOs' approach. First, the HAOs used the computer more than do many agencies. Enrollment-interview forms were batched, keypunched, and entered onto magnetic tape to establish an initial record for each client. All subsequent transactions were entered as updates to that record, and payments were adjusted automatically. Second, the HAOs devoted more effort to error control than is usual in similar programs. All assertions of fact by clients had to be either documented (the HAOs kept photocopies of the documentation) or verifiable by third parties. All interview forms were computer-edited and then manually reviewed to catch any errors made by the interviewers. Third, although shared by many welfare agencies, the HAOs' pattern of recertifying eligibility every six months was unique among housing programs; until 1982, HUD's Sec. 8 and public housing programs recertified nonelderly tenants annually and the elderly biennially. Fourth, the HAOs tried to minimize psychic costs for clients undergoing means tests. Interviews were conducted by appointment in private rooms, and the interviewers were trained to treat clients respectfully as they itemized their economic difficulties.

Payments

This function entailed preparing and mailing monthly allowance checks; suspending or terminating payments in response to determinations of ineligibility or rule violations; and adjusting payment amounts to reflect recertification results, previous underpayments or overpayments, or security deposit advances.

In the HAOs, this function was almost completely automated. In disbursing payments, for example, there were no manual operations. An addressed mailing envelope containing a check made out to the recipient in the appropriate amount was, in total, a product of the computer.

Housing Certification

Allowance payments were not authorized unless and until a client's dwelling met program standards. The major staff activity for this function, therefore, was housing evaluation in both the intake and maintenance phases. Specific subfunctions were:

- Initial evaluations. Inspecting enrollees' housing units; informing them of the results; reevaluating units after repairs were attempted; processing evaluation results and lease agreements; and authorizing payments to those whose housing qualified.
- Annual and move-related evaluations. Annually inspecting dwellings occupied by recipients; inspecting units to which recipients planned to move; informing recipients of evaluation results; reevaluating failed units after repairs had been attempted; and processing results.

The most unusual aspect of the HAOs' housing certification function was the emphasis given to quality control. Five percent of all regular evaluations were repeated by the evaluation supervisor or his assistant; discrepancies were recorded and analyzed; and the analysis provided the basis for regular feedback to the staff.

Housing certification also included client services that, like housing evaluation, would not be required in a direct cash-transfer program. Again, we distinguish services provided during intake from those provided thereafter:

- Enrollee services. Providing voluntary group counseling and legal services (in discrimination cases) to help enrollees obtain certifiable housing.
- Recipient services. Providing voluntary group counseling, literature on housing maintenance, and legal services for discrimination cases to help recipients maintain residence in certifiable housing.

When EHAP was initiated, some advocated making program services more comprehensive—including, for example, agency participation in client negotiations with landlords, or in repairing deficient dwellings. In the Supply Experiment, services were purposely limited, in part to test the ability of participants to meet program housing requirements without them.

Administrative Support

HAO administrative support activities included general management, press and community relations, staff training, management reporting, budgeting and accounting, personnel management, secretarial and clerical services, and purchasing and equipment maintenance—activities required in almost all local government agencies. The HAOs attempted to follow the best of modern business practices in each of these areas.

Their efforts in two areas were noteworthy and unusual for a government assistance program. First, they took staff training quite seriously, developing training manuals and requiring all new staff to attend both general seminars on overall HAO purposes and procedures and training courses for their particular jobs. Training was most rigorous for personnel assigned to eligibility and housing certification functions; employees had to demonstrate proficiency in simulated interviews or evaluations before they were allowed to handle regular workloads. Second, the HAOs developed statistical reporting systems for most aspects of administrative performance, and used them in day-to-day management.

ADMINISTRATIVE EFFECTIVENESS

Administrative goals are distinct from program goals. The program was designed to ease the housing expense burdens of low-income households and to improve the quality of their housing by offering conditional benefits to all eligible households. Such a program could be administered effectively even if few took up the offer or if participants' circumstances were not materially improved. Conversely, the program might succeed despite poor administration.

The HAOs had two administrative goals: to perform their functions effectively, and to do so efficiently. In this section, we discuss the effectiveness of the HAOs' performance; in the next, we discuss their efficiency.

We suggest three tests of administrative effectiveness:

- Workload processing. Expediting administrative actions associated with intake, maintenance, and terminations so that changes in applicants' or enrollees' statuses are quickly reflected in their payments.
- Program integrity. Making sure that eligible applicants are permitted to enroll and that each enrolled household gets the assistance to which it is entitled—and no more.
- Client and community relations. Cultivating good relations with clients by minimizing their paperwork, helping them understand and appreciate program rules and procedures, and safeguarding their privacy; forestalling friction with local governments and the general community of nonparticipants.

These goals often pull in opposing directions. Reducing paperwork for clients, for example, might eliminate effective error controls. Overzealous error control, on the other hand, might substantially increase operating cost as well as inconvenience clients. The task for the HAOs was to achieve the proper balance.

Workload Processing

Of the three performance goals, promptness ought to be the easiest to achieve. An open-enrollment program, however, was a challenge because the scale was large and workloads were hard to predict. By the end of their second year, the HASE programs were the largest public assistance programs in Brown and St. Joseph counties, serving more beneficiaries than even the local Aid to Families with Dependent Children (AFDC) programs. During the first five years,[1] the two HAOs together accepted 59,300 applications, enrolled 29,800 applicants, and authorized 23,100 enrollees for payments; they administered 113,400 means tests and 79,100 housing evaluations, and disbursed 428,300 allowance checks (Table 8.1).

Large backlogs at various stages of intake or maintenance were undesirable even if the work eventually got done. Maintenance backlogs never accumulated at either HAO. In each of the 60 program months for which we have data, allowance payment checks always were mailed in time to reach recipients by the first of the next month (although there were a few close calls), and each cohort of recipients due for eligibility or housing recertification was processed without holdovers to the following month. This achievement reflected a firm administrative policy: If workloads expanded beyond HAO capacity at any point, resources were to be shifted to maintenance activity first, allowing the backlogs to develop in intake. We considered it critical to program discipline (both internal and external) that everyone be able to expect payments and recertifications on time.

Because of this policy, backlogs appeared only in intake functions. Under normal conditions, we expected enrollment to take about 1.5 months, including time to receive, screen, and process the application; schedule and conduct the enrollment interview; and then check and enter the results into permanent records. We used this standard to evaluate the size of HAO intake backlogs. Specifically, we measured how often the total number of cases in process at the end of a quarter (application submitted but enrollment results not yet entered in the computer) exceeded intake capacity (half the number of cases the HAO actually processed over the quarter).[2]

---

[1]These totals are larger than those given in Ch. III (25,000 enrollees and 20,000 recipients) for two reasons. Administrative statistics for St. Joseph County were collected for three months beyond the nominal end of year 5, adding about 1,000 enrollees; and in both sites, the administrative analysis treated a reinstatement as the equivalent of a new enrollment. Altogether, about 3,500 households dropped out of the program but were subsequently reinstated.

[2]Our measure of intake capacity is the best we could devise, given the fungibility of resources between intake and maintenance. The measure reflects both the resources actually used for intake during the preceding quarter, and their productivity then. However, the assumed average processing time for backlogged cases is somewhat arbitrary, so that the measure may systematically over- or understate intake capacity. Such an error does not affect time-series comparisons of relative backlogs.

We subsequently tabulated elapsed times from application to enrollment for households that applied during calendar 1977. For those who completed the enrollment process, the median elapsed time was 20 days in both sites, a figure we take to be the norm for the system when the applicant was responsive to the HAO's requests for interviews or information. Averages were higher (40 days in Brown County, 29 in St. Joseph County) because some applicants delayed enrolling for as long as a year.

Table 8.1

ADMINISTRATIVE WORKLOADS: HOUSING ALLOWANCE PROGRAMS THROUGH YEAR 5, BY SITE

Workload Item	Program Year[a]					Total
	1	2	3	4	5	
Brown County						
Intake						
Applications	5,893	3,832	2,753	2,800	2,828	18,106
Interviews	4,326	2,763	2,036	1,971	1,945	13,041
Participation agreements	3,104	1,985	1,701	1,654	1,756	10,200
Housing evaluations	4,285	2,947	2,700	3,125	3,224	16,281
Payment authorizations	2,313	1,676	1,488	1,412	1,499	8,388
Maintenance						
Recertifications:						
Semiannual	1,050	3,012	3,276	3,470	3,660	14,468
Annual	122	1,926	2,360	2,723	2,956	10,087
Special	--	258	429	412	556	1,655
Housing evaluations	59	2,578	3,069	3,429	3,208	12,343
Payments (recipient-years)	939	2,492	3,201	3,346	3,600	13,578
Terminations						
Enrolled, never paid	167	524	280	265	249	1,485
Received payments	122	898	1,138	1,160	1,261	4,579
St. Joseph County						
Intake						
Applications	10,053	8,807	6,816	6,501	9,021	41,198
Interviews	7,219	6,199	4,664	4,580	6,029	28,691
Participation agreements	4,425	4,341	3,413	3,290	4,130	19,599
Housing evaluations	6,398	6,041	5,718	4,691	5,806	28,654
Payment authorizations	3,006	3,293	2,796	2,466	3,106	14,667
Maintenance						
Recertifications:						
Semiannual	2,162	4,376	5,928	5,922	5,825	24,213
Annual	80	2,522	4,290	4,520	4,717	16,129
Special	391	790	709	692	760	3,342
Housing evaluations	169	3,127	5,465	6,120	6,902	21,783
Payments (recipient-years)	1,254	3,780	5,232	5,672	6,178	22,116
Terminations						
Enrolled, never paid	345	900	1,065	763	903	3,976
Received payments	204	1,303	1,775	2,206	2,179	7,667

SOURCE: HAO management information reports for indicated periods. See Kingsley and Schlegel, 1982, Sec. II, for details.

NOTE: Administrative statistics for St. Joseph County were collected for three months beyond the nominal end of year 5, adding about 1,000 enrollees; and in both sites, the administrative analysis treated a reinstatement as the equivalent of a new enrollment. Altogether, about 3,500 households dropped out of the program but were subsequently reinstated.

[a] For Brown County, the five-year period is 1 July 1974 through 30 June 1979. For St. Joseph County, the five-year period is 1 January 1975 through 31 March 1980.

We found that the Brown County HAO exceeded this standard only once during its first five years, three months after enrollment began. The St. Joseph County HAO, however, had a quite different experience. The number of cases in the enrollment process there exceeded the 1.5-month processing capacity 75 percent of the time, even in years 2 through 5; it was more than double that capacity 25 percent of the time.

Although the HAO might have hired more staff in order to reduce the backlog, it was unclear how long the flow of applications would continue. If the flow diminished, newly hired staff might have to be terminated before training expenses were amortized. These concerns were shared by HUD officials who resisted proposals for staff expansion. In hindsight, we think all parties were too cautious.

With respect to the first goal—prompt workload processing—the Brown County HAO's performance must be seen as virtually faultless over the first five years. Even with what we now consider to be excessive intake backlogs, we think the St. Joseph County HAO's performance was also quite solid. Intake waiting times never provoked public complaints, nor dampened the HAO's local reputation for effectiveness—a reputation based on its consistently prompt performance of its maintenance workload.

Program Integrity

Errors in an HAO client's records are functionally important only if they affect his allowance payments. Most such errors occur because a client deliberately or accidentally misreported information used by the HAO to calculate his entitlement; or because the HAO's staff erred either in transcribing the data or in subsequent computations. Many such errors were caught before they affected payments, by third-party verification of clients' submissions or by routine computer checks or manual reviews; but not all errors were recognizable as such. These procedures were augmented by special sample audits designed to learn how much error survived routine error controls. Below, we analyze both the total and uncorrected errors.

Table 8.2 presents our estimates of the sources, incidence, and fiscal effects of errors affecting payments in each site during the program's middle years. We estimate that client misreporting affected payments in 2 to 3 percent of all enrollment interviews and annual recertifications. Staff errors occurred more frequently—in 7 to 10 percent of enrollments and annual recertifications.

The consequences of these errors are measured in two ways. Gross payment errors show the average amount (without regard for sign) by which actual payments differed from true entitlements, a measure of

Table 8.2

Payment Errors in Initial and Annual Eligibility Certifications: Housing Allowance Programs, by Site

Type of Error and Disposition	Type of Certification, by Site			
	Brown County		St. Joseph County	
	Initial	Annual	Initial	Annual
Percent of Cases with Errors				
Client misreporting:				
Total	3.1	2.8	2.3	1.8
Uncorrected	.2	.5	.6	.9
Staff errors:				
Total	6.8	7.1	10.1	8.4
Uncorrected	1.0	2.7	4.4	3.0
Gross Error per Recipient-Year ($)				
Client misreporting:				
Total	9.25	6.42	7.81	4.91
Uncorrected	.05	1.24	1.25	2.36
Staff errors:				
Total	14.97	5.72	18.56	7.06
Uncorrected	5.04	1.87	5.51	2.16
Net Error per Recipient-Year ($)				
Client misreporting:				
Total	2.96	3.79	5.22	4.35
Uncorrected	.03	.99	1.33	2.36
Staff errors:				
Total	9.62	-1.30	5.53	2.60
Uncorrected	5.03	-1.45	3.13	1.98
Net Error as Percent of Annual Payments				
All errors	1.4	.3	1.2	.8
Uncorrected errors	.6	(*a*)	.5	.5

SOURCE: Estimated from sample studies of HAO case records conducted by HAO staffs. See Rizor, 1982, for details.

NOTE: See text for definition of error-types and methods of estimating error incidence. Gross errors are averaged without regard for sign; net errors are averages of offsetting overpayments and underpayments. For initial errors, the base is the first year of recipiency; for annual errors, the base is all subsequent years of recipiency. Consequently, initial and annual errors are not additive.

[a]Less than 0.1 percent.

program integrity or "fairness." Net payment errors show the balance between over- and underpayments, a measure of the HAO's fiscal gain or loss due to error.

The typical misreporting error was large. In St. Joseph County enrollment, for example, the typical error in the client's favor, if uncorrected, would have led to an overpayment of $394 in a year's time, and the typical error in the HAO's favor to a $338 annual underpayment. But the gross error would have been small because misreporting errors were rare, and the net error would have been even smaller because errors resulted in both overpayments and underpayments. The gross error due to misreporting in St. Joseph County averaged $7.81 during the first year of enrollment, and the net error averaged $5.22. The corresponding values for Brown County were $9.25 and $2.96 per recipient-year.[3] Staff errors were typically smaller but more common than misreporting errors, and they too tended to balance, especially for annual recertifications.

Third-party verification of a substantial fraction of clients' submissions caught and corrected about 90 percent of the misreporting errors in Brown County that affected payments by more than $10 per month[4] and about 60 percent of such errors in St. Joseph County. Routine checks on staff work caught and corrected about 75 percent of staff errors in Brown County and 60 percent in St. Joseph County. Overall, less than 5 percent of all clients were paid either more or less than they were entitled to during a typical year.

Our estimates of uncorrected error are based on sample audits conducted after routine error control procedures were completed. We can be fairly sure that these audits found all or nearly all uncorrected staff errors, since those errors leave an "audit trail." The sample audit of client submissions, conducted by an independent accounting firm, included reinterviews with the clients, third-party verification of reported incomes, and systematic searches for unreported sources of income. The auditors were satisfied that they had overlooked little if any unreported income (Tebbets, 1979).

---

[3]Initial errors affected payments during a client's first year of enrollment, and annual errors affected only subsequent payments, so the two types of error cannot be added. They can be roughly averaged by assuming that one-third of all recipient-years pertain to new enrollees.

[4]Client misreporting errors were not corrected by the HAOs unless they would change monthly payments by $10 or more. Because smaller apparent errors were never discussed with clients, some may not be errors, merely misunderstandings. Examination of third-party verification records indicates that most of the smaller apparent errors would have affected payments by less than $5 monthly and that overreporting was nearly as common as underreporting. The cost of correcting all such errors would clearly have exceeded the net payment error they entailed.

The fiscal effect of uncorrected error was negligible. Clients in St. Joseph County were overpaid by about $5 per recipient-year, or 0.5 percent of total payments. Clients in Brown County were overpaid by about $2 per recipient-year, or about 0.2 percent of total payments.[5]

Available evidence suggests that this record is enviable. A study of the national AFDC program during the first half of 1976, for example, found payment errors in 25 percent of all cases reviewed, and estimated that net overpayments amounted to an average of $216 per recipient-year, or 8 percent of the average payment.[6] The AFDC quality-control program has since led to improvements in many areas, but the HAO rates (under 1 percent in both sites) still were well below the lowest AFDC regional average (4 percent) in 1978 (Griffiths and Callahan, 1980).

HAO efforts in catching and correcting errors played a relatively small part in achieving this level of accuracy. For example, initial errors at the HAOs, if uncorrected, would have resulted in net overpayments of 1.4 percent in Brown County and 1.2 percent in St. Joseph County, well below the AFDC rates cited above. This does not mean, however, that the HAOs do not deserve credit. We cannot measure "potential" error, but Harrar, 1976, suggests that in means tests generally, initial error may be substantially above the reported rates for the AFDC program. We believe that the HAOs' major accomplishment in error control was preventing errors, by thorough enrollment and recertification interviews (see discussion in Rizor, 1982, Sec. V).

Allowance program integrity, of course, depended on accuracy and consistency in housing evaluations as well as in means tests. A detailed study of this function covering the period October 1975 through August 1976 shows that for both HAOs, the overall result (pass or fail) of quality-control reevaluations differed from those of the original evaluations in only 1.5 percent of all cases (Tebbets, 1979). Overall determinations can differ if there is a discrepancy in any one of 80 possible entries on the typical evaluation form. Using a subsample, Tebbets found that differences on individual entries occurred 0.1 percent of the time in Brown County and 0.4 percent of the time in St. Joseph County.

---

[5]The figures in this paragraph are averages of initial and annual payment errors; see note 2, above.

[6]The study was based on a sample audit of 45,000 cases, conducted by the Social and Rehabilitation Service, U.S. Department of Health, Education, and Welfare, during the first half of 1976; findings were reported in a news release dated 16 December 1976. We computed average dollar amounts of net overpayments by applying the reported 8-percent net overpayment rate to national benefit and caseload data for fiscal year 1976 (Executive Office of the President, 1978, p. 347).

Client and Community Relations

The evidence on the HAOs' relations with their clients and host communities was presented in Ch. VII. Survey respondents (both clients and nonclients) gave high approval ratings to HAO administration in both sites, even following administrative actions adverse to their interests. Those who had the most contact with the HAOs were the most favorably disposed toward the institutions and their staffs.

ADMINISTRATIVE EFFICIENCY

Both HAOs rate high marks for meeting their performance goals, but how high a price did they have to pay for that achievement? They did spend a considerable amount of money administering the program; together, $13.6 million in the five-year experimental period (Table 8.3). Administrative expenses averaged $1.1 million per year in Brown County, $1.6 million in St. Joseph County. In both sites, almost exactly two-thirds of these expenses went for staff salaries and fringe benefits.

Data presented this way, however, tell us nothing about efficiency. To evaluate HAO administrative expenditures, we need to calculate cost per unit of output or service provided.

Measuring Efficiency

Measuring the efficiency of HAO administration required an accounting system that would allow us to allocate expenses to the administrative functions described earlier in this chapter. The system was installed in April 1976 (21 months after open enrollment began in Brown County; 12 months in St. Joseph County). It is described fully in Kingsley and Schlegel, 1979 and 1982.

Because personnel expenses make up such a large proportion of the total, the way they are allocated is important. HAO employees distributed their work hours each day among a set of detailed activity codes.[7] Hours by activity can be translated into salary and fringe dollars that can then be aggregated by function.

Different methods were used for nonpersonnel expenses. Some of these were clearly chargeable to only one direct function; e.g., advertising bills were appropriately charged only to outreach. Others could

[7]The system had 68 different activity codes but only a few applied to any one staff member at any time. Time sheets were reviewed by supervisors to ensure conformity to specifications.

Table 8.3

ANNUAL ADMINISTRATIVE EXPENSE AND ALLOWANCE PAYMENTS: HOUSING ALLOWANCE PROGRAMS THROUGH YEAR 5, BY SITE

Type of Expense	Annual Amount ($000), by Program Year					Five-Year Total
	1	2	3	4	5	
Brown County						
Administration:						
Salaries and benefits	686	706	772	720	685	3,569
Offices and equipment[a]	109	118	111	109	110	556
Supplies	63	64	59	53	54	294
Other	382	202	115	136	135	969
Total	1,240	1,089	1,056	1,018	985	5,388
Allowance payments	744	1,902	2,780	3,022	3,486	11,934
Total expense	1,983	2,992	3,837	4,040	4,471	17,323
St. Joseph County						
Administration:						
Salaries and benefits	878	1,117	1,140	1,171	1,243	5,549
Offices and equipment[a]	136	146	163	165	166	776
Supplies	90	113	101	93	102	498
Other	342	274	237	307	221	1,381
Total	1,445	1,649	1,641	1,736	1,733	8,204
Allowance payments	1,255	3,047	4,595	5,121	6,315	20,334
Total expense	2,701	4,696	6,236	6,875	8,049	28,539

SOURCE: Tabulated from HAO accounting records. See Kingsley and Schlegel, 1982, for details.
NOTE: All expenses are in current dollars.
[a]Rental payments only. Purchases are included with "Other."

be distributed as direct charges among several functions based on related information; e.g., data on automobile mileage by purpose of trip offered a reasonable basis for distributing local travel expenses. Yet others could not reasonably be allocated as direct charges so were grouped as indirect administrative expense. Because of the smaller scale of operations in Brown County, functions were less differentiated, and a larger share of total costs was classified as indirect administrative expense.

Once all expenses were allocated, we divided by appropriate workload measures for each function. For example, from April through December 1976, the Brown County HAO spent $29,584 directly on annual recertification interviews and conducted 1,662 such interviews, implying a cost of $17.80 per case.[8] Since the denominators (workload measures) for each maintenance function differ, we cannot simply aggregate function costs like these to yield an overall measure of the cost of maintenance; we used the recipient-year as a common unit of account. We found that over the long term, the Brown County HAO conducted 0.87 annual interviews per recipient-year.[9] Thus the direct cost of those interviews was $15.49 per recipient-year (*$17.80* × *0.87*).

For intake costs, however, it does not make sense to use recipient-years as the denominator. When the program is growing rapidly and intake dominates HAO workloads, intake costs per recipient-year would be high. When the program has reached steady state (only enough intake to replace terminations), intake cost per recipient-year would be much lower, even with no change in the efficiency of intake activity. It is more appropriate to relate the cost of intake to its own direct output—the number of new recipients added to the program. We calculated the cost per case processed for each intake function and then multiplied by the number of such cases required to yield one new recipient.

Direct costs of program operations, however, tell only part of the story. To estimate total administrative costs for intake and maintenance, respectively, we factored in expenses for administrative support functions in proportion to direct costs.[10] For the reason given earlier, these indirect costs were slightly higher per dollar of direct cost in Brown County than in St. Joseph County.

Costs of Client Intake and Maintenance

Cost data consistent with this framework are presented in the last two columns of Table 8.4, covering the period April 1976 through June 1979.

[8]In this and all subsequent calculations of administrative costs in this chapter, costs are expressed in constant 1976 dollars for consistency with other presentations of costs in EHAP (see, for example, U.S. Department of Housing and Urban Development, 1980).

[9]The number of recipient-years of program service provided by the HAO is the equivalent of 12 months of recipient status regardless of the number of households involved. If, during a given year, two households received payments for 6 months and two others for 9 months, the yield would be 2.5 recipient-years (30 recipient-months divided by 12).

[10]For comparability with other programs, experimental support costs must be excluded. The allocation of costs to this category was conservative; i.e., the costs of some activities mandated only by experimental needs were left in the intake and maintenance categories because we did not have sufficient data to allow us to remove them reliably (see Kingsley and Schlegel, 1979).

Table 8.4

ADMINISTRATIVE EXPENSE BY FUNCTION: HOUSING ALLOWANCE PROGRAMS BY SITE, 1976-79

Period	Annualized Expense in 1976 Dollars (000)				Intake Cost ($) per New Recipient[a]	Maintenance Cost ($) per Recipient-Year[a]
	Program Operations		Experimental Support	General Administration		
	Intake	Maintenance				
Brown County						
Apr-Dec 1976	206	218	168	508	209	137
Jan-Jun 1977	132	216	137	481	210	143
Jul-Dec 1977	116	212	140	508	163	129
Jan-Jun 1978	108	199	124	472	161	122
Jul-Dec 1978	102	197	119	466	157	120
Jan-Jun 1979	97	165	67	441	146	110
St. Joseph County						
Apr-Dec 1976	473	262	178	756	275	137
Jan-Jun 1977	510	279	205	740	281	112
Jul-Dec 1977	339	306	151	725	233	112
Jan-Jun 1978	257	345	128	697	254	114
Jul-Dec 1978	364	326	202	661	256	104
Jan-Jun 1979	264	316	83	666	197	109

SOURCE: Calculated from HAO accounting records and management information reports. See Kingsley and Schlegel, 1982, for details.

[a]Costs include direct expense as shown under "Program Operations" plus a prorated share of general administrative expense; experimental support expenses are excluded.

Looking first at maintenance cost per recipient-year, we note that it was nearly the same in the two sites, and declined over time in much the same way. Intake costs per new recipient also declined over time, but were consistently higher in St. Joseph County.

Intake cost more initially in St. Joseph County partly because the HAO there spent more on outreach and enrollee services as a matter of policy; and partly because fewer applicants there ended as recipients, so that intake workloads were higher per new recipient. Controlling for these factors (eliminating outreach and service costs and using the Brown County intake yield factors in both sites), we find very little difference in the efficiency of remaining intake functions.

Costs by Function

The costs of administering each intake and maintenance function during the steady-state period are shown in Table 8.5. Clearly, means-test administration (enrollment and eligibility recertification) is the most costly. In Brown County, it accounted for 60 percent of all intake costs and 63 percent of all maintenance costs; 48 percent and 58 percent in St. Joseph County. As would be expected, given their different natures, annual recertifications cost more than twice as much as did semiannuals.

Housing certification is the next most expensive function. Housing evaluation accounted for between one-fifth and one-third of all costs. Service costs were negligible in Brown County, comparatively small in St. Joseph County.

Total Administrative Cost per Recipient-Year

To characterize overall HAO efficiency, we needed a summary measure that brought together the costs of intake and maintenance. We estimated the total administrative cost per recipient-year by amortizing intake costs per new recipient over the average duration of recipiency and adding that annualized cost to the average annual maintenance cost per recipient-year.

Data on recipient attrition during the first two years of the program enabled us to estimate that the average Brown County recipient would remain in the program for 3.67 years after the initial payment authorization.[11] The full administrative cost for the typical recipient,

[11]Duration of recipiency was modeled from data on early cohorts of enrollees whose attrition during the first five program years could be observed. The model specified attrition as a negative exponential function of time, a form that yields a mean value for

Table 8.5

STEADY-STATE ADMINISTRATIVE COSTS BY FUNCTION: HOUSING ALLOWANCE PROGRAMS, BY SITE

	Cost in 1976 Dollars		Percent of Total Cost	
Function	Brown County	St. Joseph County	Brown County	St. Joseph County
Intake Cost per New Recipient				
Outreach	5.18	46.08	3.3	20.0
Enrollment:				
Screening and scheduling	22.43	27.70	14.3	12.0
Interview and information sessions	44.12	46.91	28.1	20.4
Error control and data processing	26.92	35.37	17.2	15.3
Housing certification:				
Housing evaluation	46.87	49.58	29.9	21.5
Data processing	8.77	12.63	5.6	5.5
Services to enrollees	2.43	12.31	1.6	5.3
Total intake cost	156.72	230.58	100.0	100.0
Maintenance Cost per Recipient-Year				
Payment operations	15.74	10.92	13.1	10.0
Eligibility recertification:				
Semiannual	21.52	14.67	17.9	13.4
Annual	46.04	39.14	38.4	35.9
Special	7.91	9.22	6.6	8.5
Housing recertification:				
Housing reevaluation	22.51	28.94	18.7	26.6
Data processing	4.90	3.92	4.1	3.6
Services to recipients	1.44	2.20	1.2	2.0
Total maintenance cost	120.06	109.01	100.0	100.0

SOURCE: Calculated from HAO accounting records and management information reports. See Kingsley and Schlegel, 1982, for details.

NOTE: Steady-state estimates are averages for July 1977 through June 1979 in each site.

therefore, would be $157 divided by 3.67 for intake plus $120 per year for maintenance—a total of $163 per recipient-year. We estimate that the average duration of recipiency in St. Joseph County is 4.28 years. Similar calculations using that average show that long-term total administrative cost there was also $163 per recipient-year.

---

duration of recipiency. Average durations estimated from the model were longer than the periods for which some cohorts were actually observed; and for some household types, longer than five years; see Table 8.7 below.

Comparison with Other Programs

In Table 8.6, we compare the administrative cost of the Supply Experiment allowance programs with the costs of other housing and welfare programs. Where sufficient data were available, we divided costs into two components: those required for basic income-transfer functions, and those required to ensure that the recipients' housing was adequate.

Consider Brown County costs as an example. Income-transfer costs there in the intake phase include the cost of all functions except housing certification (*$157 − $58 = $99* per new recipient). But if there were no housing requirements, all enrollees would automatically have become recipients. The Brown County HAO enrolled 1.17 households for every one finally authorized for payment; thus, without housing requirements intake cost would have been $85 per new recipient ($99 divided by 1.17), or (dividing by the 3.67-year average duration of recipiency again), $23 per recipient-year. In the maintenance phase, subtracting housing recertification costs from the total leaves $90 per recipient-year (*$120 − $30*). The total income-transfer cost was thus $113 per recipient-year (*$23 + $90*), and by implication, the residual $50 was the additional administrative cost required to earmark the transfer for housing. In St. Joseph County, income-transfer costs were somewhat lower and housing requirements costs somewhat higher. The intersite averages were $108 for income-transfer, and $55 for housing requirements.

HAO total costs were substantially below even the lowest cost recorded among the seven agencies administering housing allowance programs in the Administrative Agency Experiment (AAE). The AAE median ($235) exceeded the $163 HAO average by 44 percent. The AAE agencies had much smaller workloads (500 to 1,500 enrollees) than the HAOs, and only renters were allowed to participate. All shared the same basic list of administrative functions as the HAOs, but were given considerable latitude in designing procedures to implement them, which accounts for the wide variation in outcomes.

Most of the cost difference between the two experiments is explained by high AAE expenditures for housing certification; the AAE median was 2.5 times the HAO average. The difference arose because most AAE agencies chose to spend substantial amounts on services to help enrollees find certifiable housing; AAE housing evaluation procedures were in fact considerably less rigorous than those employed by the HAOs (see Kingsley, Kirby and Rizor, 1982).

The AAE median income-transfer cost was only 25 percent higher than the HAO average, but AAE processing requirements here were less demanding. First, where the HAOs recertified client eligibility

Table 8.6

Administrative Costs of Selected Housing and Welfare Programs

Program	Cost per Recipient-Year (1976 $)		
	Income Transfer	Housing Certification	Total
Supply Experiment			
Brown County	113	50	163
St. Joseph County	103	60	163
Average	108	55	163
Administrative Agency Experiment[a]			
Most expensive site	202	275	403
Least expensive site	92	61	194
Median	133	138	235
Sec. 8 Existing Housing			
0-49 recipients	(*b*)	(*b*)	216
50-99 recipients	(*b*)	(*b*)	191
100-299 recipients	(*b*)	(*b*)	170
300-499 recipients	(*b*)	(*b*)	214
500-999 recipients	(*b*)	(*b*)	191
1,000+ recipients	(*b*)	(*b*)	296
Average	(*b*)	(*b*)	190
Aid to Families with Dependent Children			
Most expensive state	582	(*c*)	582
Least expensive state	77	(*c*)	77
National average[d]	295	(*c*)	295

SOURCES: Supply Experiment data are from Table 8.5; Administrative Agency Experiment data are from U.S. Department of Housing and Urban Development, 1980, and Maloy, Madden, and others, 1977; Sec. 8 data are from Coopers and Lybrand, 1981; AFDC data are from Campbell and Bendick, 1977.

NOTE: Costs for each program were converted to 1976 dollars. Intake costs for the Supply and Administrative Agency experiments and for the Sec. 8 program are amortized over the estimated average duration of recipiency (4 years). AFDC costs for determining eligibility and administering payments for fiscal 1976 were divided by average monthly caseload during that year; costs for social services to recipients were excluded.

[a] Seven sites, excluding Jacksonville, Florida, where operating experience was unusual. Income transfer, housing certification, and total entries are for different sites, so the components do not add to the total.

[b] Not available.

[c] Not applicable.

[d] Average of state costs, each weighted by caseload.

once every six months, the AAEs required only annual recertifications for nonelderly recipients and biennial recertifications for the elderly. Second, although some AAE agencies had formal procedures for error control, none was as thorough as the HAOs' procedures.

HAO costs were also well below the administrative costs estimated for a sample of agencies operating Sec. 8 Existing Housing programs. This component of the broader Sec. 8 program was HUD's fastest growing vehicle for housing assistance in the late 1970s. It operated like a housing allowance program, but with three major differences. First, as in the AAE, only renters could participate. Second, the administering agency contracted with landlords for the occupancy of specific dwellings by program participants, and the subsidy was paid to the landlord rather than to the tenant. Third, subsidies equaled the difference between the tenant's income-based rent-paying ability and his actual rent, whereas HAO benefits were based on a standard cost of adequate housing.

These differences gave Sec. 8 agencies several additional administrative tasks to perform. In the intake phase, funds were spent on outreach for landlords as well as for tenants, and on negotiating contracts and rent levels with landlords who decided to participate. In the maintenance phase, Sec. 8 agencies had additional responsibilities reviewing landlord eviction requests, inspecting and accounting for the vacated housing units of landlords who still had active contracts, and renegotiating rents and other contract terms as conditions changed.

All of this implies that a Sec. 8 program ought to have cost more to administer than an allowance program at the same level of efficiency. However, there is a compensating factor. Section 8 eligibility recertification requirements were the same as noted above for the AAE. Thus, the Sec. 8 agencies had much less work to do in this major maintenance function than the HAOs.

The AFDC program, of course, did not have housing certification requirements to administer, so it is appropriate to compare AFDC costs with HAO income-transfer costs only. HAO costs averaged $108 per recipient-year, 37 percent of the 1976 national AFDC average, and lower than the AFDC averages for all but two states. It appears that the other housing programs (AAE and Sec. 8) also spent less than AFDC in administering income-transfer functions, but they required less than half of the eligibility recertifications performed by either the HAOs or the typical AFDC office.

Although the AAE and Sec. 8 served client populations much like those served in the Supply Experiment, AFDC clients were overwhelmingly single parents. It is therefore appropriate to compare AFDC administrative costs with HAO costs for that subset of recipients. From entries in Table 8.7, below, we estimate that the HAOs served single parents (both renters and owners) at an average cost of $189 per recipient-year, including housing certification, or about $130 for income-transfer functions alone. This figure may be compared with $295, the national average of AFDC costs.

DETERMINANTS OF PERFORMANCE

The HAOs effectively met their administrative goals as the housing allowance programs got under way, and they either maintained high standards of performance or improved upon them as time went on. Compared with other transfer programs, the HAOs' costs per recipient-year were low, indicating relative efficiency as well as effectiveness. Their achievement was not just getting their work done on schedule, controlling errors, maintaining good client and community relations, or cutting administrative costs, but rather, accomplishing all these tasks simultaneously. There are many things the HAOs could have done better, but on the whole their records are encouraging counters to current skepticism about the effectiveness and efficiency of social programs.

The HAOs were organized and supervised by The Rand Corporation as part of a highly visible social experiment. Is their experience relevant to the world of regular program operations? We judge that there were enough similarities to regular programs to make the search for broader lessons worthwhile. First, the allowance programs were far larger than the usual experimental program. Second, although the excitement associated with the project gave the HAOs an edge over local governments in recruitment, more than 95 percent of the employees in both HAOs were recruited locally and HAO salary structures were comparable to those of local agencies. Third, like public agencies, the HAOs were not driven by the profit motive or the pressures of competitive markets; they were nonprofit institutions whose funding was assured for a ten-year period.

In looking back over their experience, we sought to identify the most important factors that affected the HAOs' ability to meet their goals, and thus to identify major determinants of administrative performance that we can generalize to other allowance programs.

Of primary importance was the intentionally limited nature of HAO administrative functions. The HAOs' two main activities—eligibility and housing certifications—shared several common features. The number of cases that had to be processed was clearly prescribed by program rules; employees could not choose to increase or decrease

Table 8.7

ADMINISTRATIVE COST PER RECIPIENT-YEAR, BY TENURE AND HOUSEHOLD COMPOSITION: HOUSING ALLOWANCE PROGRAM IN BROWN COUNTY

Household Composition	Average Duration of Recipiency (years)	Administrative Cost (1976 $)		
		Intake Cost per New Recipient	Maintenance Cost per Recipient-Year	Total Cost per Recipient Year
		Renters		
Nonelderly				
Single, no children	2.93	154	117	170
Single, with children	2.94	144	124	173
Couple, no children	1.25	162	131	261
Couple, with children	1.55	178	128	243
All nonelderly	2.61	154	123	182
Elderly				
Single	3.99	142	111	147
Couple	4.87	154	121	153
All elderly	4.13	146	113	148
All renters	2.99	153	121	172
		Owners		
Nonelderly				
Single, no children	6.17	161	126	153
Single, with children	2.41	154	121	185
Couple, no children	2.24	177	118	197
Couple, with children	1.53	202	124	255
All nonelderly	2.65	173	123	188
Elderly				
Single	7.72	150	115	135
Couple	4.71	211	118	162
All elderly	6.72	168	116	141
All owners	5.00	172	119	153

SOURCE: Estimated by HASE staff from accounting records and management information reports of the Brown County HAO through June 1978.

NOTE: Estimates for each type of household were derived by multiplying its function-specific workloads by each function's average cost, and summing over all intake and all maintenance functions. Total cost per recipient-year was calculated by adding annual maintenance cost to annualized intake cost; intake costs are amortized over the average duration of recipiency. Function costs are averages for July 1977 through June 1979.

their workloads. Written guidelines for handling individual cases limited employees' discretion and thereby sped processing as well as ensuring consistency in the application of standards. Because of these characteristics, it was easier to measure (and therefore to control) output, quality, and productivity than it would have been with more complex functions.

In contrast, many functions typically associated with housing program administration are open-ended and harder to control; these include, for example, checking and auditing the work of private builders; managing housing projects (selecting tenants, controlling vacancies, making repairs); and negotiating with landlords on behalf of low-income households. Here, there are no clear standards as to how much time should be allocated to a given task, and it is harder to measure performance to everyone's satisfaction. Certainly, there are more opportunities for things to go wrong.

In addition to administrative simplicity, we identified three other major determinants of administrative performance, which we analyze in the remainder of this chapter:

- The mix of household types in the participant population.
- The specification of administrative rules and procedures for both the eligibility- and housing-certification functions of the HAOs.
- Several managerial and institutional factors, including staff training, quality control, and management reporting systems.

In discussing each, we first note how it affects administrative performance. Then, we assess options that might have improved that performance in the Supply Experiment. Finally, we draw lessons relevant to the implementation of a national housing allowance program or administrative improvement in other programs.

THE PARTICIPANT MIX

As we began our analysis of administrative costs, we expected scale to be a significant variable, but it was not. As we have seen, unit costs in the St. Joseph County program were nearly the same as those in the Brown County program, yet St. Joseph County's recipient population was on average 62 percent larger. Although unit costs declined in both sites as the programs grew in size, cross-site analysis persuades us that experience, not scale, was the reason (Kingsley and Schlegel, 1982, Sec. III). The main effect of scale was a difference between sites in the ratio of direct to overhead costs; in the smaller program, a somewhat larger share of total cost was booked as overhead, implying less specialization of function. Thus it appears that economies of scale are negligible for programs serving from 3,000 to 6,500 current recipients.

The Effect of Attrition on Administrative Cost

If scale is unimportant, then administrative cost in a mature program will vary roughly in proportion to workload. We find that a substantial part of the HAOs' workloads was attributable to applicants who were screened out or voluntarily dropped out before qualifying for payments. Among those who qualified for payments, some stayed in the program much longer than others. During both the intake and maintenance phases of participation, attrition varied with household characteristics. Moreover, the cost of some administrative procedures, such as enrollment, varied with the complexity of household incomes or other circumstances. For all these reasons, administrative cost per recipient-year varied among household types by a factor of 2.

Brown County will serve as an example. To obtain one new recipient there, the HAO had to receive, screen, and process 1.94 applications, conduct 1.35 enrollment interviews, enroll 1.17 households, and administer 2.18 housing evaluations. Only 52 percent of Brown County's applicants ever qualified for payments; among those who did, some dropped out or lost their eligibility at the first semiannual recertification, whereas others were still receiving payments at the end of the fifth program year. The average duration of recipiency, estimated from the experience of early enrollees, was 3.67 years.

Attrition and Household Characteristics

We measured the workloads generated by various types of households in each site, and found substantial variations. For example, among homeowner applicants in Brown County 100 interviews of single elderly persons yielded 90 enrollees, whereas 100 interviews of elderly couples yielded only 52 enrollees; the lower yield for couples reflected the fact that many who applied were ineligible but had not been screened out before the interview. Among renters who enrolled, 13 percent of the single parents but 25 percent of the couples with children dropped out before qualifying for payments, so that the work entailed in enrolling them was unproductive.

Classifying applicants by housing tenure and household composition, we have estimated how those characteristics affect administrative cost in each site (Kingsley and Schlegel, 1982). The results for Brown County are shown in Table 8.7.

The first column of the table shows the estimated average duration of recipiency among those who qualified for payments, the factor used to amortize intake costs. That duration varied from 1.25 years for renter couples without children to 7.72 years for elderly single homeowners. The second column shows the unamortized intake costs per new recipient, ranging from $142 to $202. Maintenance costs per recipient-year, shown in the third column, varied less with household characteristics—from $111 to $131 for the groups shown.

Combining amortized intake costs with annual maintenance costs, we obtain total cost per recipient-year, shown in the last column of the table. By this measure, the most expensive households to serve were nonelderly couples with or without children, whether renters or owners; the main reason was their very short average duration of recipiency. The least expensive were the elderly, whether renters or owners, couples or singles; and also the nonelderly single homeowners. Again, the critical factor was average duration of recipiency.

To estimate the overall effect of attrition on administrative cost, we averaged the cost and workload requirements presented earlier for the two HAOs, then modified the workload ratios to simulate a world in which there was zero attrition (Kingsley and Schlegel, 1982, Sec. IV). If every applicant were eventually authorized for payment, only one application, one interview, and one enrollment would be needed per new recipient. Intake costs per new recipient would drop from the cross-site average of $194 to $130. Thus, perfect preinterview screening of applicants would at most reduce intake costs by one-third.

If no recipients ever left the program, maintenance costs per recipient-year would rise slightly, but intake costs would be amortized to the vanishing point. Total administrative costs per recipient-year, actually $163, would drop to $134 regardless of attrition rates in the intake phase. Choosing enrollees so as to lengthen the average duration of recipiency by a year, a more plausible possibility, would reduce administrative cost per recipient-year by only 2.5 percent.

Policy Implications

Variations in workload and cost relationships by participant groups were strikingly similar in Brown and St. Joseph counties. This suggests that we can generalize at least some of our findings. We do not assert, for example, that in all areas the cost of administering a housing allowance program for elderly single homeowners would be 52 percent of the cost for nonelderly renter couples without children, as it was in Brown County. But we do believe that in all programs that administer means tests and housing certifications, costs for the former will be significantly lower than those for the latter.

The main value of this analysis for other programs should be as a guide for budgeting. It would clearly be a mistake to provide the same administrative resources to a Sec. 8 Existing Housing program serving 1,000 elderly households as to one serving 1,000 nonelderly couples.

Another policy implication concerns the targeting of housing assistance programs. We see that young couples generated the highest administrative cost in the Supply Experiment allowance programs. This is because, as a group, their household circumstances and incomes were relatively unstable; brief periods of eligibility followed the loss of a job or an illness, and many in such circumstances applied for assistance. Certainly, it would be inappropriate to exclude anyone from the program simply because of age or household composition; yet we doubt that the extra cost of earmarking housing assistance for short-term participants is justified.

It is now generally believed (see Mulford, 1979) that families decide how much they will spend for housing based on their longer-term income expectations, not their immediate rate of income. When income drops because of unemployment, housing expenditures are not likely to be reduced until the family has exhausted its savings and capacity to borrow. Usually, reemployment relieves the family's financial problems before they become acute. Housing allowances certainly help such families through episodes of insecurity, but have little effect on their housing consumption. For their financial problems, unemployment compensation seems a more appropriate remedy than housing allowances.

Recessions in 1974 and 1980 caused program enrollments to swell in both of our sites, and during those periods, the temporarily unemployed made up a larger proportion of all recipients than they did during the steady-state conditions we have discussed above. Because they reported little or no income, their allowance entitlements were above average. The following hypothetical calculation gives some idea of the fiscal consequences for the allowance program.

Assuming a one-third increase in short-term unemployed recipients, and assuming they all had characteristics like the nonelderly renter couples without children for whom we presented data above, program outlays per recipient-year would increase by 14 percent. Counting the effect of increases both in number of recipients and average cost, the total monthly outlays would increase by 51 percent.

Fiscal planning for the program would certainly be greatly simplified if it were possible to exclude households who would be only briefly eligible.[12]

RULES AND PROCEDURES FOR ELIGIBILITY CERTIFICATION

Eligibility certification is the major administrative function of a housing allowance program, so how it is accomplished can significantly affect program success. For example, we saw that the HAOs recertified household eligiblity more than twice as often as would be required under Sec. 8 program rules. If they had adopted the Sec. 8 approach, administrative costs would have been reduced significantly, but erroneous payments would surely have increased. Which approach is best?

The two HAOs conducted eligibility certifications under the same set of rules and procedures, with only minor modifications, over a five-year period. Clearly, we could have learned more about the costs and benefits of different administrative options had the HAOs conducted formal experiments with different techniques. Nonetheless, five years of operating experience, even under the same rules, provides insight into what is workable and what is not. The paragraphs below present our conclusions. In some cases, we have data to demonstrate our point. In the others, we rely on a consensus of judgment among Rand's staff and senior HAO managers. The discussion is structured around six essential features of any eligibility certification system:

- Extent of intake application screening (e.g., none vs. intensive).
- Specification of income-accounting rules (e.g., general vs. specific).
- Form of means test (e.g., interview vs. mail-back questionnaire).
- Frequency of recertification (e.g., semiannually vs. annually).
- Type and extent of error control (e.g., 100 percent verification vs. sample verification).
- Form of record management (e.g., automated vs. manual).

[12]One way would be to delay housing assistance until six to nine months after the loss of a primary source of income. Another would be to use the household's income over the last full year (rather than the current rate of income as the HAOs did) as the basis for eligibility determinations.

Intake Application Screening

In its first year of operation, the Brown County housing allowance program enrolled only 53 percent of its applicants (27 percent dropped out before the interview and 20 percent either dropped out or were found to be ineligible at the interview). To improve its yield, the HAO began more intensive preapplication screening, asking potential applicants questions when they first called the HAOs, to help determine whether they were eligible. Conditions did improve. In the steady-state period, 60 percent of all applicants were enrolled (31 percent dropping out before the interview and 9 percent at the interview).

The St. Joseph County HAO had even lower yields in its first year; 28 percent dropped out before the interview and 28 percent at the interview, leaving 44 percent enrolled. The HAO did not adopt Brown County's intensive screening approach, but tried more intensive follow-up to get more applicants to turn up at the interview. These efforts did not work. By the steady-state period, the proportion dropping out before the interview actually increased (to 33 percent). Even without intensive screening, the proportion dropping out at the interview decreased somewhat (to 19 percent), leaving 48 percent enrolled.

We draw three conclusions: First, we can envision no technique for forestalling applications from ineligibles that would not also discourage applications from eligible households. Second, preapplication screening is worthwhile so long as its cost per rejected applicant does not approach that of a full interview (about $50 per case; see Table 8.5). Third, efforts to get more applicants to attend the interview are probably not cost-effective. From HASE surveys, we estimate that among those who dropped out before the interview, 69 percent in Brown County and 82 percent in St. Joseph County were ineligible a few months after they applied.

Income-Accounting Rules

There is a sizeable literature on the merits of various income-accounting rules (see, for example, Zais, Melton, and Berkham, 1975). This is not the place to present our views on the equity or incentive effects of particular specifications. Three comments on their administration are warranted, however.

First, we emphasize the importance of making the rules understandable and unambiguous. To do this, we need to ensure that they operate in conjunction with acceptable documentation. Suppose an applicant is employed and the rule simply requires the interviewer to determine his "current rate of income" from that job. If the applicant works irregular hours, he and the interviewer could spend a long time debating how to calculate the current rate. The HAO manuals went further, specifying for such a case: "Use pay stubs covering at least six of the past eight weeks to determine an average income per pay period; multiply the average times the number of pay periods per year." Arbitrary, yes, but this method eliminates debate. It was less likely that the applicant would return later and say "Another interviewer at the HAO gave one of my coworkers more benefits and he gets the same wage I do." Since the HAOs kept photocopies of all documentation, a subsequent auditor could quickly and clearly determine whether the interviewer had applied the rule correctly. Asking the question, "How can this be documented?" was a critical step in designing the rules initially; where the answer was "It can't," we usually reconsidered our approach.

Second, we note the benefits of a "no exceptions" policy. Regardless of how unfair an interviewer thought the application of a rule was in a particular case, neither he nor any of his superiors was permitted to grant an exception. This policy would have led to institutional explosions, however, if another channel had not been open. The interviewer could tell the client, "I think this rule is not fair to you, and while I have to apply it today, I will talk to my supervisor about changing the rule to take into account cases like yours." In the first year of HAO operations, many such changes were proposed and reviewed by HAO managers, Rand, and HUD. Some were made, but others were not because no one could devise an alternative that would work better across the board. In subsequent years, the number of proposals for changes dropped off. One indication that the process worked well is that in five years of program operations at both HAOs, no client ever requested a formal hearing (at which an independent panel would judge whether HAO staff had applied specific rules in accord with general program standards). We are confident that exceptions would have been impossible to control had they been allowed; that the "no exceptions" rule was vital to maintaining efficiency as well as program integrity.

Third, we review some advantages of a "prospective income" accounting system like the one used by the HAOs. In this type of system, when the interviewer's calculations show that a client is entitled to receive $80 per month, that is precisely what the client will receive until a required recertification shows an adjustment is warranted (unless an initial error is discovered). In a retrospective system (often advocated for welfare reform; see Allen, 1973), the agency must obtain data on the client's actual income over the period, and to the extent that it differs from the "best estimate" made initially, the client may have to pay back some portion of what he had received. If the period between recertifications is short (say one month), the adjustment may not be large, but it could be substantial with semiannual recertifications.

Retrospective systems have been advocated because they are more accurate and should save the government money. We do not assert that such savings would be insignificant, but we do suggest that they be balanced against two substantial costs. First, there is the burden for the administrating agency. HAO managers occasionally had to recover overpayments from their clients; they not only considered this their most time-consuming and onerous task, but were seldom able to collect the full amounts due. Such collection tasks would have been frequent with a retrospective system. Second, a retrospective system imposes a burden of uncertainty on the client, who cannot know, except retrospectively, how much of his benefit he will be allowed to keep.

The foregoing discussion on income accounting points up the importance of certainty as a guiding principle in effective program administration. In HAO income accounting, both staff and clients always knew exactly where they stood. We think this may have been as important a factor as considerate treatment in clients' positive evaluations of the program's administration.

Form of Elicitation

The HAOs determined eligibility from data obtained during a face-to-face interview with each applicant. As soon as the interview was scheduled, the applicant was sent a brochure explaining program rules and the purpose of the interview, as well as a list of the documents (e.g., paycheck stubs, bank statements) that he should bring to the HAO on the appointed day.

The interview was conducted by a trained enroller, who followed a standard pattern of questions to obtain information about place of residence, household composition, assets, income, deductions, and housing expenses. As each question about financial items came up, the applicant was asked to show the relevant documentation. If the documentation was not available, the applicant was asked to sign forms that authorized the HAO to verify the data with appropriate third parties. When the enrollment form was complete, the applicant was asked to sign it, certifying that the information he provided was accurate and complete.

In this context, the interviewer was able to verify the applicant's understanding of income-accounting terms and rules, probe unclear responses, and emphasize (explicitly and implicitly) that the HAO would be aggressive about catching and correcting errors. From the way they responded, it was clear that few applicants could have filled out an enrollment form properly without the interviewer's guidance, even if detailed instructions had been provided. As we noted earlier, we cannot measure the error prevented by this approach, but our considered judgment is that it outweighed by far any additional administrative cost implied. It not only prevented error in enrollment data, but also set a tone that we believe prevented error in subsequent recertifications.

With a thorough initial interview, we saw less risk in using a less expensive mail-back questionnaire for the semiannual recertification. The questionnaire was computer-generated: It showed the client the responses he had given to household composition and income questions in the last interview and asked him only to indicate any changes. Sample verifications of returned questionnaires give them good marks for accuracy (Rizor, 1982).

In the Supply Experiment, we scheduled a complete interview for each annual recertification. Such annual interviews might not be needed in a national program, however. For groups whose household statuses change infrequently, it might be possible to use two or three mail-back recertifications between interviews without significant losses in accuracy.

Frequency of Recertification

The frequency with which an income-transfer program recertifies client eligibility and entitlement ought to relate to the frequency of change in client circumstances. If an agency recertifies too often, it will incur a substantial administrative cost in order to make only a few adjustments in payments. On the other hand, increasing the interval between recertifications will save administrative expense but permit more erroneous payments.

Although the HAOs required recertifications much more frequently than did the Sec. 8 program, they by no means had the most rigorous requirement among income-transfer programs. Allen, 1973, and Kershaw, 1973, recommended monthly recertification for the AFDC program, and that approach is now being tested in a number of states (see Crespi, Kaluzny, and Tidwell, 1978). The results generally (although not conclusively in our view) suggest that monthly reporting may work best for AFDC. Even so, what works there may not be optimal for housing assistance programs. The decision should depend on the relationship between administrative costs and payment savings in the program at hand.

If recertifications yielded minimal changes in eligibility or allowance entitlements, we would conclude that the periods between them could be extended. This conclusion is not warranted for the Supply Experiment's programs. In both sites, about 70 percent of all semiannual recertifications and over 90 percent of all annuals caused terminations or entitlement changes. Terminations followed 10 to 15 percent of all semiannuals and annuals initiated in both sites. Semiannuals reduced monthly allowance entitlements per 100 cases reviewed by $1,200 in Brown County and $1,800 in St. Joseph County. Annuals reduced outlays per 100 cases reviewed by $1,500 to $1,600 in both sites.

In both sites, the results differ considerably depending on age of household head. Although both the elderly and nonelderly were about as likely to experience a negative payment change (either downward adjustment or termination), the nonelderly were much more likely to be terminated. The difference in the effect on payments is striking. Annual recertifications for 100 elderly households in Brown County reduced monthly outlays by $500; the comparable reduction for nonelderly households was $2,200. The difference is similar in St. Joseph County annuals and in semiannuals in both sites, and applies equally to renters and homeowners.

Information derived from this analysis and the cost model presented earlier permits us to estimate the fiscal outcomes of alternative recertification schedules. Table 8.8 presents the estimated effects of two alternatives for Brown County renters. Program costs are calculated per recipient-year, including both administration and allowance payments.

In the first option, we assume the recertification standards of the Sec. 8 program. Nonelderly renters would be recertified only once each year. Administrative cost per recipient would decline by $26, but payments would increase by $133, producing a net increase in outlays of $107 (9 percent). Under this option, the elderly would be recertified only once every two years. Administrative costs for them would decline by $51, but payments would increase by $95, producing a net outlay increase of $44 (5 percent). Clearly, this change in recertification intervals would not have been cost-effective.

The second alternative retains the current semiannual requirement for nonelderly recipients, but makes two changes for the elderly. First, they would be recertified only once each year. Second, every other annual recertification would be done by mail-back questionnaire rather than complete interview. This approach would increase program efficiency, but only marginally: Administrative expenses decline by $37 and payments increase by $31, yielding a net savings of $6 per hundred elderly recipients (less than 1 percent).

Table 8.8

HOW RECERTIFICATION FREQUENCY AFFECTS PROGRAM COST: HOUSING ALLOWANCE PROGRAM FOR RENTERS IN BROWN COUNTY

Age of Household Head	Annual Cost per Recipient (1976 $)			Cost Index (Base Case = 100)		
	Administration	Allowance Payments	Program Cost	Administration	Allowance Payments	Program Cost
Base Case: Actual Recertification Frequencies						
Nonelderly	182	989	1,171	100.0	100.0	100.0
Elderly	148	791	939	100.0	100.0	100.0
All renters	172	941	1,113	100.0	100.0	100.0
Option 1: Sec. 8 Recertification Frequencies						
Nonelderly	156	1,122	1,278	85.7	113.4	109.1
Elderly	97	886	983	65.5	112.0	104.7
All renters	141	1,063	1,204	82.0	113.0	108.2
Option 2: Recertify Elderly Annually						
Nonelderly	182	989	1,171	100.0	100.0	100.0
Elderly	111	822	933	75.0	103.9	99.4
All renters	164	947	1,111	95.3	100.6	99.8

SOURCE: Estimated by HASE staff from accounting records and management information reports of the Brown County HAO. For additional details, see Kingsley, Kirby, and Rizor, 1982.

NOTE: In the base case, all recipients undergo semiannual recertification of eligibility and adjustment of entitlement to reflect current income and household size. Under Option 1, nonelderly recipients are recertified annually and elderly recipients are recertified biennially. Under Option 2, nonelderly recipients are recertified semiannually and elderly recipients are recertified annually. Fiscal outcomes for Options 1 and 2 were estimated from the Brown County's experience with terminations and payment adjustments following semiannual recertifications.

Error-Control Options

When HAO administrative systems were being designed, we thought that third-party verification (to discover reporting errors) and record review (to discover staff errors) would be the most important error-control techniques. We now see that what happened in the enrollment interview was more important.

The HAOs' reliance on client-provided documentation deserves emphasis in this context. The practice did require one additional expense (making photocopies for HAO files), but on the whole, it saved administrative cost. When clients provided ample documentation, the interview went smoothly and took less time. We believe that requiring documentation prevented many inadvertent errors, whose correction would have added to administrative costs later in the program. We encountered no forged documents.[13]

Given error prevention in the interview, there was not much error left for the other control techniques to correct. Our calculations show that the relationship between the cost of administering these techniques and the net payment error they corrected was almost identical in both sites. Verification just about broke even in the strict fiscal sense. Per recipient-year, it cost $2.81 and saved $2.84 in Brown County, and it cost $2.76 and saved $2.46 in St. Joseph County. Staff data review, however, was far from cost-effective. In Brown County, it cost $12.34 and saved $1.14 per recipient-year. In St. Joseph County, it cost $12.87 and saved $1.05.

The results suggest that neither of these techniques should be implemented in a national program exactly as they were in the Supply Experiment; yet, we would strongly recommend against dropping them entirely. We are confident that because both client and HAO interviewer knew during the interview that these error-control techniques would be applied later, initial error was significantly reduced. It should be possible, though, to reduce sample sizes and thereby cut administrative costs without offsetting increases in payment errors.

Examining verification results, we found that because of HAO sampling rules, elderly clients were most likely to need verification;[14] yet the net payment error found and corrected by that process was negligible. In Brown County, for example, verifications for the elderly cost $3.14 per recipient-year as against a net savings of one cent. If sampling rules were adjusted so that only 5 percent of all enrollment and recertification cases for the elderly were verified, cost for them would decline to 16 cents per recipient-year with no measurable change in payments. Average verification cost for all clients would be reduced

[13]An independent audit showed that the risk of forgery was negligible. The auditors sent photocopies of over 1,000 randomly selected pieces of documentation back to the people who supposedly had prepared them (employers, doctors, etc.). In no case had the documentation been forged (see Tebbets, 1979, Sec. VI).

[14]Verification sampling rates varied inversely with the proportion of income that was adequately documented, and the elderly were often unable to document their primary income source, Old Age and Survivors Insurance or Supplemental Security Income. The reason was simply that the Social Security Administration did not routinely provide its clients with benefit statements either attached to monthly checks or as annual reports.

from \$2.81 to \$1.77—not a very substantial change in relation to total HAO administrative cost, but one worth implementing nonetheless.

Larger efficiency improvements are possible by drastic reductions in staff data review. Suppose that instead of reviewing every case, the HAOs randomly selected five percent for routine review, plus two percent for special circumstances (e.g., all cases completed by new employees during their first month on the job). Again using Brown County data, we estimate that administrative cost would decline to 86 cents and errors corrected to 8 cents per recipient-year. The \$11.48 reduction in costs would be offset by only a \$1.06 increase in uncorrected net payment error. In a program with 1,000 recipients, this change would save \$10,420 per year.

Records Management

Earlier, we noted that both HAOs used the same computer system to maintain means-test data, adjust payments, and record other administrative transactions for all clients. The system provided many benefits. Built-in edit routines remedied many simple clerical errors, and the internal discipline of the accounts prevented others. For example, the system printed out the clients' names, addresses, and identification numbers on most forms; mistakes in copying, so common in manual record-keeping, were thus averted. More broadly, system protocols prevented not only interviewers, but also the two HAOs, from following different rules. There was only one set of procedures, and the system would not accept entries that did not conform. Regular system outputs included automatic reminders to staff when follow-up actions were required, and automatic counts of various transactions and their characteristics for use in management reporting. Clearly, the administrative cost of records management was considerably less than it would have been if the same tasks had been performed manually, given the same quality standards. In fact, we doubt that it would have been feasible to perform them all manually.

Had this book been issued five years ago, we would have recommended that a computer system similar to that used by the HAOs be considered for all larger agencies if a national housing allowance program were to be implemented. But times have changed; the HAO system is now technologically obsolete.

If the system were being designed today, data processing economics would allow us to move beyond batch processing. During enrollment and recertification interviews, HAO staff would key responses directly into a terminal, and the computer would edit them immediately. At the end of the interview, the computer would print out a hard-copy record for the client's signature; then, on command, the interview data would be stored in the proper format for a client record. Such an automated system would shorten the interview, facilitate data review and verification, and eliminate the need for some file-maintenance staff and all data-entry staff. In consequence, administrative cost per recipient-year should decline significantly.

In the 1980s, such sophisticated data-processing systems should be feasible in small as well as large agencies that administer allowance or Sec. 8 programs.

RULES AND PROCEDURES FOR HOUSING CERTIFICATION

Here, we review rules and procedures governing the HAOs' housing certification function as we have reviewed them for the eligibility certification function above, asking whether any alternative rules and procedures would have improved the HAOs' performance. We look at five features of housing certification:

- Specification of program housing standards.
- Form of housing evaluation.
- Frequency of housing reevaluation.
- Extent of quality control.
- Extent of housing services provided.

We close by suggesting a broader framework for evaluating the benefits of housing certification as performed by the HAOs in relation to its costs.

Specification of Housing Standards

Here, as with our earlier discussion of income-accounting standards, we note only administrative implications. Two conclusions are similar to those for income-accounting.

First, we believe that a successful housing certification process depends on standards that can be applied without much ambiguity. In designing the standards for the Supply Experiment, we tried to limit the amount of discretion left to the evaluator. Evaluators rated a specified list of items in each housing unit; and for each item, we specified as clearly as was feasible the grounds for acceptance or rejection. When the presence or absence of a physical feature was at issue, clear specification was easy; but for many hazardous conditions, we had to defer to evaluators' judgments as to the seriousness of observed conditions. Nonetheless, we believe we did substantially reduce the likelihood of costly wrangling with participants about acceptance ratings.

Second, we applied a "no exceptions" policy to housing evaluations. As with means tests, evaluators or clients could question a standard, but evaluators could not grant exceptions for individual households. Again, the policy led to a number of adjustments to the standards in the first year or so, but requests for changes decreased thereafter. AAE agencies did permit exceptions in housing certification and found it difficult to control erosion of their standards (see Hamilton, 1979).

Third, we think that administrative and political factors limit the stringency of housing standards that can be applied in a mass evaluation program. The funds available for local code enforcement usually allow the agencies to inspect only a small fraction of the units in their communities each year; the same is true for Sec. 8 Existing Housing programs so far. In contrast, the Supply Experiment allowance programs evaluated about two-thirds of all rental dwellings (including about four-fifths of all substandard dwellings) in Brown County during the first five years of operations.

The Supply Experiment's housing standards concerned health and safety, not appearances or unessential conveniences. Because so many dwellings were being evaluated, the local political establishment paid attention. General pressure to maintain the standards sometimes vied with pressure to relax them in individual cases, since failure meant denying assistance to needy households. In such cases, Rand and the HAO usually had to argue forcefully that relaxing standards would allow clients to live in dangerous or unhealthy homes. Where smaller programs might be able to apply standards not essential to health and safety, we doubt that such standards would be politically acceptable for a large-scale program.

Form of Evaluation

To determine whether a dwelling meets a given set of standards, someone has to inspect it and record the results. HAO experience suggests two guidelines for housing evaluations in other programs.

First, prescribe a clear step-by-step routine for evaluators to follow as they go through a housing unit, and reinforce the discipline of the routine by the design of the evaluation form. The sequence of the form should follow the sequence of the evaluation, and the listing of blanks to be filled in should ensure that the evaluator takes note of all physical characteristics that can affect program quality standards. This approach was critical to consistency and efficiency in Supply Experiment evaluations.

Second, we would advise that only trained evaluators be used. Only a few HAO evaluators had inspection experience prior to joining the HAO staff, but all received considerable training once employed. Some were also "cross-trained" (e.g., they developed skills in housing evaluation in addition to conducting interviews or reviewing data), but none was permitted to inspect dwellings before demonstrating competence in that job.

In some AAE agencies, evaluations were performed by staff generalists (employees not trained in evaluation) or by participants (Hamilton, 1979). We believe that both approaches create serious risks likely to outweigh any potential savings in a large-scale program. Our ability to operate the program successfully in Brown and St. Joseph counties depended heavily on the credibility of the evaluation system. Community leaders in both sites took the enforcement of our standards seriously; and political difficulties would have ensued if allowance determinations had been based on inspections by participants who obviously had a vested interest in the outcome.

Frequency of Reevaluation

In the Supply Experiment, annual reevaluations were required. Although they did not have programs that lasted long enough to test options, AAE researchers share the judgment that evaluations once each year are appropriate (Hamilton, 1979). Earlier, we examined options for the interval between eligibility recertifications. Are there reasons to investigate alternative cycles for housing reevaluation?

The principle should be the same: Recertification frequency should be related to the frequency with which circumstances change. If some groups seldom fail their annual housing reevaluations (i.e., the quality of their housing does not often change), the time between reevaluations for them might be extended. However, failure rates at annual recertifications were present for all groups in the Supply Experiment. Among the nonelderly in both sites, the rate was at least 25 percent; it ran as high as 59 percent for single renters with children in St. Joseph County. Rates for the elderly were lower—9 to 24 percent—but not low enough, in our judgment, to justify lengthening the interval between reevaluations.

The annual reevaluation requirement worked well in the Supply Experiment. Participants and the public understood it easily, and generally seemed to accept it as reasonable. Anecdotal evidence suggests that many participants appreciated having yearly independent assessments that pointed up deficiencies in their dwellings they might otherwise not have noticed. Recognizing the cost of more frequent reevaluations and the possible credibility loss associated with a longer cycle, we judge that annual reevaluations are a sensible recommendation for Sec. 8 and other national housing programs.

Quality Control

HAO experience suggests that a formal quality-control program is essential to an effective housing evaluation system. Data from the Supply Experiment show that errors in pass-fail determinations were seldom made by evaluators in either site (see Tebbets, 1979, Sec. IV). We believe that the quality-control program had a great deal to do with that result, imposing a valuable discipline on the evaluation staff. A secondary benefit was that program managers could confidently assert to the public that the standards were strictly enforced, thus reducing the program's vulnerability to criticism.

The Role of Housing Services

When the Supply Experiment began, both HAOs invited participants to attend information sessions to learn about program housing requirements and to become more skillful housing consumers. Topics included home-repair techniques, tips on moving and purchasing a house, lease agreements, and fair-housing law. The Brown County HAO stopped the sessions after a few months because participant interest was low. The St. Joseph County HAO continued to offer them, but no more than a small fraction of all recipients attended. Free legal services were also available to participants who felt they had been discriminated against in their search for better housing, but again, few people made use of them.

This evidence, coupled with the fact that about 80 percent of all enrollees qualified for payments, makes it clear that services were not important to the success of the allowance program. It would have been a costly error to have made services mandatory for all enrollees—a view generally corroborated by research on the AAE, where mandatory services were attempted (see Hamilton, 1979, Ch. 3).

Nonetheless, services might have helped some of the 20 percent of all enrollees who dropped out before they met the program's housing requirements. We were not able to actually test the effects of targeting services to this group, but we did survey a 1,222-household sample to find out (a) the actions they took attempting to qualify for payments and (b) whether their circumstances at termination suggested they might have been candidates for additional service.

We found that a surprisingly small percentage made any effort to meet program housing requirements (Table 8.9). Among enrollees who never qualified for payments, about 15 percent of all renters and 27 percent of all homeowners attempted to repair their preenrollment dwellings; about 19 percent of the renters (but few owners) searched for another unit; and 16 percent of the renters (again few owners) actually moved.

About half of the renters and 70 percent of the owners took no action at all. The reader might suppose that everyone in this group had failed an initial evaluation and had decided that repairing or moving to get into the program would not be worth the effort. But two-fifths of the renters and a fifth of the owners in this group never obtained evaluations of their enrollment dwellings, and a few renters who had passed their evaluations did not qualify because either they or their landlords refused to sign the HAO-required lease agreement.[15]

The bottom panel of Table 8.9 shows that only 35 to 50 percent of these households might have been candidates for special services. There are several reasons why services would not have been warranted for the majority. Among the renters, about a fifth had become ineligible by the time they dropped out; 16 percent, although still formally eligible, had a change in circumstances (usually a new job or other increase in income) that caused them to decide they did not need the allowance anymore. Another 16 percent refused to move, even though program rules required them to do so to qualify for payments. Finally, 10 percent had become dissatisfied with the program—in many cases because they thought the allowance was too small to be worth the trouble. Among the homeowners, a much larger percentage dropped out because they were dissatisfied with the program; fewer terminated because they refused to move or because their incomes increased.

We categorized survey respondents as potential candidates for services if they named problems with moving or making repairs as one of their reasons for termination (even if it was not the primary reason). Among them, a modest number of renters, but a sizeable proportion of homeowners, said that their problems were financial only. They needed cash in order to repair their homes or move, but they did not need advice or technical help. For a larger proportion (in all groups except St. Joseph County owners), money was not the problem. They needed technical help in searching for a new unit or in making repairs. Some respondents were physically able to take the required

---

[15]The evaluation statuses of enrollees who took no action were about the same as for all enrollees in the sample; but note that the first panel of Table 8.9 covers the entire sample.

Table 8.9

Circumstances of Enrollees Who Never Qualified for Payments: Housing Allowance Programs in Brown and St. Joseph Counties

Item	Percentage Distribution of Households			
	Brown County		St. Joseph County	
	Renters	Owners	Renters	Owners
Housing Evaluation Status				
No evaluation completed[a]	31	14	51	21
Enrollment dwelling failed	58	86	42	79
Enrollment dwelling passed	11	--	7	--
All cases	100	100	100	100
Action Taken to Qualify for Payments				
No action reported	53	76	45	66
Attempted to repair	14	24	16	29
Moved to another dwelling	14	--	19	2
Searched for another dwelling	19	--	20	4
All cases	100	100	100	100
Potential Candidates for Special Services				
Services not warranted:				
Ineligible	24	24	17	17
No longer interested[b]	16	10	14	8
Unwilling to move[c]	16	7	16	7
Dissatisfied with program[d]	10	20	10	18
Services might help:				
Financial problems only	3	14	8	26
Technical problems only	29	25	33	8
Financial and technical problems	3	--	2	16
All cases	100	100	100	100

SOURCE: Tabulated by HASE staff from records of a survey of 1,222 households that enrolled between June 1976 and December 1978, but never qualified for payments. See Kingsley, Kirby, and Rizor, 1982, for details of the EENP Survey. Percentages may not add exactly to 100 because of rounding.

[a]Mostly cases in which no evaluation was ever requested, but includes some evaluations requested but never completed because of obstacles interposed by either the client or the property's owner.

[b]Lost interest because of household circumstances that changed after enrollment. Some incorrectly thought they were no longer eligible.

[c]Had to move in order to qualify, but were unwilling to do so.

[d]Thought the allowance payment was too small, objected to paperwork or invasion of privacy, etc.

action themselves but did not know how to go about it. Others needed more direct assistance. The number indicating that they needed both financial and technical help was quite small.

The fact that a number of these households reported financial or technical problems in qualifying for payments does not indicate that they would have accepted assistance from the HAO, or if they did, that the services would have ensured their conversion to recipient status. We have no rigorous evidence on these points, but responses to one survey question cast doubt about the payoff from a targeted service program. The potential candidates were asked whether they thought the HAOs should have offered them more advice or help in making repairs or finding a new place to live. Only 37 percent of them (44 percent of those with financial problems only and 27 percent of those with technical problems only) answered affirmatively.

We now turn to the question how the HAOs might have designed a targeted service-delivery system. The first task would be to select a method for targeting. If the candidates shared similar characteristics, they could be identified and the service arranged for at the time of the enrollment interview. However, their characteristics are diverse. It would be very difficult to pick them out from among all enrollees.

Another approach would be to wait for a time: Allow all enrollees to try to meet program housing requirements on their own, and after a reasonable period, find out who is having problems. The St. Joseph County HAO experimented with this approach. Three months after enrollment, the staff tried to contact enrollees who had not yet been authorized for payment. Out of 773 such cases, the HAO was able to reach (by phone or mail) only 49 percent. The nature of the problems and service needs of those contacted generally conformed to findings from the survey described above. It is reasonable to assume that few of those the HAO was unable to contact would have been helped by services of the type provided by the HAOs.

There is a method for delivering financial assistance that proved efficient in Brown and St. Joseph counties. The HAOs offered advances on allowance payments to cover security deposits for renters moving to new locations. The advances averaged $174; amounts were repaid with deductions from the new recipients' next six monthly allowance payments. A few of these recipients dropped out of the program before the advance had been fully repaid, and the HAOs often had trouble collecting the remaining balances in these instances. However, the aggregate repayment rate was surprisingly high for a public assistance program.

Given reasonable amounts required for repairs or moving expenses, there appears to be no need for a front-end *grant* for these purposes. The HAOs could offer *advances* to be repaid by subsequent deductions, and expect few losses. There are, however, two other potentially serious administrative difficulties.

First, how would the HAOs ascertain that the amount of an advance requested for repairs was reasonable? They might review contractors' bids, thereby becoming involved in clients' repair transactions; the administrative problems and liability could be significant. Alternatively, the HAOs might simply limit the amount of repair advances (say to $200); enrollees who said that their dwellings needed more expensive work could be referred to other agencies offering rehabilitation loans and grants.

A more serious risk is that incentives for other enrollees might change if the HAOs offered front-end financing to those who "needed" help. Without that resource, most enrollees who had to repair their dwellings in order to qualify for payments did so without HAO assistance. If it became known that the HAO would provide front-end financing, how many would discover that they too needed such help? How many would decide to use contractors rather than do the work themselves? How many would "pad" the cost estimates?

We do not know the answers to these questions, but we think the risks to some of the allowance program's most beneficial features are high enough to warrant very careful tests of any proposal for front-end financing.

Agency staff could provide technical assistance of two types: (a) counseling (providing information and advice), and (b) direct assistance (participating directly in the enrollees' negotiations with landlords, repair contractors, or lenders; doing repair work for the enrollee; or accompanying the enrollee in his search for a new dwelling).

Some evidence from the St. Joseph County follow-up program suggests that assistance of the first type is not likely to be effective. When the St. Joseph County staff contacted enrollees who had not met program housing requirements, they asked if the enrollee would like advice on how to solve the problems they were having. About 60 percent accepted. The staff believe that this advice enabled enrollees who otherwise would not have done so to meet program requirements. The statistical results, however, are not encouraging. The ultimate conversion rates for the enrollees who received such counseling were compared with those of earlier enrollees who had not met program requirements three months after enrollment. The aggregate rate for both groups was about the same: Roughly one-third were subsequently authorized for payments. A comparison of rates for different types of households showed that this outcome was not the result of compositional differences.

The only direct assistance offered to enrollees in the St. Joseph County project was free auto transportation in the search for new housing; the demand was negligible. We have no evidence on the real demand for, or effectiveness of, other direct assistance techniques. We point out, however, that all of the other direct techniques would represent a significant role change for HAO staff; again, the additional administrative complexity and liability implied are factors that deserve careful evaluation.

To summarize, we have found that only a small fraction of all enrollees are potential candidates for service (in Brown County, 7 percent of the renters and 6 percent of the owners; in St. Joseph County, 13 percent of the renters and 8 percent of the owners). We have also shown that designing an effective targeted-services program is not easy.

We conclude that a national demand-oriented housing assistance program (Sec. 8, housing allowances or vouchers) could be quite effective if the administering agencies provided no responsive services to the participants whatsoever. This is not to say that many low-income households do not need extra help in securing and maintaining decent housing, but only that the administering agencies in a national subsidy program need not provide it. In the Supply Experiment, we are sure that many among the 80 percent of all enrollees who qualified for payments did obtain extra help, but they were able to obtain this assistance from friends or other local groups and agencies not affiliated with the program directly. Federal policy might be better focused on how to encourage the development of such local resources.

MANAGERIAL AND INSTITUTIONAL FACTORS

Thus far, we have argued that the simplicity of the allowance program's administrative design contributed substantially to the HAOs' effectiveness. The households that applied for assistance were responsible for meeting program housing requirements (making repairs, moving, negotiating with landlords) without direct help from the HAO staff, and as we have seen, almost all were successful at it. This left the HAOs with more controllable tasks to perform: certifying eligibility and housing, and disbursing payments.

We have seen that the cost of operating these administrative functions depends primarily on attrition rates. The higher the percentage of applicants who drop out before becoming recipients, the larger the intake workload the HAO will have to process, and therefore, the higher the intake cost per new recipient. Higher recipient attrition rates in the maintenance phase increase workloads in more expensive functions as compared with less expensive ones, and thus somewhat increase maintenance cost per recipient-year. Amortizing intake costs over the average duration of recipiency shows us that high recipient attrition rates cause a dramatic increase in total administrative cost per recipient-year. Different types of clients have different probabilities of attrition (the rates by household type and housing tenure were remarkably consistent in the two sites); thus, the composition of the applicant and recipient populations considerably affects administrative workloads and costs.

We have also seen that changes in the rules and procedures governing major HAO functions could have had a marked effect on costs and program integrity. However, we found that the particular combination of rules and procedures the HAO started with proved effective overall; there are few things we would change in hindsight.

None of these factors, however, guaranteed good performance. Had the HAO staff been less diligent, the outcomes might have been quite different; backlogs, error rates, administrative costs, and client frustration all could have increased significantly. What caused the HAOs to persevere?

Some Natural Advantages

Part of the explanation no doubt lies in some advantages the HAOs had over typical government agencies. First, the excitement associated with a nationally visible experiment helped the HAOs recruit a top-quality staff. Second, the HAO governing boards cared about efficiency and exhibited this concern by regularly taking stock of program costs and errors and by encouraging efficiency improvements. Because the HAOs were private, nonprofit corporations, they were freer to create incentives for performance than are most agencies. The HAO boards and top managers had more flexibility in hiring and firing, and they were able to tie salary adjustments directly to worker performance.

We do not believe, however, that these advantages tell all or even most of the story; there were a number of other factors. Most important were the management techniques that the HAOs applied in the three areas discussed below—techniques that could well be more widely adopted by local agencies that administer housing and income-transfer programs.

Staff Training

All HAO employees underwent formal training when they joined the staff. Training for those who would work in means-test administration, housing certification, and financial management was most extensive. Employees were required to perform successfully in numerous simulated interviews, data reviews, housing evaluations, or accounting transactions before they were assigned regular workloads. They periodically attended review sessions to learn new rules or techniques and confirm their understanding of existing procedures. In the training sessions, the reasons behind HAO rules and procedures were explained, as well as the mechanics of their application. Training also emphasized sensitivity in dealing with participants, suggesting specific ways to handle common problems.

HAO managers always considered the benefits derived from training to far exceed its cost. Bendick, 1978, has shown that the error rate in the national AFDC program could noticeably be reduced if all local agencies had staff training programs.

Quality Control

HAO staff working in means-test administration, housing evaluation, and financial management knew that samples of their weekly output would be checked by other employees, and that some of their work would be checked again by external auditors. Regular management use of the quality-control results thus heightened motivation. Similarly, summary statistics were reported and discussed in staff meetings, and employees' error rates figured prominently in their annual salary reviews.

Management Reporting Systems

Special emphasis was given to the design of HAO management information systems. Rand and HAO managers worked together to devise performance measures that would be credible to staff as well as to overseers. Efforts were made to rely on computer-generated numbers wherever possible, so that the staff would not feel over-burdened in preparing management reports. Report formats were carefully designed to display important changes prominently, so they would not be missed in a sea of details.

We believe these tools were perhaps more important than initial staff quality in achieving the HAOs' administrative objectives. This motivational power of information is too often discounted.

Consider the motivations of a section supervisor whose unit's productivity is unambiguously reported at the end of each week. If the line on the graph turns down, everyone (his colleagues, his boss and his boss's boss) will know. He has good reason to take the steps necessary to prevent the downturn or, if he cannot, to explain why.

The HAOs' directors reviewed and acted on weekly performance reports for individual units. The HAOs' trustees received monthly summaries and discussed general trends in board meetings, but seldom questioned the supervisor handling performance at the section level. On the whole, we found that the reporting systems made the task much easier for higher levels of management. It was important for top management to get regular reports and to be aware of problems, but they did not need to intervene in section affairs unless the supervisor called for help. The HAO reporting systems provided incentives for supervisors to detect and try to solve emerging problems themselves, before those problems showed up in the statistics.

CONCLUSIONS

In the preceding pages, we have shown that the HAOs performed their administrative functions effectively and, compared with other transfer programs, efficiently. Intake and maintenance workloads were processed promptly, program rules were reliably enforced, payment and housing evaluation errors were rare, and good relations were maintained with both clients and the host communities. Administrative costs per recipient-year were lower than for other programs with comparable functions—in some comparisons, much lower. Nearly everyone who has visited the HAOs in Brown and St. Joseph counties has been impressed by the pleasant surroundings and high staff morale.

Some observers credit the HAOs' administrative success to a "hothouse" environment: Relative to a national program, the experimental program was small enough so that both its staffing and administration could be given special attention by its sponsors, who were well aware of its visibility. We agree that the outcome reflects concerted effort by Rand and HUD to create the conditions for administrative success; but we also think that many of those conditions are replicable in national programs. Below, we explain that judgment.

Program Design

First, it is important to note that the design of the allowance program simplified the HAOs' administrative tasks, as compared with most housing assistance programs. Because clients were responsible for finding their housing in the private market, for negotiating the terms and conditions of occupancy, and for arranging repairs, the HAOs were able to concentrate on functions that were amenable to clear rules and management control—principally, administering means tests and housing evaluations, and disbursing payments. Except for outreach, HAO staff had no entrepreneurial functions, and seldom had occasion to *negotiate* with clients or others.

Although many observers were skeptical that clients could handle their responsibilities under this program design, the experiment revealed few problems in their performance; indeed, by some performance measures, clients were more efficient than public agencies (see Ch. V, "Program Evaluation"). We think that other federal programs that provide services directly to their clients should consider whether, within the framework of their objectives, a similar devolution of responsibilities is possible. If so, program administration could be simplified substantially for them, also.

Administrative Design

The HAOs' limited functions provided the opportunity for an administrative design that proved to be unusually effective and efficient. Administrative functions were governed by detailed rules consistently applied to all cases. The staffs were thoroughly trained in their duties, their work was checked, and individual performances were regularly reviewed and appropriately rewarded. A management information system supplied current data on workloads, performance, and cost to all levels of management. Because of these features, failures in performance could be spotted quickly and their causes diagnosed and corrected; and early evidence of workload and productivity trends made planning easier.

The administrative style that worked so well for the HAOs is not appropriate for all organizations. Those whose success depends on creativity, for example, would not be well-served by an administrative system that imposed standard operating procedures on their staffs. Those whose success depends on making "deals" with outside parties would be ill-advised to insist on strict accounting for time spent in negotiation. But a program whose functions are routine can benefit greatly from a carefully designed administrative system that stresses standard procedures and strict accountability for performance.

Careful administrative design is as feasible for large, permanent programs as for "hothouse" experiments—indeed more so, inasmuch as design costs can be spread over a larger operating base. We think that the administrative problems of many government programs reflect a remediable lack of systematic administrative plans, some illustrative details of which were offered earlier in this chapter. We hasten to add that detailed regulations, common enough in government programs, do not necessarily reflect forethought about their administrative consequences—how they will affect transactions between staff and clients, the reliability of record systems, the measurement of staff performance, and so on.

Staffing

A large part of the HAOs' administrataive success is attributable to their able and dedicated staffs. As noted, these staffs were recruited locally at prevailing wages; but we judge that the experimental nature of the program and its public visibility helped the HAOs to recruit able people. Such inducements are generally available to new programs, whether or not they are formally experimental; and even in an experimental program such as housing allowances, the initial excitement does not last for long.

What counts over the longer run, we think, are personnel policies that discriminate between better and worse performance, and distribute rewards appropriately. It is in this connection that public agencies seem to be at a disadvantage relative to organizations like the HAOs. On the one hand, public agencies usually apply political as well as technical tests in choosing upper-level management; and on the other hand, lower-level staff are protected by civil service rules that often seem better designed to protect employees' vested interests than to encourage good performance. Although these personnel problems are most visible in public agencies, many private corporations suffer from them also.

In fact, the HAOs faced both problems—pressures for political appointments, and resistance to performance tests for employment or advancement. Their ability to overcome these pressures reflected several circumstances. First, the HAOs were governed by trustees who were insulated from the larger political process; none, for example, were concurrently or even customarily candidates for or incumbents of public office. Second, as new organizations outside of government, the HAOs were able to devise their own personnel policies rather than being obligated to accept an existing system that carried the burden of accumulated compromise.

According to one close observer of the HAOs, himself an experienced manager of government programs, a crucial factor in the HAOs' administrative success was the quality and dedication of their trustees. The administrative design provided the trustees with more precise and more timely information about agency operations than is available to most similar boards (e.g., commissioners of local housing authorities), but the trustees also had the skills and interest to use this information constructively. Their insistence on high performance standards was transmitted through the HAO directors to the staffs, reverberating throughout the organization.

For us, the lesson is that successful staffing starts at the top: It depends on the interests and intentions of those who have the power of appointment. In government, that power is bestowed by the voters, from whose judgment there is no appeal.

Granted the staffing problems of public agencies, there remains the possibility that staff performance could be improved by administrative reforms that did not directly challenge either civil service job rights or the political test for upper-level appointments. We think that some of the devices that worked well in the HAOs could be implemented in public agencies, and would both enable and motivate better staff performance. Specifically, a management information system that regularly provides clear measures of individual performance, both as to output and error rate, is consistent with the civil service "merit" principle, though opinions may differ as to the appropriateness of any specific measure. Management decisions would surely be improved by clear and current reports on agency performance, even though managers were appointed from among the politically acceptable.

In short, despite the institutional differences between the HAOs and regular public agencies, we think that the administrative techniques that were successful in the Supply Experiment should and could be more widely applied.

REFERENCES

Allen, Jodie T., "Designing Income Maintenance Systems: The Income Accounting Problem," in *Studies in Public Welfare,* Paper No. 5, Part 3, Congress of the United States, Subcommittee on Fiscal Policy of the Joint Economic Committee, U.S. Government Printing Office, Washington, D.C., 12 March 1973.

Bendick, Marc, Jr., Abe Lavine, and Toby H. Campbell, *The Anatomy of AFDC Errors,* The Urban Institute, UI-5902-1, Washington, D.C., April 1978.

Campbell, Toby H., and Marc Bendick, Jr., *A Public Assistance Data Book,* The Urban Institute, UI-5902-02, Washington, D.C., October 1977.

Coopers and Lybrand, *Administrative Fee Study; Section 8 Existing Housing Program; Vol. I—Technical Report,* Coopers and Lybrand, Washington, D.C., March 1981.

Crespi, Irving, Richard L. Kaluzny, and Billy Tidwell, *Final Report: A Survey of Participants in the Denver Monthly Reporting Experiment,* Mathematica Policy Research, Princeton, N.J., 30 June 1978.

Executive Office of the President, Office of Management and Budget, Appendix to *The Budget of the United States Government, Fiscal Year 1978,* U.S. Government Printing Office, Washington, D.C., p. 347.

Griffiths, Andrew S., and Edward Callahan, *Income Verification in Subsidized Housing Programs: The Utility of Techniques from Welfare Programs,* Urban Systems Research & Engineering, Inc., Cambridge, Mass., August 1980.

Hamilton, William L., *A Social Experiment in Program Administration: The Housing Allowance Administrative Agency Experiment,* Abt Books, Cambridge, Mass., 1979.

Hamilton, W. L., David W. Budding, and W. L. Holshouser, Jr., *Administrative Procedures in a Housing Allowance Program: The Administrative Agency Experiment,* Abt Associates, Inc., Cambridge, Mass., 28 March 1977.

Harrar, William S., *The Accuracy of Self-Administered Reporting,* Rural Income Maintenance Experiment Final Report, Vol. II, Institute of Research on Poverty, University of Wisconsin, Madison, 1976.

Holshouser, William L., Jr., Bradford S. Wild, M. G. Trend, William L. Hamilton, Rex Warland, and Frederick Temple, *Supportive Services in the Administrative Agency Experiment,* Abt Associates, Inc., Cambridge, Mass., 28 February 1977.

Katagiri, Iao, and G. Thomas Kingsley, eds., *The Housing Allowance Office Handbook,* The Rand Corporation, N-1491-HUD, July 1980.

Kershaw, David N., "Administrative Issues in Establishing and Operating a National Cash Assistance Program," in *Studies in Public Welfare,* Paper No. 5, Part 3, Congress of the United States, Subcommittee on Fiscal Policy of the Joint Economic Committee, U.S. Government Printing Office, Washington, D.C., 12 March 1973.

Kershaw, David N., and Roberton C. Williams, Jr., "Administrative Lessons," in Katharine L. Bradbury and Anthony Downs, eds., *Do Housing Allowances Work?,* The Brookings Institution, Washington, D.C., 1981.

Kingsley, G. Thomas, *Allowance Program Administration: Interim Findings,* The Rand Corporation, N-1277-HUD, December 1979.
Kingsley, G. Thomas, and Priscilla M. Schlegel, *Analyzing Allowance Program Administrative Costs: Account Structures and Methodology,* The Rand Corporation, N-1276-HUD, December 1979.
——, *Housing Allowances and Administrative Efficiency,* The Rand Corporation, N-1741-HUD, May 1982.
Kingsley, G. Thomas, Sheila Nataraj Kirby, and W. Eugene Rizor, *Administering a Housing Allowance Program: Findings from the Housing Assistance Supply Experiment,* The Rand Corporation, N-1846-HUD, May 1982.
Maloy, Charles M., J. Patrick Madden, David W. Budding, and William L. Hamilton, *Administrative Costs in a Housing Allowance Program: Two-Year Costs in the Administrative Agency Experiment,* Abt Associates, Inc., Cambridge, Mass., 1 February 1977.
Mulford, John E., *Income Elasticity of Housing Demand,* The Rand Corporation, R-2449-HUD, July 1979.
Rizor, W. Eugene, *Income Certification in an Experimental Housing Allowance Program,* The Rand Corporation, N-1740-HUD, forthcoming 1982.
Stucker, Jennifer L., "The Importance of Income Verification in the Section 8 Housing Assistance Payments Program," in *Occasional Papers in Housing and Community Affairs,* Vol. 6, U.S. Department of Housing and Urban Development, Office of Policy Development and Research, U.S. Government Printing Office, Washington, D.C., December 1979.
Tebbets, Paul E., *Controlling Errors in Allowance Program Administration,* The Rand Corporation, N-1145-HUD, August 1979.
U.S. Department of Housing and Urban Development, *Experimental Housing Allowance Program Conclusions: The 1980 Report,* U.S. Department of Housing and Urban Development, Office of Policy Development and Research, Division of Housing Assistance Research, U.S. Government Printing Office, Washington, D.C., February 1980.
Wynn, Mark, "Costs of Functions Performed in the Sec. 8 Existing Housing Program," Unpublished paper, U.S. Department of Housing and Urban Development, Office of Policy Development and Research, February 1981.
Zais, James P., C. Reid Melton, and Mark Berkham, *A Framework for the Analysis of Income Accounting Systems in EHAP,* The Urban Institute, WP-216-17, Washington, D.C., 7 July 1975.
Zais, James P., and John Trutko, *Integrated Analysis of Administration of Housing Allowance Programs,* The Urban Institute, WP-216-31, Washington, D.C., September 1976.

IX. LESSONS FROM THE SUPPLY EXPERIMENT

From conception to completion, the Supply Experiment lasted ten years, during which time public and legislative attention focused on a series of housing problems, policies, and programs: a crisis in public housing management, the Sec. 8 housing assistance program, community development block grants, environmental regulation of housing development, real-estate speculation, rent control, condominium conversion, mortgage interest rates, and the threatened insolvency of savings and loan associations. As this chapter is written, housing allowances, now known as "housing vouchers" or "housing payments," have reemerged into the arena of public discussion.[1]

By virtue of its purposes and design, the Supply Experiment was the longest and largest part of HUD's Experimental Housing Allowance Program. Our analysts have been able to ponder not only the data we gathered in Brown and St. Joseph counties, but reports from the Demand and Administrative Agency experiments, and national data from the Annual Housing Survey conducted by the Bureau of the Census. Because of that perspective, it is especially appropriate for us to distill lessons for public policy from our experience in the Supply Experiment; and those lessons should be especially pertinent to imminent federal decisions about housing vouchers.

As is usually the case in research, the lessons we learned were not all anticipated in the experimental charter. As the experiment progressed, it became clear to us that many prior assumptions about the housing circumstances of the poor, their attitudes toward housing assistance, the way housing markets work, and what other housing programs accomplish were no longer if ever correct. Our annual surveys of the housing markets of Brown and St. Joseph counties, unprecedented in scope and detail, presented us with a number of unexpected findings, both challenging our preconceptions and enabling us to seek explanations. Program data obtained from the HAOs were similarly rich in unexpected empirical observations and amenable to analysis, both with respect to the behavior of participants and the administration of the program. Finally, our experience in designing and conduct-

---

[1]In April 1982, the President's Commission on Housing proposed that a "Housing Payments Program,...coupled with housing supply assistance through the Community Development Block Grants program, should replace future commitments to build or substantially rehabilitate units under Federal housing programs."

ing the experiment taught us lessons worth passing on to those who might embark on such enterprises in the future.

In the following pages, we briefly note what we regard as important lessons that might be missed by readers of the preceding chapters of this book, because those chapters focus on the specific questions that formed our research charter. As will be seen from the citations offered, these lessons are grounded in systematic evidence; but drawing lessons from experience often entails unprovable inferences. In this chapter, we permit ourselves the latitude of informed judgment that helps to make sense of the array of facts at our disposal. Most of our comments bear on housing policy (the housing circumstances of the poor, how housing markets work, what housing programs accomplish); but we also offer advice on program design and administration. The chapter closes with lessons we learned about conducting large social experiments.

THE HOUSING CIRCUMSTANCES OF THE POOR

Much discourse on federal housing policy is based on two widely held beliefs: (a) that most poor people live in seriously substandard dwellings, and (b) that they do so because they cannot afford adequate housing. Evidence from the Supply Experiment strongly qualifies both propositions.

Housing Quality

Although the experimental allowance programs did not evaluate all dwellings occupied by low-income households in Brown or St. Joseph counties, it evaluated enough to allow us to speak with confidence about low-income housing conditions.[2] During the first two program years, before many dwellings had been repaired and recycled through the evaluation process, 49 percent of all initial evaluations in Brown County and 55 percent in St. Joseph County rated the enrollee's dwelling as unacceptable.

However, relatively few of the failed dwellings were truly dilapidated, lacked basic domestic facilities, or were severely overcrowded (see

---

[2]During the first five program years, the HAOs evaluated two-thirds of all rental dwellings in Brown County and half in St. Joseph County; and about a tenth of all owner-occupied homes in each site. This sample of the housing stock was strongly biased toward low-income housing, since evaluations were performed only for eligible households that had enrolled in the program. We estimate that over half of all households poor enough to be eligible for assistance enrolled in the program, and the enrollees were drawn disproportionately from the lower income ranges of the eligible population.

Table 9.1). Most of the defects reported by the HAOs' evaluators were easily remediable health or safety hazards; for example, the most common defect in both sites was lack of a handrail on an interior staircase. Other common problems were broken or unopenable windows, leaky plumbing, unsafe electrical installations, and poorly vented space heaters. Although about 16 percent of the dwellings were failed for overcrowding (more than two persons per habitable bedroom), about a third of these were dwellings with enough space but inadequate heat, light, ventilation, or privacy in one or more of the

Table 9.1

SPECIFIC DEFECTS IN ENROLLEES' DWELLINGS: INITIAL EVALUATIONS THROUGH PROGRAM YEAR 2, BY SITE

Type of Defect	Defects per 100 Dwellings[a]			
	Brown County		St. Joseph County	
	Renter	Owner	Renter	Owner
Inadequate Living Space				
Too few habitable rooms or bedrooms	18	15	23	13
Inadequate Facilities				
Kitchen (lacking any of 7 items)	6	5	16	8
Bathroom (lacking any of 8 items)	15	14	30	17
Hazardous Conditions				
Exterior property area (4 items)	3	3	3	2
Building exterior:				
Stairs, porches, railings	6	7	3	3
Windows	10	7	20	13
Other (4 items)	4	3	6	4
Building interior:				
Stairs, railings	23	31	35	34
Other (7 items)	7	8	11	8
Utility systems (4 items)	12	11	17	7
All defects	104	104	164	109

SOURCE: Tabulated by HASE staff from HAO records through June 1976 for Brown County and December 1976 for St. Joseph County.

NOTE: Entries are based on initial evaluation records for 4,213 enrollment dwellings in Brown County and 5,782 in St. Joseph County. Any defect tabulated here caused the dwelling to be rated not acceptable.

[a]Because some entries cover more than one item on the evaluation form, "defects per 100 dwellings" is not necessarily equivalent to "percent of dwellings with indicated defect."

bedrooms; such rooms were not counted by the HAOs as habitable space.

The remediability of these defects is evidenced by enrollees' responses to evaluation failures. About 57 percent of the renters and 78 percent of the owners whose enrollment dwellings failed their initial evaluations arranged to repair those dwellings. Nearly all the work was done by the owners or occupants of the failed dwellings, or by their friends; professional contractors were hired for less than 15 percent of all repair jobs (see Ch. VI, Fig. 6.5). The average cost of these required repairs, including an imputed wage for unpaid labor, was about $100 for renters and $90 for homeowners. Cash outlays were considerably less.[3]

The findings in our sites are broadly consistent with the evidence of recent national surveys of housing quality, evidence somehow overlooked in most policy debates. For example, the 1978 Annual Housing Survey (AHS) reports that 98 percent of all occupied dwellings in the United States contain all the plumbing fixtures needed for a healthy domestic life, and 96 percent have at least one room per occupant. The AHS does not include an HAO-style inspection that would identify the health and safety hazards so common in our sites, but the AHS questions on housing condition yield answers that imply results similar to those we found in Brown and St. Joseph counties.

Our conclusion is that low-income housing, both in HASE sites and elsewhere in the nation, is nearly all structurally sound, equipped with essential plumbing and kitchen equipment, and rarely seriously overcrowded. Most of its defects could readily and inexpensively be corrected by routine maintenance that is within the competence and purse of the occupants themselves. The health and safety hazards we found in enrollees' homes are also often present in the homes of more prosperous households, where they are regarded as minor inconveniences or hazards that ought to be attended to—someday.

There are, of course, people who do live in dilapidated dwellings that lack toilets or baths or refrigerators, and sleep five or six persons per room. But these are now rare cases—too rare to be reasonably addressed by a broadly targeted program of housing improvement. Whether it is an urgent national priority to remedy the common health and safety hazards that do not much concern the occupants of defective dwellings is essentially a political question; but as we decide it, we should realize that remedying those hazards probably would not

---

[3]We have also estimated repair costs for unrepaired dwellings. They were higher than for repaired dwellings, but not enough higher to alter our conclusion that most failed dwellings were easily and inexpensively repairable. See Ch. V for further discussion of the kinds of repairs made by participants, and their costs.

dramatically affect the health, morale, or social performance of the poor.[4]

Housing Expenditures

One reason for the basically good quality of dwellings in Brown and St. Joseph counties was that even the poor spent substantial amounts on their housing. From market surveys, we estimated the gross rents at which dwellings meeting HAO standards were available in each site. As shown in Table 9.2, the average renter participant was spending at least that amount when he enrolled, and the average owner participant was spending considerably more.[5] Although these participants were drawn exclusively from the lower half of each community's income distribution, the average housing expenditure of the renter participants approached the marketwide median rent in each site.

These housing expenditures were surely burdensome for low-income households. For example, among renter participants in St. Joseph County, the average income at enrollment was $3,500 and the average gross rent expenditure was $1,850, or 52 percent of income. For owners with an average income of $5,000, the housing expense burden was 43 percent.[6]

Although housing expense burdens are not usually calculated for homeowners (because of the complexity of the data required), national data on low-income renters consistently reveal comparably high housing expense burdens. Oddly, that fact has often served as the premise for the proposition that if poor people had more money, they would buy better housing.

Our data speak strongly against that conclusion, both for program

---

[4]There is little scientific evidence about the effects of housing conditions on health or social adjustment. By far the best study was conducted by Daniel M. Wilner and his associates (1962). It exhaustively analyzes effects on slum dwellers of moving into new public housing in Baltimore, and finds evidence of small but significant improvements in health, morale, and social performance (relations with neighbors, success in school, etc.), especially for children.

[5]See Lowry, Woodfill, and Repnau, 1981, and Lowry, Woodfill, and Dade, 1981, for the methods used to estimate the "standard cost of adequate housing" on which allowance entitlement was based. See Helbers, 1980, for the estimation of homeowner housing expense, which includes the opportunity cost of equity investment as well as direct expenses. Enrolled owners spent more than enrolled renters essentially because their dwellings were larger relative to household size.

[6]These figures are based on enrollment records for all enrollees who qualified for payments during the first three program years. Owners' incomes include the same imputed return on home equity that is counted as a housing expense. See Table 5.8 in Ch. V for "without-program" expense burdens for those receiving payments at the end of year 3; the burdens estimated there are slightly higher than those cited above.

Table 9.2

PREENROLLMENT HOUSING EXPENSE COMPARED WITH THE STANDARD COST OF ADEQUATE HOUSING: ENROLLEES THROUGH PROGRAM YEAR 3, BY SITE

Household size (persons)	Brown County			St. Joseph County		
	Standard Cost ($/mo.)	Average Expense/ Standard Cost		Standard Cost ($/mo.)	Average Expense/ Standard Cost	
		Renter	Owner		Renter	Owner
1	120	1.03	1.63	108	1.19	1.55
2	142	1.11	1.43	135	1.08	1.30
3-4	169	1.01	1.43	157	1.05	1.24
5-6	185	1.00	1.30	173	1.04	1.15
7+	196	1.01	1.11	184	1.01	1.04
All sizes	153	1.03	1.42	143	1.08	1.25

SOURCE: Tabulated by HASE staff from HAO records through June 1977 in Brown County and December 1977 in St. Joseph County.

NOTE: The standard cost of adequate housing was estimated for each site from rental market surveys before enrollment began. The figures shown here were derived by inflating those estimates to prices current at the midpoint of the period covered by the enrollment data; the inflation factors were derived from Stucker, 1981, and Lindsay and Lowry, 1980.

For renters, expenses are gross rents reported at the time of enrollment. For owners, expenses include mortgage interest, real-estate taxes, maintenance and repair, fuel and utilities, and the opportunity cost of the owner's equity investment. Because these are low-income owners, the tax benefits of ownership are minimal.

participants and nonparticipants. Analysis of HASE household survey records yields estimates of the income elasticity of housing demand ranging from 0.11 to 0.22 for renters, depending on site, mobility status, and whether current or "permanent" income is specified; and from 0.28 to 0.51 for homeowners (Mulford, 1979). The most pertinent of these estimates imply that doubling a renter's income would typically cause him to increase his housing expenditures by about 15 percent; and doubling an owner's income would typically cause him to increase his housing expenditures by about 37 percent.[7]

[7]These computations are based on cross-site averages of Mulford's permanent income elasticities: 0.19 for renters, 0.45 for owners (Mulford, 1979, Table 5). Estimates of the income elasticity of housing demand have been falling over the past decade as better data were analyzed, but only one other study has yielded estimates as low as Mulford's (ibid., Table 1). It should also be noted that these low cross-sectional

In the experimental program, renters' incomes were augmented by about a fourth and owners' incomes by about a sixth (see Ch. V, Table 5.1). Both renters and owners increased their housing expenditures by about 8 percent. For renters, only half that increase would be predicted from their income change; the other half was because of program standards that impelled participants to correct (by repairing or moving) housing defects they would otherwise have tolerated. For owners, the total increase was only slightly larger than would be predicted from their income change, but was more focused on repairs and improvements than we expected: After allowing for required repairs, voluntary repairs substantially exceeded what owners with comparable incomes normally spend.[8]

Even so, renters typically spent only 16 cents and owners 21 cents of each allowance dollar on extra housing consumption; about four-fifths of all allowance payments were used by recipients to reduce their housing expense burdens—in other words, spent on nonhousing consumption.

We conclude from this evidence that low-income households in our sites and probably elsewhere would much prefer help with their present housing expenses to any substantial increase in their housing consumption. It does not necessarily follow that the taxpayer who contributes to low-income housing assistance programs should share that view; but if the public purpose is a substantial change in the pattern of low-income housing consumption, unrestricted cash grants are not the answer. The desired consumption change as well as the means to pay for it must be imposed on the beneficiary.

HOW HOUSING MARKETS WORK

The main reason for conducting the Supply Experiment was that a number of influential observers believed or feared that a full-scale housing allowance program would drive up the price of housing for

---

elasticities for individual households are consistent with the long-run constancy of budget shares spent for housing. The assumption that makes them consistent is a consumption function of the form,

$$H = \alpha \overline{Y}^{\lambda} Y^{1-\lambda}$$

where H = housing consumption and Y = income. In this function, λ is the long-run elasticity and $(1 - \lambda)$ is the cross-sectional elasticity.

[8]In addition to estimating the income elasticity of total housing expenditures on the general population of homeowners (with the results cited above), we estimated the income elasticity of their repair expenditures (Helbers and McDowell, 1982). The latter seems more relevant than the former to the short period of program participation that we could observe, in which few homeowners (2.2 percent in Brown County and 1.4 percent in St. Joseph County) changed residences.

both participants and other consumers. The general reasoning was that housing allowances would increase the demand for housing services, but would not augment the supply. Especially in markets where vacancy rates were already low, competition for better dwellings would then cause prices to rise sharply. (Barnett and Lowry, 1979, review preexperimental predictions.)

The evidence presented in Ch. VI demonstrates that a full-scale program did not have that undesirable effect in either Brown County's tight market or St. Joseph County's loose market. The absence of the predicted price increases is partly explained by the fact that program-induced housing demand was substantially less than most of us expected, for reasons discussed above. But it also appears that the supply of housing services is more flexible than it was generally believed to be.

Investigating the reasons for the outcomes we observed in Brown and St. Joseph counties led us to new insights about the structure and functioning of housing markets, especially rental markets. These insights and their significance for housing policy are discussed below.

Supply Responsiveness

If the only feasible supply response to program-induced housing demand had been the construction of new dwellings, even the modest demand increases caused by the program would have caused substantial short-run price increases. In the rental market, the increased demand was substantially met by redistributing vacancies and by improvements to the existing stock of dwellings.

The Price Elasticity of the Occupancy Rate. When the effective demand for rental housing increases in a local market, newly formed households occupy formerly vacant dwellings, and existing households move from small or poor-quality dwellings to larger or better ones. Such events increase the total amount of housing service sold to and consumed by renters, without any change in the inventory of rental dwellings. In the course of these events, landlords may also raise rents; but unless the vacancy rate is very low, competition between the owners of occupied and vacant dwellings serves to keep the rent increases modest.

At baseline in Brown and St. Joseph counties, we encountered rental vacancy rates that differed dramatically; yet the rents charged for similar dwellings in the two sites were nearly identical (see Ch. II, Tables 2.6 and 2.7). First using HASE data and later using Annual Housing Survey data for a national sample of 59 metropolitan areas, we estimated the price elasticity of the occupancy rate—that is, by how much the occupancy rate typically increases in reponse to a given increase in the market price of rental housing. The results based on AHS data are displayed in Fig. 9.1; those data indicate that relatively small price increases will call forth unoccupied dwelling space until the occupancy rate reaches about 95 percent (vacancy rate equals 5 percent); thereafter, the supply responsiveness to price changes drops off sharply.[9]

Housing Deterioration, Optimal Maintenance, and Improvements. Housing services are produced by capital-intensive technology; in Brown County, for example, over half the cost of producing rental housing services was payment for the use of structural capital.[10]

Absent regular maintenance, the productivity of residential capital declines rapidly. For a mixed-age sample of rental dwellings in our sites, we estimate that the deterioration rate under conditions of zero maintenance would be about 8 percent annually (Rydell and others, 1981, Appendix C).

To offset that deterioration and improve their dwellings, property owners spend considerable amounts on repair, replacement, and improvements. In our sites, annual outlays for these purposes averaged $280 per rental dwelling and $500 per owner-occupied home (1973 dollars), or about 17 percent of the total value of the flow of housing services and 2.5 percent of property value (see Table 9.3). Nationally, such outlays (including the value of unpaid labor) account for about 44 percent of annual gross investment in housing (Helbers and McDowell, 1982).

Logically, the maintenance policy pursued by the owner of a residential property ought to reflect the flow of services he wants to get from the property. For a rental property, that desired flow of services should in turn reflect the perceived future demand for them (as reflected in the price they command) and the cost of maintenance. From HASE data, we estimate that the price elasticity of demand for maintenance or improvement of existing dwellings should be about 1.2. This estimate implies that if the market price of rental housing services were to rise by 10 percent relative to the cost of maintenance

---

[9]The chart is based on a regression of the average price per unit of rental housing service in each metropolitan area against a transformation of the rental occupancy rate. The price variable was the value of a hedonic rent index estimated by The Urban Institute (see Follain and Malpezzi, 1980) and evaluated for a standard bundle of housing and neighborhood characteristics in each area. Our regression model, too complex for specification here, also included an estimate of the long-run price elasticity of supply and equilibrium occupancy rate for each place. See Rydell, 1982, for details.

[10]Neels, 1982, Tables 3 and 4. This estimate excludes the payments attributable to land, but includes property taxes and insurance on improvements as capital costs.

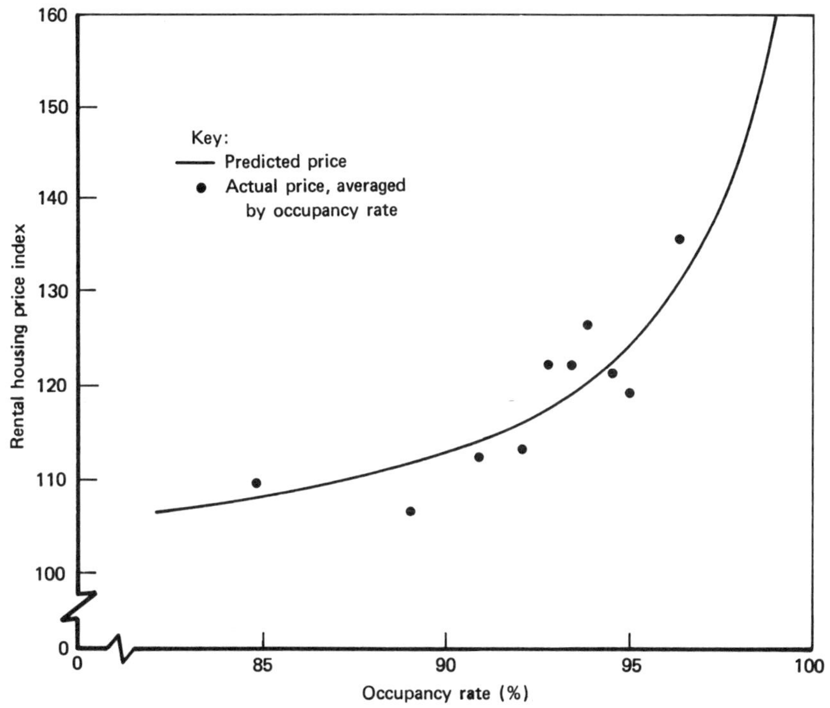

SOURCE: Adapted from Rydell, 1982, Fig. 3.2.

Fig. 9.1—Price of rental housing services as a function of the occupancy rate: 59 SMSAs, 1974-76

inputs, landlords would increase those inputs by 12 percent.[11] If they also increased their inputs of energy (fuels) and labor (building services) in the same proportions, the output of housing services would increase by 2 percent, implying a price elasticity of supply from the existing stock of 0.2.

In the short run, landlords can also accommodate a demand shift by varying the factor mix—for example, using more current inputs such as energy or labor with the existing stock of capital. With a fixed quantity of capital, we estimate that a 10-percent increase in both

[11]See Rydell and others, 1981, Appendix C, for the underlying model. The diminishing returns parameter (λ) in Eq. C.11 transforms to a price elasticity for maintenance (ϵ), although that result is not shown. The transformation is

$$\epsilon = 1/(1 - \lambda).$$

Table 9.3

VALUE OF REPAIRS AND IMPROVEMENTS TO RESIDENTIAL PROPERTIES, BY SITE AND TYPE OF PROPERTY: 1973-77

Site and Type of Property	Average Annual Investment per Dwelling ($)			Percent of Investment Applied to:		Total Investment as Percent of:	
	Cash Outlay	Unpaid Labor[a]	Total	Repair or Replacement	Improvement[b]	Gross Rent[c]	Property Value[d]
Brown County							
Rental	200	86	286	68	32	17.8	2.3
Homeowner	426	69	495	60	40	16.1	2.1
St. Joseph County							
Rental	188	92	280	76	24	17.4	3.2
Homeowner	435	65	500	74	26	17.3	2.5

SOURCE: Tabulated by HASE staff from integrated records of the annual surveys of landlords, tenants, and homeowners in each site.

NOTE: Entries are based on 444 rental properties and 386 homeowner properties in Brown County with complete four-year records, 1973-76; and 539 rental properties and 293 homeowner properties in St. Joseph County with complete four-year records, 1974-77. Expenses for rental properties include outlays reported by tenants. Each year's reported expenses were deflated to 1973 dollar equivalents and averaged over four years. Annual investment for individual properties is highly variable from year to year.

[a] Valued at the current minimum wage.

[b] Major outlays for remodeling, adding rooms, installing air conditioning, landscaping, paving, etc.

[c] For rental properties, contract rent plus utilities paid by tenants; for homeowner properties, total housing expense excluding opportunity cost of owner's equity investment.

[d] Average of estimates by three alternative methods.

energy and labor inputs would expand output by 2.8 percent. Moreover, the technology of housing services production is flexible enough to accommodate substantial increases in current inputs without encountering seriously diminishing returns.[12] Thus, a further 10-percent increase in current inputs would expand the quantity of housing services by only a little less than 2.8 percent.

Because the demand shift prompted by the housing allowance program was small, we were unable to obtain direct statistically significant estimates of repair response to marketwide price changes. But a general analysis of housing service production functions, based on our surveys of rental properties and owner-occupied homes, yields evidence that a housing assistance program need not add to the stock of dwellings or replace old dwellings with new ones in order to increase the flow of services available to consumers. As shown above, repairs and improvements and changes in operating policies can respond rapidly and helpfully to demand shifts, thus moderating their price effects.

Housing Submarkets

Estimates of the probable effects of government intervention in local housing markets usually entail either explicit or implicit assumptions as to the division of a local market into essentially noncompeting submarkets. In the case of the Supply Experiment, we and others worried about the possibility that program-induced demand would drive up housing prices in the submarkets heavily patronized by program participants even if the rest of the market were unaffected. Various studies have proposed the existence of separate submarkets by location (central-city vs. suburban), race (black vs. white), type of structure (apartments vs. single-family houses), and tenure (rental vs. ownership).

Distinguishing submarkets is not easy. Conceptually, a housing submarket consists of a collection of housing suppliers and demanders who trade in dwellings or housing services for which there are no close substitutes.[13] For example, high-rise apartments are not usually considered close substitutes for single-family houses by either the single adults who prefer apartments or the families with children who

---

[12]Neels, 1981, estimates that the elasticities of substitution between energy and capital and between labor and capital are about 2.0 or higher, increasing with building size. A value of 2.0 implies that the factor mix could be changed by 10 percent from the optimum (which depends on current factor-price ratios) with a 5-percent loss in technical efficiency.

[13]Technically, the cross-elasticities of both supply and demand must be low between dwellings in different submarkets.

prefer houses; nor can dwellings of one kind be easily converted to dwellings of the other kind. It therefore seems possible that the mutual adjustment of supply and demand would proceed independently in each submarket, and that different submarket prices for housing services could therefore coexist.

We searched assiduously in Brown and St. Joseph counties for evidence of submarket structure. What we found instead was a continuous gradation of household preferences and dwelling configurations such that there were no sharp breaks in the chain of substitutability. For example, though high-rise apartments may be poor substitutes for single-family houses, they do compete with low-rise apartments, which compete with duplexes, which compete with single-family houses. The chain of substitutability is strong enough to forestall sharp differences in the prices paid for housing attributes that are common to all submarkets, for example, the extra rent charged for an extra bedroom (Barnett, 1979; Noland, 1980).

Although the flow prices of housing attributes were close to uniform across each of our metropolitan housing markets, it is important to add that stock prices were not. The most remarkable difference was between rental dwellings in central South Bend and elsewhere in St. Joseph County. After adjusting rents and values to control for differences in age of buildings and types of structures (Rydell, 1979, Table 1), we obtained the following values for 1974:

	Average Gross Rent ($/unit/year)	Average Property Value ($/unit)	Average Vacancy Rate (%)[a]
Central South Bend	1,727	6,862	13.2
Rest of county	1,732	9,315	6.1

[a]Percent of potential gross rent lost because of vacancies.

Given the same rents for comparable dwellings in the two areas, but sharply higher vacancy rates in central South Bend, it follows that rental revenue per dwelling will be lower there; and our calculations show that after subtracting operating costs (about the same in each area), net operating returns differ by enough to warrant the different property values shown.[14]

[14]Theoretically, the market value of rental property should equal the present value of the expected future stream of net operating return, discounted at the market rate of interest.

A sharp difference in both rental and homeowner vacancy rates between central South Bend and the remainder of St. Joseph County was evident in the 1970 Census of Housing and persisted through the four years (1974-77) of our surveys there. That rents did not fall in central South Bend must have inhibited the redistribution of vacancies across submarket boundaries. Over the long run, we expect vacancy rates to be realigned by the withdrawal of residential capital from central South Bend (e.g., by demolishing persistently vacant buildings); but the continuing shift of housing demand away from central South Bend will surely make market adjustment a lengthy process.

If it is generally true that rents do not fall in neighborhoods that are out of favor with consumers, that fact has important implications for the futures of such neighborhoods. For renters, no price concessions are offered to offset the disadvantages of the neighborhood, so renters are unlikely to return there. The case may be different for homebuyers. As with rental properties, the prices of single-family houses offered for sale in central South Bend were much lower than for comparable houses elsewhere. A venturesome homebuyer could therefore get more housing for his money if he were willing to accept less neighborhood, and were indifferent to the possibility that the value of his property might decline further. The rejuvenation of deteriorating neighborhoods may thus hinge on a shift from rental to owner-occupancy, the possibilities for which vary with the typical configuration of buildings in such a neighborhood.

We conclude that geographically delineated *investment* submarkets (as distinguished from *consumption* submarkets) are important features of local housing markets, and should be taken into account when planning intervention strategies. Sharply different vacancy rates can persist for long periods in different neighborhoods because housing prices (rents in particular) are insufficiently flexible to balance supply and demand marketwide.

WHAT HOUSING ALLOWANCES DO—AND DON'T DO

Although the Supply Experiment's results should quiet the general concern about undesirable market disturbances that might result from a national housing allowance program, those results raise some very pointed questions about housing assistance programs generally. Nearly everyone expected the experimental program to have a larger effect on participants' housing consumption than it did, and some expected a conspicuous improvement in the general quality of low-income neighborhoods. Below, we summarize our own sense of the ways in which a national housing allowance program would serve the objectives of national housing policy.

The Goals of National Policy

No one can speak authoritatively about those objectives except the U.S. Congress. By induction from 50 years of housing legislation, we can list six recurring themes of policy to guide our assessment of housing allowances. Historically, federal policy has entailed balancing the following objectives:

- Promoting improved housing for the poor, viewed as a way of bettering their lives and improving their social performances.
- Promoting neighborhood improvement by replacing or remodeling dilapidated dwellings, viewed as a form of civic housekeeping that improves the condition of urban life and thereby attracts the households and businesses needed for urban vitality.
- Promoting the racial and economic integration of residential neighborhoods, viewed both as a benefit to disadvantaged minorities and as a contribution to social and political stability.
- Promoting home ownership, viewed as a vehicle for family financial security and as a social stabilizer.
- Promoting housing construction, viewed as a way of creating socially useful employment, especially during periods of economic recession.
- Promoting the liquidity of housing investments, viewed as an important element of a sound national credit structure.

Over the years, these objectives have been pursued by a kaleidoscope of programs, sometimes working at cross-purposes. No single program could seriously address all objectives simultaneously, although hope springs eternal that ways can be found to make federal dollars do triple duty.

Improving the Housing Circumstances of the Poor

Housing allowances directly address only the first objective listed. By definition, low-income families cannot afford a socially adequate standard of living, but they choose different economies in order match their living standards to their budgets. Some poor people live in inexpensive and inadequate dwellings; others are adequately housed by dint of spending half or more of their incomes for housing. Allowances are flexible enough to remedy whichever circumstance applies to a particular case.

Program Effectiveness. The evidence from our experimental sites is that most of the poor live in fairly good dwellings but spend large fractions of their incomes for housing. Thus, it is appropriate for a housing assistance program to devote more resources to budgetary relief than to housing improvement.

On average, the recipients of housing allowances increased their housing expenditure by about 8 percent, of which only 4 percent was typically required to meet minimum quality standards. The largest increases, averaging 21 percent, were for the minority of renters who moved from failed dwellings that were overcrowded or difficult to repair.

However, using housing expenditure to measure the change in participants' housing may miss the point. The features of a dwelling that are vested with the public interest are not necessarily those that are valued in the marketplace and thus reflected in rents or home prices. The health and safety hazards enumerated in local housing codes (and on HAO evaluation forms) did not much affect the market values of dwellings, either because the hazards did not greatly concern the occupants or potential occupants of those dwellings or because the defects were inexpensive to remedy. Only the program's space requirements focused on a housing attribute that is highly valued in the marketplace.

Using standards based on a national model housing code, the HAOs failed about half of all enrollees' dwellings. The inducement of a housing allowance persuaded most enrollees in substandard dwellings to remedy the defects or move to homes that met the standards. However, the initial repairs and moves were not enough; each year, about a fifth of recipients' dwellings in Brown County and a third in St. Joseph County drifted below program standards. Nearly all were repaired to avoid suspension of payments. In steady state, we estimate that participation in the program increased the chances that an eligible household would be adequately housed from about 48 to 78 percent for renters and from 57 to 87 percent for owners—a gain in each case of 30 percentage points.[15]

---

[15]The standards are detailed in Appendix C, below. Estimates of the steady-state condition of participants' housing are derived in Mulford and others, 1982, Appendix D; Table 2.2, ibid., summarizes the results.

Put simply, what an allowance program does for housing quality is to enforce local housing codes by offering an incentive payment for compliance rather than by punishing violators. The incentive payment works because it considerably exceeds the cost of compliance for all but the worst dwellings. We estimate that participants allocated about a fifth of their allowances to additional housing expenditure, including compliance costs. Aside from whatever value they placed on their improved housing, they reaped a net cash gain from participation that averaged roughly $800 annually for renters and $600 for homeowners.

If one accepts the traditional federal standard that the housing expenses of low-income families should not exceed a fourth of income, those cash transfers were not excessive. Under the most conservative interpretation of this rule, the average renter participant's housing expense dropped from 49 to 28 percent of gross income; as that rule is applied in the public housing program, the without-program ratio of housing expense to income for the same renter would be 62 percent, reduced by participation to 36 percent.[16]

Program Efficiency. However one weights the housing improvement and income transfers achieved by housing allowances, the program is notably efficient in its use of public funds. We estimate that 85 cents of each federal dollar directly benefited program participants; the remainder went mostly for program administration.

We know of no other low-income housing assistance program that approaches this record (see Table 9.4). Public housing is plagued by high development and operating costs which, by one recent estimate, amount to twice the market value of the housing services provided (Mayo and others, 1980). The Sec. 8 Existing Housing program is similar in concept to housing allowances, but at least in its early years did not control price increases effectively; landlords of dwellings entering the program obtained rent increases averaging 26 percent

[16]Under the Brooke Amendment, public housing rents were limited to 25 percent of adjusted gross income, the adjustments allowing for age of head, household size, and certain special expenses. Similar rules were applied to most other low-income housing assistance programs during the 1970s. In these applications, the federal rent subsidy was not counted either as income or housing expense. The comparable calculation for the allowance program is (actual gross rent minus allowance) divided by nonallowance adjusted gross income. See Ch. V, Table 5.11 for details.

Recent actions by Congress and HUD foreshadow a move to a higher norm for low-income housing expense burdens—probably 30 percent of adjusted gross income. Recipients of housing allowances would have higher average burdens even if benefits were still calculated under the 25-percent rule, because the typical participant spends more than the standard cost for his housing.

Table 9.4

Destination of Program Dollars in Selected Rental Housing Assistance Programs

Destination of Program Dollars	Percent of Program Dollars			
	Public Housing	Sec. 8 Existing	Housing Allowances	Income Maintenance
Beneficiary				
Program participants	34	57	85	89
Other consumers[a]	6	--	-2	-1
Builders, landlords, administrators[b]	60	43	17	12
Total	100	100	100	100
End Use				
Housing consumption[c]	8	10	15	7
Other consumption[c]	92	90	85	93
Total	100	100	100	100

SOURCE: Comparisons of public housing, housing allowances, and income maintenance are from Rydell, Mulford, and Helbers, 1980 (also summarized above, Table 5.17). Comparison with Sec. 8 is based on Rydell and Mulford, 1982, and additional data from their sources.

NOTE: Estimates are for programs serving a standard population of renter participants and providing the same average participant benefit. Programs differ with respect to the estimated cost to the government of supplying the standard benefit, the allocation of those costs, and the division of benefits between housing and other consumption. Accounting conventions used here differ slightly from those in Table 5.17, in order to simplify presentation of results.

[a]Program activities may affect the price of housing to nonparticipants. Positive entries reflect reduced market prices and negative entries reflect higher market prices, resulting in both consumption changes and budget reallocations for nonparticipants. Their gains and losses are balanced by landlords' gains and losses, included in the third entry of each column.

[b]Includes above-market development and operating cost (public housing), above-market rent charged by participating landlords (Sec. 8), and program administration (all programs). See also note *a*.

[c]Estimated net increase in consumption by both participants and nonparticipants due to the program. Payments enumerated in note *b* are assumed to result only in nonhousing consumption.

(Rydell, Mulford, and Helbers, 1980), and those price increases absorbed 30 percent of total program funds without benefit to participants; administrative costs accounted for another 13 percent (Ch. VIII, Table 8.6).

As noted in Ch. V, assistance to low-income families in the form of unrestricted cash grants would have a greater transfer efficiency than do housing allowances; we estimate that 89 percent of the federal cost would end as benefits to participants. We also note, however, that such an approach would yield less increase in housing consumption and would not significantly affect housing quality as measured by public standards (see Ch. V, Tables 5.15 and 5.16).

Housing Allowances and Other Housing Policy Objectives

Although allowances are effective and efficient remedies for the housing quality and expense problems of low-income families, they do not contribute much to the other objectives of federal policy listed above. At least during the first five years of program operations in our experimental sites, we were unable to identify either neighborhood improvements that could be linked to the program (although many residents perceived some improvement) or substantial changes in the pattern of racial and economic segregation. The program did enable a few hundred renters who would not otherwise have qualified for mortgage credit to purchase homes, and added marginally to employment in the residential repair industry. We do not think the liquidity of housing investments was affected.

From about 1960 to 1980, neighborhood improvement and racial integration were generally accepted as the highest priorities among these policy objectives. Both have proven to be intractable to a formidable array of ameliorative programs. The experience with urban renewal in the 1950s was that neighborhoods could be improved only by removing their low-income residents and rebuilding for a more prosperous population. The Model Cities program of the 1960s tried nearly every conceivable combination of physical and social rehabilitation without conspicuous success. Although Fair Housing legislation and court decisions have established the right of racial minorities to buy or rent anywhere they can afford housing (and public sentiment has generally supported that right), indexes of segregation in U.S. cities are at best falling very slowly.[17]

It may be that solutions to these problems will come only through redefinition of the problems and corresponding changes in our ideas about the satisfactory solutions. At any rate, we would not expect a national housing allowance program to do much more than enable low-income households to afford safe and decent housing on condition that they occupy such housing. Possibly, the program's implicit training in standards of home maintenance would have a long-run cumulative effect on the physical appearance of low-income neighborhoods and on the morale of neighborhood residents in and out of the program, but the experimental evidence does not warrant such a prediction. Certainly, the allowance program widens the range of dwellings

---

[17]On urban renewal, see Wilson, 1966 (especially the articles by Martin Anderson and Herbert Gans and the rebuttals thereto); Congressional Research Service, 1973; and McFarland, 1977. On the Model Cities program, see Haar, 1975; on residential integration, see Taueber and Taueber, 1965; and Schnare, 1977. For general reviews, see Gorham and Glazer, 1976; and Lowry, 1980.

affordable to participants belonging to racial minorities and so could facilitate the gradual desegregation of our cities; but we suspect that the desegregation of private and government employment and the consequent changes in the economic and social status of minorities will have much more influence on residential integration than a transfer program aimed at low-income members of these minorities.

Who Gets Help

Because the experimental housing allowance program offered cash payments to eligible households, nearly everyone expected a high participation rate among those who were eligible. Although enrollment grew rapidly during the first two program years, it leveled off by the end of the third year, when only 40 percent of those currently eligible were enrolled and only 33 percent were actually receiving payments.[18]

The surprisingly low participation rate raises three important questions about a national housing allowance program:

- In a permanent program, would participation rise beyond the level indicated by the experimental program?
- Does participant self-selection support or frustrate program objectives?
- Are these results inherent in the allowance concept or do they depend on some easily modifiable detail of the experimental program?

Below, we address these questions in turn.

Participation in a Permanent Program. It is important to distinguish between the incidence of eligibility and the participation rate among eligibles. The incidence of eligibility for a national program would certainly vary in different places, as it did between HASE sites; and could be raised or lowered substantially by changing the income limits or categorically excluding specific groups (for instance, homeowners or nonelderly single persons).[19] Here, we deal first with the issue of participation among those eligible by HASE standards, given also the benefit formula and housing standards of the Supply Experiment.

[18]These figures exclude single persons under 62 who were admitted to eligibility in August 1977; see Ch. IV, "Households Excluded from Analysis." The enrollment and recipiency series plotted in Ch. III, Fig. 3.1, include the newly eligible nonelderly singles who comprised about a third of new enrollees during the fourth and fifth program years, so show more growth than would have occurred under fixed eligibility rules.

[19]National estimates of eligibility under the standards applied in the experimental program range from 19 percent of all households (Repnau and Woodfill, 1980, Table A-1) to 24 percent (Sepanik, Hendricks, and Heinberg, 1975).

We think that a permanent national program designed like the experimental one would achieve only slightly higher participation rates than those we found. The main reasons for expecting any higher level of participation in a permanent national program are wider knowledge of program details, more favorable attitudes toward participation, and prompter enrollment by newly eligible households. As compared with the experience in Brown and St. Joseph counties, there is little room for improvement in these respects.

Figure 9.2 shows the distribution of eligibles by participation status and the reasons why the majority of eligibles in each site were not enrolled and receiving payments. (The figure somewhat transcends the evidence as to reasons for nonparticipation, but we are confident that its details are close to the mark.)[20] Given universal knowledge of the program, we estimate that participation would have increased by about 6 percentage points in Brown and St. Joseph counties. Substituting positive for negative attitudes toward assistance from government would increase participation by less than 2 percentage points.

About 9 percent of those currently eligible were not receiving payments because they had not yet but would eventually enroll, or because they had enrolled but had not yet qualified for payments. Part of the delay was attributable to HAO processing procedures, but most of it was due to the fact that newly eligible households did not usually apply promptly for assistance even though they knew about the program. If the allowance program had been a more familiar source of help, the newly needy might have moved more quickly.

If all three of these obstacles to participation were attenuated in a permanent national program, we can imagine that participation might rise by 5 to 10 percentage points. A larger increase could only be achieved by program changes that affected the main reasons for nonparticipation: the expectation of low benefits and unwillingness to meet the program's housing standards.

Because the allowance formula causes benefits to decrease smoothly to zero as income rises, there was necessarily a large group of households that were nominally eligible but entitled to only small payments. In Brown and St. Joseph counties, about 10 percent of all eligibles were entitled to less than $20 and 30 percent were entitled to

---

[20]The figure is adapted from a more cautious presentation in Ch. IV, summarized in Table 4.12. The category labeled "Other" is an estimate of the joint effects of lack of information, delay, poor housing, and negative attitudes toward assistance from government. The category labeled "Low benefits" is a residual, encompassing all reasons for nonparticipation that we could not identify statistically. Because of the structure of the allowance program, we could not distinguish the effect of benefit amount from the effect of self-perceived need for assistance.

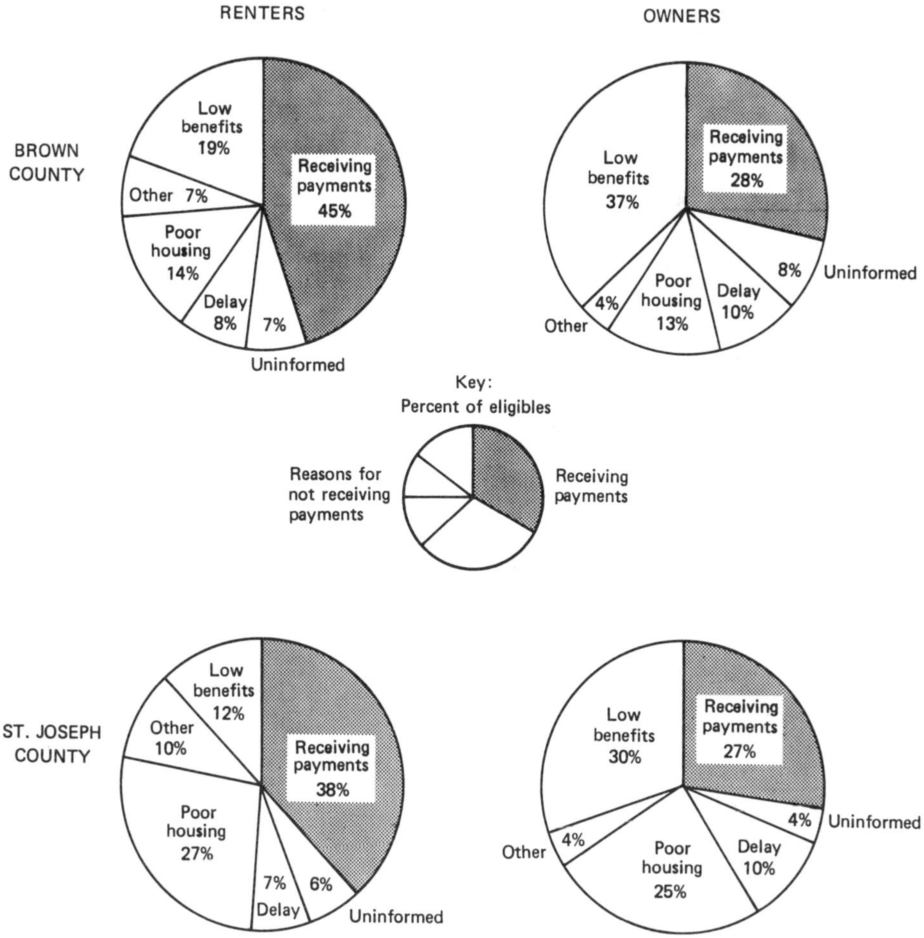

SOURCE: Adapted from Table 4.12.

Fig. 9.2—Distribution of eligible households by recipiency status and reasons for not receiving payments: renters and owners in each site

less than $30 monthly. Moreover, 15 percent of the eligible households in Brown County and 28 percent in St. Joseph County could expect their eligibility to last for less than a year—and these were the very households whose entitlements were smallest.

The expectation of low benefits operated primarily to inhibit enrollment. Those whose dwellings were below standard did not often on that account fail to enroll; but once their dwellings had been evaluated and they were informed that they must either repair or move, those in the worst dwellings often dropped out of the program. In Brown County, a fifth of those whose initial repair bills would have been over $100 were unwilling either to repair or move, so never qualified for payments. In St. Joseph County, the corresponding dropout rate was about 40 percent (see Ch. IV, Table 4.10).

We will later discuss program changes that might affect participation. Before leaving the present discussion, we should add a note of caution about outcomes under existing program rules. During the fifth program year, enrollment began to grow again in both experimental sites. By June 1981, the number of participants had increased by 21 percent over the end-of-year-5 level in Brown County and by 34 percent in St. Joseph County. Because our last household surveys were conducted in 1977 and 1978, we cannot tell how much of the new growth reflects growth in the eligible population (because of changing economic conditions), and how much was caused by the factors discussed above.[21] This recent program growth would repay more analysis than it has received.

Participation Self-Selection and Program Objectives. The allowance program's eligibility standards were designed, however imperfectly, to encompass the neediest households in each experimental site. Need was defined jointly by income and household size, with a separate constraint as to assets. Applying these standards, we were not surprised to learn that single parents and elderly persons together comprised from two-thirds (Brown County) to three-fourths (St. Joseph County) of all eligibles, or that the eligibility rate for nonwhites was twice the rate for whites (see Ch. IV, Table 4.1). Less expected was the finding that over half of all eligibles in each site were homeowners—despite the fact that we included an imputed return on home equity as income.

Within the eligible population, participation rates differed substantially for renters and owners; for whites and nonwhites; and for

[21]HAO staff believe that much of the growth has been due to increased unemployment in the sites, which temporarily increases the number of eligibles. The income limits for participation and benefits at each level of income have been increased regularly to keep up with inflation, but those changes may have inadvertently widened eligibility. It is also possible that familiarity with the program has increased the willingness of eligible households to enroll.

households headed by couples and single persons, old and young persons, and parents and childless persons (see Table 9.5). However, we traced most such differences to underlying differences between groups as to the benefits and costs of participation or attitudes toward government assistance. Once these variables are controlled, the only significant household characteristic is the presence or absence of children: Families with children are more likely to participate, all other things equal.

Table 9.5

CHARACTERISTICS OF RECIPIENTS AND RECIPIENCY RATES AT THE END OF YEAR 3, BY SITE

Characteristic	Percent of All Recipients		Recipients as Percent of All Eligibles	
	Brown County	St. Joseph County	Brown County	St. Joseph County
Housing Tenure				
Renter	58	38	45	38
Owner	42	62	28	27
Household Composition				
Single parent	32	31	46	39
Elderly single person	35	43	56	37
Young couple, young children	12	5	21	12
Other nonelderly couple	10	7	25	22
Elderly couple	11	14	23	24
Race of Head				
White non-Latin	97	78	(*a*)	29
Other	3	22	(*a*)	36
All cases	100	100	36	31

SOURCE: Adapted from Sec. IV, Tables 4.3 and 4.4.

NOTE: Entries exclude single persons under 62 who became eligible in August 1977.

[a] Distribution of eligibles by race was not estimated for Brown County, where over 98 percent of all household heads were non-Latin whites.

The underlying determinants of participation suggest a model of rational choice in which housing improvements are not much valued. Eligibles and enrollees seem to balance the expected stream of cash payments against the expected trouble and out-of-pocket expense of meeting housing standards. Their decisions may also be influenced by perceptions of need that covary with expected benefits and are clearly influenced by predispositions concerning the proper role of government.

We doubt that a strong case could be made for forcing help on those who, even though needy, disdain assistance from their government. Nor does it seem appropriate to worry overmuch about financial aid to those who, though eligible, do not consider themselves needy. The low participation rate (17.5 percent) for eligibles with monthly entitlements under $20 undoubtedly reflects their disinterest in such small sums, but surely also reflects less than urgent need for any benefit at all. Similarly, many who expected to be eligible for only a short time did not bother to apply. By selecting themselves out of the program, the marginally eligible saved administrative expense with little consequence for program objectives.

More troublesome is the evidence that those in the worst housing were, on average, least likely to qualify for payments. That outcome is curious, both because repair estimates for dropouts seldom exceeded a few hundred dollars and because allowance entitlements were, on average, substantially larger for those facing the larger repair costs. We calculate that most of the dropouts could have repaired their substandard dwellings and recouped the cost from their first few allowance payments (Shanley and Hotchkiss, 1980, Table 3.11); and the renters among them could have avoided expensive repairs by moving.

Among all who were living in substandard housing when they enrolled, about 20 percent failed to repair or move, so never qualified for payments. Although universal compliance with the housing standards would obviously have contributed more to the program's housing objectives, 80 percent compliance seems a considerable accomplishment, given the well-known perversity of human responses to incentives.[22]

In the comparable part of the Housing Allowance Demand Experiment, housing evaluation failures were more common than in the Supply Experiment, required repairs were on average more expensive, and the dropout rate was higher. Analysts of that experiment have concluded that the neediest households among their enrollees were less likely to participate than those higher up the income scale, mostly because of repair obstacles (Kennedy and MacMillan, 1980).

Although we too found that repair costs were on average higher for the needier families, the participation outcome was different. Among eligible households entitled to $120 or more per month, participation was 2.5 times as great as among those entitled to less than $20. There is absolutely no question that in the Supply Experiment, the tilt of

[22]Counting those who were already occupying adequate dwellings when they enrolled, compliance was about 90 percent.

participation was toward the needier. It is also clear, however, that more of the neediest would have participated in the absence of housing requirements.

Program Changes That Might Affect Participation. If a national allowance program is ever created by Congress, it will surely differ from the experimental program in many details. Eligibility standards may be made more or less inclusive, the benefit formula may be changed, the housing requirements may be differently specified, and the relationships between the administering agency, the participating households, and suppliers of housing may be altered. Absent a specific proposal, it would be fruitless to speculate about the effects on participation of all the conceivable changes. However, three points seem worth making here for consideration by those who may participate in planning a national program.

First, there is every reason to suppose that larger benefits relative to income and household size would encourage more eligibles to participate, and smaller benefits would discourage participation. The analysts of the Demand Experiment have estimated quantitative relationships between benefit levels and participation (Kennedy and MacMillan, 1980). The Supply Experiment was not designed to produce such estimates, but our data are at least generally consistent with the Demand Experiment's findings on this point.

Second, the nominal participation rate could be sharply altered by limiting eligibility to those with substantial allowance entitlements, but the actual number of participants would not be much affected. If, for example, the income limit for enrollment had been set at a level corresponding to a monthly entitlement of $50, the participation rate in the Supply Experiment would probably have risen to about 45 percent, because those with lower entitlements, unlikely to enroll in any case, were no longer counted as eligibles. Such a change, however, would be more cosmetic than functional, and has other disadvantages. For example, participants with incomes just below the eligibility limit would be made better off by the program than ineligibles whose incomes were just above the limit.

Third, the exact specification of housing standards is a very important factor in the outcome of a housing allowance program. Although the standards used in the Supply and Demand experiments had the same general intent—to specify the minimum levels of housing quality needed for health, safety, and decency—and drew on the same precedents, slight differences in wording and evaluation style led to substantial differences in results when the same set of dwellings were evaluated under each experiment's rules (Valenza, 1977). The different failure rates would have been unimportant if all failures were easily remediable; but a dwelling that fails because its windows are too small or its ceilings are too low by a few inches is unlikely to be repaired.

We strongly recommend additional research and field testing for housing standards that are applied in both federal housing assistance programs and local codes. Those in common use represent a consensus of expert opinion; but their premises are largely untested, and their consequences in the field are, except for the EHAP experiments, poorly documented.

OPERATING A LOW-INCOME ASSISTANCE PROGRAM

Federal programs offering various kinds of assistance to low-income persons or households face similar administrative tasks. They must decide who is eligible to participate, recruit and enroll the eligibles, determine how much and what kind of help each client should get, and see that the assistance is delivered on schedule. If the assistance is conditional or involves third-party providers of services, the performances of clients and providers must also be monitored.

The housing allowance offices in Brown and St. Joseph counties faced these tasks and others special to a housing assistance program. As documented in Ch. VIII, their administrative performances were in most respects exemplary. Although the reasons for their success must be inferred (because we did not field-test an array of administrative alternatives), we think that this experience offers valuable lessons for the administration of both a national housing allowance program and other transfer programs, especially those dealing with clients whose circumstances change rapidly.

The lessons fall under three headings: program features that simplify administration; administrative style; and the management of staff-client relationships. When stated as general principles, these lessons are likely to strike the reader as self-evident. Whether or not they are generally recognized as sound principles, they are commonly ignored in practice or subordinated to other considerations. We think they deserve reassertion.

Program Features That Simplified Administration

An important aspect of the housing allowance concept, reflected in the experimental program, is the division of labor between clients and program administrators. In most housing assistance programs, a public authority builds, buys, leases, or manages residential property; or else enters into contracts with private developers or owners whose performance is supervised, regulated, or audited by the public authority. The assisted household is rarely a party to these transactions; the public authority, when it is not itself the landlord, acts on the client's behalf. In contrast, the HAOs did not deal with housing suppliers at all, and had no contingent liability to them or for their performances. Program participants conducted their own housing transactions on the private market without supervision, intermediation, or assistance from the HAOs, which checked only on the physical characteristics of the dwellings that clients chose and reported evaluation outcomes only to those clients.

This division of labor greatly simplified program administration, both by reducing the number of functions to be performed and by assigning to the HAOs the functions that were most amenable to routine performance and strict accountability for outcomes. Except in acquiring office space and hiring, the HAOs rarely had occasion to *negotiate* with anyone. Instead, their managers were able to focus on four major administrative functions: outreach, eligibility certification, housing evaluation, and disbursement. Of these functions, only outreach resisted routine procedures.

While simplifying formal administration, this division of labor placed greater responsibility for program outcomes on the program's clients, relying on the incentive of a conditional transfer and the clients' problem-solving abilities to attain program objectives. Other parts of this book deal at length with how well clients did at arranging for dwelling repairs, finding alternative dwellings, and negotiating rents or home purchases. We think they demonstrated considerable skill at tasks which, after all, are part of the common experience of American households. In any case, they did well enough to encourage reflection on possible devolution of responsibility and discretion in other assistance programs.

Administrative Style

The administrative system developed by the HAOs can be seen in retrospect to have embodied three salient principles:

- Administrative functions were governed by detailed rules consistently applied to all cases.
- The staffs were thoroughly trained in their duties, their work was checked, and individual performances were regularly reviewed and appropriately rewarded.
- A management information system supplied current data on

workloads, performance, and cost to all levels of management.

This administrative style has characteristic tensions and limitations, but we are nonetheless impressed by its effectiveness. For example, both eligibility certification and housing evaluation required HAO staff to reach conclusions affecting allowance payments, based either on client-supplied evidence or direct observation. Overly general guidelines, subject to different interpretations, can turn such processes into negotiating rather than fact-finding sessions. On the other hand, meticulously detailed rules never apply fairly to all cases; yet they cease to be rules if staff are given leave to overlook them in particular cases.

We think that carefully specifying the relevant evidence and rules on which a determination must rest—and allowing no exceptions—speeded the work, made checking it feasible, and reduced the potential friction between clients and staff. Yet it was also important to provide outlets for dissatisfaction. The HAOs encouraged their staffs to propose rule changes, many of which were accepted; and offered clients a formal procedure for appealing staff decisions (rarely used).

The high morale and productivity of HAO staffs reflected both the emphasis given to thorough training (employees *felt* competent) and the clarity of performance standards. Both the quantity and quality of work accomplished could be and was tracked for most individual employees, and the results were regularly reviewed by their immediate supervisors. The HAOs had an advantage in personnel matters over most public agencies in not being bound by civil service rules that subordinate merit to job protection; and they used that freedom constructively. But even within a civil service system, we think that better training and better performance scorecards are possible and would improve both morale and output.

The HAOs' administrative style would have been infeasible without the support of a good management information system to keep administrators at all levels abreast of workloads, output, work quality, and cost. A good system is one that accepts information from records that would be kept in any case and generates timely reports that highlight operationally important facts and figures. Such systems require considerable planning to devise; but, once installed and debugged, they can operate routinely as part of a machine records system.

Staff-Client Relations

The HAOs' dealings with applicants and participants were remarkably friendly compared with other assistance programs that require means tests and checks on client performance. We attribute this outcome to three interrelated factors: high staff morale; clear program rules; and procedures deliberately designed to protect the clients' dignity and minimize the inconveniences attendant on transactions with the agency.

To protect clients' dignity, enrollment interviews were conducted in comfortable private rooms, without distracting interruptions, by staff trained to elicit information without bullying. Guarantees of confidentiality were explicit and scrupulously observed. The interviews and housing evaluations were individually scheduled to suit clients' convenience, a procedure that added measurably to direct costs because broken appointments were common. Yet the HAO directors believe that these extra efforts paid off in willing cooperation by the clients. Our household surveys indicate that those who dealt with the HAOs usually thought well of their staffs even in the face of adverse determinations on issues of eligibility, entitlement, and housing acceptability.

Experimental versus Operating Programs

Nearly everyone who has visited the HAO offices in Brown and St. Joseph counties has been impressed by the pleasant surroundings and high staff morale. The operating statistics presented in Ch. VIII attest to the effectiveness and efficiency of HAO operations, but few observers seem persuaded that the techniques that succeeded in these experimental programs would flourish in a public agency operating a permanent program. Reservations about the transferability of HASE administrative features usually rest on the issue of staff quality.

We think that the HAOs did indeed recruit exceptionally able staffs, many of whom were attracted by the idea of participating in a highly visible experiment. But it is worth noting that 95 percent of all personnel were recruited locally and that HAO pay-scales were aligned to prevailing local standards for comparable work. In short, able people are available and can be recruited by inducements other than high pay. We think that the value of participating in an experiment would have palled quickly had the administrative style of the program been either less supportive or less demanding of HAO staffs; and we think that administrative style could be applied much more widely than it is today.

SOCIAL EXPERIMENTS AND PUBLIC POLICY

According to HUD's Office of Policy Development and Research, the total budget for the Experimental Housing Allowance Program is $153 million, partly for research and partly for allowance payments. The Supply Experiment alone accounted for just over half that total. Rand spent $41 million for research (including field surveys); during the first five years of program operations, the HAOs spent $14 million for program administration and $32 million for allowance payments.[23]

It is appropriate to wonder whether such an expensive social experiment was worthwhile, and whether social experiments in general are effective and efficient tools for policy analysis. We think that such questions can be debated indefinitely, because there is no good way to measure the full public benefit accruing from experimental findings, even when they are known to have affected public policy. However, we can note that the scale of federal housing assistance is such that even modest improvements in policy or program design based on experimental findings could easily save enough to pay for EHAP.[24]

Rather than joining that debate, we think it will be more fruitful to close this volume by reflecting on our experience of planning, conducting, and reporting on the Supply Experiment, for the benefit of those who may undertake either social experiments or similar large research projects in the future.

Designing a Social Experiment

Although most advocates of social experiments stress the virtues of a specific statistical method (cf. Reichen and Boruch, 1974), it is perhaps more important that an experiment can be tailored to illuminate specific policy issues. Most policy analysis rests on theoretical models whose parameters are uncertain, on data collected for other purposes,

[23]Estimates of EHAP costs as of April 1980 are reported in Struyk and Bendick, 1981, Table 12.1; they include an additional $12 million budgeted for the Brown and St. Joseph counties' housing allowance programs through 1984. Rand's connection with those programs ended in 1979, and its research contract with HUD expired in September 1981. The Demand and Administrative Agency experiments were completed earlier, so are fully accounted for at $31 million and $22 million, respectively. Another $7 million is attributed to overall design and integrated analysis, for a total of $158 million. However, HUD informs us that they expect the total cost (including the remaining cost of the HASE allowance program) to be $153 million.

[24]For one example, see pp. 96-8 of Henry Aaron, "Policy Implications: A Progress Report," in Bradbury and Downs, 1981. For another, see Rydell, Mulford, and Helbers, 1980, pp. 14-16. For an outsider's appraisal of EHAP, see Frieden, 1980: for a semidetached view, see Raymond J. Struyk, "Social Experimentation and Public Policy," in Struyk and Bendick, 1981. The Bradbury-Downs volume also contains specific critiques of the Supply Experiment; see John F. Kain, "A Universal Housing Allowance Program," and Downs and Bradbury, "Conference Discussion."

or on observation and analysis of fortuitous events. A well-designed experiment can produce an appropriately structured event (experimental stimulus) under conditions that allow the most pertinent observations of its consequences.

In the case of the Supply Experiment, we began by agreeing with HUD on the salient research questions, then worked backward through the appropriate design of the experimental stimulus and its context to the agenda of data collection and analysis. Thus, the design of our survey samples and instruments derived from the formal specification of analytical models that, in the experimental context, would yield answers to specific questions.

As can be seen from our early design reports (cf. Lowry, 1980), that process, though systematic, entailed considerable guesswork: Optimal design depends on the unknown structure of the empirical world. Although a design can be somewhat protected against empirical uncertainty by redundancy (larger samples, longer survey instruments, multiple sources of information on the same event), such precautions are costly. Risks must continually be balanced against budget constraints that fluctuate with circumstances wholly unrelated to the experiment.

The Supply Experiment was singularly fortunate in having roughly two years to work out the details of the experiment before large-scale field operations began. Thereafter, practical urgencies preempted all our energies for several years, leaving little time for reflection on broader issues. In any case, commitments necessarily made to sponsors, subcontractors, program clients, and the general public increasingly narrowed the options for design changes. We cannot overemphasize the importance of thorough planning *before* field operations begin.

Although analytical models were prespecified to guide data collection, the final analysis of the experimental data bore only a family resemblance to initial plans. That outcome did not surprise us; analytical methods are the most flexible component of empirical research. As we found better ways to analyze the data we had collected, we applied them; but major changes in data collection to fit a new analytical plan would have been infeasible in a project so driven by its schedule of annual fieldwork and so dependent on the continuity of data over time.

Conducting Field Experiments

Conducting a large field experiment requires an organization that delegates and fixes responsibility, teamwork between diverse talents, tight scheduling, and a reliable system of records.

At peak, the Supply Experiment employed about 200 individuals, equivalent to a full-time staff of 120 persons. These figures do not include the HAO staffs (about 130 persons at peak) or the staffs of survey subcontractors who conducted the fieldwork. Our technical tasks included designing office procedures and machine record systems for the HAOs, constructing and testing survey instruments, selecting survey samples, overseeing fieldwork, editing completed questionnaires, organizing the data into research files, compiling codebooks and auditing the files, conducting statistical analyses on the data, and writing and editing reports.

Simultaneously, we were engaged in more or less continuous negotiations with HUD (both with the Office of Policy Development and Research, which had jurisdiction over the research, and HUD's regional office, which had jurisdiction over the allowance program); the Office of Management and Budget, whose approval was required for each survey instrument; the survey subcontractors; local housing authorities in Brown and St. Joseph counties, which were conduits for program funds; and the local governments within whose jurisdiction and by whose consent programs were conducted.

We established the basic division of functions—allowance program operations, research design and analysis, and survey fieldwork—quite early in the life of the experiment. Within each functional area, however, tasks were progressively differentiated and dispersed among different teams and individuals as we came to understand the size and complexity of our undertaking.

Different tasks require different skills, and cooperative effort between people whose skills and outlooks differ requires mutual education. Good researchers rarely have either the temperament or the skills needed to manage operations; and good operations managers are unlikely to have a deep appreciation of research issues. Individuals who are meticulous about details often lack broader vision or analytical imagination; and those who possess the latter qualities are often careless of detail.

It was imperative but difficult to devise a routine system of communication between those performing different but interrelated tasks. At one level, group managers met regularly to make policy and assess progress; but what seemed like minor technical decisions within the context of (say) questionnaire editing might have large consequences for an analytical plan with which the editors were unfamiliar. We succeeded in establishing the general principle that procedural rules and technical decisions should all be documented and reviewed, but found that sending copies of everything to everyone was self-defeating. Instead, each functional group produced a weekly list of all its documents, correspondence, and internal memoranda that could be scanned by others to see if topics of interest to the reader were included.

Internal documentation was critical for another reason. In a long project, staff turns over. Only a handful of Rand employees worked continuously on the Supply Experiment from beginning to end. Documentation provided the institutional memory that was essential to continuity of action and consistency of purpose.

The most difficult management problem, and the main source of friction between Rand and HUD, was getting tasks done on schedule, so that contingent tasks could proceed. At HUD's wise insistence, we developed formal, integrated schedules to plan, track, and report progress. However, nearly every new task took longer than expected, frustrating both the responsible parties and those who depended on the results. Much management time was spent devising ways around bottlenecks and rescheduling subsequent events.

A saving feature of the enterprise was that most tasks were repetitive, so that once mastered, they could be reduced to routine. By the time of the third year of program operations and the fourth wave of surveys, we had models for nearly every operation and procedure. Many of these models seem to us readily adaptable to other projects entailing program operations or field data collection, and indeed some were adopted by other studies conducted at Rand. We strongly urge anyone beginning a project of this kind to thoroughly investigate the documentation of HASE and other social experiments for procedural models that might save the effort of reinvention.

Managing Large Data Bases

By the standards of social science research, the Supply Experiment generated a great deal of data. HASE files include administrative records of up to five years' duration on over 25,000 households that enrolled in the allowance programs; over 18,000 interviews with households and 8,000 with landlords, covering countywide populations over four annual surveys; and auxiliary records on some 4,000 residential properties and 200 neighborhoods (see Appendix B for details). Over half of the research budget and much of the intellectual energy of the Supply Experiment was spent on collecting, editing, organizing, storing, and documenting these data so that they would be useful to HASE analysts and subsequently to the general public.

There are many different ways to botch a large data base of this type. They include vague sampling protocols, ambiguous questionnaires, sloppy fieldwork, careless editing, inaccessible file structures, accidental damage to records, or insufficient technical documentation. The HASE data are far from perfect, but we are frankly proud of both their quality and accessibility. Achieving that outcome was greatly facilitated by adherence to four principles guiding data preparation and management; we recommend them to our readers.

First in importance is comprehensive accountability. From sample selection through archived final master file, every operation that contributed to the existence or nonexistence of a record or data entry was positively recorded. We maintained machine records that traced the field history of every sample element (residential properties, individual buildings and dwellings, household heads, and landlords) through four years of surveying. For every entry in each final master file, we maintained a complete audit trail through all stages of data preparation, back to hard copy. Frequent accounting checks during file preparation forestalled losing or mislabeling data and exposed procedural flaws so that they could be remedied in subsequent operations.

Second was dividing the data into functionally independent files. We used a system of computer processing and file storage that both forced completion of the work on individual files and made the files independently accessible and usable. Thus, the records for each annual survey (household, landlord, residential building, neighborhood) in each site were archived and documented as separate master files, each accessible with standard software. Problems with one file did not inhibit the use of others.

Third was meticulous documentation of variables and files. Each file is accompanied by a codebook that repeats each question from the survey instrument, defines all permissible entries in the response field, and abstracts pertinent detail from interviewer training guides and editing instructions. For each derived variable added to survey files, the codebook specifies the construction algorithm. Finally, the actual distribution of responses ("marginals") is shown for each variable. Users of the file are thus able to determine what each variable means and what values they will encounter, so can judge the variable's usefulness to their proposed analysis. In addition, each file is documented by an audit report that appraises the completeness and reliability of the data, and warns the user of special problems with the file.

The fourth principle is redundant storage. Until final master files were archived, documented, and analytically exercised, we retained not only the hard-copy sources of our machine-readable records, but also the intermediate tape files produced at successive stages of data preparation. Preliminary and final master files were duplicated as soon as they were created; the duplicates were safely stored offsite and periodically checked for readability. There were few instances in which files were accidentally damaged, but predecessor files, including hard-copy sources, were regularly consulted to diagnose or correct errors in subsequent processing.

Despite the elaborate system of edit checks and file audits, data defects were often unnoticed until a file was analyzed. Organizing the data to fit a conceptual framework revealed many otherwise invisible inconsistencies or implausibilities. After the first round of analysis, we added another step in file preparation, systematically constructing and auditing the derived variables that would be most often used. That process substantially improved data quality. However, as long as the data are in use, observant analysts are likely to discover hitherto unnoticed defects.

Bringing Experimental Findings To Bear on Public Policy

The Supply Experiment was designed to answer specific questions about the market and community effects of a full-scale housing allowance program, questions that were prompted by both Congressional and Executive dissatisfaction with existing methods of delivering low-income housing assistance (see Ch. I, "Historical Background"). The HASE charter was subsequently broadened to include research on eligibility and participation, effects on participants, and program administration.

Arriving at the answers summarized in this volume took ten years, during most of which other issues of federal housing policy preoccupied the national attention. Yet, the research program was sustained through four presidential administrations by six successive secretaries of HUD, some of whom clearly had no interest in housing allowances as a tool of federal policy.

We do not think the experiment's survival through all these changes was due merely to bureaucratic inertia. We know of several occasions on which HUD reviewed the future of EHAP, with its termination as an explicit option. EHAP survived because its research findings were perceived by successive administrations with different policy predilections as broadly relevant to federal housing policy, not just as an evaluation of a particular program.

EHAP began to influence federal housing policy a decade ago, when the staffs of HUD's Office of Policy Development and Research, the research contractors, and interested scholars were planning the several experiments. Designing the experiments forced us to ask and try to answer such questions as: What is low-income housing assistance meant to accomplish, and how can we tell if it has succeeded? In what respects does the public interest in the housing circumstances of the poor differ from the preferences of low-income households? Why does the private market fail to provide socially acceptable housing for the poor? That there was initially so little consensus on the answers was sobering to all concerned.

During the experiments, the research contractors reported what they were learning about the housing circumstances of the poor, their responses to offers of financial assistance, their contrivances for solving their housing problems, and the structure and functioning of local housing markets. Some of these interim findings resolved formerly open questions; other findings challenged conventional wisdom, or supported it. In consequence, both the premises and logic of housing policy debate were gradually altered. The influence of EHAP can be detected in both the vocabulary and paradigms of housing discourse.

Publication of final reports on each of the EHAP experiments—the present volume is the last such report—and two book-length reviews of experimental findings (Struyk and Bendick, 1981; Bradbury and Downs, 1981) brings the research cycle to its close. That these events coincide with a renewed political interest in "housing vouchers" is neither pure cause-and-effect nor pure coincidence. The efficient cause was a change in presidential administration, which prompted a review of policy options. That housing allowances were chosen by the new administration surely reflects its confidence that the ten-year research program has clarified both the strengths and weaknesses of the allowance concept to the degree that an informed choice could be made.

Whether or not a national allowance program is legislated, we are confident that EHAP research will continue to exert a powerful influence on housing policy: It has articulated the criteria for judging low-income housing assistance programs and provided benchmarks against which other programs, existing or proposed, will inevitably be judged.

REFERENCES

Barnett, C. Lance, *Using Hedonic Indexes to Measure Housing Quantity,* The Rand Corporation, R-2450-HUD, October 1979.

Barnett, C. Lance, and Ira S. Lowry, *How Housing Allowances Affect Housing Prices,* The Rand Corporation, R-2452-HUD, September 1979.

Bradbury, Katharine L., and Anthony Downs, eds., *Do Housing Allowances Work?,* The Brookings Institution, Washington, D.C., 1981.

Congressional Research Service, Library of Congress *The Central City Problem and Urban Renewal Policy,* U.S. Government Printing Office, Washington, D.C., 1973.

Follain, James R., Jr., and Stephen Malpezzi, *Dissecting Housing Value and Rent: Estimates of Hedonic Indexes for Thirty-Nine Large SMSAs,* The Urban Institute, Washington, D.C., February 1980.

Frieden, Bernard J., "Housing Allowances: An Experiment That Worked," *The Public Interest,* No. 59, Spring 1980.

Friedman, Joseph, and Daniel H. Weinberg, *The Demand for Rental Housing: Evidence from a Percent of Rent Housing Allowance,* Abt Associates, Inc., Cambridge, Mass., June 1980.

Haar, Charles M., *Between the Idea and the Reality: A Study in the Origin, Fate, and Legacy of the Model Cities Program,* Little, Brown and Company, Boston, 1975.

Helbers, Lawrence, *Measuring Homeowner Needs for Housing Assistance,* The Rand Corporation, N-1094-HUD, October 1980.

Helbers, Lawrence, and James L. McDowell, *Determinants of Housing Repair and Improvement,* The Rand Corporation, R-2777-HUD, forthcoming, 1982.

Katagiri, Iao, and G. Thomas Kingsley, eds., *The Housing Allowance Handbook,* The Rand Corporation, N-1491-HUD, July 1980.

Kennedy, Stephen D., and Jean MacMillan, *Participation under Alternative Housing Allowance Programs: Evidence from the Housing Allowance Demand Experiment,* Abt Associates, Inc., Cambridge, Mass., 1980.

Lindsay, D. Scott, and Ira S. Lowry, *Rent Inflation in St. Joseph County, Indiana, 1974-78,* The Rand Corporation, N-1468-HUD, November 1980.

Lowry, Ira S., ed., *The Design of the Housing Assistance Supply Experiment,* The Rand Corporation, R-2630-HUD, June 1980.

Lowry, Ira S., "The Dismal Future of Central Cities," in Arthur P. Solomon, ed., *The Prospective City,* The MIT Press, Cambridge, Mass., 1980.

Lowry, Ira S., Barbara Woodfill, and Tiina Repnau, *Program Standards for Site I,* The Rand Corporation, N-1058-HUD, January 1981.

Lowry, Ira S., Barbara Woodfill, and Marsha A. Dade, *Program Standards for Site II,* The Rand Corporation, N-1079-HUD, April 1981.

McFarland, M. Carter, "The Rehabilitation and Revival of Decayed or Decaying Neighborhoods," in Congressional Research Service, Library of Congress, *Subsidized Housing: Where Do We Go from Here?,* U.S. Government Printing Office, Washington, D.C., 1977.

Mayo, Stephen K., Shirley Mansfield, David Warner, and Richard Zwetchkenbaum, *Housing Allowances and Other Rental Housing Assistance Programs—A Comparison Based on the Housing Allowance Demand Experiment;* Part 1: *Participation, Housing Consumption, Location, and Satisfaction;* Part 2: *Costs and Efficiency,* Abt Associates, Inc., Cambridge, Mass., 1980.

Mulford, John E., *Income Elasticity of Housing Demand,* The Rand Corporation, R-2449-HUD, July 1979.

Mulford, John E., James L. McDowell, Lawrence Helbers, Michael P. Murray, and Orhan M. Yildiz, *Housing Consumption in a Housing Allowance Program,* The Rand Corporation, R-2779-HUD, forthcoming, 1982.

Neels, John Kevin, *The Derived Demand for Energy in the Production of Housing Services,* Unpublished doctoral dissertation, Cornell University, January 1981.

Neels, Kevin, *The Economics of Rental Housing,* The Rand Corporation, R-2776-HUD, forthcoming, 1982.

Noland, Charles W., *Assessing Hedonic Indexes for Housing,* The Rand Corporartion, N-1305-HUD, May 1980.

President's Commission on Housing, *The Report of the President's Commission on Housing,* U.S. Government Printing Office, Washington, D.C., 1982.

Reichen, Henry W., and Robert F. Boruch, eds., *Social Experimentation: A Method for Planning and Evaluating Social Intervention,* Academic Press, New York, San Francisco, and London, 1974.

Repnau, Tiina, and Barbara M. Woodfill, *Additional Estimates of Enrollment and Allowance Payments under a National Housing Allowance Program,* The Rand Corporation, N-1044-HUD, July 1980.

Rydell, C. Peter, *Price Elasticities of Housing Supply,* The Rand Corporation, R-2846-HUD, forthcoming, 1982.

——, *Shortrun Response of Housing Markets to Demand Shifts,* The Rand Corporation, R-2453-HUD, September 1979.

Rydell, C. Peter, C. Lance Barnett, Carol E. Hillestad, Michael P. Murray, Kevin Neels, and Robert H. Sims, *The Impact of Rent Control on the Los Angeles Housing Market,* The Rand Corporation, N-1747-LA, August 1981.

Rydell, C. Peter, and John E. Mulford, *Consumption Increases Caused by Housing Assistance Programs,* The Rand Corporation, R-2809-HUD, April 1982.

Rydell, C. Peter, John E. Mulford, and Lawrence Helbers, *Price Increases Caused by Housing Assistance Programs,* The Rand Corporation, R-2677-HUD, October 1980.

Sepanik, Ronald J., Gary Hendricks, and John D. Heinberg, *Simulations of National Housing Allowances: An Application of the Trim Model,* The Urban Institute, Washington, D.C., February 1975.

Schnare, Anne B., *Residential Segregation by Race in U.S. Metropolitan Areas: An Analysis across Cities and over Time,* The Urban Institute, Washington, D.C., 1977.

Shanley, Michael G., and Charles M. Hotchkiss, *The Role of Market Intermediaries in a Housing Allowance Program,* The Rand Corporation, R-2659-HUD, December 1980.

Stucker, James P., *Rent Inflation in Brown County, Wisconsin: 1973-78,* The Rand Corporation, N-1134-HUD, March 1981.

Struyk, Raymond J., and Marc Bendick, Jr., eds., *Housing Vouchers for the Poor,* The Urban Institute Press, Washington, D.C., 1981.

Taueber, Karl E., and Alma F. Taueber, *Negroes in Cities,* Aldine Press, Chicago, 1965.

Valenza, Joseph J., *Program Standards in the Experimental Housing Allowance Program: Analyzing Differences in the Demand and Supply Experiments,* The Urban Institute, Washington, D.C., 1977.

Wilner, Daniel M., and others, *The Housing Environment and Family Life,* The Johns Hopkins Press, Baltimore, 1962.

Wilson, James Q., ed., *Urban Renewal: The Record and the Controversy,* The M.I.T. Press, Cambridge, Mass., 1966.

Appendix A

SELECTED PUBLICATIONS OF THE HOUSING ASSISTANCE SUPPLY EXPERIMENT

This appendix lists 32 reports, 116 notes, and 20 professional papers prepared by Rand's staff for the Housing Assistance Supply Experiment. The list is a selection from over 279 documents published by HASE during its ten-year history, and encompasses all aspects of experimental design and research findings. Nearly all HASE publications not listed here are codebooks and audit reports documenting the HASE data files; these are listed separately in Appendix B.

The list is topically organized as follows:

- General Reports
- Final Topical Reports
- Research Design
- Program Design
- Program Analysis
- Market and Community Response to Program
- General Market Analysis
- Housing Cost and Price Indexes

Most topics are subdivided to help readers with specific interests locate the pertinent documents. Within each subdivision, documents are listed by publication series (R = report, N = note, P = professional paper) and number. Except for general reports, documents that deal substantially with more than one subject are listed under all pertinent headings.

Many of the documents listed here were initially published as working notes (WN series) designed for prompt communication of research results to HUD. During 1980 and 1981, those of more than passing interest were republished as notes (N series) for general distribution. Entries for these documents include the original publication number and date. Titles appearing in earlier lists but not shown here have been superseded by other documents or withdrawn because they are obsolete.

All documents listed here are available to the public from Rand or from nearly 350 libraries that subscribe to Rand publications. Many of them are also available from the National Technical Information Service (NTIS) and HUD User.[1]

GENERAL REPORTS

R-1659-HUD. *First Annual Report of the Housing Assistance Supply Experiment.* October 1974.

R-1959-HUD. *Second Annual Report of the Housing Assistance Supply Experiment.* May 1976.

R-2151-HUD. *Third Annual Report of the Housing Assistance Supply Experiment.* February 1977.

R-2302-HUD. *Fourth Annual Report of the Housing Assistance Supply Experiment.* May 1978.

R-2434-HUD. *Fifth Annual Report of the Housing Assistance Supply Experiment.* June 1979.

R-2544-HUD. *Sixth Annual Report of the Housing Assistance Supply Experiment.* May 1980.

R-2880-HUD. *Experimenting with Housing Allowances: Executive Summary. The Final Comprehensive Report of the Housing Assistance Supply Experiment.* Ira S. Lowry. April 1982.

N-1215-HUD. *A Topical Guide to HASE Research.* Ira S. Lowry. June 1979.

P-5567. *The Housing Assistance Supply Experiment: An Overview.* Ira S. Lowry. January 1976.

P-5976. *An Overview of the Housing Assistance Supply Experiment.* Ira S. Lowry. September 1977.

P-6075. *Early Findings from the Housing Assistance Supply Experiment.* Ira S. Lowry. January 1978.

P-6455. *Housing Allowances: Lessons from the Supply Experiment.* Ira S. Lowry. March 1980.

P-6696. *Delivering Housing Assistance to Low-Income Households.* Ira S. Lowry. October 1981.

FINAL TOPICAL REPORTS

R-2659-HUD. *The Role of Market Intermediaries in a Housing Allowance Program.* Michael G. Shanley, Charles M. Hotchkiss. December 1980.

---

[1]The address of NTIS is Springfield, Virginia 22151. The address of HUD User is P.O. Box 280, Germantown, Maryland 20767.

R-2720-HUD. *Price Effects of a Housing Allowance Program.* C. Peter Rydell, Kevin Neels, C. Lance Barnett. Forthcoming (1982).

R-2775-HUD. *The Economics of Rental Housing.* Kevin Neels. Forthcoming (1982).

R-2776-HUD. *Measuring Neighborhood Change due to Housing Allowances.* Carol E. Hillestad, James L. McDowell. Forthcoming (1982).

R-2779-HUD. *Housing Consumption in a Housing Allowance Program.* John E. Mulford, James L. McDowell, Lawrence Helbers, Michael P. Murray, Orhan M. Yildiz. Forthcoming (1982).

R-2783-HUD. *Eligibility and Participation in a Housing Allowance Program.* Grace M. Carter, James C. Wendt. Forthcoming (1982).

N-1846-HUD. *Housing Allowance Program Administration: Findings from the Supply Experiment.* G. Thomas Kingsley, Sheila Nataraj Kirby, W. Engene Rizor. May 1982.

RESEARCH DESIGN

General Design

R-2630-HUD. *The Design of the Housing Assistance Supply Experiment.* Ira S. Lowry (ed.). June 1980.

N-1025-HUD. *Testing the Supply Response to Housing Allowances: An Experimental Design.* Ira S. Lowry, C. Peter Rydell, David M. de Ferranti. February 1981. (First issued as WN-7711-UI, December 1971.)

N-1027-HUD. *Preliminary Design for the Housing Assistance Supply Experiment.* Ira S. Lowry. July 1980. (First issued as WN-7866-HUD, June 1972.)

N-1030-HUD. *Phase II Price Controls and the Housing Assistance Supply Experiment.* David B. Lewis. February 1981. (First issued as WN-7888-HUD, July 1972.)

N-1031-HUD. *Failure Mode Analysis for the Housing Allowance Program.* Robert A. Levine. February 1981. (First issued as WN-7895-HUD, July 1972.)

N-1036-HUD. *Contingency Planning for the Supply Experiment.* Ira S. Lowry. October 1980. (First issued as WN-7980-HUD, October 1972.)

N-1037-HUD. *Supplemental Design Papers for the Housing Assistance*

Supply Experiment. Housing Assistance Supply Experiment Staff. October 1980. (First issued as WN-7982-HUD, July 1972.)

N-1052-HUD. *General Design Report: Supplement.* Ira S. Lowry (ed.). December 1980. (First issued as WN-8364-HUD, August 1973.)

N-1053-HUD. *Proceedings of the General Design Review of the Housing Assistance Supply Experiment.* Housing Assistance Supply Experiment Staff. January 1981. (First issued as WN-8396-HUD, October 1973.)

N-1060-HUD. *Market Intermediaries and Indirect Suppliers: Reconnaissance and Research Design for Site I.* William G. Grigsby, Michael Shanley, Sammis B. White. July 1980. (First issued as WN-8577-HUD, February 1974.)

N-1087-HUD. *Market Intermediaries and Indirect Suppliers: First Year Report for Site II.* Sammis B. White. December 1979. (First issued as WN-9020-HUD, August 1977.)

N-1089-HUD. *Market Intermediaries and Indirect Suppliers: Reconnaissance and Research Design for Site II.* William G. Grigsby, Michael Shanley, Sammis B. White. July 1980. (First issued as WN-9026-HUD, May 1975.)

N-1106-HUD. *Are Further Survey Cycles Needed in Site I?* Ira S. Lowry. March 1981. (First issued as WN-9541-HUD, July 1976.)

N-1138-HUD. *Completing the Supply Experiment.* Housing Assistance Supply Experiment Staff. May 1981. (First issued as WN-10223-HUD, June 1978.)

P-4645. *Housing Assistance for Low-Income Urban Families: A Fresh Approach.* Ira S. Lowry. May 1971.

P-5302. *The Housing Assistance Supply Experiment: Tensions in Design and Implementation.* Ira S. Lowry. September 1974.

Site Selection

N-1026-HUD. *Site Selection for the Housing Assistance Supply Experiment: Stage I.* Housing Assistance Supply Experiment Staff. July 1980. (First issued as WN-7833-HUD, May 1972.)

N-1033-HUD. *Site Selection for the Housing Assistance Supply Experiment: SMSAs Proposed for Site Visits (A Briefing).* Housing Assistance Supply Experiment Staff. July 1980. (First issued as WN-7907-HUD, August 1972.)

N-1041-HUD. *Collected Site Selection Documents: Housing Assistance Supply Experiment.* Robert Dubinsky. July 1980. (First issued as WN-8034-HUD, January 1973.)

Survey Sample Design and Sample Selection

N-1040-HUD. *Sample Design for the Housing Assistance Supply Experiment.* Timothy M. Corcoran, Eugene C. Poggio, Tiina Repnau. October 1980. (First issued as WN-8029-HUD, November 1972.)

N-1043-HUD. *Preliminary Description of Sample-Selection Procedure.* Eugene C. Poggio. May 1981. (First issued as WN-8101-HUD, January 1973.)

N-1045-HUD. *The Effects of Nonresponse on Record Completion in a Panel of Residential Properties.* Timothy M. Corcoran. December 1980. (First issued as WN-8174-HUD, April 1973.)

N-1047-HUD. *Sample-Selection Procedures for Site I.* Eugene C. Poggio. December 1980. (First issued as WN-8201-HUD, March 1973.)

N-1049-HUD. *The Role of Household Survey Data in the Supply Experiment.* Adele R. Palmer (ed.). January 1981. (First issued as WN-8218-HUD, March 1973.)

N-1061-HUD. *Sample Selection Procedure for St. Joseph County, Indiana.* Sandra H. Berry. Daniel A. Relles, Eugene Seals. May 1981. (First issued as WN-8588-HUD, January 1974.)

N-1064-HUD. *Sampling Nonresidential Properties: Site I.* Timothy M. Corcoran. December 1980. (First issued as WN-8623-HUD, March 1974.)

N-1065-HUD. *Survey Sample Design for Site I.* Timothy M. Corcoran. February 1981. (First issued as WN-8640-HUD, March 1974.)

N-1066-HUD. *Selecting the Baseline Sample of Residential Properties: Site I.* Eugene C. Poggio. February 1981. (First issued as WN-8645-HUD, March 1977.)

N-1067-HUD. *Characteristics of the Residential Baseline Survey Samples for Site I.* Tiina Repnau. March 1981. (First issued as WN-8682-HUD, May 1974.)

N-1090-HUD. *Selecting the Baseline Sample of Residential Properties: Site II.* Daniel A. Relles. May 1981. (First issued as WN-9027-HUD, October 1975.)

N-1107-HUD. *Selecting the Permanent Panel of Residential Properties, Site I.* Timothy M. Corcoran. April 1981. (First issued as WN-9575-HUD, April 1978.)

N-1109-HUD. *Selecting the Permanent Panel for Residential Properties, Site II.* Timothy M. Corcoran. April 1981. (First issued as WN-9577-HUD, April 1977.)

Survey Instruments and Field Procedures

N-1028-HUD. *Preliminary Description of Survey Instruments.* Housing Assistance Supply Experiment Staff. July 1980. (First issued as WN-7883-HUD, June 1972.)

N-1071-HUD. *The Screening Instrument and Supplementary Forms: Site I.* HASE Survey Group. March 1981. (First issued as WN-8688-HUD, July 1974.)

N-1072-HUD. *Interviewer Training Manual for the Site I Screening Survey.* HASE Survey Group. May 1981. (First issued as WN-8689-HUD, November 1974.)

Survey Audit Plans and Statistical Methods

N-1050-HUD. *Compensating for Landlord Nonresponse in the Housing Assistance Supply Experiment.* Adele R. Palmer. December 1980. (First issued as WN-8268-HUD, June 1973.)

N-1063-HUD. *Baseline Audit Plan.* Leonard G. Chesler, David M. de Ferranti, William L. Dunn, Joseph A. Grundfest, Richard E. Stanton. February 1981. (First issued as WN-8612-HUD, February 1974.)

N-1070-HUD. *Accounting and Auditing Procedures for Rental Property Financial Data.* Therman P. Britt, Jr. March 1981. (First issued as WN-8687-HUD, August 1974.)

N-1096-HUD. *A Plan for Analyzing Nonresponse Bias: Survey of Landlords, Baseline, Site I.* C. Peter Rydell, Richard E. Stanton. April 1981. (First issued as WN-9211-HUD, August 1975.)

N-1136-HUD. *Using Weights to Estimate Population Parameters from Survey Records.* Daniel A. Relles. May 1981. (First issued as WN-10095-HUD, April 1978.)

Data Management

N-1029-HUD. *Data Management System: Part I, Fieldwork Data and Data Transfer Specifications.* Gerald Levitt. July 1980. (First issued as WN-7885-HUD, July 1972.)

N-1034-HUD. *Data Management System: Part II, The Management of Data for Analysis.* Gerald Levitt. February 1981. (First issued as WN-7953-HUD, August 1972.)

N-1042-HUD. *Data Management System for the Housing Assistance Supply Experiment.* Colleen M. Dodd, Misako C. Fujisaki, Gerald Levitt. July 1980. (First issued as WN-8054-HUD, November 1972.)

N-1062-HUD. *Baseline Data Systems Design, Implementation, and Operation Report.* Gerald Levitt (ed.). May 1981. (First issued as WN-8611-HUD, March 1974.)

N-1098-HUD. *HASE Data Systems: The HASE Audit and Analysis Support Package (HAASP).* Eric Harslem, Michel Rogson. May 1981. (First issued as WN-9292-HUD, November 1975.)

N-1131-HUD. *HAMISH Update System: Input Form Specifications.* Zahava B. Doering, Susan Welt. May 1981. (First issued as WN-10029-HUD, January 1978.)

N-1132-HUD. *Sample Maintenance Office Procedures Manual.* Susan Welt. May 1981. (First issued as WN-10039-HUD, January 1979.)

N-1133-HUD. *HAMISH Survey Support System: Technical Description.* Zahava B. Doering, Susan Welt. May 1981. (First issued as WN-10057-HUD, May 1978.)

P-5494-1. *Documentation in Social Science Experiments.* Michel M. Rogson. January 1976.

PROGRAM DESIGN

General Design

N-1027-HUD. *Preliminary Design for the Housing Assistance Supply Experiment.* Ira S. Lowry. July 1980. (First issued as WN-7866-HUD, June 1972.)

N-1038-HUD. *Funding Housing Allowances for Homeowners under Sec. 235.* Mack Ott. July 1980. (First issued as WN-8025-HUD, November 1972.)

N-1051-HUD. *The Housing Allowance Program for the Supply Experiment: First Draft.* Robert Dubinsky (ed.). January 1981. (First issued as WN-8350-HUD, August 1973.)

N-1056-HUD. *Funding Homeowner Assistance in the Supply Experiment: Problems and Prospects.* Ira S. Lowry. January 1981. (First issued as WN-8489-HUD, November 1973.)

Program Standards

N-1058-HUD. *Program Standards for Site I.* Ira S. Lowry, Barbara Woodfill, Tiina Repnau. January 1981. (First issued as WN-8574-HUD, January 1974.)

N-1073-HUD. *Equity and Housing Objectives in Homeowner Assistance.* Ira S. Lowry. March 1981. (First issued as WN-8715-HUD, June 1974.)

N-1079-HUD. *Program Standards for Site II.* Ira S. Lowry, Barbara Woodfill, Marsha A. Dade. April 1981. (First issued as WN-8974-HUD, February 1975.)

N-1084-HUD. *The Section 8 Housing Assistance Program: Notes on Eligibility and Benefits.* Barbara Woodfill. April 1981. (First issued as WN-8999-HUD, February 1975.)

N-1102-HUD. *Inflation in the Standard Cost of Adequate Housing: Site I, 1973-1976.* Ira S. Lowry. October 1979. (First issued as WN-9430-HUD, March 1976.)

N-1116-HUD. *Rent Inflation in St. Joseph County, Indiana: 1974-77.* James P. Stucker. November 1979. (First issued as WN-9734-HUD, September 1977.)

N-1134-HUD. *Rent Inflation in Brown County, Wisconsin: 1973-78.* James P. Stucker. March 1981. (First issued as WN-10073-HUD, August 1978.)

N-1468-HUD. *Rent Inflation in St. Joseph County, Indiana, 1974-78.* D. Scott Lindsay, Ira S. Lowry. November 1980.

Program Estimates

N-1032-HUD. *Preliminary Estimates of Enrollment Rates and Allowance Costs.* Barbara Woodfill. February 1981. (First issued as WN-7901-HUD, July 1972.)

N-1035-HUD. *Estimates of Eligibility and Allowance Entitlement under Alternative Housing Allowance Programs.* Barbara Woodfill, Tiina Repnau. July 1980. (First issued as WN-7974-HUD, September 1972.)

N-1044-HUD. *Additional Estimates of Enrollment and Allowance Payments under a National Housing Allowance Program.* Tiina Repnau, Barbara Woodfill. July 1980. (First issued as WN-8167-HUD, March 1973.)

N-1054-HUD. *Estimates of Eligibility, Enrollment, and Allowance Payments in Green Bay and Saginaw: 1974 and 1979.* Barbara Woodfill, Tiina Repnau, Ira S. Lowry. December 1980. (First issued as WN-8439-HUD, September 1973.)

N-1057-HUD. *Program Size and Cost for Site I: New Data from the Screener Survey.* Ira S. Lowry, Barbara Woodfill, Tiina Repnau. January 1981. (First issued as WN-8547-HUD, December 1973.)

Program Administration

N-1048-HUD. *The Housing Allowance Office: Functions and Procedures.* Alan Greenwald, David B. Lewis. December 1980. (First issued as WN-8209-HUD, March 1973.)

N-1100-HUD. *Review of the Relationship between the Housing Assistance Supply Experiment and Other Types of Assisted Housing Programs.* Robert Dubinsky, William G. Grigsby, Karen G. Watson. March 1981. (First issued as WN-9390-HUD, February 1976.)

N-1491-HUD. *The Housing Allowance Office Handbook.* Iao Katagiri, G. Thomas Kingsley (eds.). July 1980.

PROGRAM ANALYSIS

Eligibility and Participation

R-2632-HUD. *Who Applies for Housing Allowances? Early Lessons from the Housing Assistance Supply Experiment.* Phyllis L. Ellickson. August 1981.

R-2780-HUD. *Measuring Eligibility and Participation in the Housing Assistance Supply Experiment.* Grace M. Carter, Steven L. Balch. September 1981.

R-2781-HUD. *How Housing Evaluations Affect Participation in a Housing Allowance Program.* Sinclair B. Coleman. April 1982.

R-2782-HUD. *The Decision to Apply for a Housing Allowance.* James C. Wendt. Forthcoming (1982).

R-2783-HUD. *Eligibility and Participation in a Housing Allowance Program.* Grace M. Carter, James C. Wendt. Forthcoming (1982).

N-1124-HUD. *Client Responses to Housing Requirements: The First Two Years.* Bruce W. Lamar, Ira S. Lowry. May 1981. (First issued as WN-9814-HUD, February 1979.)

N-1125-HUD. *Eligibility and Enrollment in the Housing Allowance Program: Brown and St. Joseph Counties through Year 2.* Lawrence W. Kozimor. January 1981. (First issued as WN-9816-HUD, August 1978.)

N-1137-HUD. *Dynamics of Participation in a Housing Allowance Program.* C. Peter Rydell, John E. Mulford, Lawrence W. Kozimor. February 1981. (First issued as WN-10200-HUD, June 1978.)

P-6187. *Participation Rates in Government Transfer Programs: Application to Housing Allowances.* C. Peter Rydell, John E. Mulford, Lawrence W. Kozimor. January 1979.

Incomes and Housing Expenditure

R-2779-HUD. *Housing Consumption in a Housing Allowance Program.* John E. Mulford, James L. McDowell, Lawrence Helbers, Michael P. Murray, Orhan M. Yildiz. Forthcoming (1982).

R-2809-HUD. *Consumption Increases Caused by Housing Assistance Programs.* C. Peter Rydell, John E. Mulford. Forthcoming (1982).

N-1208-HUD. *How Low-Income Renters Buy Homes.* Michael G. Shanley, Charles M. Hotchkiss. August 1979.

N-1456-HUD. *How Housing Allowance Recipients Adjust Housing Consumption.* John E. Mulford, George D. Weiner, James L. McDowell. August 1980.

Housing Conditions and Housing Improvement

R-2779-HUD. *Housing Consumption in a Housing Allowance Program.* John E. Mulford, James L. McDowell, Lawrence Helbers, Michael P. Murray, Orhan M. Yildiz. Forthcoming (1982).

R-2809-HUD. *Consumption Increases Caused by Housing Assistance Programs.* C. Peter Rydell, John E. Mulford. Forthcoming (1982).

N-1124-HUD. *Client Responses to Housing Requirements: The First Two Years.* Bruce W. Lamar, Ira S. Lowry. May 1981. (First issued as WN-9814-HUD, February 1979.)

N-1198-HUD. *Housing Allowances and Housing Improvement: Early Findings.* James L. McDowell. September 1979.

N-1306-1-HUD. *Effects of the HAO Lead-Based Paint Hazard Standard.* James L. McDowell. June 1980.

N-1456-HUD. *How Housing Allowance Recipients Adjust Housing Consumption.* John E. Mulford, George D. Weiner, James L. McDowell. August 1980.

N-1774-HUD. *Measuring Housing Quality: Evidence from St. Joseph County.* Orhan M. Yildiz, John E. Mulford. Forthcoming (1982).

P-6076. *Housing Repair and Improvement in Response to a Housing Allowance Program.* James L. McDowell. May 1978.

Residential Mobility

R-2776-HUD. *Measuring Neighborhood Change due to Housing Allowances.* Carol E. Hillestad, James L. McDowell. Forthcoming (1982).

R-2779-HUD. *Housing Consumption in a Housing Allowance Program.* John E. Mulford, James L. McDowell, Lawrence Helbers, Michael P. Murray, Orhan M. Yildiz. Forthcoming (1982).

N-1144-HUD. *Residential Mobility of Housing Allowance Recipients.* Mark D. Menchik. October 1979.

N-1456-HUD. *How Housing Allowance Recipients Adjust Housing Consumption.* John E. Mulford, George D. Weiner, James L. McDowell. August 1980.

P-6434. *Using Administrative Records To Study Mobility: The Case of the Housing Assistance Supply Experiment.* Mark D. Menchik. January 1980.

Participants' Attitudes

R-2259-HUD. *Public Perceptions of Housing Allowances: The First Two Years.* Phyllis L. Ellickson, David E. Kanouse. September 1979.

P-5960. *How the Public Views Housing Allowances.* Phyllis L. Ellickson, David E. Kanouse. August 1978.

Program Administration

N-1145-HUD. *Controlling Errors in Allowance Program Administration.* Paul E. Tebbets. August 1979.

N-1276-HUD. *Analyzing Allowance Program Administrative Costs: Accounting Structures and Methodology.* G. Thomas Kingsley, Priscilla M. Schlegel. December 1979.

N-1277-HUD. *Allowance Program Administration: Interim Findings.* G. Thomas Kingsley. December 1979.

N-1740-HUD. *Income Certification in an Experimental Housing Allowance Program.* W. Eugene Rizor. Forthcoming (1982).

N-1741-HUD. *Housing Allowances and Administrative Efficiency.* G. Thomas Kingsley, Priscilla Schlegel. May 1982.

N-1846-HUD. *Housing Allowance Program Administration: Findings from the Supply Experiment.* G. Thomas Kingsley, Sheila Nataraj Kirby, W. Eugene Rizor. May 1982.

MARKET AND COMMUNITY RESPONSE TO PROGRAM

Market Response

R-2452-HUD. *How Housing Allowances Affect Housing Prices.* C. Lance Barnett, Ira S. Lowry. September 1979.

R-2453-HUD. *Shortrun Response of Housing Markets to Demand Shifts.* C. Peter Rydell. September 1979.

R-2659-HUD. *The Role of Market Intermediaries in a Housing Allowance Program.* Michael G. Shanley, Charles M. Hotchkiss. December 1980.

R-2677-HUD. *Price Increases Caused by Housing Assistance Programs.* C. Peter Rydell, John E. Mulford, Lawrence Helbers. October 1980.

R-2720-HUD. *Price Effects of a Housing Allowance Program.* C. Peter Rydell, Kevin Neels, C. Lance Barnett. Forthcoming (1982).

R-2776-HUD. *Measuring Neighborhood Change due to Housing Allowances.* Carol E. Hillestad, James L. McDowell. Forthcoming (1982).

N-1102-HUD. *Inflation in the Standard Cost of Adequate Housing: Site I, 1973-1976.* Ira S. Lowry. October 1979. (First issued as WN-9430-HUD, March 1976.)

N-1116-HUD. *Rent Inflation in St. Joseph County, Indiana: 1974-77.* James P. Stucker. November 1979. (First issued as WN-9734-HUD, September 1977.)

N-1134-HUD. *Rent Inflation in Brown County, Wisconsin: 1973-78.* James P. Stucker. March 1981. (First issued as WN-10073-HUD, August 1978.)

N-1338-HUD. *Supply Response to the Housing Allowance Program.* C. Peter Rydell. October 1980.

N-1339-HUD. *How Housing Allowances Affect Housing Markets: Supply Experiment Interim Findings.* Wayne D. Perry. August 1980.

N-1468-HUD. *Rent Inflation in St. Joseph County, Indiana, 1974-78.* D. Scott Lindsay, Ira S. Lowry. November 1980.

P-5564. *Measuring the Supply Response to Housing Allowances.* C. Peter Rydell. January 1976.

P-6184. *Expected and Actual Effects of Housing Allowances on Housing Prices.* C. Lance Barnett. January 1979.

Community Attitudes

R-2190-HUD. *Public Knowledge and Evaluation of Housing Allowances: St. Joseph County, Indiana, 1975*. Phyllis L. Ellickson. February 1978.

R-2259-HUD. *Public Perceptions of Housing Allowances: The First Two Years*. Phyllis L. Ellickson, David E. Kanouse. September 1979.

R-2475-HUD. *Landlord Knowledge and Evaluation of Housing Allowances: St. Joseph County, Indiana, 1975*. David E. Kanouse. May 1980.

P-5960. *How the Public Views Housing Allowances*. Phyllis L. Ellickson, David E. Kanouse. August 1978.

Site Monitor Reports

N-1085-HUD. *Brown County Press Coverage of the Housing Assistance Supply Experiment and the Allowance Program: December 1972-December 1974*. Earl S. Carter (comp.). May 1981. (First issued as WN-9015-HUD, March 1975.)

N-1086-HUD. *South Bend Press Coverage of the Housing Assistance Supply Experiment and the Allowance Program: January 1974-December 1974*. Earl Carter (comp.). May 1981. (First issued as WN-9016-HUD, March 1975.)

N-1220-HUD. *Monitoring the Housing Allowance Program in St. Joseph County, Indiana: July-September 1974*. Michael Shanley. March 1981. (First issued as WN-9723-HUD, December 1977.)

N-1221-HUD. *Monitoring the Housing Allowance Program in St. Joseph County, Indiana: September 1974-March 1975*. Nancy O'Nell, Michael Shanley. March 1981. (First issued as WN-9724-HUD, December 1977.)

N-1222-HUD. *Monitoring the Housing Allowance Program in St. Joseph County, Indiana: April-August 1975*. Nancy O'Nell, Michael Shanley. March 1981. (First issued as WN-9725-HUD, December 1977.)

N-1223-HUD. *Monitoring the Housing Allowance Program in St. Joseph County, Indiana: September-December 1975*. Nancy O'Nell, Michael Shanley. March 1981. (First issued as WN-9726-HUD, December 1977.)

N-1224-HUD. *Monitoring the Housing Allowance Program in St. Joseph County, Indiana: January-June 1976*. Nancy O'Nell, Michael Shanley. April 1981. (First issued as WN-9727-HUD, December 1977.)

N-1225-HUD. *Monitoring the Housing Allowance Program in St. Joseph County, Indiana: July-September 1976*. Nancy O'Nell, Wim Wiewel. April 1981. (First issued as WN-9728-HUD, December 1977.)

N-1226-HUD. *Monitoring the Housing Allowance Program in St. Joseph County, Indiana: October-December 1976*. Nancy O'Nell, Wim Wiewel. May 1981. (First issued as WN-10086-HUD, January 1979.)

N-1227-HUD. *Monitoring the Housing Allowance Program in St. Joseph County, Indiana: January-March 1977*. Wim Wiewel, Nancy O'-Nell. May 1981. (First issued as WN-10139-HUD, February 1979.)

GENERAL MARKET ANALYSIS

Market Structure and Condition

R-2453-HUD. *Shortrun Response of Housing Markets to Demand Shifts*. C. Peter Rydell. September 1979.

N-1082-HUD. *Rental Housing in Site I: Characteristics of the Capital Stock at Baseline*. C. Peter Rydell. November 1979. (First issued as WN-8978-HUD, August 1975.)

N-1083-HUD. *Rental Housing in Site I: Market Structure and Conditions at Baseline*. C. Peter Rydell, Joseph Friedman. October 1979. (First issued as WN-8980-HUD, April 1975.)

N-1135-HUD. *Vacancy Duration and Housing Market Condition*. C. Peter Rydell. October 1979. (First issued as WN-10074-HUD, January 1978.)

P-6008. *Effects of Market Conditions on Prices and Profits of Rental Housing*. C. Peter Rydell. September 1977.

Housing Demand

R-2449-HUD. *Income Elasticity of Housing Demand*. John E. Mulford. July 1979.

R-2650-HUD. *The Demand for Housing Space and Quality*. C. Lance Barnett, Charles W. Noland. July 1981.

N-1091-HUD. *Housing Choices and Residential Mobility in Site I at Baseline*. Kevin F. McCarthy. October 1979. (First issued as WN-9029-HUD, August 1976.)

N-1094-HUD. *Measuring Homeowner Needs for Housing Assistance*. Lawrence Helbers. October 1980. (First issued as WN-9079-HUD, February 1978.)

N-1119-HUD. *Housing Choices and Residential Mobility in Site II at Baseline*. Kevin F. McCarthy. October 1979. (First issued as WN-9737-HUD, September 1977.)

N-1192-HUD. *Estimated Effects of Increased Income on Homeowner Repair Expenditures*. Lawrence Helbers. November 1979.

N-1542-HUD. *Families, Housing, and the Demand for Energy*. Kevin Neels. April 1981.

P-5565. *The Household Life Cycle and Housing Choices*. Kevin F. McCarthy. January 1976.

P-6473. *Housing Search and Consumption Adjustment*. Kevin McCarthy. April 1980.

Housing Supply

R-2775-HUD. *The Economics of Rental Housing*. Kevin Neels. Forthcoming (1982).

R-2777-HUD. *Determinants of Housing Repair and Improvement*. Lawrence Helbers, James L. McDowell. Forthcoming (1982).

R-2846-HUD. *Price Elasticities of Housing Supply*. C. Peter Rydell. Forthcoming (1982).

N-1704-HUD. *Revenue and Expense Accounts for Rental Properties*. Kevin Neels. March 1982.

N-1744-HUD. *Specification Bias in Housing Production Functions*. Kevin Neels. May 1982.

N-1774-HUD. *Measuring Housing Quality: Evidence from St. Joseph County*. Orhan M. Yildiz, John E. Mulford. Forthcoming (1982).

P-6587. *Measuring Capital's Contribution to Housing Services Production*. Kevin Neels, C. Peter Rydell. February 1981.

Market Intermediaries

N-1060-HUD. *Market Intermediaries and Indirect Suppliers: Reconnaissance and Research Design for Site I*. William G. Grigsby, Michael Shanley, Sammis B. White. July 1980. (First issued as WN-8577-HUD, February 1974.)

N-1087-HUD. *Market Intermediaries and Indirect Suppliers: First Year Report for Site II*. Sammis B. White. December 1979. (First issued as WN-9020-HUD, August 1977.)

N-1089-HUD. *Market Intermediaries and Indirect Suppliers: Reconnaissance and Research Design for Site II*. William G. Grigsby, Michael Shanley, Sammis B. White, July 1980. (First issued as WN-9026-HUD, May 1975.)

N-1101-HUD. *Market Intermediaries and Indirect Suppliers: First Year Report for Site I*. Sammis B. White. November 1979. (First issued as WN-9400-HUD, September 1976.)

N-1208-HUD. *How Low-Income Renters Buy Homes*. Michael G. Shanley, Charles M. Hotchkiss. August 1979.

Residential Mobility

R-2451-HUD. *Housing Search and Mobility*. Kevin F. McCarthy. September 1979.

N-1091-HUD. *Housing Choices and Residential Mobility in Site I at Baseline*. Kevin F. McCarthy. October 1979. (First issued as WN-9029-HUD, August 1976.)

N-1119-HUD. *Housing Choices and Residential Mobility in Site II at Baseline*. Kevin F. McCarthy. October 1979. (First issued as WN-9737-HUD, September 1977.)

P-5565. *The Household Life Cycle and Housing Choices*. Kevin F. McCarthy. January 1976.

P-6473. *Housing Search and Consumption Adjustment*. Kevin McCarthy. April 1980.

P-6487. *A Three-Stage Model of Housing Search*. Kevin McCarthy. May 1980.

Neighborhood Studies

N-1055-HUD. *Neighborhoods in Brown County*. Bryan C. Ellickson. December 1980. (First issued as WN-8468-HUD, November 1973.)

N-1077-HUD. *Index to the Site I Maps*. Doris Dong. March 1981. (First issued as WN-8819-HUD, August 1974.)

N-1127-HUD. *Index to the Site II Maps*. Housing Assistance Supply Experiment Staff. May 1981. (First issued as WN-9901-HUD, December 1977.)

N-1205-HUD. *Neighborhoods in St. Joseph County, Indiana*. John E. Bala. September 1979.

P-6225. *Hungarian-Americans in St. Joseph County, Indiana: Implications of Ethnicity for Social Policy*. Wim Wiewel. March 1979.

HOUSING COST AND PRICE INDEXES

Hedonic Indexes

R-2450-HUD. *Using Hedonic Indexes To Measure Housing Quantity.* C. Lance Barnett. October 1979.

N-1069-HUD. *Using Hedonic Indexes To Measure Supply Response to Housing Allowances.* C. Lance Barnett. March 1981. (First issued as WN-8686-HUD, August 1976.)

N-1305-HUD. *Assessing Hedonic Indexes for Housing.* Charles W. Noland. May 1980.

Cost-of-Production Indexes

N-1088-HUD. *Indexing the Cost of Producing Housing Services: Site I, 1973.* Charles W. Noland. April 1981. (First issued as WN-9022-HUD, January 1977.)

N-1117-HUD. *Indexing the Cost of Producing Housing Services: Site I, 1973-74.* Charles W. Noland. April 1981. (First issued as WN-9735-HUD, April 1977.)

N-1118-HUD. *Indexing the Cost of Producing Housing Services: Site II, 1974.* Charles W. Noland. April 1981. (First issued as WN-9736-HUD, May 1977.)

N-1129-HUD. *Indexing the Cost of Producing Housing Services in Site I, 1973-75.* Charles W. Noland. April 1981. (First issued as WN-9979-HUD, June 1978.)

N-1130-HUD. *Indexing the Cost of Producing Housing Services in Site II, 1974-75.* Charles W. Noland. May 1981. (First issued as WN-9980-HUD, May 1978.)

N-1627-HUD. *Indexing the Cost of Producing Housing Services for Site I, 1973-76.* Charles W. Noland. September 1981.

N-1653-HUD. *Indexing the Cost of Producing Housing Services in Site II, 1974-77.* Charles W. Noland. February 1982.

Rent Indexes

N-1102-HUD. *Inflation in the Standard Cost of Adequate Housing: Site I, 1973-1976.* Ira S. Lowry. October 1979. (First issued as WN-9430-HUD, March 1976.)

N-1116-HUD. *Rent Inflation in St. Joseph County, Indiana: 1974-77.*

James P. Stucker. November 1979. (First issued as WN-9734-HUD, September 1977.)

N-1134-HUD. *Rent Inflation in Brown County, Wisconsin: 1973-78.* James P. Stucker. March 1981. (First issued as WN-10073-HUD, August 1978.)

N-1468-HUD. *Rent Inflation in St. Joseph County, Indiana, 1974-78.* D. Scott Lindsay, Ira S. Lowry. November 1980.

Appendix B

DATA FILES AND DOCUMENTATION AVAILABLE FROM THE HOUSING ASSISTANCE SUPPLY EXPERIMENT

The research findings of the Housing Assistance Supply Experiment are based primarily on administrative records from five years of allowance program operations in Brown and St. Joseph counties, and on four annual marketwide surveys of residential properties in each county. Rand has organized the data thus collected into user-oriented research files and documented them for public use. The files and documentation have been deposited with the Housing Research Data Center, sponsored by HUD and operated by Data Use and Access Laboratories (DUALabs), Arlington, Virginia. Persons interested in access to these files should contact the Housing Research Data Center.

The HASE data base consists of 40 machine-readable files. The 8 *program files* contain information from HAO administrative records about clients and program operations during the program's first five years. The 32 *survey files* reflect information collected in the HASE surveys of residential properties and neighborhoods conducted about the same time. We used the program data to monitor the program itself; the survey data informed us about program effects on the surrounding housing market. The program files should be useful to analysts interested in housing allowances, income transfers, or program administration. The survey files should be useful to those interested in housing characteristics and consumption patterns, residential repair and rehabilitation, residential mobility, rental property management and finance, or housing market structure and dynamics.

To protect the privacy of HAO clients and survey respondents, some entries in these files were suppressed or transformed prior to delivering them to DUALabs. In our judgment, these changes do not materially reduce the usefulness of the data to researchers.

The *User's Guide to HASE Data,* Refs. 1-3, provides technical guidance for accessing and manipulating the data in these files, as well as a topical index of the variables in each. Below, we offer more general descriptions of the files that will enable the reader to assess their relevance to his research interests.

PROGRAM FILES

The program files were compiled from data collected on various HAO administrative forms. Some of the data were gathered to meet HASE research needs; most served HAO administrative needs in monitoring the flow of clients through the program, maintaining records of entitlement and allowance payments, and documenting housing evaluations. The HAOs entered the completed forms into their automated systems and periodically sent the resulting administrative data files to Rand. We recompiled them into four cumulative files for each site: client characteristics file (CCF), housing characteristics file (HCF), recertification characteristics file (RCF), and client history file (CHF).

The program files contain records for every program applicant and client through the first five years of HAO operations, covering the periods 17 June 1974 through 30 June 1979 for Brown County (Site I) and 17 December 1974 through 4 January 1980 for St. Joseph County (Site II).

In all four program files, each logical record pertains to a specific client. Records in the client, housing, and recertification characteristics files are of fixed length, though the amount of data per HCF and RCF record depends on the number of the client's housing and recertification transactions, respectively. In the client history file, each logical record may contain many physical records of different lengths and types. Table B.1 indicates the number of logical records in each file and the types of clients represented.

Table B.1

CLIENT GROUPS REPRESENTED IN THE PROGRAM FILES

File	Group	Number of Records	
		Site I	Site II
CCF	Applicants	16,670	34,657
	Applicants interviewed for eligibility	11,802	23,017
	Clients ever enrolled	9,133	16,126
	Clients enrolled at end of year 5	4,136	7,367
HCF	Clients ever enrolled	9,133	16,126
RCF	Clients ever enrolled	9,133	16,126
CHF	Applicants	16,670	34,657

SOURCES: Refs. 4-9, 14.

File Contents

The detailed contents of the files are given in Tables B.2 through B.5. A general idea is best conveyed by a brief review of the client's course through the program. Each applicant was screened for program eligibility on the basis of his application form and enrollment interview. The contents of those forms appear in the client characteristics file, along with the client's characteristics and enrollment status at the time of his last transaction before the end of the five-year period (see Table B.2).

If an applicant was found eligible, his housing unit was evaluated according to program standards. If the unit failed to meet the standards, the client could repair it or move to better quarters. In either case, he had to request another housing evaluation for the new or repaired unit. If the unit passed the evaluation, allowance payments were authorized. The housing characteristics file documents all housing evaluations; these include the initial evaluation of the enrollment unit, inspections of other units the client considered occupying or had moved into, reevaluations of repaired units, and annual recertification evaluations (see Table B.3).

For a client to remain in the program, his household had to continue to meet eligibility tests and comply with the HAO's administrative regulations. Any changes in household characteristics affecting eligibility or the amount of the allowance payment were recorded either as they became known or during the annual recertification process. All such changes, other corrections or revisions of the client's records, and changes in client status or payments because of administrative policies (such as the periodic revision of benefit schedules) are recorded in the recertification characteristics file (see Table B.4).

To allow for both detailed and cursory views of the entire process, the client history file combines all information from the other three files[1] into a single comprehensive dossier for each client, and adds a new record summarizing the client's program history (see Table B.5).

File Documentation

The HASE *User's Guide* (Ref. 3) describes the origin, structure, and contents of the program files, presents a topical index of the variables

[1]The CHF also contains a few specialized variables from HAO administrative files that do not appear in any other analysis file. Because the size and complexity of the CHF make it somewhat cumbersome to use, the CCF, HCF, and RCF were retained to facilitate data processing for analysis designs that do not require the full range of client data.

Table B.2

CONTENTS OF THE CLIENT CHARACTERISTICS FILE

Topic	Information Recorded
1. Client identification	Client ID, previous client ID, housing unit ID at close of file. Neighborhood code and census tract of housing unit at preliminary application, enrollment, and close of file.
2. Eligibility and participation	Dates and circumstances of preliminary application, enrollment interview, and most recent client recertification and housing unit reevaluation. Dates and reasons for enrollment, termination, and reinstatement. Number of housing evaluation requests and number of acceptable housing units.
3. Household characteristics	Total household size, number of eligible household members at preliminary application, enrollment, and last recertification or close of file. For each household member: age, sex, race, and relationship to head of household. Family structure, life-cycle stage, assets, including value of house, income, and occupation.
4. Housing characteristics and expenses	Tenure at preliminary application, enrollment, and close of file; whether unit is owned, rented, federally subsidized; date of lease, move-in date, monthly expenses for rent, mortgage, interest, utilities, taxes, insurance and maintenance for residences at enrollment and close of file; physical characteristics of dwelling; nonresidential use of property.
5. Allowance payments	Date payments authorized, maximum entitlement, number of authorizations, amount of last monthly payment, total gross and advance payments, date of last payment change; current annual cost of housing.

SOURCE: Adapted from Ref. 4, p. 4.
NOTE: Each client record contains 665 variables.

they contain, and offers guidance for using the files and selecting and linking records.

The client, housing, and recertification characteristics files are documented more specifically in a series of codebooks and audit reports. The codebooks, one per file in each site (Refs. 4-9), define each variable and present a frequency distribution of its values; they also

Table B.3

CONTENTS OF THE HOUSING CHARACTERISTICS FILE

Topic	Information Recorded
1. Evaluation information	For each evaluation: presence of administrative forms, completion status, previous action, form serial number, request date, number and date of contacts and appointments, evaluation date, evaluation type and reason (payment authorization annual reevaluation, correction, update, etc.). Dates for HAO action on evaluation, unit certification, special reevaluation for paint deficiency, and payment authorization. Number of evaluations per client.
2. Unit identification	Unit ID, neighborhood and census tract, occupancy status, lease date for rental unit.
3. Building and unit characteristics	Building type and description: number of residential units, levels, basements, porches, commercial or industrial units; siding and roofing materials, roof type, garage spaces, other buildings on property, location of evaluated unit in the building, type of access, ratings for building exterior and interior, presence of flaking or peeling paint; total number of rooms in unit, habitable rooms and bedrooms, presence of bath and kitchen facilities, bath and kitchen adequacy, maximum occupancy.
4. Repair data	Unit improvements since the last evaluation: item repaired, type and location of repair, who did it, who paid for it, cost of individual repairs, and total cost.
5. Evaluation results	Habitability rating, summary condition rating, special review determination, adequacy of space for occupants, evaluation finding, overall acceptability.
6. Client characteristics	All variables from the client characteristics file (see Table B.2), plus tenure at the time of evaluation and payment authorization, whether client is receiving payments; monthly housing expenses: rent, utilities, mortgage interest, real estate taxes, insurance, maintenance, and other housing expenses.

SOURCE: Adapted from Ref. 5, p. 3.

NOTE: Each client record contains header information, plus 35 segments of 215 variables each. Each segment contains data for one housing evaluation, ordered chronologically; unused segments are blank.

Table B.4

CONTENTS OF THE RECERTIFICATION CHARACTERISTICS FILE

Topic	Information Recorded
1. Interview information	Length of interview, transaction type, recertification type, date of interview, signature date, processing date, effective date of information.
2. Housing characteristics	Neighborhood and census tract, unit type, uses of property, appliances and furniture provided, mortgage status, full rent or not, utilities paid for.
3. Household characteristics	Eligibility status, total size of household, family structure, life-cycle stage, tenure, move-in date, assets, income, home value, allowance entitlement.
4. Housing expenses	Rent, utilities, interest, taxes, insurance, maintenance, total housing expenses, mortgage principal and interest.
5. Client characteristics	Summary of information from the client characteristics file (see Table B.2).

SOURCE: Adapted from Ref. 6, p. 3.

NOTE: Each client record contains header information, plus 40 segments of 120 variables each. Each segment contains data for one recertification transaction, ordered chronologically; unused segments are blank.

reproduce the various HAO administrative forms on which the data were originally recorded.[2]

To assess and improve the quality of the data, we subjected them to computerized and manual checks at every stage of recompiling the HAO administrative files into program files. Suspected errors were investigated and corrected or replaced with an audit code signifying the absence of usable data. Those procedures and their results are described in four audit reports, two for each site, covering cumulative CCF, HCF, and RCF data as of year 3 and again as of year 5 (Refs. 10-13). File users are encouraged to review those reports to better understand the files and the quality of information they contain.

[2]The codebooks reflect file contents prior to privacy protection. To conceal clients' identities, the values of certain variables were suppressed or transformed (see Ref. 3, Appendix A); the codebook definitions and response codes for those variables no longer apply. In addition, some data errors were discovered too late for codebook publication, though the files themselves were corrected.

Table B.5

CONTENTS OF THE CLIENT HISTORY FILE

Topic	Information Recorded
1. Digital client history	Chronological summary of every transaction pertaining to each client while in the program. Location of supporting detail elsewhere in the file. Indicators for selecting clients with similar characteristics to form analytic subsamples.
2. Client characteristics	(Table B.2)
3. Housing characteristics	(Table B.3, topics 1-5)
4. Recertification characteristics	(Table B.4, topics 1-4)
5. Payment suspensions and reauthorizations	Circumstances and timing of payment suspensions and subsequent reauthorizations.
6. Exceptional payment adjustments	Circumstances and timing of payment adjustments not covered by normal HAO computer algorithms.

SOURCE: Ref. 14.

NOTE: Each client record (dossier) can contain up to seven types of physical records of different lengths, and as many of each type as are needed to document the client's participation history.

The client history file is documented separately in a report that combines the functions of user's guide, codebook, and audit report (Ref. 14).

SURVEY FILES

To determine how the program affected the local housing market and community, Rand conducted four annual cycles of field surveys in the two sites.[3] The first or baseline wave of the surveys was conducted in 1974 in Brown County (Site I) and in 1975 in St. Joseph County (Site II), in each case just before the allowance program began enrolling clients. Figure B.1 depicts the timing of all surveys in relation to the allowance program.

The survey agenda was large and complex. Separate but linked surveys of landlords, households (tenants and homeowners), and residential buildings were addressed to a panel of residential properties in

[3]In Brown County, Mathematica, Inc. conducted the first survey wave as subcontractor to Rand; the National Opinion Research Center (NORC) conducted waves 2 through 4. In St. Joseph County, all waves were conducted by Westat, Inc.

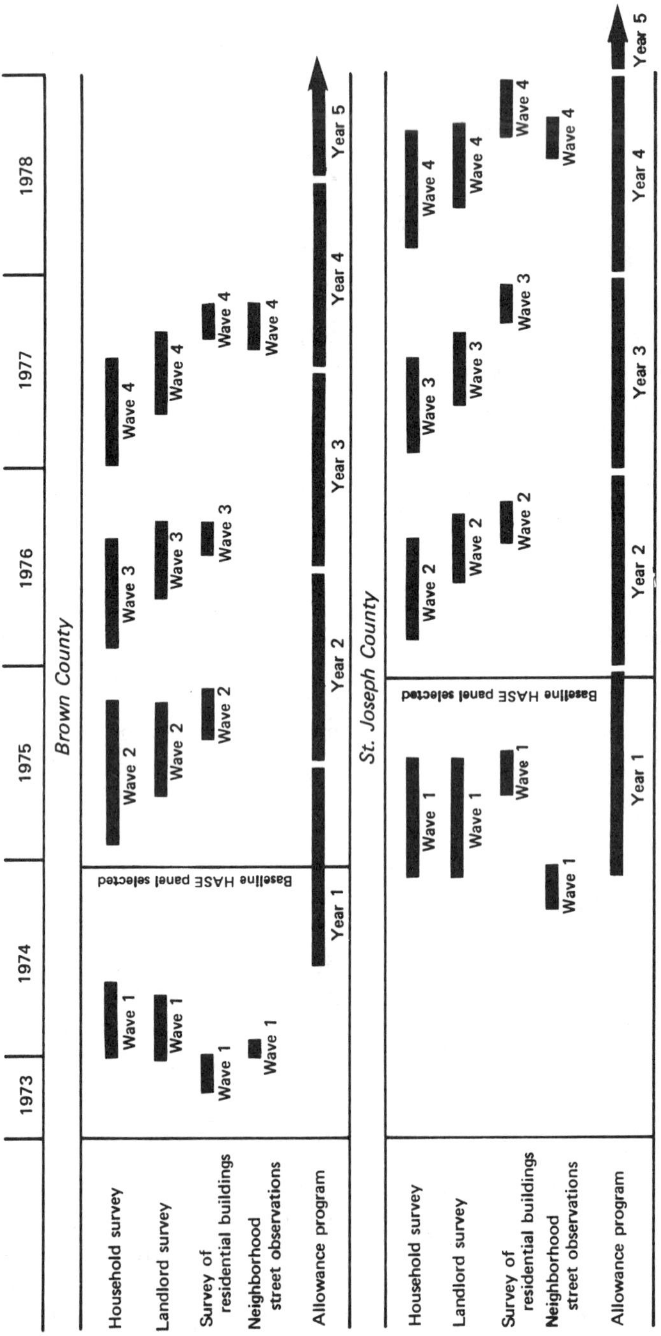

Fig. B.1—Timing of HASE survey fieldwork in relation to allowance program, by site

each site. Neighborhood surveys covered the entire county, with HASE-defined neighborhoods and street segments as units of observation.

The Panel of Residential Properties

The basic sample element was the property, the smallest unit of real estate for which an owner maintained a separate account. The sampling frame consisted of all residential tax parcels in each county. From them we chose a stratified probability sample, surveyed those properties at baseline, then selected the HASE panel of about 2,000 properties in each site from survey records with complete baseline data.[4]

To select the panel, properties surveyed at baseline were stratified by tenure (rental or ownership), location (urban or rural), number of dwelling units (1, 2-4, 5+), and rent or value (tercile or quartile of the countywide distribution). Rooming houses and mobile homes were in separate strata. Each stratum was then sampled to yield a panel with the desired composition. Each year after baseline a sample of properties newly converted to residential use was surveyed and added to the panel to keep it representative of the current housing market.

The classical problem with longitudinal panels is attrition, or loss of sample elements over time. Our sample elements were properties, parcels of land that are never physically lost. They can be subdivided or merged and converted to a different tenure or nonresidential use, but those were phenomena we wanted to observe. After the baseline HASE panel was selected, attrition was generally limited to cases for which we were unable to complete an annual interview with both the property's owner and some of its tenants. Such properties remained in the panel to be resurveyed the following year.

File Preparation

At the end of fieldwork for a given survey, the completed questionnaires were sent to Rand, where verbatim responses were coded and all responses were entered into machine-readable records, which were then edited and collated into a preliminary master file. We next

---

[4]Housing units on empaneled properties were designated for the household survey; on large properties, only a sample of all dwellings was empaneled. All buildings containing empaneled dwellings were covered in the survey of residential buildings. Sample selection is described in more detail in Ref. 1.

audited that file to assess the completeness and quality of the data. Auditors accounted for the sample by reconciling each record received from the field with the master sample list, checked response distributions in search of implausible values, and calculated weights for individual records so that they would collectively represent the sampled populations. We also augmented the file with derived variables, consisting of transformations of original survey responses, data from other sources, and sample-selection indicators. After running error checks on the derived variables, we archived the augmented file as a final master file.

Survey Results

The survey cycles produced 16 files for each site: four each for the landlord, household, and residential building surveys (waves 1 through 4), and two each for the neighborhood local sources and street observation surveys (waves 1 and 4).

Table B.6 displays the number of records in each file—for both the total sample and the "field-complete" subset representing completed interviews or observations. Completion rates for the landlord and household interview surveys are lower than those for the residential building and neighborhood surveys because the latter depended on direct observation or secondary research and did not require the cooperation of a respondent.[5] The incomplete records in the interview surveys are about evenly divided between cases in which fieldworkers were unable to contact the desired respondent despite repeated attempts and cases in which a contacted respondent refused to grant an interview.

The data available for longitudinal analysis can be gauged by the number of properties and rental units for which we obtained complete data for three and four waves (see Table B.7). Although we empaneled about the same number of properties in each site, higher nonresponse rates and more vacancies in St. Joseph County resulted in fewer longitudinally complete records there.

File Contents

Below, we describe the information contained in the files for each survey.

---

[5]Completion rates for the wave 1 landlord survey are high because they reflect completion rates for subsequently empaneled properties rather than all properties in the baseline sample; except for a few cases in St. Joseph County, field completion was a criterion for empanelment.

Table B.6

Summary of Records on HASE Survey Files

Survey Wave	Brown County (Site I) Total Number of Records	Brown County (Site I) Number of Field-Complete Records[a]	Brown County (Site I) Completion Rate[b]	St. Joseph County (Site II) Total Number of Records	St. Joseph County (Site II) Number of Field-Complete Records[a]	St. Joseph County (Site II) Completion Rate[b]
Landlord Survey						
Wave 1	1,320	1,320	1.00[c]	1,417	1,404	.99[c]
Wave 2	1,360	1,105	.81	1,444	915	.63
Wave 3	1,347	935	.69	1,394	935	.67
Wave 4	1,314	910	.69	1,346	831	.62
All waves	5,341	4,270	.80	5,601	4,085	.73
Household Survey						
Wave 1	3,293	2,712	.82	3,559	2,066	.58
Wave 2	3,389	2,472	.73	3,603	1,958	.54
Wave 3	3,541	2,360	.67	3,696	2,143	.58
Wave 4	3,621	2,424	.67	3,686	2,103	.57
All waves	13,844	9,968	.72	14,544	8,270	.57
Residential Building Survey						
Wave 1	2,153	2,116	.98	2,515	2,366	.94
Wave 2	2,225	2,075	.93	10	6	.60
Wave 3	139	107	.77	140	131	.94
Wave 4	2,325	2,263	.97	2,557	2,429	.95
All waves	6,842	6,561	.96	5,222	4,932	.95
Neighborhood Local Sources Survey						
Wave 1	108	108	1.00	86	86	1.00
Wave 4	108	108	1.00	86	86	1.00
All waves	216	216	1.00	172	172	1.00

Table B.6—continued

Neighborhood Street Observation Survey

Wave 1	8,084	8,084	1.00	12,152	12,152	1.00
Wave 4	9,315	9,256	.99	12,933	12,852	.99
All waves	17,399	17,340	1.00	25,085	25,004	1.00

SOURCE: Tabulated by HASE staff from the final master files for all surveys.

[a]Records representing completed interviews or observations.

[b]Field-complete records divided by total records.

[c]These rates are extremely high because the wave 1 files consist only of the records for empaneled properties (not all properties in the larger baseline sample), and field completion was a criterion for empanelment.

Survey of Landlords. The survey of landlords elicited a detailed description of the ownership, management, and finances of the rental properties in the sample. The instrument was designed to enable us to learn how the owners of rental properties responded to the market stimulus provided by the allowance program.

In each wave, the interview sought a record of landlord rental revenues and expenses for building maintenance and operation during the preceding year, including a detailed account of repairs and improvements and their costs. We also gathered data on mortgage financing, property ownership and management, property and tenant characteristics, landlord-tenant relationships, and plans for the property. Finally, we sought landlords' impressions of the allowance program and how it had affected them.

The landlord survey files each contain about 2,800 survey variables and 200 derived variables.[6] Table B.8 describes the information contained in the files.

Household Survey. From the current tenants of each rental property in the sample, we sought a description of the interior features and condition of the dwelling, the amounts of contract rent and any other housing expenses, and an evaluation of the dwelling, the landlord, and the neighborhood. As background for analysis, we also obtained information on household composition and family characteristics, income, education, and occupation. An important element of

[6]Throughout this discussion, the numbers of survey and derived variables we cite per file are averages; the actual numbers vary because of instrument revisions and changing analytic needs.

Table B.7

AVAILABILITY OF LONGITUDINAL DATA FROM HASE SURVEYS OF RESIDENTIAL PROPERTIES

	Elements Represented by Field-Complete Records			
	Brown County		St. Joseph County	
Sampling Element	3 Waves	4 Waves	3 Waves	4 Waves
Rental property	800	501	554	248
Rental unit	1,261	621	712	264
Homeowner property	501	376	405	288

SOURCE: Calculated by HASE staff from the final master files of landlord and household surveys, all waves.

NOTE: To qualify for enumeration here, *rental properties* had to be represented by field-complete records in both the landlord survey (landlord respondent) and household survey (at least one tenant respondent--not necessarily the same one each wave); *rental units* on empaneled properties had to be represented by complete records for the owner of the property and the current occupant of that specific unit; vacant units are excluded. *Homeowner properties* required complete data from only the owner, responding to the household survey. Properties and units that were merged or subdivided are excluded from this account.

the first interview with a given household[7] was a five-year residential and employment history for each household head, including household, housing, and employment characteristics at the time of each move.

The interview for homeowners covered similar ground but also included detailed questions on mortgage financing and housing expenses similar to those addressed to landlords.

[7]Each year, we interviewed the *current* residents of empaneled dwellings; households that moved after such an interview were not followed to their new residences. Because the panel of dwellings was annually updated by sampling new construction, each year's sample of households can be weighted to represent the current countywide population of households.

Table B.8

CONTENTS OF THE LANDLORD SURVEY FILES

Topic	Information Recorded
Verification	Verification of owner and type of ownership. Number and relationship of owners. Names of other respondents appointed to answer certain sections of the instrument.
Acquisition and ownership	How property was acquired; reason for acquisition; purchase price. Capital improvements made by previous owner.
Experience and activity in real estate	Number of rental properties owned in county; percentage of income derived from real estate; length of time owner active in real estate; nature of other business involvement. Participation in property owners, real estate, or other organizations. Knowledge of tenant organizations.
Property description	Changes in property since previous year. Number and age of buildings; number and size of residential units; number of commercial units and mobile homes. Average monthly rent for each type of residential unit.
Income	Income received from property. Losses due to vacancies and bad debts. Type and amount of federal housing assistance received (Site II).
Expenses	Types of employees, wages, rent discounts. Use of management firm, lawyers, accountants, brokers, and other professional assistance. Office expenses. Utility costs.
Repairs and improvements	Expenses for remodeling, decorating, appliance replacement and repair, and repair work of all kinds. Description of each repair to determine whether it was operating or capital expense. Materials and labor costs. Imputed value of time spent by owner and unpaid workers on property's management and maintenance.

Table B.8—continued

Topic	Information Recorded
Mortgage, taxes, and insurance	Costs and terms associated with all mortgages, taxes, and property insurance.
Tenants	Turnover rates, evictions, tenant complaints, lease policies, and satisfaction with tenants.
Neighborhood	Characteristics of the neighborhood and perceptions of change. Satisfaction with neighborhood as place to own rental property.
Plans for property	Condition of residential buildings on the property. Plans for capital improvements. Owner's evaluation of future market value and financial return from the property.
Attitudes	Respondent's knowledge of and attitude about the housing allowance program.
Previous owner's account	For portion of the year property was owned: income and expenses for property management, maintenance, repairs, improvements, mortgages, taxes, and insurance.

SOURCE: Adapted from Ref. 48, p. 6.

Both tenants and homeowners were asked about their perceptions of the allowance program and its effects on their housing and neighborhoods. Since the sample included both program participants and nonparticipants, both views are represented.

The household survey files each contain about 4,400 survey variables and 250 derived variables. Table B.9 describes the contents of the files.

Survey of Residential Buildings. Through direct observation, the survey of residential buildings gathered data on the physical characteristics and condition of residential buildings, the properties on which they stood, and their immediate neighborhoods. The survey instrument was designed to detect alterations or improvements, changes in the physical condition or use of the property, and changes in the neighborhood.

Observers conducted the survey from on the sampled property unless the resident objected or access was physically impeded. Then, they attempted the observation from an off-property vantage point.

Table B.9

CONTENTS OF THE HOUSEHOLD SURVEY FILES

Topic	Information Recorded
Introduction	Primary characteristics of housing unit--type of residence, tenure of respondent, (tenant, homeowner, mobile home resident, lodger).
Characteristics	Description of residence and its condition. Respondent's level of satisfaction with various aspects of the dwelling. Perception of neighborhood characteristics. Proximity to friends and relatives. Tenant's relations with landlord.
Housing expenses	For tenants, contract rent and special considerations affecting rent. For homeowners, date and method of acquiring property, costs and terms associated with all mortgages and taxes. For all respondents, costs of utilities, major remodeling, other repairs and improvements, and insurance.
Mobility history	Location, housing characteristics, expenses, and dates of previous residences; perception of former neighborhood and reasons for moving to present address. Methods used to find present dwelling and costs of moving.
Employment history	Industry, occupation, and wage rate of respondent and spouse for present and previous jobs. Time, distance, and mode of travel to work. (Separate data for male and female heads of household.)
Household composition, income, and ethnicity	For all regular members of the household: name, age, sex, relationship to respondents, school enrollment, and grade. Household income by source. Ethnic background.
Evaluation of housing allowance program	Respondent's knowledge of and attitudes about the housing allowance program.

SOURCE: Adapted from Ref. 44, p. 3.

Observations were restricted to the exteriors of all buildings and the interior public areas (e.g., hallways, lobbies) of multiunit structures.

The files from the survey of residential buildings each contain about 840 survey variables and 175 derived variables. Table B.10 describes the files' contents.

Neighborhood Survey. The neighborhood survey gathered information on the physical characteristics of the entire county in each site, with HASE-defined neighborhoods and street segments as the units of observation. (A street segment is both sides of a length of

Table B.10

CONTENTS OF THE RESIDENTIAL BUILDING SURVEY FILES

Topic	Information Recorded
Nature of use and tenancy	Building status (inhabitable or uninhabitable), indications of vacancies, presence of commercial or industrial uses, evidence of marketability (vacant buildings).
Physical characteristics of building	Type and layout of structure, placement on lot, observability, principal construction materials.
Related tenant facilities	Availability of garage, carport, and on- or off-street parking. Quality of landscaping, presence of swimming pool, condition of sidewalks.
Exterior condition of building	Presence and condition of exterior items (roof, wall surfaces, doors, windows and screens, porches, foundations, paving, etc.) and overall state of repair.
Interior condition of public areas in multiunit dwellings	Presence and condition of interior items (doors, floors, walls and woodwork, windows, ceilings, lighting fixtures, mailboxes, stairways, banisters, elevator, door locks, fire alarms, and extinguishers), and overall state of repair and cleanliness.
Characteristics of immediate neighborhood	Land uses, vehicular traffic, street lighting, pedestrian walkways, street maintenance, litter, abandoned automobiles and buildings. For other residential buildings in the area, characteristic types, comparative size, age, and landscaping. Beneficial and detrimental features of neighborhood (noise, odors, physical hazards, parks, ponds, woodlands, etc.).

SOURCE: Adapted from Ref. 52, p. 3.

street between intersections.) Neighborhood survey data contributed to analyses of the neighborhood effects of the allowance program, and helped explain differences in the views and behavior of the landlords, tenants, and homeowners interviewed in our other surveys.

We divided each county's territory into mutually exclusive neighborhoods whose boundaries often conformed to those of 1970 census tracts and local planning districts. In the urbanized portion of the county, neighborhoods were small and configured so as to contain relatively homogeneous populations and housing stocks; rural neighborhoods were larger and less homogeneous. Most neighborhoods contained 1,000 to 4,000 residents.

The survey had two parts corresponding to the two observation units. For the local sources survey, fieldworkers compiled data on land-use and public facilities in each neighborhood from records maintained by local agencies; for the street observation survey, fieldworkers recorded the characteristics of each street segment by direct observation. The two parts had separate instruments and produced separate data files (see Table B.11). The local sources files contain 500 survey variables and 20 derived variables each; the street observation files contain 115 survey variables and 10 derived variables each.

File Documentation

The HASE survey files are documented in the *User's Guide*, codebooks, and audit reports.

The *User's Guide* (Ref. 2) describes the origin, structure, and contents of the files in detail, presents a topical index of the variables they contain, and offers guidance for selecting, linking, and weighting records for analytic purposes.

Each file is specifically documented in one or more codebooks that define and present response distributions for every variable, and reproduce the corresponding question from the survey instrument.[8]

There are three types of codebooks. The 14 attitude-module codebooks (Refs. 15-28) document the portions of the landlord and household files reporting respondents' knowledge of and attitudes toward the allowance program. Separate codebooks are warranted because the attitude module of the instrument was designed and administered

[8]The codebooks reflect file contents prior to privacy protection. To conceal respondents' identities, the values of certain variables were suppressed or transformed (see Ref. 2, Appendix A); the codebook definitions and response frequencies for those variables no longer apply. In addition, some data errors were discovered after codebook publication, and the findings of sample accounting necessitated some changes in sample sizes. As a result, response distributions in the codebooks will not necessarily agree with those calculated from the corrected files.

Table B.11

CONTENTS OF THE NEIGHBORHOOD SURVEY FILES

Topic	Information Recorded
	Local Sources Survey
Land uses	Acreage devoted to a selected list of land uses.
Access to facilities and services	Number of facilities (institutional, recreational, religious, educational, commercial) and distance of nearest facility from neighborhood center; church membership and weekly attendance; availability of public and private utility services.
Soil	Effect of soil limitations on residential improvement.
Highways, arterials, public streets, planned highways, and railroads	Description of federal and state routes, major arterials, local streets, planned highways, and railroads, including route-miles.
Bodies of water	Description of lakes, rivers, and streams, including total surface acres, location, and use (swimming, fishing, etc.).
Air and noise pollution	Severity of particulate matter; average noise level. Location of pollution monitoring equipment.
School, crime, and employment statistics	Name and type of school, design capacity, enrollment, teacher-pupil ratios, number of dropouts, and achievement test code and score. Number of major crimes. Number of employers and employees; unemployment statistics.
	Street Observation Survey
Quality and condition ratings	Ratings for residential buildings and landscaping, vacant lots, streets, sidewalks, and overall cleanliness.
Special features	Presence of construction in progress and abandoned buildings or vehicles.
Land uses	Presence of a selected list of land uses or estimates of the percentage of street segment devoted to each land use listed.

SOURCE: Refs. 41, 42, 55, 56.

NOTE: This is a composite description. The contents of individual files vary according to the availability or applicability of data.

differently from the rest of the instrument. The 28 main-survey codebooks (Refs. 29-56) document the rest of the survey files. Twenty-five supplemental codebooks (Refs. 57-81) define every derived variable added to the files, cite the survey or other source variable(s), specify the construction logic, and provide response distributions.

Finally, 30 audit reports (Refs. 82-111) describe the procedures and results of error checks, sample accounting, calculation of weights, and tests for nonresponse bias in each file. Two of the reports detail the special audit procedures for attitude data in the household survey files (Ref. 110) and in the landlord survey files (Ref. 111).

REFERENCES

1. R-2692/1-HUD. *User's Guide to HASE Data, Vol. 1: Overview.* E. Wayne Hansen and Christine D'Arc. April 1982.
2. R-2692/2-HUD. *User's Guide to HASE Data, Vol. 2: The Survey Files.* Patricia Boren. April 1982.
3. R-2692/3-HUD. *User's Guide to HASE Data, Vol. 3: The Program Files.* Ann W. Wang. April 1982.
4. N-1417-HUD. *Codebook for the HAO Client Characteristics File: Site I, Year 5.* Ann W. Wang. October 1980.
5. N-1419-HUD. *Codebook for the HAO Housing Characteristics File: Site I, Year 5.* Ann W. Wang. February 1981.
6. N-1421-HUD. *Codebook for the HAO Recertification Characteristics File: Site I, Year 5.* Ann W. Wang. March 1981.
7. N-1418-HUD. *Codebook for the HAO Client Characteristics File: Site II, Year 5.* Ann W. Wang. September 1981.
8. N-1420-HUD. *Codebook for the HAO Housing Characteristics File: Site II, Year 5.* Ann W. Wang. September 1981.
9. N-1422-HUD. *Codebook for the HAO Recertification Characteristics File: Site II, Year 5.* Ann W. Wang. September 1981.
10. N-1149-HUD. *Audit of the HAO Analysis Files, Site I, Year 3.* Ann W. Wang. May 1979.
11. N-1318-HUD. *Audit of the HAO Analysis Files, Site II, Year 3.* Ann W. Wang. October 1979.
12. N-1423-HUD. *Audit of the HAO Analysis Files, Site I, Year 5.* Ann W. Wang. November 1981.
13. N-1424-HUD. *Audit of the HAO Analysis Files, Site II, Year 5.* Ann W. Wang. Forthcoming.
14. N-1711-HUD. *The HAO Client History File.* Charles A. Hubay and Clairessa Cantrell. Forthcoming.

15. N-1368-HUD. *Codebook for the Attitude Module of the Household Survey, Site I, Wave 2*. Patricia Boren. January 1980.
16. N-1345-HUD. *Codebook for the Attitude Module of the Household Survey, Site I, Wave 3*. Patricia Boren. January 1980.
17. N-1370-HUD. *Codebook for the Attitude Module of the Household Survey, Site I, Wave 4*. Patricia Boren. March 1980.
18. N-1363-HUD. *Codebook for the Attitude Module of the Landlord Survey, Site I, Wave 2*. Roger Johnston, Patricia Boren. January 1980.
19. N-1364-HUD. *Codebook for the Attitude Module of the Landlord Survey, Site I, Wave 3*. Patricia Boren. February 1980.
20. N-1365-HUD. *Codebook for the Attitude Module of the Landlord Survey, Site I, Wave 4*. Patricia Boren, Christina Witsberger. March 1980.
21. N-1123-HUD. *Codebook for the Attitude Module of the Survey of Tenants and Homeowners, Site II, Baseline*. Phyllis L. Ellickson, HASE Survey Group. May 1981. (First issued as WN-9802-HUD, November 1977.)
22. N-1143-HUD. *Codebook for the Attitude Module of the Survey of Tenants and Homeowners, Site II, Wave 2*. Patricia Boren. May 1981. (First issued as WN-10432-HUD, March 1979.)
23. N-1371-HUD. *Codebook for the Attitude Module of the Household Survey, Site II, Wave 3*. Patricia Boren. June 1980.
24. N-1372-HUD. *Codebook for the Attitude Module of the Household Survey, Site II, Wave 4*. Patricia Boren. August 1980.
25. N-1122-HUD. *Codebook for the Attitude Module of the Landlord Survey, Site II, Baseline*. Phyllis L. Ellickson, David E. Kanouse, HASE Survey Group. May 1981. (First issued as WN-9801-HUD, April 1978.)
26. N-1142-HUD. *Codebook for the Attitude Module of the Landlord Survey, Site II, Wave 2*. Patricia Boren, Roger Johnston. May 1980. (First issued as WN-10422-HUD, February 1979.)
27. N-1366-HUD. *Codebook for the Attitude Module of the Landlord Survey, Site II, Wave 3*. Patricia Boren, Christina Witsberger. July 1980.
28. N-1367-HUD. *Codebook for the Attitude Module of the Landlord Survey, Site II, Wave 4*. Patricia Boren, Christina Witsberger. August 1980.
29. N-1074-HUD. *Codebook for the Survey of Tenants and Homeowners, Site I, Baseline*. HASE Survey Group. March 1981. (First issued as WN-8809-HUD, December 1975.)

30. N-1190-HUD. *Codebook for the Household Survey, Site I, Wave 2*. Patricia Boren. July 1979.
31. N-1309-HUD. *Codebook for the Household Survey, Site I, Wave 3*. Patricia Boren. November 1979.
32. N-1358-HUD. *Codebook for the Household Survey, Site I, Wave 4*. Patricia Boren. March 1980.
33. N-1080-HUD. *Codebook for the Baseline Landlord Survey in Site I*. Ann W. Wang, Doris Crocker, Stephanie Schank. May 1981. (First issued as WN-8976-HUD, March 1975.)
34. N-1189-HUD. *Codebook for the Survey of Landlords, Site I, Wave 2*. Patricia Boren. June 1979.
35. N-1349-HUD. *Codebook for the Survey of Landlords, Site I, Wave 3*. Patricia Boren. February 1980.
36. N-1351-HUD. *Codebook for the Survey of Landlords, Site I, Wave 4*. Patricia Boren. February 1980.
37. N-1075-HUD. *Codebook for the Baseline Survey of Residential Buildings in Site I*. Ann W. Wang, Charles W. Noland. March 1981. (First issued as WN-8810-HUD, February 1975.)
38. N-1191-HUD. *Codebook for the Survey of Residential Buildings, Site I, Wave 2*. Patricia Boren. August 1979.
39. N-1405-HUD. *Codebook for the Survey of Residential Buildings, Site I, Wave 3*. Patricia Boren. March 1980.
40. N-1354-HUD. *Codebook for the Survey of Residential Buildings, Site I, Wave 4*. Patricia Boren. March 1980.
41. N-1076-HUD. *Codebook for the Survey of Neighborhoods, Site I, Baseline*. HASE Survey Group. March 1981. (First issued as WN-8811-HUD, June 1977.)
42. N-1361-HUD. *Codebook for the Survey of Neighborhoods, Site I, Wave 4*. Patricia Boren, Carol Hillestad. March 1980.
43. N-1112-HUD. *Codebook for the Survey of Tenants and Homeowners, Site II, Baseline*. HASE Survey Group. April 1981. (First issued as WN-9651-HUD, April 1977.)
44. N-1139-HUD. *Codebook for the Survey of Tenants and Homeowners, Site II, Wave 2*. Patricia Boren. May 1981. (First issued as WN-10293-HUD, October 1978.)
45. N-1359-HUD. *Codebook for the Household Survey, Site II, Wave 3*. Patricia Boren. May 1980.
46. N-1360-HUD. *Codebook for the Household Survey, Site II, Wave 4*. Patricia Boren, Deborah Wesley. August 1980.
47. N-1104-HUD. *Codebook for the Survey of Landlords, Site II, Baseline*. HASE Survey Group. April 1981. (First issued as WN-9444-HUD, July 1976.)

48. N-1140-HUD. *Codebook for the Survey of Landlords, Site II, Wave 2.* Patricia Boren. May 1981. (First issued as WN-10294-HUD, December 1978.)
49. N-1352-HUD. *Codebook for the Survey of Landlords, Site II, Wave 3.* Patricia Boren. June 1980.
50. N-1353-HUD. *Codebook for the Survey of Landlords, Site II, Wave 4.* Patricia Boren, Deborah Wesley. July 1980.
51. N-1126-HUD. *Codebook for the Survey of Residential Buildings, Site II, Baseline.* HASE Survey Group. May 1981. (First issued as WN-9895-HUD, September 1977.)
52. N-1355-HUD. *Codebook for the Survey of Residential Buildings, Site II, Wave 2.* Patricia Boren. June 1980.
53. N-1356-HUD. *Codebook for the Survey of Residential Buildings, Site II, Wave 3.* Patricia Boren. July 1980.
54. N-1357-HUD. *Codebook for the Survey of Residential Buildings, Site II, Wave 4.* Patricia Boren, Deborah Wesley. August 1980.
55. N-1128-HUD. *Codebook for the Survey of Neighborhoods, Site II, Baseline.* HASE Survey Group. April 1981. (First issued as WN-9949-HUD, December 1977.)
56. N-1362-HUD. *Codebook for the Survey of Neighborhoods, Site II, Wave 4.* Patricia Boren, Carol Hillestad. August 1980.
57. N-1373-HUD. *Supplemental Codebook for the Baseline Household Survey, Site I.* Evelyn C. Casper. October 1980.
58. N-1374-HUD. *Supplemental Codebook for the Household Survey, Site I, Wave 2.* Sally Trude, Evelyn Casper, Roberta Allen. January 1980.
59. N-1375-HUD. *Supplemental Codebook for the Household Survey, Site I, Wave 3.* Evelyn Casper, Roberta Allen, Sally Trude. February 1980.
60. N-1376-HUD. *Supplemental Codebook for the Household Survey, Site I, Wave 4.* Roberta Allen, Evelyn Casper, Sally Trude. March 1980.
61. N-1381-HUD. *Supplemental Codebook for the Baseline Survey of Landlords, Site I.* Kenneth Wong, Patricia Boren. September 1980.
62. N-1382-HUD. *Supplemental Codebook for the Survey of Landlords, Site I, Wave 2.* Kenneth Wong, Patricia Boren, Sally Trude. January 1980.
63. N-1383-HUD. *Supplemental Codebook for the Survey of Landlords, Site I, Wave 3.* Kenneth Wong, Patricia Boren. February 1980.

64. N-1384-HUD. *Supplemental Codebook for the Survey of Landlords, Site I, Wave 4.* Kenneth Wong, Patricia Boren. March 1980.
65. N-1389-HUD. *Supplemental Codebook for the Survey of Residential Buildings, Site I, Wave 2.* Sally Trude, Patricia Boren, Beverly Lowe. January 1980.
66. N-1390-HUD. *Supplemental Codebook for the Survey of Residential Buildings, Site I, Wave 3.* Patricia Boren, Sally Trude. March 1980.
67. N-1391-HUD. *Supplemental Codebook for the Survey of Residential Buildings, Site I, Wave 4.* Patricia Boren, Sally Trude. March 1980.
68. N-1590-HUD. *Supplemental Codebook for the Baseline Survey of Neighborhoods, Site I.* Carol Hillestad. December 1980.
69. N-1377-HUD. *Supplemental Codebook for the Household Survey, Site II, Baseline.* Evelyn C. Casper. December 1980.
70. N-1378-HUD. *Supplemental Codebook for the Household Survey, Site II, Wave 2.* Evelyn C. Casper, Roberta Allen. May 1980.
71. N-1379-HUD. *Supplemental Codebook for the Household Survey, Site II, Wave 3.* Roberta Allen, Evelyn Casper. July 1980.
72. N-1380-HUD. *Supplemental Codebook for the Household Survey, Site II, Wave 4.* Evelyn C. Casper, Roberta Allen. August 1980.
73. N-1385-HUD. *Supplemental Codebook for the Baseline Survey of Landlords, Site II.* Patricia Boren, Kenneth Wong. December 1980.
74. N-1386-HUD. *Supplemental Codebook for the Survey of Landlords, Site II, Wave 2.* Patricia Boren, Kenneth Wong. May 1980.
75. N-1387-HUD. *Supplemental Codebook for the Survey of Landlords, Site II, Wave 3.* Patricia Boren, Kenneth Wong. July 1980.
76. N-1388-HUD. *Supplemental Codebook for the Survey of Landlords, Site II, Wave 4.* Patricia Boren, Kenneth Wong. August 1980.
77. N-1392-HUD. *Supplemental Codebook for the Baseline Survey of Residential Buildings, Site II.* Patricia Boren. November 1980.
78. N-1393-HUD. *Supplemental Codebook for the Survey of Residential Buildings, Site II, Wave 2.* Patricia Boren. June 1980.

79. N-1394-HUD. *Supplemental Codebook for the Survey of Residential Buildings, Site II, Wave 3.* Patricia Boren. June 1980.

80. N-1395-HUD. *Supplemental Codebook for the Survey of Residential Buildings, Site II, Wave 4.* Patricia Boren. August 1980.

81. N-1596-HUD. *Supplemental Codebook for the Baseline Survey of Neighborhoods, Site II.* Carol Hillestad. December 1980.

82. N-1097-HUD. *Audit of the Baseline Household Survey in Site I.* Lawrence Helbers. October 1979. (First issued as WN-9229-HUD, February 1979.)

83. N-1081-HUD. *Audit of the Baseline Landlord Survey in Site I.* Richard E. Stanton, Therman P. Britt. October 1979. (First issued as WN-8977-HUD, June 1977.)

84. N-1078-HUD. *Audit Report for the Baseline Survey of Residential Buildings in Site I.* Larry A. Day. December 1979. (First issued as WN-8973-HUD, January 1976.)

85. N-1115-HUD. *Audit of the Baseline Neighborhood Survey in Site I.* C. Lance Barnett. October 1979. (First issued as WN-9732-HUD, April 1977.)

86. N-1282-HUD. *Audit of the Neighborhood Survey, Site I, Wave 4.* Carol E. Hillestad. November 1979.

87. N-1108-HUD. *Audit of the Baseline Survey of Tenants and Homeowners in Site II.* John E. Mulford. October 1979. (First issued as WN-9576-HUD, August 1978.)

88. N-1121-HUD. *Audit of the Baseline Landlord Survey in Site II.* Richard E. Stanton, Therman P. Britt. October 1979. (First issued as WN-9739-HUD, February 1979.)

89. N-1120-HUD. *Audit of the Baseline Survey of Residential Buildings in Site II.* Larry A. Day, Charles W. Noland. October 1979. (First issued as WN-9738-HUD, December 1977.)

90. N-1113-HUD. *Audit of the Baseline Neighborhood Survey in Site II.* John E. Bala. October 1979. (First issued as WN-9709-HUD, September 1977.)

91. N-1416-HUD. *Audit of the Survey of Neighborhoods, Site II, Wave 4.* Carol E. Hillestad. August 1980.

92. N-1398-HUD. *Audit of the Landlord Survey, Site I, Wave 2.* John W. Dawson. February 1981.

93. N-1404-HUD. *Audit of the Survey of Residential Buildings, Site I, Wave 2.* Beverly F. Lowe. May 1981.

94. N-1410-HUD. *Audit of the Household Survey, Site I, Wave 2.* Carole Beauchemin. Forthcoming.

95. N-1399-HUD. *Audit of the Landlord Survey, Site I, Wave 3.* Roger Johnston. Forthcoming.
96. N-1411-HUD. *Audit of the Household Survey, Site I, Wave 3.* FDG Staff. Forthcoming.
97. N-1400-HUD. *Audit of the Landlord Survey, Site I, Wave 4.* FDG Staff. Forthcoming.
98. N-1406-HUD. *Audit of the Survey of Residential Buildings, Site I, Wave 3.* Sandra S. Figge. May 1981.
99. N-1474-HUD. *Audit of the Survey of Residential Buildings, Site I, Wave 4.* Sandra S. Figge. Forthcoming.
100. N-1412-HUD. *Audit of the Household Survey, Site I, Wave 4.* FDG Staff. Forthcoming.
101. N-1401-HUD. *Audit of the Landlord Survey, Site II, Wave 2.* John W. Dawson, and Roger Johnston. Forthcoming.
102. N-1413-HUD. *Audit of the Household Survey, Site II, Wave 2.* FDG Staff. Forthcoming.
103. N-1402-HUD. *Audit of the Landlord Survey, Site II, Wave 3.* FDG Staff. Forthcoming.
104. N-1414-HUD. *Audit of the Household Survey, Site II, Wave 3.* FDG Staff. Forthcoming.
105. N-1403-HUD. *Audit of the Landlord Survey, Site II, Wave 4.* FDG Staff. Forthcoming.
106. N-1407-HUD. *Audit of the Survey of Residential Buildings, Site II, Wave 2.* Sandra S. Figge. Forthcoming.
107. N-1408-HUD. *Audit of the Survey of Residential Buildings, Site II, Wave 3.* Sandra S. Figge. Forthcoming.
108. N-1409-HUD. *Audit of the Survey of Residential Buildings, Site II, Wave 4.* Sandra S. Figge. Forthcoming.
109. N-1415-HUD. *Audit of the Household Survey, Site II, Wave 4.* FDG Staff. Forthcoming.
110. N-1173-HUD. *Audit of the Household Attitude Survey, Site II, Wave 2.* Marsha Baran. July 1979.
111. N-1329-HUD. *Audit of the Landlord Attitude Survey, Site II, Wave 2.* Roger Johnston. September 1980.

Appendix C

THE HOUSING ALLOWANCE PROGRAM'S HOUSING STANDARDS

In order to qualify for allowance payments, an enrollee had to occupy a dwelling that met minimum standards for space, equipment, and condition. These standards were enforced by periodic housing evaluations conducted by HAO staff. An evaluation was conducted shortly after a household enrolled, annually on the enrollment anniversary, and each time an enrollee moved.

The typical evaluation required 30 to 40 minutes to complete. The evaluator visited all accessible areas of the dwelling and the "common" areas of multiple dwellings, as well as touring the outside of the dwelling and its grounds. While on site, the evaluator completed a lengthy rating form, counting the rooms and checking each for habitability. He also inspected structural features that might pose health or safety hazards, the accessible portions of the heating, electrical, and plumbing systems, the operability of kitchen and bathroom equipment, and the arrangements for storage of foodstuffs and combustibles.

The HAOs' evaluators were carefully trained to follow uniform procedures in rating each aspect of the dwellings they evaluated, and their work was checked by independent reevaluations conducted on a sample of dwellings (see Ch. VIII). Below, we list the 38 standards that were applied to each dwelling. Failure of any of these standards made a dwelling unacceptable. If the occupants repaired an unacceptable dwelling, the failed features were reinspected by HAO staff to determine whether they had been adequately repaired.

HAZARDS TO HEALTH AND SAFETY

Exterior Property Area

1. Sanitation and Storage

   Heavy accumulations of litter, trash, garbage, or other debris that may harbor insects, rodents, or other pests; that are combustible; that hamper emergency access; or that create a safety or health hazard.

2. Grading and Drainage

   Presence of hazardous conditions, including cases in which topography and the absorptive capacity of the soil cause drainage or seepage into the building or standing water that might damage the structure or its contents or create unsanitary conditions.

3. Trees and Plant Material

   Presence of hazardous conditions, including cases in which the property is so heavily overgrown that natural light is blocked from the structure and normal access is impeded; the presence of noxious plants that endanger the health of the occupants; or vines or trees that threaten to damage the building or endanger its occupants.

4. Accessory Structures and Fences

   Presence of hazardous conditions, including cases in which such structures and fences have severe structural defects and are located close enough to the main building or to areas of normal human activity on the lot that their potential collapse endangers the occupants.

Building Exterior

5. Foundation

   Presence of hazardous conditions, including foundations with severe structural defects or that are penetrable by water so that the structural safety of the building is threatened.

6. Exterior Walls and Surfaces

   Presence of hazardous conditions in the exterior walls and surfaces of the building, including severe leaning, buckling, or sagging; major holes or missing sections; or excessive cracking such that there is a danger of structural collapse or of significant damage to the interior of the structure from the elements.

7. Roofs, Chimneys, Gutters, and Downspouts

   Presence of hazardous conditions on the roof, chimney, gutters, or downspouts of the building, including sagging or buckling, major holes or missing sections such that there is a danger of collapse or significant damage to the interior of the structure from the elements.

8. Stairs, Porches, and Railings

   Presence of hazardous conditions, including severe structural defects, broken or missing steps, or the absence of a handrail for six or more consecutive steps or the absence of railings around a porch that is four feet or more from the ground.

9. Windows

   Presence of hazardous conditions, including missing or broken window panes and heavily damaged or rotted sashes that allow loss of heat or severe weather damage to the interior of the unit or threaten the safety of the occupants.

10. Doors and Hatchways

    Presence of hazardous conditions, including missing or broken doors that allow loss of heat or severe weather damage to the interior of the unit or threaten the safety of the occupants.

Building and Unit Interior

11. Exits

    Presence of hazardous conditions, including lack of one exit from the unit and at least two safe exits from the residential building leading to open space outside the building.

12. Sanitation and Storage

    Presence of hazardous conditions, including significant accumulations of litter, trash, garbage, or other debris that may harbor insects, rodents, or other pests; that are combustible; or that hamper emergency entrance or exit. Unsafe storage of flammable materials.

13. Walls

    Presence of hazardous conditions in the interior walls of the unit or the public spaces of the building, including severe buckling, major holes or missing sections, evidence of persistent moisture, dry rot, or insect damage such that there is a potential for structural collapse or other threats to safety.

14. Ceiling

    Presence of hazardous conditions, including severe buckling, sagging, major holes or missing sections, evidence of persistent moisture, dry rot, or insect damage such that there is a potential for structural collapse or other threats to safety.

15. Floors

    Presence of hazardous conditions of floors in the unit or the public spaces of the building, including severe buckling, noticeable movement under walking stress, major holes or missing sections, evidence of persistent moisture, dry rot, or insect damage such that there is a potential for structural collapse or other threats to safety. Floors of bathroom and kitchen must be of properly installed impervious materials so as to prevent leakage of water that would damage the structural system or create other threats to safety.

16. Stairs and Railings

Presence of hazardous conditions in the stairs and railings of the unit or the public spaces of the building, including severe structural defects, broken or missing steps, absence of railings around open steps or absence of a handrail for six or more consecutive steps.

17. Toilet and Bath Facilities

Presence of hazardous conditions, including severely damaged, broken, or cracked fixtures that endanger the users or that may result in leakage or flooding. Major leaks around base of toilet.

18. Kitchen Facilities

Presence of hazardous conditions, including a severely damaged or broken stove, sink, or refrigerator that endangers the users or that may result in gas or water leakage, fire, or electrical shock.

19. Water Heater

Presence of hazardous conditions, including the absence of a hot water heater, inadequate hot water, or heater not connected or inoperable; gas leakage, danger of flooding, vent pipe seriously cracked or broken, allowing unexpended gases to escape into the unit; improper or no venting for exhaust gases; lack of temperature pressure valve; tagged by utility company as unsafe.

20. Plumbing System

Presence of hazardous conditions relating to the plumbing system of the unit or public areas of the building, including the absence of a plumbing system, or any condition in which clean water is not distributed effectively to all fixtures in the unit and waste from them is not carried to a public system or other disposal mechanism; where there are major cracks or broken pipes, improperly sealed joints, and other defects that cause leakage and threats to health and safety.

21. Heating System

Presence of hazardous conditions in the heating system in the unit or the building, including absence of an acceptable primary source of heat; breakage or damage to the source of heat, ducts, or fixtures such that heat is not available or not adequately distributed to the unit; potential for fire or other threats to safety; vent pipe seriously cracked or broken, allowing unexpended gases to escape into unit; portable electric room heaters serving as primary sources of heat; unvented room heaters that burn gas, oil, or other flammable liquids.

22. Electrical System

Presence of hazardous conditions in the electrical system of the unit, in public areas in the building, or in the exterior property area, including absence of an electrical system; exposed, non-insulated, or frayed wires; improper connections, insulation, or grounding of any component of the system; the overloading of capacity such that there is an immediate hazard of electrocution or fire; or wires in or near standing water or other unsafe places. These requirements apply to cable and equipment outside of the building as well as all components of the electrical system within the unit.

ESSENTIAL FACILITIES

Kitchen Facilities

23. Ceiling Height

The ceiling of the room in which the kitchen facilities are located must be at least 6′6″ high over at least 35 square feet of room area.

24. Natural Light

There must be sufficient light in the kitchen, either from natural or artificial sources, to permit normal domestic activities.

25. Ventilation

There must be at least one openable window or other device that provides ventilation for the kitchen.

26. Fixtures and Outlets

The kitchen must have two separate, properly installed electric convenience outlets or one electric convenience outlet and one ceiling or wall electric light fixture with a safe switching device.

27. Hot and Cold Sink

The kitchen must contain a sink with hot and cold running water.

28. Cooking Range

The kitchen must contain a working cooking range consisting of at least one burner and an oven.

29. Refrigerator

The unit must have a working refrigerator.

Bathroom Facilities

30. Ventilation

    There must be an openable window or a mechanical system to provide ventilation for the bathroom.

31. Fixtures and Outlets

    The bathroom must contain a properly installed electric convenience outlet or one ceiling or wall light fixture with a safe switching device.

32. Heating

    The bathroom must have a permanent source of heat.

33. Flush Toilet

    The bathroom must contain a working flush toilet.

34. Hot and Cold Sink

    The bathroom must contain a working sink complete with hot and cold running water fixtures.

35. Hot and Cold Tub or Shower

    The bathroom must contain either a bathtub or shower with operating hot and cold running water fixtures.

36. Privacy

    The toilet and bathtub or shower must have some form of enclosure to ensure privacy.

OCCUPANCY

37. Minimum Number of Habitable Rooms

    A habitable room is one that has:

    - Floor area of 70 square feet or more.
    - Ceiling height of at least 6′6″ over at least 35 square feet of floor area.
    - Natural light from at least one window facing directly outdoors or onto a sunporch that is strong enough during daylight hours to permit normal domestic activities without artificial light.
    - Adequate ventilation from at least one openable window or mechanical device.
    - At least one properly installed and working electric convenience outlet.
    - Adequate heat from a source other than a portable electric heater.

- No special adaptations for use as a kitchen, bathroom, or utility room.

In addition, a bedroom must have:

- Rigid walls, secured in position from floor to ceiling, including a doorway with a door, curtain, or other screening device.

Pursuant to these definitions, there must be a minimum number of habitable rooms that varies depending on the total number of persons residing in the unit. There must be one bedroom for every two persons, except that seven or more persons only require four bedrooms. If there are three or more persons occupying the unit, there must be one habitable room in addition to the kitchen, bathroom, and bedrooms to serve as a general living area.

LEAD-BASED PAINT

38. Lead-Based Paint Hazards (authorized January 1977)

Absence of cracked, scaled, chipped, peeled, or loose paint on surfaces accessible to children, in dwellings that are occupied or frequently visited by children under seven years of age. The surfaces subject to this provision include all exterior surfaces, whether or not accessible. Faulty paint is not tested for lead content, but is presumed hazardous.

Appendix D

TRUSTEES AND DIRECTORS OF THE HOUSING ALLOWANCE OFFICES

The experimental housing allowance programs in Brown and St. Joseph counties are operated by nonprofit corporations (housing allowance offices, or HAOs) whose boards of trustees were initially composed of members of The Rand Corporation and local citizens. These boards appoint the officers of the HAOs and review their budgets and operating policies. The trustees serve without compensation.

At the end of the five-year experimental period, Rand members resigned from the boards and were replaced by local citizens. Under their guidance, the allowance programs will continue until 1984.

Below, we list the trustees and directors of each HAO through May 1982, and indicate their periods of service.

THE HOUSING ALLOWANCE OFFICE OF BROWN COUNTY, INC.
Green Bay, Wisconsin

Trustees

Daniel J. Alesch (1973-present; *Chairman*, 1973-present)
Robert Dubinsky (1973-76)
G. Thomas Kingsley (1973-80)
George F. Kress (1973-78)
Roger Levien (1973-74)
Charles E. Nelson (1973-79)
Gustave H. Shubert (1973-79)
Barbara R. Williams (1973-79)
Robert C. Nelson (1974-77)
Philip J. Hendrickson (1976-present)
Ruth Clusen (1977-78)
Judith Crain (1978-present)
John M. Rose (1978-present)
Gerald Prindiville (1980-present)

Directors

Theodore H. Bauer (1973-75)
W. Eugene Rizor (1976-79)
Lars Larsen (1979-present)

THE HOUSING ALLOWANCE OFFICE, INC.
South Bend, Indiana

Trustees

Charles F. Crutchfield (1974-present; *Chairman*, 1980-present)
Robert Dubinsky (1974-76)
G. Thomas Kingsley (1974-80)
Charles E. Nelson (1974-80)
Franklin D. Schurz, Jr. (1974-present)
Michael F. Shea (1974-76; *Chairman*, 1974-76)
Gustave H. Shubert (1974-80)
Thomas W. Weeks (1974-80; *Chairman*, 1976-80)
Barbara R. Williams (1974-80)
Martha LaSane (1978-present)
Ernestine M. Raclin (1978-present)
Roland W. Chamblee, Sr. (1980-present)
Josephine Curtis (1981-present)
William G. Huys (1981-present)
Henry Jackson (1981-present)
Mary Jaicomo (1981-present)

Directors

Charles F. Lennon, Jr. (1974-78)
Hollis E. Hughes, Jr. (1978-present)

Appendix E

RAND'S STAFF FOR THE HOUSING ASSISTANCE SUPPLY EXPERIMENT, 1972-81

The Housing Assistance Supply Experiment began its formal existence in April 1972 with a staff of ten professionals engaged in planning the experiment and screening potential sites. By September 1974, when the experiment was under way in two sites and a large volume of field survey data was being processed, the staff had grown to the equivalent of 110 full-time workers. They were located in Washington, D.C.; Santa Monica, California; Green Bay, Wisconsin; and South Bend, Indiana. From 1979 through 1981, the staff decreased in size as various phases of site operations, data preparation, and analysis were completed.

At peak, slightly more than half the staff were professional-rated employees or consultants, most of them working full-time on the project. The remainder provided the administrative and clerical support without which a project could not function.

Below, we list the project's professional staff and indicate the main responsibilities or contributions of each member. Because responsibilities and job titles changed continuously in response to shifting workloads and professional growth of staff members, it is difficult to give as clear a picture as we would like of the contributions of each person. The first listing singles out for special mention those with major management responsibilities. There later follows a complete alphabetical list.

Many more Rand employees than are listed in this appendix contributed in important ways to the Supply Experiment. Rand's nonprofessional support staff was indispensible, but naming all who worked at least part-time on HASE over a ten-year period is infeasible. Thus, the listings here were limited to professional-rated staff who were formally committed to work for HASE.

To design administrative procedures for the housing allowance program, Rand enlisted the help of several subcontractors: Abt Associates, American Management Systems, Arthur Young and Company, Development Associates, Goldberg Marchesano and Associates, and the National Civil Service League. The staffs of these organizations were extremely helpful to us.

PROGRAM MANAGERS

Program Director

Charles E. Nelson (1972-80)
G. Thomas Kingsley (1980-81)

Deputy Director

G. Thomas Kingsley (1974-80)

Principal Investigator

Ira S. Lowry (1979-81)

GROUP MANAGERS

Design and Analysis

Ira S. Lowry (1972-78)

Analysis

C. Lance Barnett (1979-81)

File Development

E. Wayne Hansen (1979-81)

Publications

Janet DeLand (1972-73)
Charlotte Cox (1974-79)
Judith A. Rasmussen (1980-81)

Surveys

Sandra H. Berry* (1972-73)
Deborah R. Hensler (1974-75)
Douglas Scott (1975-80)

Survey Data Preparation

Carolyn Ivie (1974)
Donald P. Trees (1974-80)

Field and Program Operations

Robert Dubinsky (1972-76)
G. Thomas Kingsley (1976-81)

Data Systems

Gerald Levitt (1972-74)
Edward H. Lipnick (1974-75)
Antoinette C. J. Shetler* (1975)
Eric F. Harslem (1975-76)
Carol A. Medine (1977)
Susan C. Augusta (1978-80)
Lynn Johnson (1980-81)

SITE MANAGERS

Site I
Brown County, Wisconsin

Daniel J. Alesch (1974-80)

Site II
St. Joseph County, Indiana

Michael F. Shea (1974-76)
Thomas Weeks (1976-81)

*Acting.

Survey fieldwork was also subcontracted. Urban Opinion Surveys, a division of Mathematica, Inc., helped with instrument design and conducted the baseline surveys in Site I. The National Opinion Research Center of the University of Chicago conducted the remaining surveys there. Westat, Inc., conducted all four annual surveys in Site II. Chilton Research Services did special surveys in both sites.

Legal advice on program design and operations was provided by the firms of Cooley, Castro, Huddleson, and Tatum (San Francisco), and Foley and Lardner (Milwaukee).

PROFESSIONAL STAFF, 1972-81

All staff members are listed alphabetically. Each entry gives a reverse chronological account of the positions held or main responsibilities of the named individual. The functional groups within HASE are abbreviated as follows:

AG	Analysis Group (1979-81)
DAG	Design and Analysis Group (1972-78)
DSG	Data Systems Group (1972-78)
FDG	File Development Group (1979-81)
FPOG	Field and Program Operations Group (1972-81)
PG	Publications Group (1972-81)
SDPG	Survey Data Preparation Group (1973-80)
SG	Survey Group (1972-80)

* * * * *

Abelson, Jane, editor, PG, 1980-81.

Abraham, Stanley C., deputy manager for reports, DAG, 1976-78.

Achtenberg, Joel, allowance program design consultant, FPOG, 1974.

Adachi, Mitsuko, computer services, SDPG, 1977.

Alesch, Daniel J., manager of Site I, FPOG, 1974-80.

Allen, Roberta M., file preparation, FDG, 1979-80.

Allen, William H., supervisor of computer services, SDPG, 1977-78.

Allison, Doris, deputy manager, SDPG, 1977-80; supervisor of data coding, editing, and control, 1977.

Althauser, Robert P., research design, DAG, 1972-73.

Anna, Katherine E., file preparation, DAG, 1976-77.

Arroyo, Michele A., instrument production supervisor, SG, 1974.

Askin, A. Bradley, research design, DAG, 1974.

Augusta, Susan C., manager, DSG, 1978-80; audit and analysis team leader, 1977; programmer, 1975-77.

Baer, Laurence, record management system, DSG, 1977; audit and analysis programmer, 1976.

Bailey, Barbara, data control, SDPG, 1979.

Bailey, Garnette, data control, SDPG, 1979-80.

Bala, John E., analyst, AG, 1979-80; analyst and audit team leader, 1976-78.

Balch, Steven L., analyst, AG and DAG, 1978-80.

Bandur, Janet, computer services, SDPG, 1976; data control and computer operations, 1974-75.

Baran, Marsha, file preparation team leader, FDG and DAG, 1978-81; file preparation, DAG, 1977.

Barnett, C. Lance, manager, AG, 1979-81; deputy manager for operations and planning, DAG, 1978; analyst 1975-77.

Barrett, Teresa E., administrative assistant, DAG, 1974-77.

Baumann, Dorothy, audit and analysis programmer, DSG, 1976-79; record management system, 1978.

Baumgartner, Stephen, deputy manager, SDPG, 1976.

Beauchemin, Carole A., sample accounting, FDG, 1979-81; sample accounting and file preparation, DAG, 1976-77.

Bedell, M. A., data administration, DSG, 1979-81; audit and analysis programmer, 1974-81.

Beerman, David A., record management system, DSG, 1975-76; sample selection programmer, 1974-75; systems development programmer, 1974.

Berry, Joseph, audit and analysis team leader, DSG, 1977-78; programmer, 1977-78.

Berry, Sandra H., assistant manager for instrument design, SG, 1974-75; acting manager, 1972-73.

Betancourt, Donna, administrative assistant, AG and FDG, 1979-81.

Bikson, Tora K., community attitudes team leader, AG, 1979-80.

Black, Joan C., audit and analysis programmer, DSG, 1974-75.

Bloomfield, Ellyn, coding and editing, SDPG, 1977-79.

Blum-Doering, Zahava, record management system design, SG, 1978; assistant manager, survey operations, 1974-77; survey instrument design, 1972-73.

Bonner, Annette, site selection, DAG, 1972.

Boothe, Janet, data control and computer operations, SDPG, 1974-75.

Boren, Patricia M., file preparation, DAG and FDG, 1978-81; codebook production, SG, 1976-79.

Both, Deborah R., housing evaluations, FPOG, 1974-81.

Brewer, Sandra H., file preparation, DAG, 1978.

Britt, Therman P., file preparation and audit, DAG, 1974-78; survey instrument design, 1973; site selection, 1972.

Buhl, Linda, coding and editing, SDPG, 1977-80.

Bush, Charles H., record management system, 1977; postbaseline system programmer, 1975-76.

Butler, Jan L., project accounting system, DSG, 1975-81; administrative assistant, 1974-81.

Campbell, Harrison S., research design, DAG, 1972-73.

Cantrell, Clairessa H., file preparation, FDG, 1979-81.

Carey, Ralph, allowance program design consultant, FPOG, 1974.

Carlson, Timothy, audit and analysis programmer, DSG, 1978-79; computer services, SDPG, 1978.

Carter, Earl, allowance program monitoring, FPOG, 1974-75; site selection, 1972-73.

Carter, Grace M., eligibility and participation team leader; AG, 1979-81; analyst, DAG, 1978.

Casper, Evelyn C., file preparation, FDG, 1979-81.

Cates, David, sample maintenance, DAG, 1976-77.

Chesler, Leonard G., deputy manager for planning and coordination, DAG, 1974-75.

Christensen, Donna, data coding and editing, SDPG, 1975.

Cohen, Donald N., systems development programmer, DSG, 1974.

Colbert, Linda L., consulting editor, PG, 1976-78.

Coleman, Sinclair B., analyst, AG, 1979-81.

Conley, Barbara, data control, SDPG, 1977-78.

Cooper, Donna R., audit and analysis programmer, DSG, 1975-77.

Corcoran, Timothy M., survey sample maintenance, DAG, 1976; survey sample design and selection team leader, 1972-75.

Corona, Antonio F., audit and analysis programmer, DSG, 1978-80.

Correa, Sylvia, allowance program design consultant, FPOG, 1974.

Cox, Charlotte, consulting editor, PG, 1980-81; managing editor, 1974-79.

Crawford, Gary, coding and editing, SDPG, 1978-80.

Crocker, Doris, supervisor for data coding, editing and control, SDPG, 1976; supervisor for data coding and editing, 1974-75.

Dade, Marsha A., analyst, DAG, 1975-76; file preparation and audit, 1974-75; survey sample selection, 1974.

D'Arc, Christine, documentation supervisor, FDG, 1979-81; consulting editor, PG, 1978.

Davidson, Elizabeth, supervisor for data coding, editing, and control, SDPG, 1977-80; data coding and editing, 1974-76.

Davis, Tom, computer services, SDPG, 1976; data control and computer operations, 1975.

Dawson, John W., sample accounting, DAG and AG, 1978-81; file preparation, 1977-78.

Day, Hallie, data control, SDPG, 1977-78.

Day, Larry A., file preparation and audit, DAG, 1974-78.

de Ferranti, David M., file preparation and audit team leader, DAG, 1974; research design, 1972-73.

DeLand, Janet, managing editor, PG, 1972-73.

Dickenson, Antoinette, program control assistant, office of the program director, 1974.

Dodd, Colleen M., record management system, DSG, 1974-76; audit and analysis programmer, 1974; data management planner, 1972-73.

Dong, Doris, cartography and graphics, DAG, 1974-77.

Douglas, John, file preparation, DAG, 1978.

Dubinsky, Robert, manager, FPOG, 1972-76; site selection, 1972.

Dunn, William L., survey audit, DAG, 1974-76.

Ebener, Patricia, survey operations director, SG, 1979; survey operations, 1974-77.

Edwards, Carol A., record management system, DSG, 1975-81.

Edwards, Kim, audit and analysis programmer, DSG, 1978-81.

Edwards, Sandra, audit and analysis programmer, DSG, 1978-79; computer and services, SDPG, 1977-78.

Ellickson, Bryan, research design, DAG, 1973.

Ellickson, Phyllis, analyst, AG and DAG, 1975-80; community attitudes team leader, 1976.

Emery, Michael H., audit and analysis programmer, 1978-80.

Emile, Loring, data coding, editing, and control, SDPG, 1975-76.

Enns, John H., deputy manager for operations and planning, DAG, 1975-77.

Ernst, Paul, resident observer for Site I, FPOG, 1975-80.

Fain, Terry, audit and analysis programmer, DSG, 1978.

Fairbrother, Edward M., supervisor of computer services, SDPG, 1977; data administration team leader, DSG, 1975-76; postbaseline system programmer, 1975; audit and analysis team leader, 1974; systems development programmer, 1974.

Fanelli, Diane, supervisor of data control and computer operations, SDPG, 1975.

Figge, Sandra S., survey accounting and file preparation, FDG, 1979-81; sample maintenance, SG, 1978.

Fisher, Marilyn, survey operations, SG, 1977-78.

Flory, Sandy, assistant supervisor for instrument production, SG, 1976-77.

Friedman, Joseph, analyst, DAG, 1974-75.

Friedman, Ellen T., administrative assistant, DAG, 1977-78.

Fujisaki, Misako C., systems development team leader, DSG, 1974; data management planner, 1972-73.

Gallimore, Patricia, computer services, SDPG, 1979-80.

Gamble, Stacy W., staff, FPOG, 1975-77.

Garfinkle, Jeffrey B., audit and analysis programmer, DSG, 1979-80.

Gayle, Tom, computer services, SDPG, 1977-78; audit and analysis programmer, DSG, 1977.

Geller, Leslie, file preparation and audit, FDG and DAG, 1978-80.

Genung, George, allowance program design consultant, FPOG, 1974.

Goff, Charlotte, instrument production, SG, 1975.

Goodchilds, Jacqueline D., analyst, AG, 1979-80.

Granoff, William J., file preparation and audit, DAG, 1975-76; survey sample design and selection, 1974-75.

Gray, Kirk, resident observer for Site I, FPOG, 1974-78.

Gray, Loretta, computer services, SDPG, 1978-79.

Green, Kathy, computer services, SDPG, 1976-77.

Greenwald, Alan F., allowance program design, FPOG, 1974-75; site selection, 1972-73.

Grigsby, William G., market intermediaries team leader, DAG, 1974-76; research design, 1972-73.

Groo, David K., staff, FPOG, 1976-77.

Grundfest, Joseph A., file preparation and audit, DAG, 1974.

Gutek, Barbara A., analyst, DAG, 1979-80.

Hackett, Karen, computer services, SDPG, 1977-79.

Hanunian, Heather A., file preparation, DAG, 1978.

Hansen, E. Wayne, manager, FDG, 1979-81.

Harrell, Wade H., audit and analysis programmer, DSG, 1975-80.

Harslem, Chris S., supervisor of computer services, SDPG, 1976-77; data control and computer operations, 1974-75.

Harslem, Eric F., manager, DSG, 1975-76.

Hatch, Dolph M., audit and analysis programmer, DSG, 1975.

Hawes, Jennifer, survey operation, SG, 1976; research assistant, 1974-75.

Hayes, Frederick O'R., allowance program design consultant, FPOG, 1974.

Helbers, Lawrence, analyst, AG and DAG, 1977-81; file preparation and audit, 1974-77.

Hensler, Carl P., analyst, AG, 1979-81.

Hensler, Deborah, manager, SG, 1974-75; survey instrument design, 1972-73.

Hillestad, Carol E., analyst, AG, 1981; sample accounting and file preparation, FDG and DAG, 1977-80.

Hirsch, Michael L., audit and analysis programmer, DSG, 1980-81.

Honig, Paul, audit and analysis programmer, DSG, 1979-81.

Hope, Nancy, instrument production supervisor, SG, 1974-78; research assistant, 1974.

Horner, Barbara, survey operations, SG, 1974.

Hotchkiss, Charles M., analyst, AG, 1978-80.

Howitt, Matthew R., audit and analysis programmer, DSG, 1979-80; computer services, SDPG, 1978-79.

Hubay, Charles A., file preparation and audit, FDG, 1979-81.

Huddlestone, Susan, computer services, SDPG, 1976; data control and computer operations, 1975.

Hummel, Katherine, administrative assistant, SG, 1979.

Hunter, Michael J., data control and computer operations, SDPG, 1974-75.

Hutchison, John, coding and editing, SDPG, 1977.

Ingram, Cheryl, coding and editing, SDPG, 1978-79.

Insley, Caroline, data coding, editing, and control, SDPG, 1976; data control and computer operations, 1974-75.

Ivie, Carolyn, manager, SDPG, 1974.

Jackson, Cheryl A., audit and analysis programmer, DSG, 1975.

Johnson, Lynn, manager, DSG, 1980-81; audit and analysis team leader, 1979; postbaseline system programmer, 1979.

Johnston, Roger H., file preparation and audit, FDG and DAG, 1978-81.

Jones, Saul E., allowance program design consultant, FPOG, 1974.

Kachner, Susan G., project accounting system, DSG, 1975-76.

Kanouse, David E., analyst, DAG, 1976-78.

Katagiri, Iao, deputy manager, FPOG, 1979-80; staff, 1976-79; file preparation and audit, DAG, 1974-76.

Kawamoto, Alicia, data control, SDPG, 1978-79.

Kellogg, Richard W., audit and analysis programmer, DSG, 1974-75.

King, Robert, survey operations, SG, 1977-79.

Kingsley, G. Thomas, program director, 1980-81; deputy program director, 1974-80; manager, FPOG, 1976-81.

Kirby, Sheila N., staff, FPOG, 1977-81.

Klimek, Joyce, survey monitor for Site I, FPOG, 1974.

Knapik, Stephanie, coding and editing, SDPG, 1978-79.

Komai, Masaaki, analyst, DAG, 1975-76.

Kozimor, Lawrence W., analyst, DAG, 1976-78.

Kuncel, Ernest E., audit and analysis programmer, DSG, 1979-81.

Lamar, Bruce W., analyst, DAG, 1977-78.

Laskey, Marlene L., file preparation, FDG, 1979-81.

Lee, Nancy, computer services, SDPG, 1979-80.

Lee, Shirley J., data administration, DSG, 1975-79.

Lenox, Janis, sample maintenance, SG, 1976-77; data coding, editing, and control, SDPG, 1975-76.

Leone, Frank, survey operations, SG, 1976-77.

Leunig, Inge, data coding, editing, and control, SDPG, 1975-77.

Levitt, Gerald, manager, DSG, 1972-74.

Lewis, David B., allowance program design, FPOG, 1972-73; site selection, 1972-73.

Lewis, Marsha, administrative assistant, SG, 1974-76.

Lindsay, D. Scott, analyst, AG, 1979-80.

Lipnick, Edward H., manager, DSG, 1974-75; postbaseline system design, 1974.

Lowe, Beverly F., sample accounting and file preparation, FDG and DAG, 1977-81.

Lowry, Ira S., principal investigator, 1979-81; manager, DAG, 1972-78.

Luxenberg, Susan Welt, sample maintenance supervisor, SG, 1976-79; survey operations, 1976; research assistant, 1975.

Maltez, Frank, computer services, SDPG, 1978-79; coding and editing, 1976-78.

Margo, Robert A., analyst, DAG, 1978.

Matyskiela, Sharon Anderson, record management system, DSG, 1975-77; sample selection programmer, 1974-76.

McCardle, Kevin, computer services, SDPG, 1977-78.

McCarthy, Kevin F., analyst, AG and DAG, 1974-80.

McDowell, James L., analyst, AG and DAG, 1977-81.

McGuire, Nanci, coding and editing, SDPG, 1977-78.

McKenzie, Kay A., administrative assistant, SG, 1979-80.

McMahon, Pam, supervisor of computer services, SDPG, 1978-80.

McMullen, Molly A., file preparation, FDG, 1979-81.

Medine, Carol A., manager, DSG, 1977; audit and analysis team leader, 1975-76.

Meers, Patricia, program control assistant, office of the program director, 1978-79; administrative assistant, SG, 1976-78.

Menchik, Mark David, analyst, DAG, 1976-78.

Miller, Douglas, data coding, editing, and control, SDPG, 1975-77.

Montes, Pilar N., audit and analysis programmer, DSG, 1979-81.

Morris, Mary E., sample accounting, FDG, 1979-80; sample maintenance, SG, 1978-79.

Moursund, Hal, program control officer, office of the program director, 1974-76; staff, FPOG, 1973-75.

Mulford, John E., participant effects team leader, AG, 1979-81; analyst, DAG, 1978.

Neelands, Jim, data control and computer operations, SDPG, 1975.

Neels, J. Kevin, analyst, AG and DAG, 1978-81.

Nelson, Charles E., program director, 1972-80.

Ninnis, Kathleen, computer services, SDPG, 1978-80.

Noland, Charles W., analyst, AG and DAG, 1974-80; allowance program and research design, 1972-73.

Oliver, Lonna Prara, data control and computer operations, SDPG, 1974.

Oliver, Lynn, audit and analysis programmer, DSG, 1978; record management system, 1977.

O'Nell, Nancy, resident observer for Site II, FPOG, 1975-80.

Onishi, Randy, computer services, SDPG, 1978.

Ott, Mack, research design, DAG, 1972-73.

Palmer, Adele R., analyst, DAG, 1976-78; research design, 1972-73.

Patrick, Robert L., project accounting system team leader, DSG, 1975-76; postbaseline system design, 1975.

Perry, Wayne D., market effects team leader, AG, 1979-80.

Pesqueira, Frank, computer services, SDPG, 1976.

Pierson, Cordell L., data administration, DSG, 1979-80; data control and computer services, SDPG, 1978-79.

Pitman, Greg, data control and operations, SDPG, 1975; data coding and editing, 1974.

Poggio, Eugene C., survey sample design and selection, DAG, 1972-74.

Post, Penny, editor, PG, 1980-81.

Rahe, Carolyn, survey design and operations, SG, 1978-80.

Rainey, Richard B., site selection, DAG, 1972.

Rasmussen, Judith A., managing editor, PG, 1980-81; consulting editor, 1979.

Reid, Charles, audit and analysis programmer, DSG, 1976.

Reiley, James S., record management system team leader, 1975-77.

Reingold, Diane, codebook production supervisor, SG, 1978-80.

Relles, Daniel A., statistical consultant, AG, FDG, and DAG, 1976-81; sample selection team leader, DAG, 1974-75.

Repnau, Tiina, sample accounting and file preparation team leader, DAG, 1976-78; survey sample design and selection, 1974-75; housing allowance program design, 1972-73.

Richardson, Sandy, computer services, SDPG, 1977.

Rizor, Eugene W., staff, FPOG, 1979-81.

Rogers, William H., statistical consultant, DAG, 1977-78.

Rogson, Michel M., postbaseline system design, DSG, 1975.

Rosenthal, Albert H., public records acquisition, DAG, 1974-78.

Rydell, C. Peter, analyst, AG and DAG, 1972-81.

Sackman, Harold, instrument design consultant, 1973-74.

Sampson, Susan, sample maintenance, SG, 1977.

Savage, Eve, research assistant, SG, 1975.

Schlegel, Priscilla M., program control officer, office of the program director, 1977-81; program control assistant, 1975-76.

Schlereth, Larry, staff, FPOG, 1979-81.

Schoeff, Diana, deputy manager, SG, 1979-80; survey design and operations, 1976-79.

Scott, Douglas, manager, SG, 1975-80.

Seals, Eugene, sample selection team leader, DSG, 1974-75.

Sender, Joel D., audit and analysis programmer, DSG, 1975-76.

Shanley, Michael G., analyst, AG and DAG, 1978-80; assistant manager of Site I, FPOG, 1976-77; resident observer for Site II, 1974-76; resident observer for Site I, 1974.

Shea, Michael F., manager of Site II, FPOG, 1974-76; staff, 1974.

Shetler, Antoinette C. J., acting manager, DSG, 1975.

Shoden, Al, data control, SDPG, 1977-79.

Soohoo, Joanne, computer services, SDPG, 1977.

Soper, Linda, audit and analysis programmer, DSG, 1977.

Spence, Barbara, data control, SDPG, 1978.

Stanton, Richard E., sample accounting and file preparation, DAG, 1974-78.

Stevenson, Joanne, computer services, SDPG, 1978-79.

Stucker, James P., analyst, DAG, 1977-78.

Sudman, Seymour, survey sampling consultant, 1972-73.

Swart, Hanny, audit and analysis programmer, 1977.

Tabor, Robert, deputy manager, FPOG, 1974-75.

Tebbets, Paul, staff, FPOG, 1975-78.

Teed, Ellen, administrative assistant, DAG, 1974.

Todd, Charles F., audit and analysis programmer, DSG, 1980-81.

Tracy, Richard L., project accounting system, DSG, 1975-76.

Trees, Donald P., manager, SDPG, 1974-80.

Trimble, Ferris E., project accounting system, DSG, 1975-76.

Trude, Sally, analyst, AG, 1981; file preparation team leader, FDG, 1979-81; file preparation, DAG, 1978.

Tuller, Mitch, computer services, SDPG, 1977-78.

Turner, Sandra, sample maintenance operations supervisor, SG, 1978-79; survey design and operations, 1978-79; data coding and editing, SDPG, 1977-78.

Velez, Patricio, audit and analysis programmer, 1978.

von Heydenreich, Edmund, record management system team leader, DSG, 1977-78.

Wagner, Helen, audit and analysis programmer, DSG, 1976-81.

Wahrman, Michael, postbaseline system programmer, DSG, 1975-78.

Wallschlager, Mary, sample maintenance operations supervisor, SG, 1977-78.

Wang, Ann W., file preparation and audit team leader, FDG, 1979-80; file preparation and audit, DAG, 1974-78.

Watson, Karen Goldfarb, staff, FPOG, 1974-75.

Way, Alice M., record management system, DSG, 1975-77.

Weeks, Thomas, manager of Site II, FPOG, 1976-81; deputy manager of Site II, 1974-76.

Weiler, Louise, audit and analysis programmer, DSG, 1979-81.

Weiner, George D., analyst, AG, 1979-80.

Weisz, Russell, computer services, SDPG, 1977-78.

Wesley, Deborah, codebook production, SG, 1978-80.

White, Sammis B., analyst, DAG, 1974-77.

White, Wesley, computer services, SDPG, 1976.

Wiewel, Wim, resident observer for Site II, FPOG, 1977-80.

Wikle, Victoria, audit and analysis programmer, DSG, 1979-80.

Wilson, Carmen, survey design and operations, SG, 1975-77; data coding and editing, SDPG, 1974.

Winter, Linda, data control and computer operations supervisor, SDPG, 1974-75.

Witsberger, Christina J., file preparation and survey audit, FDG and DAG, 1978-81.

Wong, Kenneth C., file preparation, FDG and DAG, 1978-81.

Woo, Edward M., sample selection programmer, DSG, 1974-75; audit and analysis programmer, 1974.

Woodfill, Barbara, analyst, DAG, 1974-75; allowance program design, 1973-74.

Yildiz, Orhan M., analyst, AG, 1979-81.

Young, Robert J., audit and analysis team leader, DSG, 1978-81; audit and analysis programmer, 1975-78; sample selection programmer, 1974.

Zycher, Benjamin, file preparation and audit, DAG, 1976.

INDEX

SELECTED LIST OF RAND BOOKS

Bagdikian, Ben H. *The Information Machines: Their Impact on Men and the Media.* New York: Harper & Row, 1971.

Brewer, Garry D., and James S. Kakalik. *Handicapped Children: Strategies for Improving Services.* New York: McGraw-Hill Book Company, Inc., 1979.

Carpenter-Huffman, P., G. R. Hall, and G. C. Sumner. *Change in Education: Insights from Performance Contracting.* Cambridge, Mass.: Ballinger Publishing Company, 1974.

DeSalvo, Joseph S. (ed.). *Perspectives on Regional Transportation Planning.* Lexington, Mass.: D. C. Heath and Company, 1973.

Greenwood, Peter W., Jan M. Chaiken, and Joan Petersilia. *The Criminal Investigation Process.* Lexington, Mass.: D. C. Heath and Company, 1977.

Kakalik, James S., and Sorrel Wildhorn. *The Private Police: Security and Danger.* New York: Crane, Russak & Company, Inc., 1977.

Lowry, Ira S. (ed.). *Experimenting with Housing Allowances: The Comprehensive Final Report of the Housing Assistance Supply Experiment.* Cambridge, Mass.: Oelgeschlager, Gunn & Hain, 1983.

Mitchell, Bridger M., Willard G. Manning, Jr., and Jan Paul Acton. *Peak-Load Pricing: European Lessons for U.S. Energy Policy.* Cambridge, Mass.: Ballinger Publishing Company, 1978.

Newhouse, Joseph P., and Arthur J. Alexander. *An Economic Analysis of Public Library Services.* Lexington, Mass.: D. C. Heath and Company, 1972.

Pincus, John (ed.). *School Finance in Transition: The Courts and Educational Reform.* Cambridge, Mass.: Ballinger Publishing Company, 1974.

Quade, Edward S. *Analysis for Public Decisions.* New York: North-Holland, 2nd edition, 1982.

Timpane, Michael (ed.). *The Federal Interest in Financing Schooling.* Cambridge, Mass.: Ballinger Publishing Company, 1978.

Walker, Warren E., Jan M. Chaiken, and Edward J. Ignall (eds.). *Fire Department Deployment Analysis, A Public Policy Analysis Case Study: The Rand Fire Project.* New York: Elsevier North Holland, Inc., 1979.

Yin, Robert K., Suzanne K. Quick, Peter M. Bateman, and Ellen L. Marks. *Changing Urban Bureaucracies: How New Practices Become Routinized.* Lexington, Mass.: D. C. Heath and Company, 1979.

ABOUT THE AUTHOR

IRA S. LOWRY is a senior economist in the Systems Sciences Department of The Rand Corporation, where he has been employed since 1963. He was educated at the University of Texas (B.A. and M.A.) and the University of California at Berkeley (Ph.D.). He has taught at The Carnegie Institute of Technology and The Massachusetts Institute of Technology. His research has related mostly to urban and regional problems in the United States, especially those related to economic development, demographic change, land use, and housing. His publications include *A Model of Metropolis* (1964), *Migration and Metropolitan Growth* (1966), *Rental Housing in New York City* (1970), *Welfare Housing in New York City* (1972), and a number of reports on the Housing Assistance Supply Experiment (1972-82). His most recently published articles are "The Dismal Future of Central Cities" (1980) and "The Science and Politics of Ethnic Enumeration" (1980).